T0217109

Lecture Notes in Artificial Intelligence 1076

Subseries of Lecture Notes in Computer Science
Edited by J. G. Carbonell and J. Siekmann

Lecture Notes in Computer Science

Edited by G. Goos, J. Hartmanis and J. van Leeuwen

Springer
Berlin
Heidelberg
New York
Barcelona
Budapest
Hong Kong
London
Milan
Paris
Santa Clara
Singapore
Tokyo

Nigel Shadbolt   Kieron O'Hara
Guus Schreiber (Eds.)

Advances in Knowledge Acquisition

9th European Knowledge Acquisition
Workshop, EKAW '96
Nottingham, United Kingdom
May 14-17, 1996
Proceedings

 Springer

Series Editors
Jaime G. Carbonell, Carnegie Mellon University, Pittsburgh, PA, USA
Jörg Siekmann, University of Saarland, Saarbrücken, Germany

Volume Editors

Nigel Shadbolt
Kieron O'Hara
University of Nottingham, Department of Psychology
University Park, Nottingham NG7 2RD, United Kingdom

Guus Schreiber
University of Amsterdam, Department of Social Science Informatics
Roetersstraat15, NL-1018 WB Amsterdam, The Netherlands

Cataloging-in-Publication Data applied for

Die Deutsche Bibliothek - CIP-Einheitsaufnahme

Advances in knowledge acquisition : proceedings / 9th
European Knowledge Acquisition Workshop, EKAW '96,
Nottingham, United Kingdom, May 14 - 17, 1996. Kieron
O'Hara ... (ed.). - Berlin ; Heidelberg ; New York ; Barcelona ;
Budapest ; Hong Kong ; London ; Milan ; Paris ; Santa Clara ;
Singapore ; Tokyo : Springer, 1996
  (Lecture notes in computer science ; Vol. 1076 : Lecture notes in
  artificial intelligence)
  ISBN 3-540-61273-4
NE: O'Hara, Kieron [Hrsg.]; European Knowledge Acquisition Workshop
  <9, 1996, Nottingham>; GT

CR Subject Classification (1991): I.2.4-6, I.2.8

ISBN 3-540-61273-4 Springer-Verlag Berlin Heidelberg New York

© Springer-Verlag Berlin Heidelberg 1996
Printed in Germany

Typesetting: Camera ready by author
SPIN 10512936   06/3142 – 5 4 3 2 1 0   Printed on acid-free paper

Preface

This volume contains the proceedings of the 1996 European Knowledge Acquisition Workshop (EKAW), held at Matlock in Derbyshire, England, May 14–17. It is the ninth EKAW to have been held, and the fourth to have the proceedings published by Springer-Verlag. Yet again, the standard of papers received has been very high, and much important work from a wide variety of nations has been reported.

EKAW, like the complementary workshops KAW (the Knowledge Acquisition Workshop at Banff, Canada) and JKAW (the Japanese Knowledge Acquisition Workshop), focuses on the acquisition of knowledge for the modelling or automation of complex problem-solving behaviour. As the complexity of the problem increases, it becomes proportionally more difficult to ensure the correctness of a model developed using *ad hoc* methods unsupported by theory. Knowledge Acquisition theory (KA) is intended to underpin model development with theories, methods, tools, and techniques for the accurate acquisition of knowledge relevant to the problem-solving behaviour.

Over the past ten years we have seen steady advances in KA research. The early years were characterised by a clear recognition of the problems associated with undertaking KA. There was, however, little articulated theory as to what techniques and methods to apply in what circumstances. Indeed, many of the KA methods were underspecified or poorly described.

Gradually, techniques and methods became consolidated and evidence began to emerge as to their varying utility across KA contexts. It was recognised early that many of the KA techniques were ripe for computer implementation. A number of individual and then increasingly integrated tool sets appeared. Some were designed to facilitate acquisition for generic problem types, others were devoted to acquisition in specific domains, whilst a third class sought to be generic across both problem types and domains.

Alongside the development of software support we saw an increasing interest in methods to model and characterise the problem solving process in such a way as to provide a framework for managing and directing the KA process The emergence of these KA methodologies has been one of the really significant contributions of KA research. These methodologies have led in turn to the development of problem solving method libraries and more recently to the establishment of knowledge repositories.

Despite this wealth of research, we must be concerned at our lack of success in influencing the wider software engineering community. The insights of KA have direct relevance to almost all software activities and yet we still see little uptake of our methods and techniques. As a discipline we must take care not to become parochial.

Increasingly, software systems are required to have knowledge-intensive components. The construction of this new generation of complex systems can be greatly enhanced by techniques developed in the KA community. For example, the notion of reusable components based on task and domain types is a powerful engineering method that can greatly enhance the software development process. This type of reuse adds a new dimension to the reuse common in, for example, object-oriented development. Our challenge for the coming years is to show the potential of KA technology to a much wider audience.

The work reported in this volume continues research into the traditional areas of KA research outlined above. It can be divided roughly into two categories. Firstly, there is research into theories of KA, about what a KA theory should look like, what components are to be expected from a theory, how much information and guidance a theory can provide (and conversely, how much is always dependent on the KA context). And secondly, there is research into particular methods or techniques of acquiring knowledge. Research of this type presented at EKAW 96 showed a number of pleasing new features. There was an increase in the number of papers concerned with the acquisition of knowledge from texts, with the automatic acquisition of knowledge from large databases, with the acquisition and representation of knowledge from groups of subjects, and with the special problems thrown up in planning domains. The remainder of the Preface describes the papers in terms of the themes discerned by the editors.

Theoretical and General Issues

In this section are the papers which deal with aspects of KA theory. The general thrust of KA theory over the past few years has been to develop generic accounts of problem-solving behaviour which can abstract away from the details of individual domains and therefore act as a template for models of actual behaviour. They provide a general *method* for problem-solving of a particular type, which then has to be applied in the individual circumstances of a domain. The papers in this section are all concerned with the properties and implications of such *problem-solving methods*.

The first group of theoretical papers is concerned with fundamental questions about the forms these problem-solving methods should take. Richard Benjamins and Christine Pierret-Golbreich (University of Amsterdam and University of Paris-Sud) propose a formal language for expressing the assumptions, or considerations that are taken into account in the decision as to whether or not to apply a problem-solving method ("Assumptions of problem-solving methods"). Dieter Fensel and Remco Straatman (University of Amsterdam) show how such assumptions, carefully chosen and represented formally, can lead to greater efficiency of the final automatic problem-solver ("Problem-solving methods"). Kieron O'Hara and Nigel Shadbolt (University of Nottingham) take a wider view of efficiency, and argue that the Generalised Directive Model methodology can lead to greater efficiency of the KA process itself ("The thin end of the wedge"). Klas Orsvärn (Swedish Institute of Computer Science) takes a case study of the use of a library of diagnostic models to model a specific application, and on the basis of the findings he reports, proposes a set of general principles that libraries of reusable problem-solving methods should adhere to ("Principles for libraries of task decomposition methods").

The second group of theoretical papers is roughly grouped around questions of language and ontology. Workers in the REVISE project (University of Amsterdam and Vrije Universiteit Amsterdam) suggest a method of comparing languages for expressing problem-solving knowledge by focusing not on the shallow linguistic properties of these languages, but by comparing the goals they try to achieve ("A purpose driven method for language comparison"). Richard Benjamins and Manfred Aben (University of Amsterdam) defend the use of formal models for expressing knowledge, as exposing ambiguities and inconsistencies, and show how a diagnostic reasoner was built using formal methods that could be proven to meet a high level specification ("A conceptual and formal model of a diagnostic reasoner"). Jan Benjamin, Pim Borst, Hans Akkermans, and Bob Wielinga (University of Amsterdam and University of Twente) suggest how libraries of reusable components, which are difficult to navigate through in complex cases, can be replaced or augmented by providing methods to help the user construct his or her own ontologies of objects ("Ontology construction for technical domains").

See also the papers by Arlanzón, Bernaras and Laresgoiti, and Cottam and Shadbolt, for discussions with relevance to the theory of problem-solving methods.

Eliciting Knowledge from Textual and Other Sources

One recurring problem in KA is the extraction of knowledge from rich but ill-structured sources, such as transcriptions of interviews with experts. Such extraction is highly time- and labour-intensive, and the development of methods of identifying the important concepts contained in such sources is increasingly becoming an active area of research. This field is only now picking up real momentum, and the papers included here may well prove highly influential.

Stéphane Lapalut (INRIA) proposes the use of a statistical method to divide texts into their "semantic contexts", and then isolate the significant terms used in those contexts ("Text clustering to help knowledge acquisition from documents"). Udo Hahn, Manfred Klenner, and Klemens Schnattinger (Freiburg University) introduce a methodology for second order reasoning about statements concerning the significance of particular concept hypotheses derived from the process of coming to understand a text, expressed in a first order terminological representation language ("A quality-based terminological reasoning model for text knowledge acquisition"). Paul R. Bowden, Peter Halstead, and Tony G. Rose (Nottingham Trent University) describe how to extract knowledge from large texts by identifying specific conceptual relations in the text, such as definition and exemplification. The conceptual information can then be extracted using combinatorial pattern-matching ("Extracting conceptual knowledge from text using explicit relation markers").

Problems are also posed when knowledge has to be extracted from non-textual sources, and interesting work is also presented about two specific instances of this. Célia Ghedini Ralha (University of Leeds) investigates the problem of extracting knowledge from the World Wide Web, a distributed multimedia hypertext system. Her work exploits spatial metaphors of hyperspace to build maps of the domain material intelligently ("Structuring information in a distributed hypermedia system"). Peter C.-H. Cheng (University of Nottingham) investigates the extraction of knowledge from diagrams, making a clear distinction between diagrammatic representations on the one hand, and the visual presentation of propositional knowledge. He shows that diagrammatic KA, though currently a neglected area, is feasible ("Diagrammatic knowledge acquisition").

Data Mining

Another type of repository of knowledge that new techniques are opening for us are large corpora or databases. The process of extracting knowledge from such bodies, called data mining, has to be automatic because of the size of the knowledge bases being mined. Hence machine learning (ML) techniques are being exploited to uncover structures that are implicit or hidden within large unstructured bodies of knowledge.

Two papers take an evaluative look at current data mining techniques. Edgar Sommer (GMD) wants to revisit the arguments about how best to measure the quality of automatically induced theories. He surveys relevant work from linguistics and psychology to develop a set of criteria to measure the 'understandability' of theories developed using ML techniques ("An approach to measuring theory quality"). Franz Schmalhofer and Christoph Kozieja (DFKI) experimentally evaluate three ML techniques, and conclude that more user-friendly conceptualizations of ML should be developed. They preview the KOALA system, which gives the user the opportunity to configure his or her ML application according to the circumstances of the application domain ("Some late-breaking news from the data mines").

A further group of papers present particular data mining tools and methods. João José Furtado Vasco, Colette Faucher, and Eugène Chouraqui (DIAM-IUSPIM) present an aid to concept hierarchy development using insights from ML and cognitive psychology. In particular, their conceptual hierarchies can be seen from multiple perspectives, on the basis that concept formation is a context-dependent process ("A knowledge acquisition tool for multi-perspective concept formation"). James Cupit and Nigel Shadbolt (University of Nottingham) address the problem that databases used for data mining often do not present their data in ways congenial for the use of ML techniques. Their CASTLE workbench redescribes databases in terms of a knowledge structure extracted using KA techniques, allowing conventional ML techniques to be used ("Knowledge discovery in databases"). Derek Sleeman and Fraser Mitchell (Aberdeen University) describe systems that are intended to operate at a higher conceptual level than standard KA techniques, thereby proving easier for domain experts to operate ("Towards painless knowledge acquisition").

Group Elicitation

A special set of problems faces the knowledge engineer who works with groups of people (e.g. groups of experts, software development teams). Such knowledge as is publicly available has to be expressed with a shared representation, which implies a plethora of issues pertaining to the evaluation of such representations, translations between competing representations, and the evaluation of the translations.

Frances Brazier, Jan Treur, and Niek Wijngaards (Vrije Universiteit Amsterdam) investigate the use of a shared task model as a basis for interactions between experts and knowledge engineers, and expert users and intelligent systems. They present a declarative compositional approach to user-centred system design ("Modelling interaction with experts"). Guy Boy (EURISCO) presents a method for constructing a shared knowledge base, combining Warfield's brainwriting technique of amassing viewpoints of particular issues, and a decision support system ("The group elicitation method").

Planning

The final group of papers concerns the particular problems posed by KA in planning domains. Janet Efstathiou (University of Oxford) describes work done in an actual industrial application to elicit the methods used by schedulers to amend schedules in an untidy world. She presents an account of the formalisation of such techniques, and shows how software support for schedule repair should be constrained ("Formalising the repair of schedules through knowledge acquisition"). Steve A. Chien (California Institute of Technology) addresses the problem of the expense of verifying and updating planning knowledge bases. He describes tools for planning KB development to detect certain classes of error in planning KBs and tools for interactive debugging of planning KBs ("Intelligent tools for planning knowledge base development and verification"). V. Arlanzón, A. Bernaras, and I. Laresgoiti (LABEIN) show how the CommonKADS library and methodology were used to develop an application in the service recovery planning domain. They pinpoint several areas where the generic components of the CommonKADS library failed to meet the requirements of their real world application ("Configuring service recovery planning with the CommonKADS library"). Hugh Cottam and Nigel Shadbolt (University of Nottingham) apply knowledge level modelling techniques to a search and rescue planning domain. In particular, they investigate the best way of using models derived from analyses of systems to acquire knowledge, and conclude that they should best be used in tandem with domain-derived knowledge level models ("Domain and system influences in problem solving models for planning").

Acknowledgements

The editors are indebted to the following who gave their time to a thorough and constructive review process, thus ensuring that EKAW'96 continues the tradition of publishing high-quality knowledge acquisition research: Stuart Aitken (University of Glasgow), Hans Akkermans (University of Twente), Nathalie Aussenac (IRIT-CNRS, Toulouse), Guy Boy (EURISCO, Toulouse), Joost Breuker (University of Amsterdam), Hugh Cottam (University of Nottingham), James Cupit (University of Nottingham), Dieter Fensel (University of Amsterdam), Brian Gaines (University of Calgary), Jean-Gabriel Ganascia (LAFORIA, Paris), Frank van Harmelen (Free University of Amsterdam), Yves Kodratoff (Univ. Paris Sud), Marc Linster (Digital Equipment Corp.), Katherina Morik (University of Dortmund), Enrico Motta (Open University), Mark Musen (Stanford University), Kieron O'Hara (University of Nottingham), Enric Plaza (IIIA-CSIC), Franz Schmalhofer (DFKI, Kaiserslautern), Guus Schreiber (University of Amsterdam), Mildred Shaw (University of Calgary), Derek Sleeman (University of Aberdeen), Maarten van Someren (University of Amsterdam), Rudi Studer (University of Karlsruhe), André Valente (USC-ISI, Marina del Rey), Walter van der Velde (Free University of Brussels), Hans Voss (GMD, Sankt Augustin), and Bob Wielinga (University of Amsterdam),

We would also like to thank Elizabeth Hextall for excellent secretarial support.

Financial support for EKAW'96 was provided by MLNet, the European Network of Excellence in Machine Learning, the Department Psychology Artificial Intelligence Group at the University of Nottingham, and the British Computer Society's Specialist Group on Expert Systems.

March 1996

Nigel Shadbolt
Kieron O'Hara
Guus Schreiber

Table of Contents

Group Elicitation

Planning

Assumptions of Problem-Solving Methods

Richard Benjamins[1] and Christine Pierret-Golbreich[2]

[1] SWI, University of Amsterdam, Roetersstraat 15, NL-1018 WB Amsterdam, the
Netherlands, richard@swi.psy.uva.nl[***]
[2] LRI, University of Paris-Sud, Bâtiment 490, 91405 Orsay Cedex, France,
pierret@lri.fr

Abstract. Assumptions of problem-solving methods refer to necessary
applicability conditions of problem-solving methods, indicating that a
problem-solving method is only applicable to realize a task, if the assumptions are met. In principle, such assumptions may refer to any kind
of condition involved in a problem-solving method's applicability, including its required domain knowledge. In this paper, we propose a conceptual organization for assumptions of problem-solving methods and
suggest a formal language to describe them. For illustration we take examples from the Propose & Revise problem-solving method and from
diagnosis.

1 Introduction and motivation

In the context of task-method frameworks [15, 25, 6, 19, 11], tasks can be realized by applying problem-solving methods (PSMs, methods). A task defines *what*
needs to be achieved (a declarative functional specification), and a PSM *how* it
has to be achieved (an operational specification). This view introduces the problem of deciding when PSMs can be applied to tasks: the *applicability problem*. A
common view is that a PSM can be applied to a task in a particular application
if some conditions are satisfied. Such conditions can be exploited during knowledge engineering, where we are concerned with knowledge-based system (KBS)
construction, and we have to decide which PSMs to include in the KBS (static
use). Applicability conditions are also useful during reasoning (dynamic use),
where they can be exploited by a meta-level reasoner that dynamically selects
PSMs for tasks. In this paper, we are interested in conditions of PSMs without
committing ourselves to how they will be used.

Several ways have been put forward to express applicability conditions. In
Knowledge Engineering, examples include "task features" [1], "assumptions"
[2, 8], "suitability criteria" [4], "resources" and "process characteristics" [14]
and "method ontologies" [10]. In dynamic reasoning, examples include "applicability conditions" [24, 23], "additional knowledge of problem solving actions"

[***] Richard Benjamins is supported by the Netherlands Computer Science Research
Foundation with financial support from the Netherlands Organization for Scientific
Research (NWO). The work has partly been supported by the HCM program, fi-
nanced by the CEC.

[17], "resources" and "process characteristics"(again) [14], "suitability criteria" (again) [3], "input/output types" and "pre/post conditions" [13] and "sponsors" [16].

Whatever the terms used, in most approaches mentioned above, applicability conditions are not more than sets of *labels* that refer to some notion assumed to be known by its interpreter (knowledge engineer or KBS). Two things seem to lack: (1) a principled organization of the applicability conditions, and (2) a well-defined language to express them in an unambiguous manner. In the rest of the paper, we will use the term *assumption* for applicability condition; a PSM is only applicable when its assumptions hold.

Making assumptions of PSMs explicit, helps us to decide whether a PSM can be (re)used in a particular situation. If we, in addition, formalize the assumptions, then it becomes possible to check automatically whether a PSM is applicable in a particular situation. From the point of view of applying the PSM, we can speak of a proof obligation which is formulated in [9] as follows:

$$domain\ knowledge \models assumptions \tag{1}$$

Such a proof requires a thorough insight in assumptions of PSMs, a suitable formal specification language, and some proof calculus. The first two form the aim of this paper.

The structure of this paper is as follows. In Section 2, we present a conceptual organization of assumptions based on their horizontal (Section 2.1) and vertical inter-relationships (Section 2.2). Section 3 presents how sorted First-Order Predicate Logic (FOPL) can be used as a language to formalize assumptions. Some example formalizations are given from the "select-propose-check-revise" method (SPCR) as discussed in [8, 9] (Section 3.1) and from diagnosis [3, 4] (Section 3.2). In Section 4, we conclude the paper.

2 A conceptual organization for assumptions

As stated in the introduction, most work dealing with PSM assumptions considers them as an unorganized set of labels. In this section, we propose a conceptual organization to understand assumptions in a principled way. The organization consists of two parts: a horizontal organization of assumptions (Section 2.1) and a vertical organization (Section 2.2).

2.1 Horizontal organization of assumptions

Assumptions of PSMs can be organized in a specialization hierarchy as shown in Fig. 1. We distinguish between the following types, and indicate what the types mean for the knowledge engineering practice.

- **Epistemological assumptions** refer to the knowledge required by the PSM. Such knowledge can concern static domain knowledge or dynamic input knowledge (cf. static and dynamic input roles in [25]).

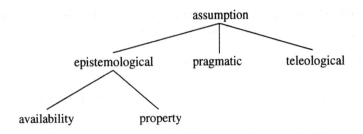

Fig. 1. A specialization organization of assumptions.

Practically: epistemological assumptions refer to knowledge that can be provided by the domain expert or knowledge engineer, or that can be produced by the KBS itself, and that is indispensable.

We divide epistemological assumptions further into two types.

- **Availability assumptions** refer to the availability of domain knowledge, for instance, a causal model. A causal model can be considered as static domain knowledge which can be described as a set of states ST related by causal relations: $r_{causal}(st_1, st_2)$, where $st_1, st_2 \in ST$. An example of dynamic input knowledge would be the availability of domain concepts that play the role of hypothesis in diagnosis. Note that we need a mapping between the domain knowledge concepts (e.g., st_1) and the concepts used by the PSM (e.g., hypothesis) to refer to the domain concepts.
- **Property assumptions** refer to properties of the domain knowledge, for instance, that a causal model is non-cyclic.

- **Pragmatic assumptions** refer to PSM requirements related to the physical context or external environment in which the system operates. For instance, a method for testing hypotheses by measuring, requires that the device is accessible for measurements. Pragmatic assumptions often show up when a KBS interacts with its environment.

    Practically: pragmatic assumptions refer to knowledge that cannot be supplied and that is indispensable.

- **Teleological assumptions** relate to the goal that the PSM has to achieve. If such assumptions are not fulfilled, then, although the PSM can be applied, the correctness of the solution cannot be guaranteed. Assuming that its teleological assumptions hold, a PSM is said to achieve a *weakened* version of the original goal, with a smaller functionality. Thus, teleological assumptions influence the functionality. An example in diagnosis is the single-fault assumption. If the task goal (the required functionality) is to find any kind of diagnosis, a particular PSM might achieve a weakening of this goal under the single-fault assumption.

> *Practically: teleological assumptions refer to knowledge that cannot be supplied. They represent a weakening of the goal.*

Our organization is beneficial for several reasons. First of all, the organization gives a better understanding of what assumptions are and where they come from. It goes without saying that we need to understand assumptions before we can formalize them.

Second, the distinction between epistemological, pragmatic and teleological assumptions has implications for the applicability problem, and in particular for formula (1). In light of our organization, we reformulate it to:

$$application\ knowledge \models epist.\ assum. \wedge pragm.\ assum. \wedge teleo.\ assum. \quad (2)$$

We divide application knowledge into (a) domain knowledge (relevant concepts and relations, both static and dynamic), (b) in external knowledge (characteristics of the specific environment in which the KBS has to operate such as "device is accessible for measurements" in diagnosis), and (c) task knowledge (the goal of a particular application, e.g., car diagnosis). Given this division of application knowledge, we identify three proof obligations for a particular PSM.

(2a) *domain knowledge $\models$ epistemological assumptions*
(2b) *external environment $\models$ pragmatic assumptions*
(2c) *task knowledge $\models$ teleological assumptions*

Proof obligation (2a) can be mechanized in a particular domain. Property epistemological assumptions refer to properties of the domain knowledge represented. Such properties can be checked automatically, such as for instance "non-cyclicness" of a network. If in addition, concept types of the domain knowledge are precisely defined (e.g., in an ontology [22]), then it is also possible to automatically check availability epistemological assumptions, such as for example the availability of a causal model.

Proof obligation (2b), on the other hand, cannot be automated. Whether a particular application satisfies the pragmatic assumptions of a PSM, has to be externally guaranteed (e.g., by an expert).

With respect to proof obligation (2c) we have to be more careful. We are currently investigating whether this proof can be established, based on a formalization of task knowledge in a specific application [12]. The question is whether such assumptions can be safely made in the context of an application task.

Table 1 and Table 2 give some assumption examples for respectively methods for diagnosis and for the SPCR-method (select-propose-check-revise).

2.2 Vertical organization of assumptions

Apart from the horizontal organization in the previous section, assumptions can also be organized along a vertical dimension. These relations are important for

Epistemological	
Availability	**Property**
-simulation rule set -fault-simulation rule set -contributor set	-no fanout structure of device model -hypothesis-set related
Teleological	**Pragmatic**
-single-fault assumption -non-intermittency assumption -independence of causes	-components replaceable -device accessible

Table 1. Assumption examples of methods in diagnosis.

Epistemological	
Availability	**Property**
-network of propose rules -set of constraints over parameter values -set of fixes	-not more than one propose rule per parameter -either propose rule or user rule for each parameter -not propose rule and user rule for same parameter -constraints define solvable problem -fixes are independent
Teleological	**Pragmatic**
-fix combinations enable a solution -property of solution is expressible as constraints over parameters -restricted search is powerful enough to find solution	-user gives complete parameter-value information -user is passive input provider -number of parameters is constant

Table 2. Assumption examples for the Select, Propose, Check & Revise method.

reasons of *consistency, completeness* and *no redundancy* when associating assumptions to PSMs. When we want to (re)use a PSM in a particular situation, we have to know the assumptions that belong to it. We could represent them extensively, that is, enumerate all assumptions for each PSM. However, this easily leads to forgetting an assumption (incompleteness), including contradictory assumptions (inconsistency), and representing the same assumption at several places (redundancy) where it could have been deduced.

To overcome these problems, we propose to exploit vertical inter-relations between assumptions to automatically generate them. Tasks, PSMs and inferences can be organized in a task-method structure (see Fig. 2). In such a structure, there are high-level and lower-level PSMs. Assumptions of high-level PSMs are partly based on assumptions of lower-level PSMs, tasks and inferences. For example in Fig. 2, method3 is part of method1. Suppose that method3 makes assumption1, then method1 also makes assumption1. In general, assumptions of lower-level PsMs are propagated upwards to higher levels. Following this line of reasoning, we can distinguish between *own* assumptions of a PsM and *propagated* ones. Propagated assumptions can be generated automatically as opposed to "own" assumptions.

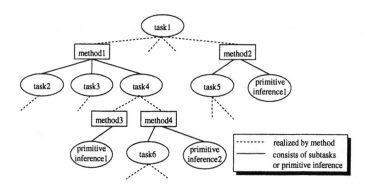

Fig. 2. A task-method structure.

"Own" assumptions of PSMs Most of the assumptions of a PsM are based on assumptions of its constituents. However, PsMs also can have assumptions of their own which do not stem from one of their constituents. Such assumptions refer to specific requirements introduced by the PsM and are related to its declarative functional specification (the PSM_{dec}). Suppose for example that we have a PsM for finding single-fault hypotheses based on multiple symptoms in a diagnosis application, and that this PsM consists of the inference "intersect". A teleological assumption of this method would be that the single-fault assumption holds. This assumption does not come from the intersect inference, because an intersection may contain any number of elements, and is therefore an "own" assumption of the method.

"Upward propagated" assumptions of PSMs A task-method structure (Fig. 2) enables upward propagation of assumptions from lower levels to higher levels. Inferences are primitives and therefore only have own assumptions. Assumptions of inferences and PsMs are propagated upwards to tasks and higher-level PsMs. Respecting the character of the task-method structure (Fig. 2), where a task may be realized by alternative methods (OR), and a method consists of subtasks/inferences (AND), the assumptions of any task or PsM can be expressed as a logical combination (AND/OR) of its own assumptions and that of its constituents. A PsM adds the logical AND of the assumptions of its constituents to its own assumptions. A task has as assumptions the OR of the assumptions of its realizing PSMs.

Fig. 3 shows an example of an AND/OR combination that represents the assumptions of the model-based hypothesis generation method (MBHG-method) [3, 4]. Note that in this case there are no pragmatic assumptions, because the PSM concerns only hypothesis generation, which requires no interaction with the environment. The combination represents the *own* and the *propagated* assumptions of the MBHG-method. The "non intermittency assumption" is an own assumption of the method. The method has three subtasks, of which the first has one assumption (device model). For the second subtask there are three alternative PSMs, which is reflected in the OR of three ANDs. The third subtask has two assumptions.

```
AND(
     teleological : non-intermittency-assumption       (PSM)
     epist-avail : device-model                        (first subtask)
     OR(                                               (second subtask)
       AND(
           teleological : independence-of-causes
           epist-avail : contributor-set
           )
       AND(
           epist-prop : fault-behavior-not-constrained
           teleological : independence-of-causes
           epist-avail : contributor-set
           )
       AND(
           teleological : single-fault-assumption
           epist-avail : contributor-set
           )
      )
     epist-avail : fault-simulation-rules-of-components  (third subtask)
     epist-avail: simulation-rules-of-components
   )
```

Fig. 3. The logical combination representing the assumptions of the MBHG-method. "Teleological" refers to teleological assumptions, "epist-avail" denote availability assumptions of the epistemological type, and "epist-prop" denote property assumptions. The task-method structure is reflected in the layout of the figure (see right-hand side).

Control knowledge of a PSM may refine the upward propagation process of low-level assumptions for assumptions concerning the availability of dynamic roles. For example, if control knowledge of a PSM assigns a particular inference as the starting inference, the assumptions of that inference are propagated to the PSM. However, if some inference I_1 of a PSM is executed before inference

I_2, and the output of I_1 is the input of I_2 and the assumption A corresponds to the dynamic input of I_2, then A is not propagated to the PSM because it will be made true by I_1 during execution of the PSM. Of course, this is not valid for assumptions corresponding to static roles, because their content is unchangeable during problem solving.

3   A language for assumptions

So far, we have used descriptive names to denote assumptions. These names are labels which give some indication of what assumptions mean, but do not define them formally. We propose sorted First-Order Predicate Logic (FOPL) as the language to formalize assumptions. FOPL, because it has well-known properties and so far has been sufficiently expressive for our purpose. We use *sorted* logic because it makes formulae easier to read and reduces their length [18]. The arguments of function and predicate symbols may have different sorts (types), and constant and function symbols also have some sort. This extension is conservative in the sense that everything that can be expressed and deduced in sorted FOPL can also be expressed and deduced in normal FOPL. An assumption is defined as ($=_{def}$) a well-formed formula in sorted FOPL.

In the rest of this paper, we first give some formalizations of assumptions from the Select, Propose, Check & Revise PSM (Section 3.1) and then from PSMs for diagnosis (Section 3.2).

3.1   Formalizations of assumptions of the SPCR-method

In this section, we introduce the necessary definitions for formalizing assumptions of the SPCR-method [8] applied to the VT-domain [26]. In a sorted logic, we can have different types (sorts) of variables, functions and relations.

Let $\mathcal{V}$ be a countable set of variables with the following sorts:
Let P be the set of variables of sort *parameter*.
Let V be the set of variables of sort *value*.
Let D be the set of variables of sort *dependency*.
Let C be the set of variables of sort *constraint*.
Let F be the variable set of sort *fix*.
Let $PList$ be the set of variables of sort *list of parameters*.

Let $\mathcal{F}$ be the set of functions $\{arg, par, val\}$ with:
$arg : D \mapsto PList$,
$par : D \mapsto P$,
$val : P \mapsto V$,
and let *user* be a constant
$user :\mapsto PList$.

Let $\mathcal{R}$ be the set of relations {*assigned, affected by, p intern, p user, propose rule, user rule*} with:

$assigned \subset P$,
$affected\ by \subset P \times P$,
$p\ intern \subset P$,
$p\ user \subset P$,
$propose\ rule \subset D$,
$user\ rule \subset D$.

Below we give the axioms for the *arg* and *par* functions of a dependency d.

$$\forall p \in P\ \exists d \in D\ \exists L \in PList\ \ arg(d) = L \wedge par(d) = p. \tag{3}$$

In words, for each parameter p, there exists a dependency rule d and the arguments of d form a list of parameters. This axiomatization suffices because we do not have to reason about the specific dependencies and parameter values, but we only need to know that there are dependencies between certain parameters.[4]

The axiom giving semantics to the relation "affected by" between two parameters p and q is as follows:

$$affected\ by(q, p) =_{def} \exists r \in P\ \exists d \in D\ (q = par(d) \wedge (p \in arg(d) \vee \\ (r \in arg(d) \wedge affected\ by(r, p)))) \tag{4}$$

In words it says that a parameter q is affected by a parameter p, if p is an argument of the dependency rule d for q, or if there is some other parameter r which is an argument of d and r is affected by p (recursive definition).

The relation $assigned \subset P$ is true for a particular p if and only if p a has a value:

$assigned(p) =_{def} \exists v \in V\ val(p) = v$.

The axioms giving semantics for the relations *propose rule* and *user rule* are respectively:

$propose\ rule(d) =_{def} \exists L \in PList\ \ arg(d) = L \wedge L \neq user$, and
$user\ rule(d) =_{def} arg(d) = user$.

The axioms giving semantics for the relations p *intern* and p *user* are respectively:

$p\ intern(p) =_{def} \exists d \in D\ p = par(d) \wedge propose\ rule(d)$, and
$p\ user(p) =_{def} \exists d \in D\ p = par(d) \wedge user\ rule(d)$.

Equipped with this language, we can now formalize the assumptions, which are taken from [8, 27].

Network-of-propose-rules. A collection of propose rules (dependencies) for parameters needs to be available, from which a parameter is selected to propose a value for. This epistemological availability assumption states that there exists at least one such parameter – propose-rule pair. The structure of the "network" (see

---

[4] In the case that specific assumptions need to know the precise relation between the parameter and the list of parameters of a dependency, it is possible to define a predicate *compute* $\subset D \times P \times PList$, which explicates this relation.

next assumption) is exploited to determine which pair to select. Since axiom (3) already states that a parameter is associated with at least one dependency, we reduce the assumption to the statement that D is not empty. For the sake of simplicity, we omit the semantics of a network.

$$network\ of\ propose\ rules =_{def} \exists d \in D \tag{5}$$

Propose-network-is-non-cyclic. The network of dependencies or propose rules should be cycle-free, that is, parameters should not depend directly or indirectly on themselves. This allows us to stratify the set of parameters to get a selection order in which parameter values can be proposed [8]. Stratification means that each parameters gets a value reflecting on how many other parameters and propose rules it depends. Parameters given by the user have value zero. If a parameter depends on itself, it would never be selected. This is an epistemological property assumption.

$$propose\ network\ is\ non\ cyclic =_{def}$$
$$\forall p, q \in P\ (affected\ by(p, q) \rightarrow \neg affected\ by(q, p)) \tag{6}$$

Where "affected by" is defined in axiom (4).

Either-propose-rule-or-user-rule-for-each-par. For each parameter there has to be either a propose rule or the parameter value is given by the user. This is an epistemological property assumption.

$$either\ propose\ rule\ or\ user\ rule\ for\ each\ par =_{def}$$
$$\forall p \in P\ \exists d \in D\ (p = par(d) \wedge (propose\ rule(d) \vee user\ rule(d))) \tag{7}$$

Not-propose-rule-and-user-rule-for-same-par. It is forbidden to have a user rule and a propose rule for the same parameter. This epistemological property assumption contributes to avoiding contradictions between values of parameters.

$$not\ propose\ rule\ and\ user\ rule\ for\ same\ par =_{def}$$
$$\forall p \in P\ (p = par(d) \rightarrow (\neg propose\ rule(d) \vee \neg user\ rule(d))) \tag{8}$$

Not-more-than-one-propose-rule-per-par. It is also forbidden to have two or more propose rules for the same parameter. Together with the previous one, this epistemological property assumption avoids contradictions between proposed values for parameters.

$$not\ more\ than\ one\ propose\ rule\ per\ par =_{def}$$
$$\forall p \in P\ \exists d \in D\ (p = par(d) \rightarrow \forall d' \in D\ (d' \neq d \wedge p \neq par(d'))) \tag{9}$$

Actually, this formalization is too simple. In the VT-domain [26], there may be several propose rules for the same parameter, however, they can never be applied at the same time [8]. For example, depending on the chosen motor, different propose rules for calculating the "peak" parameter have to be applied.

Parameters-dependent. Two parameters p, q are dependent if either p is affected by q, or q is affected by p. We define:

$$parameters\ dependent(p, q) =_{def}$$
$$affected\ by(p, q) \lor affected\ by(q, p) \tag{10}$$

Parameters-independent. Parameters are independent if no two parameters are dependent. If this epistemological property assumption does not hold, one cannot change the value of one parameter without changing the value of the other.

$$parameters\ independent =_{def} \forall p, q \in P\ \neg parameters\ dependent(p, q) \tag{11}$$

Where "parameters-dependent" is defined in definition (10).

User-gives-complete-par-val-information. Some parameter values have to be provided by the user. It is assumed that the user indeed provides values for all these parameters, otherwise the PsM does not work. This is a pragmatic assumptions.

$$user\ gives\ complete\ par\ val\ information =_{def}$$
$$\forall p \in P\ (p\ user(p) \rightarrow assigned(p)) \tag{12}$$

3.2 Formalizations of PsMs for diagnosis

The formalizations presented in this section are based on informal descriptions from literature on diagnosis and on [3, 4]. In the example formalizations, we are concerned with model-based diagnosis, where the cause of a fault is identified by reasoning about a model of the device. A device model consists of components with simulation rules that calculate values of output parameters of components based on inputs. Similarly to the SPCR-method, we can formalize assumptions of methods for diagnosis.[5]

Let $\mathcal{V}$ be a countable set of variables with the following sorts:
Let P be the set of variables of sort *parameter*.
Let SR be the set of variables of sort *set of simulation rules*.
Let O be the set of variables of sort *observation*.
Let $PList$ be the set of variables of sort *list of parameters*.
Let $comp$ be the set of variables of sort *component*.
Let h (hypothesis) be the set of variables of sort *set of comp*.
Let H (hypothesis set) be the set of variables of sort *set of h*.
Let Int be the set of variables of sort *integer*.

---

[5] We only define the symbols which are needed in the example formalizations.

Let $\mathcal{F}$ be the set of functions $\{arg, par, card\}$ with:
$arg : SR \mapsto PList$,
$par : SR \mapsto P$,
$card : H \mapsto Int$.

Let $\mathcal{R}$ be the set of relations $\{affected\ by, explains, \prec\}$ with :
$affected\ by \subset P \times P$,
$explains \subset H \times SR \times O$,
$\prec \subset H \times H$.

The axioms for the *arg* and *par* functions for the simulation rules are identical to axiom (3) provided that we rename d to sr (see assumption "simulation rules of components" (13)). *affected by* has been defined in axiom (4). The relation *explains* is not defined formally here, but expresses that a set of components (i.e, a hypothesis) is an explanation for some observations taking into account the simulation rules [7, 20]. The $\prec$ relation stands for the subset relation.

Simulation-rules-of-components. In order to perform model-based diagnosis, we need to have a device model (epistemological availability). In our case, this is a collection of simulation rules.

$$simulation\ rules\ of\ components =_{def} \exists sr \in SR \qquad (13)$$

As one can notice, this is equal to the assumption "network-of-propose-rules" as defined in (5), if we substitute d by sr. Actually, simulation rules can be considered as the dependencies or propose rules of the SPCR-method; both calculate values of parameters based on input parameters. This is the reason why we did not redefine *arg* and *par* for diagnosis. They are already defined in axiom (3).

Independence-of-causes. This teleological assumption is relevant in case of multiple faults. A multiple fault is a composite hypothesis, that is, a hypothesis consisting of several components. The assumption states that an individual cause (component) explains a set of observations regardless of what other causes (components) are being considered. In other words, it means that if a hypothesis h explains some observations O taking into account the simulation rules SR and $h \prec h'$, then h' also explains O.

$$independence\ of\ causes =_{def} \forall h, h' \in H\ \forall o \in O\ \forall sr \in SR$$
$$(h \prec h' \wedge (explains(h, sr, o) \rightarrow explains(h', sr, o))) \qquad (14)$$

h' should at least explain the same observations as h, but may explain more.

Single-fault-assumption. Single faults are hypotheses (i.e., sets of components) that contain exactly one element, that is, their cardinality is one. This teleological assumption is relevant when information from several symptoms is intersected to find the common fault.

$$single\ fault\ assumption =_{def} \forall h \in H\ card(h) = 1 \qquad (15)$$

Hypotheses-related. A hypothesis is defined as a set of components. We speak about related components if their parameter values are dependent on each other, that is, when a change in the parameter of one component causes a change in the parameter of the other. For example, a light bulb is related to the power supply because the amount of light emitted by the bulb depends on the voltage of the power supply. Such a change in parameters is always the result of the application of simulation rules (which describe the behavior of components in terms of parameters). In other words, two hypotheses (components) are related, when their parameters are affected by each other.

This implies that we can use the "affected by" relation which is defined between two parameters (axiom (4)), also for two hypotheses. The only difference is that we have to substitute d with sr, p with h_1 and q with h_2. Notice however that this correspondence between parameters and hypotheses is only true, if the hypotheses are single-fault hypotheses (formalized in (15)). Only in that case a hypothesis consists of one element (component), which is needed because the affected-by relation is defined between two elements. We define:

$$hypotheses\ related(h_1, h_2) =_{def}$$
$$affected\ by(h_1, h_2) \lor affected\ by(h_2, h_1) \tag{16}$$

Notice that this definition is the same as "parameters-dependent" (10), and we could have used that one instead.

Hypothesis-set-related. This is an epistemological property assumption of a PSM whose goal is to discard a set of hypotheses based on the test result of one hypothesis. In order to do this, all hypothesis pairs in the hypothesis set have to be related to each other. This assumption uses the definition given in (16).

$$hypothesis\ set\ related =_{def} \forall h_i, h_j \in H\ hypotheses\ related(h_i, h_j) \tag{17}$$

3.3 Support for knowledge acquisition

Once we have formalized assumptions, advanced support for method selection in knowledge acquisition becomes feasible because we can semi-automatically decide whether a PSM is applicable. In order to do this, we have to show that the logical combination (see Section 2.2) of the PSM's assumptions is true in the application knowledge at hand. In Section 2 we claimed that currently only epistemological assumptions can be verified automatically (in the domain knowledge). We have performed a small experiment in which we translated the formalized epistemological assumptions into Prolog and automatically checked them in a sub-part of the VT-domain [26]. The approach turned out to work quite well, which made us believe that such support is possible.

4 Conclusions

Assumptions of PSMs are a relatively new area in the field of Knowledge Engineering. In such areas, theory development usually starts with an inductive phase, in which case studies are analyzed and generalized. This is the approach followed in this paper. Based on the literature and on experience with PSMs for diagnosis and the Propose, Select, Check & Revise method, we have proposed an organization of assumptions which distinguished between three types: assumptions which refer to the required domain knowledge of a PSM (*epistemological*); assumptions that refer to the pragmatic aspects of the application domain and environment (*pragmatic*); and assumptions that relate to the goal to be achieved (*teleological*). Epistemological assumptions can be further divided into those referring to the *availability* of domain knowledge, and those referring to *properties* of domain knowledge. Further research is needed to see whether the proposed organization holds across different domains.

A relevant conclusion for the knowledge engineering practice is that epistemological assumptions can be verified automatically, while the pragmatic assumptions have to be guaranteed externally (by a domain expert). Teleological assumptions are still an open question in this respect, on which we currently are working. Automatic verification opens the way to automatically decide on the applicability of PSMs.

The here proposed organization of assumptions of PSMs is related to ideas put forward by other groups [19, 5, 1, 11, 10, 4]. The epistemological task features in [1] are similar to our epistemological assumptions, the difference being that task features describe features of the world, while assumptions refer to a requirement of a method. We make however a further distinction between availability and property assumptions, which bears similarity to the distinction between syntactic and semantic assumptions in [21]. Pragmatic assumptions are reminiscent of the pragmatic aspect in [19], pragmatic task features in [1], and environmental suitability criteria in [4]. Teleological assumptions are less frequently distinguished in the literature. However, in [9], they explicitly consider the relation between a task goal to be achieved and a PSM's competence, implying that the functionality of a PSM can be weaker than that of the task goal. Teleological assumptions seem to capture this weakening also.

Whereas in the literature, so far, assumptions have been described informally (in natural language), we have shown how sorted First-Order Predicate Logic can be used to formalize them. The formalization allows us to define assumptions in a clear and unambiguous manner. The language proposed has been sufficient for the examples, but further work is required to formalize other assumptions.

While formalizing, it turned out that some assumptions from different domains (i.e., diagnosis and Propose & Revise) have similar forms. This was the case with assumptions about simulation rules and propose rules (dependencies), and about hypotheses and parameters. This is an interesting result because it suggests that some assumptions can be defined in a domain-independent manner, which might facilitate their acquisition. However, we suspect many other assumptions to be domain specific. More research is required to verify to what extent assumptions can be formalized in a domain-independent manner.

Acknowledgment

Dieter Fensel and Xavier Talon are acknowledged for discussions on some topics in this paper.

References

1. A. Aamodt, B. Benus, C. Duursma, C. Tomlinson, R. Schrooten, and W. Van de Velde. Task features and their use in commonkads. Technical Report KADS-II/T1.5/VUB/TR/014/1.0, Free University of Brussels & University of Amsterdam & Lloyd's Register, 1992.

2. J. M. Akkermans, B. J. Wielinga, and A. Th. Schreiber. Steps in constructing problem-solving methods. In B. R. Gaines and M. A. Musen, editors, *Proceedings of the 8th Banff Knowledge Acquisition for Knowledge-Based Systems Workshop. Volume 2: Shareable and Reusable Problem-Solving Methods*, pages 29-1 – 29-21, Alberta, Canada, January 30 – February 4 1994. SRDG Publications, University of Calgary.

3. V. R. Benjamins. *Problem Solving Methods for Diagnosis*. PhD thesis, University of Amsterdam, Amsterdam, The Netherlands, 1993.

4. V. R. Benjamins. Problem-solving methods for diagnosis and their role in knowledge acquisition. *International Journal of Expert Systems: Research and Applications*, 8(2):93–120, 1995.

5. B. Chandrasekaran. Design problem solving: A task analysis. *AI Magazine*, 11:59–71, 1990.

6. B. Chandrasekaran, T. R. Johnson, and J. W. Smith. Task-structure analysis for knowledge modeling. *Communications of the ACM*, 35(9):124–137, 1992.

7. L. Console and P. Torasso. Integrating models of the correct behaviour into abductive diagnosis. In L. C. Aiello, editor, *Proc. ECAI-90*, pages 160–166, London, 1990. ECCAI, Pitman.

8. D. Fensel. Assumptions and limitations of a problem-solving method: A case study. In B. R. Gaines and M. A. Musen, editors, *Proceedings of the 8th Banff Knowledge Acquisition for Knowledge-Based Systems Workshop*, Alberta, Canada, 1995. SRDG Publications, University of Calgary.

9. D. Fensel, R. Straatman, and F. van Harmelen. The mincer metaphor: a new view on problem-solving methods for knowledge-based systems. Technical report, SWI, University of Amsterdam, Amsterdam, 1995.

10. J.H Gennari, S.W Tu, T.E Rotenfluh, and M.A. Musen. Mapping domains to methods in support of reuse. *International Journal of Human-Computer Studies*, 41:399–424, 1994.

11. C. Pierret-Golbreich. TASK model: a framework for the design of models of expertise and their operationalization. In B. R. Gaines and M. A. Musen, editors, *Proceedings of the 8th Banff Knowledge Acquisition for Knowledge-Based Systems Workshop*, pages 37.1–37.22. SRDG Publications, University of Calgary, 1994.

12. C. Pierret-Golbreich. Modular and reusable specifications in knowledge engineering: Formal specification of goals and their development. In *Workshop on Knowledge Engineering Methods and Languages (KEML)*, 1996.

13. C. Pierret-Golbreich and I. De Louis. Task: Task centered representation for expert systems at the knowledge level. In *Proc. of the 8th AISB-conference*. Springer-Verlag, 1991.

14. C. Pierret-Golbreich and X. Talon. An algebraic specification of the dynamic behavior of knowledge-based systems. In B. R. Gaines and M. A. Musen, editors, *Proceedings of the 9th Banff Knowledge Acquisition for Knowledge-Based Systems Workshop*, Alberta, Canada, 1995. SRDG Publications, University of Calgary.

15. A.R. Puerta, J. Egar, S. Tu, and M. Musen. A multiple-method shell for the automatic generation of knowledge acquisition tools. *Knowledge Acquisition*, 4:171–196, 1992.

16. William F. Punch and B. Chandrasekaran. An investigation of the roles of problem-solving methods in diagnosis. In *Proc. of the Tenth International Workshop: Expert Systems and their Applications*, pages 25–36, Avignon, France, 1990. EC2.

17. M. Reinders and B. Bredeweg. Strategic reasoning as a reflective task. In *Proceedings of IMSA-92*, pages 159–163, 1992.

18. M. Schmidt-Schauß. *Computational Aspects of an Order-Sorted Logic with Term Declarations*. Springer-Verlag, Berlin, Germany, 1989. Lecture Notes in Artificial Intelligence No. 395.

19. L. Steels. Components of expertise. *AI Magazine*, 11(2):28–49, Summer 1990.

20. A. ten Teije and F. van Harmelen. An extended spectrum of logical definitions for diagnostic systems. In *Proceedings of DX-94 Fifth International Workshop on Principles of Diagnosis*, 1994.

21. A. ten Teije and F. van Harmelen. An extended spectrum of logical definitions for diagnostic systems. *Computational Intelligence*, 1995. Submitted.

22. G. van Heijst. *The Role of Ontologies in Knowledge Engineering*. PhD thesis, University of Amsterdam, May 1995.

23. K. van Marcke. A generic tutoring environment. In L. C. Aiello, editor, *Proc. of the Ninth European Conference on Artificial Intelligence*, pages 655–660, London, UK, 1990. Pitman.

24. J. Vanwelkenhuysen and P. Rademakers. Mapping knowledge-level analysis onto a computational framework. In L. Aiello, editor, *Proc. ECAI-90*, pages 681–686, London, 1990. Pitman.

25. B. J. Wielinga, W. Van de Velde, A. Th. Schreiber, and J. M. Akkermans. The CommonKADS framework for knowledge modelling. In B. R. Gaines, M. A. Musen, and J. H. Boose, editors, *Proc. 7th Banff Knowledge Acquisition Workshop*, volume 2, pages 31.1–31.29. SRDG Publications, University of Calgary, Alberta, Canada, 1992.

26. G. Yost. Configuring elevator systems. Technical report, Digital Equipment Corporation, 111 Locke Drive (LMO2/K11), Marlboro MA 02172, 1992.

27. Z. Zdrahal and E. Motta. An in-depth analysis of propose & revise problem solving methods. In B. R. Gaines and M. A. Musen, editors, *Proceedings of the 9th Banff Knowledge Acquisition for Knowledge-Based Systems Workshop*, Alberta, Canada, 1995. SRDG Publications, University of Calgary.

Problem-Solving Methods:
Making Assumptions for Efficiency Reasons

Dieter Fensel & Remco Straatman[1]

Department of Social Science Informatics (SWI), University of Amsterdam, The Netherlands

{fensel I remco}@swi.psy.uva.nl, http://www.swi.psy.uva.nl/usr/dieter/home.html

Abstract. In this paper we present the following view on problem-solving methods for knowledge-based systems: Problem-solving methods describe an *efficient reasoning strategy* to achieve a goal by introducing *assumptions* about the available domain knowledge and the required functionality. Assumptions, dynamic reasoning behavior, and functionality are the three elements necessary to characterize a problem-solving method.

1   Introduction

The concept *problem-solving method* (PSM) is present in a large part of current knowledge-engineering frameworks (e.g. GENERIC TASKS [Chandrasekaran et al., 1992]; ROLE-LIMITING METHODS [Marcus, 1988], [Puppe, 1993]; KADS [Schreiber et al., 1993] and CommonKADS [Schreiber et al., 1994]; the METHOD-TO-TASK approach [Musen, 1992]; COMPONENTS OF EXPERTISE [Steels, 1990]; GDM [Terpstra et al., 1993]). Libraries of PSM are described in [Benjamins, 1993], [Breuker & Van de Velde, 1994], [Chandrasekaran et al., 1992], and [Puppe, 1993]. In general a PSM describes which reasoning steps and which types of knowledge are needed to perform a task. Such a description should be domain and implementation independent. Problem solving methods are used in a number of ways in knowledge engineering: as a guideline to acquire problem-solving knowledge from an expert, as a description of the main rationale of the reasoning process of the expert and the knowledge-based system, as a skeletal description of the design model of the knowledge-based system, and to enable flexible reasoning by selecting methods during problem solving.

However, a question that has not been answered clearly is the relation between PSMs and *efficiency* of the problem-solving process. Most descriptions of PSM frameworks do point to PSMs as being somehow related to efficiency, however no framework makes this relation explicit. Others claim to have no concern for efficiency since their PSMs are only used to capture the expert's problem-solving behavior. But one must be aware that experts also have to solve the task given their real-life limitations. In fact a large part of expert-knowledge is concerned exactly with efficient reasoning given these limitations. The conceptualization of a domain from an expert differs from the conceptualization of a novice as the former reflects the learning process which yields to efficiency in problem solving.

According to us the main point of a PSM is: *providing the desired functionality in an efficient fashion*. In general, most problems tackled with knowledge-based systems are inherently complex and intractable, i.e., their time complexity is NP-hard (see e.g. [Bylander, 1991], [Bylander et al., 1991], and [Nebel, 1995]).[2] A PSM has to describe not just a realization of the functionality, but one which takes into account the

1. Supported by the Netherlands Computer Science Research Foundation with financial support from the Netherlands Organization for Scientific Research (NWO).

constraints of the reasoning process and the complexity of the task. The constraints have to do with the fact that we do not want to achieve the functionality *in theory* but rather *in practice*. When this relation between PSMs and efficiency is ignored or kept as an implicit notion, both the selection and design of PSMs cannot be performed in an informed manner. Besides the efficiency in terms of computational effort of a PSM, there are further aspects which can influence design decisions of appropriate PSM: The efficiency of the entire knowledge-based system, the optimality of the combined problem solver user and system (e.g. minimizing the number of tests a patient has to suffer from in medical diagnosis), and efficiency of the development process of the knowledge-based system.[3]

After stating the claim that PSMs provide functionality in an efficient way, the next question then is: how could this be achieved if the problems are intractable in their general form? In our view, the way problem solving methods achieve efficient realization of functionality is by making *assumptions*. The assumptions put restrictions on the context of the PSM, such as the domain knowledge and the possible inputs of the method or the precise definition of the functionality (i.e., the goal which can be achieved by applying the PSM). These restrictions enable reasoning to be performed in an efficient manner.

The role that assumptions play in the efficient realization of functionality suggests that the process of designing PSMs must be based on these assumptions. [Akkermans et al., 1993] and [Wielinga et al., 1995] introduce a general approach that views the construction process of PSMs for knowledge-based systems as an assumption-driven activity. A formal specification of a task is derived from informal requirements by introducing assumptions about the problem and the problem space. This task specification is refined into a functional specification of the PSM by making assumptions about the problem-solving paradigm and the available domain theory. Further assumptions are introduced in the process of defining an operational specification of the method. A task is decomposed into declaratively described subtasks and the data and control flow between these subtasks are defined. We will use this approach as a general framework and try to make it more concrete. Our focus lies thereby on assumptions which are related to efficiency of a PSM. We propose to view the process of constructing a PSM for a given function as the process of incrementally adding assumptions that enable efficient reasoning. Summarizing, we want to make the following claims in this paper:

- PSMs are concerned with *efficient* realization of functionality. This is an important characteristic of PSMs and should be dealt with explicitly.
- PSMs achieve this efficiency by making *assumptions* about resources provided by their context (such as domain knowledge) and by assumptions about the precise definition of the task. It is important to make explicit these assumptions to reason about PSMs.
- The process of *constructing* PSMs is assumption-based. During this process assumptions are added that facilitate efficient operationalization of the desired functionality.

One type of assumptions of a PSM defines the relation between the method and the domain knowledge which is required by it. These assumptions describe the domain dependency of a PSM in domain-independent terms. The assumptions can be viewed

---

2. Exceptions are classification problems which have often known polynomial time complexity (see [Goel et al., 1987]).

3. See [Landes & Studer, 1995] for a discussion of further non-functional requirements which could influence design decisions.

as an index of a method since a method can only be chosen if its assumptions are fulfilled by domain knowledge. We can then view the assumptions as proof obligations for the domain knowledge. The assumptions can also define goals for the knowledge acquisition process. Making explicit the assumptions of a PSM about the domain knowledge is a way to deal with the *interaction problem*. The interaction problem [Bylander & Chandrasekaran, 1988] states that domain knowledge cannot be represented independently of how it will be used in reasoning. Vice versa, a PSM and its specific variants cannot be constructed independently of assumptions about the available domain knowledge. Developing reusable PSMs as well as reusable domain theories requires the explicit representation of the assumptions of the method about the domain knowledge; *and* the explicit representations of properties of the domain knowledge that can be related to these assumptions.

Ontologies (i.e., meta-theories of domain theories) are proposed as a means to explicitly represent the commitments of a domain theory (cf. [Top & Akkermans, 1994], [Wielinga & Schreiber, 1994]). Ontologies introduce generic terminologies which are instantiated by a domain theory. These generic terminologies can be viewed as representations of the ontological commitments of a domain theory and could define a link to the assumptions of a PSM.

The paper is structured as follows: In section 2 we discuss why and how PSMs introduce efficient reasoning and section 3 sketches the different parts of PSMs as well as their relationships.

2   Why Are Problem-Solving Methods Necessary

We use the task parametric design and the PSM propose & revise to illustrate the main points of our paper. We use this example since our experiences in the Sisyphus-II project inspired our current point of view. Sisyphus-II [Schreiber & Birmingham, 1996] aimed at comparing different approaches to knowledge engineering. The task is to configure a vertical transportation system (an elevator) which was originally described in [Marcus et al., 1988] who developed the PSM propose & revise to solve this configuration task.

In the following, we formally define the task parametric design. Then, we define a PSM generate & test that can theoretically be used to solve this task. This method can be derived straightforwardly from the task specification. Because this method is very inefficient, we then discuss a more efficient PSM propose & revise as introduced by [Marcus, 1988] and [Marcus et al., 1988]. Propose & revise weakens the task and makes additional assumptions about available domain knowledge in order to gain efficiency. The purpose of this section is neither to define the appropriate way to specify the task parametric design nor the PSM propose & revise; their only use is to illustrate our ideas on PSM.

2.1   A Definition of Parametric Design

A parametric design problem can be defined by a problem space, requirements, constraints, and a preference (see [Tank, 1992] for more details). The *problem space* describes the space which contains all possible designs. The definition of the problem space is domain-specific knowledge. Further, a finite set of *requirements* is assumed to be given by the user. A design that fulfils all requirements is called a *desired design*. In addition to the case-specific user input, a finite set of *constraints* model additional conditions for a valid design. These constraints are domain knowledge describing the regularities in the domain in which the design is constructed. A design that fulfils all constraints is called a *valid design*. A design that is desired and valid is called a *solution*. The *preference* defines a preference function on the problem space and can be used to discriminate between different solutions.

In the case of *parametric* design, a design artifact is described by a set of attribute-value pairs. Let $A_1,..., A_n$ be a fixed set of parameters (i.e. attributes) with fixed ranges $R_1,...,R_n$.

Def 1. Problem Space
   The *problem space* is the cartesian product $R_1 \times ... \times R_n$

Def 2. Requirements and Constraints
   The set of *requirements* and *constraints* are represented by two relations R and C on the problem space defining subsets of the problem space.

Def 3. Possible designs, desired design, valid design, solution
   A *possible design* is an element of the problem space, a *desired design* is an element of R, a *valid design* is an element of C, and a *possible solution* is an element of R and C.

By applying the *preference P*, an *optimal solution* is selected out of all solutions.

Def 4. Preference
   The *preference P* is a partial function on all possible designs.

Def 5. Optimal solution
   An *optimal solution* is a solution for which no other solution exists which has a higher preference value.

In general, several optimal solutions could exist. Therefore, one can further distinguish whether the user gets all of them or a non-deterministic selection of some. This definitions can be extended by introducing priorities on requirements and constraints, or by distinguishing between constraints which always hold and constraints which should hold etc, but this is beyond the scope of this paper.

2.2   A Non-Efficient Solution by Generate & Test

A straightforward operationalization of the declarative task specification can be achieved by applying a variant of `generate` & `test`. The method defines four different inferences and four different types of knowledge that are required by it. The inference structure of this method is given in Fig. 1.

- The inference action `generate` requires knowledge that describes what constitutes a possible design.
- The inference action `R-test` requires knowledge that describes what constitutes a desired designs.
- The inference action `C-test` requires knowledge that describes what constitutes a valid design.
- The inference action `select` requires knowledge that evaluates solutions, i.e., knowledge that describes what constitutes a preferred design.

We have to complete the operational method description by defining its control. Again we do this in a straightforward manner (see Fig. 2). The control flow specifies the following reasoning process: First, all possible designs are derived. Second, all valid designs are derived. Third, all desired designs are derived. Fourth, valid and desired designs are intersected. Fifth, an optimal solution is selected. The sequence of the second and third steps is arbitrary and could also be specified as parallel activities.

The advantage of this method is that it clearly separates the different types of knowledge that are included in the functional specification of the parametric design task. On the other hand, it is precisely this separation that prevents the development of an efficient problem-solver. The knowledge about what is a correct (i.e., valid and desired) and good solution is clearly separated from the generation step, and there is no

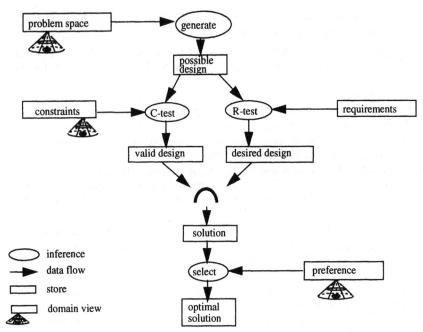

Fig. 1   Inference structure of *generate &test*.

feedback from the results of the test and evaluation step.This method is clearly not very efficient as it has to derive and test all possible designs (i.e., the complete problem space). Still, the method is able to realize the functionality specified by the task if the problem space is finite. With respect to infinite problem spaces, three remarks could be made.

(1) At the knowledge level in its original sense, one should abstract from all computational concerns like limited space or computation time by describing a completely rational agent. Therefore, it is not at all clear whether an infinite search space should be regarded as a problem. In fact the problem of tractability of the method arises not only for infinite search spaces, but also for finite spaces, because the size of the space increases exponentially with the number of parameters and their ranges. Dealing with the size of the search space therefore immediately leads to *limited* rationality[4]. Even for realistic settings with finite search spaces, no computational agent can be implemented that realizes the method in an acceptable way.

(2) One can always transform each infinite search space into a finite one by making some pragmatic assumptions. These domain and task-specific assumptions improve the efficiency of our method by reducing the search space.

> *possible design* := **generate**$_{all}$;
> *valid design* := **C-test**(*possible design*);
> *desired design* := **R-test**(*possible design*);
> *solution* := *valid design* ∩ *desired design*;
> *optimal solution* := **select**(*solution*)

Fig. 2   Control flow I of *generate &test*.

---

4. Decision procedures with perfect rationality try to find an optimal solution, whereas decision procedures with limited rationality reflect also on the costs to find such an optimal solution.

```
repeat
    possible design := generate_one;
    valid design := C-test(possible design);
    desired design := R-test(possible design);
    solution := valid design ∩ desired design;
    acceptable solution := select(solution)
until ∅ ≠ acceptable solution
```

Fig. 3   Control flow II of *generate &test*.

(3) One could think of *reducing the functionality of the method*. In the task description (see Def. 5), we required that an optimal solution should be found. A weaker definition of the functionality of the method is to require that an *acceptable solution* is a solution which has a preference higher than some threshold t.

Def 6. Acceptable solution

    An *acceptable solution* is a solution s with $P(s) > t$.

We also see here the problem of using worst-case analysis: In the worst case it takes the same effort to find an optimal solution (i.e., a global optimum), or an acceptable solution as defined now. The technique of weakening the task definition to improve the efficiency of the computation is commonly used. A well-known example from the field of model-based diagnosis is the *single-fault assumption* [de Kleer & Williams, 1987]. It assumes that the symptoms of a device are caused by one fault. This can be used to improve the efficiency of the methods, but prevents these methods from dealing with situations where the device suffers from several faults.

The weakened functionality of Def. 6 enables us to define a new control flow for the method that allows the method to deal with infinite problem spaces (see Fig. 3).

The sequence of the four inference actions is repeated until an acceptable solution is found. The inference action `generate` should now derive one possible design per step, which is further on treated by the two test steps and the `select` step. For each given probability $0 < \alpha < 1$ one can guarantee that the method finds a solution (if one exists) in finite time with probability greater than $1 - \alpha$ if each element of the problem space has the same chance to get proposed by `generate`.

Making the search finite by introducing domain-specific assumptions or reducing the functionality by weakening the solution criteria transforms `generate & test` into a method that can solve the problem in theory. Still we cannot expect to get an agent which solves this task in a realistic amount of time by implementing the method. We have not really described a PSM but rather a kind of uninformed theorem prover. Arbitrary generated designs are tested whether they are desired, valid, and preferred or not. Still, we have an operational description of how to achieve the goal. From the point of view that one does not want to care about efficiency, this could be a legal point to describe the essence of the reasoning process of a system that solves the task. For example, [Rouveirol & Albert, 1994] define a knowledge level model of machine-learning algorithms by applying the `generate & test` scheme and [Bredeweg, 1994] uses it to define a top-level view on the diagnostic task.

2.3   An Efficient Solution with Propose & Revise

The main advantages of `generate & test` as it is developed above are:
- It requires only the knowledge given by the functional specification, and the four types of knowledge (considering the requirements as knowledge) are clearly separated: each inference uses precisely one knowledge type. The description of the problem space is used in the generation step, the requirements and the constraints are used in two test steps, and the preference is used in the select step.

- Its inference structure is cycle-free. That is, its operational specification does not contain feedback loops that introduce non-monotonicity into the reasoning process.

Generate & test leads to a precise and clear distinction of different conceptual types of knowledge and defines the dynamic behavior of the problem-solving process in a highly understandable manner. On the other hand, these advantages are precisely the reasons that cause the inefficient problem-solving behavior. The PSM propose & revise as discussed in [Marcus et al., 1988] adds efficiency to the problem-solving process by regarding the given properties of generate & test as disadvantages, and introducing static and dynamic feedback into the problem-solving process. An expert has learned which design decisions led to desired, valid, and preferred solutions and which did not. Therefore, expertise compiles test knowledge into the generation step. New types of knowledge arise that enable the efficient generation of solutions.

- Generate & test requires only the knowledge given by the functional specification: An expert includes feedback based on experience from solving earlier design problems. In generate & test the knowledge about what is a desired, correct, and preferred solution is clearly separated from the generation step: A much more clever strategy is to use these knowledge types to guide the generation step of possible designs.
- There is no dynamic feedback in generate & test from the results of the test and evaluation step of a given design: If a design derived during problem solving is not a solution, a new design is derived in the next step. Dynamic feedback would include the reported shortcomings of the first proposed design as guidance for its modification by the next derived design.

The use of the test and evaluation knowledge as guidance for the generation step and the use of the feedback of the test step as input for the generation step are precisely the main improvements which are incorporated into the propose & revise method. In a pessimistic manner this can be expressed as destroying the clear conceptual distinctions of generate & test. Optimistically, this can be viewed as introducing new types of knowledge which glue these different aspects together, thereby adding expertise.

The generate step becomes decomposed into two different activities. The propose step derives an initial design based on the requirements and the revise step tries to improve an incorrect design based on the feedback of the C-test step. To this end, it uses the meta-information that this design is incorrect as well as constraint violations reported by C-test. We get the following conceptual structure of the method (see Fig. 4): The propose step requires knowledge which enables it to derive desired designs using the requirements as input. The revise step requires knowledge which enables it to fix constraint violations of desired designs. Additionally it uses the reported violations to guide the repair process. Revise delivers an acceptable solution as its output. The third inference action C-test requires constraints to check desired designs. As output it derives the set of constraints violated by a design.

Propose & revise requires a number of assumptions to justify its I/O behavior with the specified task. Propose & revise as described in [Marcus et al., 1988] does not require an R-test. That is, designs are not checked on the requirements. Propose is assumed to derive desired designs, instead of possible designs as delivered by the generate step. It is also assumed that the revise step delivers designs that are desired (i.e., this would be an assumptions about the domain specific repair knowledge) or that requirements violations which are not fixed by it must be accepted (i.e., this would weaken the functionality of the method).[5] Finally, propose & revise does not contain a selection of a solution using the preferences. That is, it is either assumed that

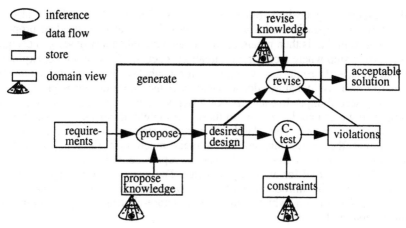

Fig. 4   Inference structure of *propose & revise*.

the propose step as well as the revise step deliver acceptable (or optimal) solutions or that the functionality of the task is reduced to finding just a solution.

When we take a closer look at `revise` by distinguishing several substeps, we see that the `C-test` inference appears also as sub-step of `revise` (cf. [Fensel, 1995a]). After applying some repair rules on an invalid design, `revise` has to check whether the given violations are overcome and whether no new violations are introduced by applying the repair rules. Again, test knowledge that was originally separated from the generation step now appears as sub-activity of it. The `revise` step causes the main computational effort of the method (and also the main effort in precisely specifying the behaviour of the method). The actual efficiency of the method therefore heavily relies on the quality of the repair rules that are required by `revise`, but also on the propose knowledge. The propose knowledge is responsible for ensuring preferred desired designs that require less repair activities. The main point of the method in gaining efficiency is not so much to get rid of the R-test and selection step, but to reduce the search space from the set of all possible designs (i.e., the complete problem space) to the set of preferred desired designs which should be nearly valid.

Two possible control flows for `propose & revise` are shown in Fig. 5. Control flow I tries to find an acceptable solution in one attempt (i.e., the assumption is that this can be done), whereas control flow II includes a loop of *propose, test,* and *revise* until an acceptable solution is found.

Control flow I of propose & revise
desired design := **propose**(*requirements*);
violations := **test**(*desired design*);
acceptable solution :=
   revise(*desired design,violations*)

Control flow II of propose & revise
repeat
   desired design := **propose**(*requirements*);
   violations := **test**(*desired design*);
   acceptable solution :=
      revise(*desired design,violations*)
until $\emptyset \neq$ *acceptable solution*

Fig. 5   Different control flow of *propose & revise*.

Stepwise propose & revise. Our current characterization of propose and revise

_____

5. One can also argue that `propose & revise` extends the competence of the method because it can modify the problem space by overwriting requirements. `Generate & test` can only search through the defined problem space.

works with complete designs. But, as discussed in [Marcus et al., 1988], it also makes sense to regard repair activities as soon as possible. That is, instead of proposing a complete design that is then repaired, we can also incrementally develop a design, and repair at each step where a constraint violations occurs. We have not yet exploited the fact that we specify propose & revise for a subclass of design tasks, namely, for parametric designs. A natural decomposition of the entire design is provided by the parameters describing it. In each propose step we can assign one or some parameters a value; and we can apply revise to these incomplete designs before we propose the next parameter values. This *divide & conquer* strategy with intermediate repairs requires that the constraints do not interact much (see [Marcus et al., 1988]). Otherwise, one always has to redo earlier repair activities when new constraint violations are reported for another parameter. The stepwise derivation of incomplete designs requires the introduction of the new inferences select-parameter and check-completeness which causes a structure-altering transformations of the original version of propose & revise.

2.4   A List of Assumptions

[Poeck et al., 1996] present a specification of propose & revise applied to the VT problem (configuring a vertical transportation system). [Fensel, 1995a] has analysed this variant of propose & revise and reported several assumptions about domain knowledge. This variant of propose & revise consists of four steps where each requires different types of knowledge.

Select. A parameter is selected which should get a value in the next propose step. In the given application domain, a set of propose rules is given. Each rule can be used to derive the value of the parameter that forms its conclusion from the values of the parameters of its premises. Each rule could be further accomplished with guards defining applicability criteria for the rule depending on already derived parameter values. The select step uses these implicitly given dependencies between the parameter as domain-specific meta-knowledge, and assumes that this network defines a partial strong ordering on the set of parameters. At each step each parameter that depends only on already computed parameters according to the applicable propose rules is regarded as a possible choice. One parameter is non-deterministically chosen from this set of possible candidates. That is, select does not make further assumptions about knowledge that would guide this second selection step. The implicit assumption is that this selection does not change performance and quality of the problem-solving process and its result.

Propose. The propose step assumes that *either precisely one applicable* propose rule *or one* user input is given to derive the value of the selected parameter. A parameter should not depend on itself (i.e., no recursive derivation rules requiring a fixpoint operation are allowed). This requirement is not as trivial as it seems to be, as it depends on the rules that become applicable during the problem-solving process.[6]

Test. The test step requires constraints that define a solvable problem and that exclude all non-valid possibilities.

Revise. The revise step is decomposed into a set of more elementary inferences. A select step non-deterministically selects one constraint violation from the set of all violations that were detected by test. Again, the implicit assumption is that this selection does not influence performance and quality of the problem-solving process

---

6. There may exist several propose rules for a parameter, but depending on the already derived values only one should be applicable (see for more details [Fensel, 1995a]).

and its result. This is a very critical assumption because the method does not backtrack from this selection. Derive computes the set of all possible fix combinations (i.e., the set of all sets of elementary fixes) that could possibly resolve the selected constraint violation. Each fix combination (i.e., each set of elementary fixes) as well as the set of all fix combinations must be finite. This requirement is not trivial because some fixes (e.g., increment the value by one) can be applied several times, and specific constraints are required to restrict the number of legal repetitions of these fixes to guaranty finiteness. From the set of all possible fix combinations one is selected by another select step. A cost function is used to guide this selection step. The application of a fix decreases the quality of a design product because it overwrites user requirements or it increases the cost of the product. The cost function defined on the fixes (more precisely on the fix combinations) must be defined in a way that reflects the preferences between possible designs. Apply applies a fix combination. It is again realized by a set of elementary inferences, because it requires the propagation of modified values according to the dependency network of parameter. The precise definition of this step and further aspects of the revise step are beyond the scope of our paper.

2.5 Resume

The propose step as well as the revise step glues together types of knowledge that were treated separately by generate & test. These new knowledge types define strong assumptions about the domain knowledge required by the method. The only reason for doing this is trying to gain *efficiency*. That is, we assume that the "refined" PSM propose & revise will be able to find a solution faster than generate & test (or a better solution in the same amount of time). Therefore, developing PSMs means to blur conceptual distinctions and to introduce assumptions about new types of domain knowledge for reasons of efficiency. The pure and very clear separation of four types of knowledge in generate & test is destroyed by forcing parts of the test and evaluation knowledge into the generation step in order to improve the efficiency of the problem-solving process. We can conclude that propose & revise provides the same or less functionality as generate & test. It makes stronger assumptions to achieve this functionality. Finally, propose & revise is much harder to understand in detail than generate & test. Especially the revise step requires several levels of refinement to define it precisely (see [Fensel, 1995a]) and "the non-monotonic nature of the *Propose and Revise* method is difficult to capture in intuitively understandable theories." [Wielinga et al., 1995]. Given this we must face the fact that the only reason why we still would prefer propose & revise is for reasons of efficiency.

2.6 Principles of Efficient Reasoning

A large part of the problem types tackled by PSMs are hard problems. This means that there is no hope of finding a method that will solve all cases in polynomial time. [Rich & Knight, 1991] even define AI as "... the study of techniques for solving exponentially hard problems in polynomial time by exploiting knowledge about the problem domain." Most PSMs in knowledge engineering implement a heuristic strategy to tackle problems for which no polynomial algorithms are known. There are basically three general approaches:

- Applying techniques to define, structure and minimize the search space of a problem. An appropriate definition of the problem space can immediately rule out most of the effort in finding a solution. In generate & test this implies the transfer from test knowledge into the generate step to shrink the problem space `generate` is working on, and to define the sequence in which possible solutions are generated. Such techniques cannot change the complexity class of a problem but can drastically change the actual behavior of a system. The ordering on different search alternatives can have a *heuristic* or a *non-heuristic* nature.

- Introducing assumptions about the domain knowledge (or the user of the system) which reduces the functionality or the complexity of the part of the problem that is solved by the PSM. In terms of complexity analysis, the domain knowledge or the user of the system is used as an oracle that solves complex parts of the problem.

- Weakening the desired functionality of the system and reducing therefore the complexity of the problem by introducing assumptions about the precise problem type. An example of this type of change is to no longer require an optimal solution, but only an acceptable one, or the single-fault assumption in model-based diagnosis (see [van Harmelen & ten Teije, 1995] for further examples in diagnostic reasoning).

The second and the third approach tackle the problem by solving a different, more restricted, problem. In the second approach this restriction is already part of the domain which implies that the provided functionality of the entire system does not change. The third approach explicitly changes the functionality. Studying these assumptions and restrictions and their influence on the efficiency defines a link to the work in complexity analysis. [Nebel, 1995] proposes different strategies to deal with complex problems. He proposes different ways to restrict the functionality of the system, but he also mentions that additional domain knowledge can change the complexity class of a problem.

3   Problem-Solving Methods: Parts and Relations

In the following, we briefly sketch the different parts of a description of a PSM. Then we discuss the relationships between these parts and between a PSM and its environment.

3.1   The Different Parts of A Problem-Solving Method

The description of a PSM consists of four main parts: a *functional specification*, a *cost description*, an *operational specification*, and its *assumptions* over available resources for the reasoning process (cf. Fig. 6). The functional specification, PSM_f, is a declarative description of the input-output behavior the PSM was designed for. The functional description can be seen as a description of what can be achieved by the PSM. The functional specification is enriched by a cost description, PSM_c, which describes the costs that are associated with using this PSM. The operational specification, PSM_o, describes how to realize the functionality in a reasoning system. The assumptions, PSM_A describe conditions under which the structure described in the operational description will achieve the functional specification (with the described costs). Given the functional description, the assumptions and the cost description, we are able to express what the utility of the PSM is. The method provides the functionality described in PSM_f with costs PSM_c and it expects domain knowledge in return that fulfils the assumptions described in PSM_A.

The functional description describes the input-output behavior of the PSM. The simplest form of *functional description* is a list of input-output tuples. However, in practice, this will often not be possible or feasible because of the size of such a specification. In practice, some form of mathematical representation of the relation between input and output is needed (see e.g. [Levesque, 1984] and [ten Teije & van

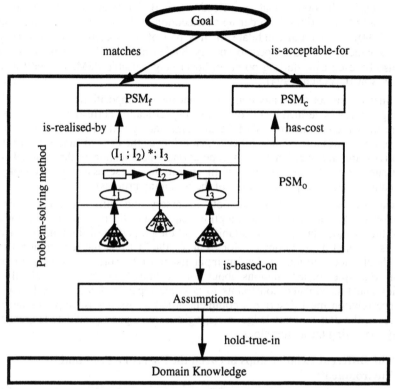

Fig. 6   The PSM and its environment.

Harmelen, 1994] for knowledge-based systems and for [Fensel, 1995b] a survey on functional specification techniques in software engineering).

The cost of a method could include the computing time, the number of interactions with the user, the costs of external tests etc., required by the method. We want to mention however, that in concern to computational complexity we are less interested in the *worst case behavior,* because a significant part of the applied methods are of a heuristic nature which do not improve the worst-case behavior. The worst case is precisely the case where the heuristics do not bring any improvement. Also, *average-case behavior* analysis often introduces assumptions about the problem distribution which are hard to justify. Therefore, we want to look at the complexity of typical cases and assume the expert as oracle that can provide typical cases.

The operational specification consists of inferences and the data- and control-flow between them. The *inferences* specify the reasoning steps that are used to accomplish the functionality of the method. They are described by their input/output relation and can be achieved by a method or a primitive inference. Inferences can be realized by either *methods* (i.e., the description of a PSM can be hierarchically composed) or *primitive inferences*. These primitive inferences are atomic reasoning steps which are not decomposed any further and are described by their input/output relation. In fact one can think of primitive inferences as a special type of problem solving method which has no operational specification. The *roles* are either *stores* that are used to act as input and output of the inferences or *domain views* in which case they get their values from the domain knowledge. A syntactical variant of first-order logic including semantical data modelling primitives is an appropriate mathematical notation for these static aspects of the operational specification (cf. [Kifer et al., 1995]). Finally, the *control* of a PSM describes the ordering of execution of the inferences. Dynamic logic [Kozen, 1990] is a natural candidate for this part of the specification. A survey of languages which were developed to specify KADS models of expertise and which could also be used as a starting point for specifying reusable PSMs can be found in [Fensel & van Harmelen, 1994].

Notice, that we do not make any claim whether the decomposition and control of the reasoning process as defined by the operational specification corresponds to the design model or the structure and control of the implementation of the PSM. The operational specification defines a reasoning process that achieves the desired functionality if the assumptions are fulfilled. That is, the operational specification is the rationalize of these assumptions or the structure of the proof that these assumption enable the functionality (under the specified costs of the reasoning process).

The assumptions of a method are both necessary and sufficient criteria for the application of the method. The assumptions can define restrictions on the possible input of the method, and on the availability and the properties of domain knowledge. Examples of input assumptions are for example the fact that the requirements for a design should not conflict, or that an input list must be sorted according to some criterion. Examples of assumptions about domain knowledge are the availability of heuristics that link violated constraints to possible repair actions, or the fact that a preference relation must describe a complete ordering. As the assumptions describe properties of the domain knowledge, meta-logic seems a good candidate language for formally specifying the assumptions.

3.2 The Different Relationships between the Parts of a PSM and its Environment

The relation between the functional specification, the operational specification, and the assumptions is essential for understanding PSMs. Given that the assumptions hold, the reasoning system defined by the operational specification will exhibit the input-output behavior specified in the functional specification. One can view *the assumptions as the missing pieces in the proof that the behavior of the method satisfies its goal*. Four types of proof obligations arise:

(1) the external relation between the goal (i.e., the task) and the functionality of the PSM has to be established. One has to ensure that the functionality of the method is strong enough to fulfil the goal if its assumptions are fulfilled.

(2) the external relation between the method and the domain knowledge has to be established. One has to ensure that the domain knowledge fulfils the assumptions of the method. Depending on the type of an assumption, we have to ensure either that the domain knowledge implies an assumption or that it does not violate it.

(3) the internal relationship between the functional and operational descriptions of the method has to be established. One has to ensure that, given the assumptions the operational description describes a way to achieve the functionality. Because the description of the operational specification requires a logic over states, we use dynamic logic [Kozen, 1990] to formalize this obligation (that ensures the termination of the program and the desired functionality):

$$\models PSM_A \rightarrow (<PSM_o> \text{true} \land [PSM_o] \, PSM_f)$$

(4) a statement about the efficiency of the method has to be made. In the ideal case, given the assumptions, each alternative operational description requires at least the same effort as the chosen one to achieve the functionality of the method.[7] A simpler obligation is to proof a lower bound for the efficiency complexity of a chosen method (see [Straatman & Beys, 1995]).

4   Conclusions

Our paper tries to answer two questions: What are problem-solving methods and why are they necessary? In a nutshell, we provided the following answer: A PSM translates a declarative goal descriptions into a set of assumptions about domain knowledge required to achieve the goal in an efficient manner. The dichotomy of a declarative goal description and an efficient implementation must be bridged by a level where one rationalizes an efficient problem solver, that is, a problem solver with limited resources. A part of expertise is knowledge about achieving goals under bounded rationality. An operational description of a problem-solving method defines the appropriate level to elicit, acquire, interpret, and model this kind of knowledge. Assumptions about domain knowledge or the precise functionality are introduced, strengthened, or modified in order to achieve efficiency. The point of view on problem-solving methods as presented in our paper defines a number of research topics.

(1) An adequate framework for describing problem-solving methods has to be established: A formal notation for the functionality of a method is required. A logic over states is needed to express the operational specification of a method. This language must be able to express control over functionally specified basic building blocks. A formal notation for the assumptions is needed. A variant of meta-logic could be used to specify the assumptions of the method. Finally, a feasible calculus must be provided to specify the computational behavior of a method.

(2) A proof calculus is necessary that enables to prove relationships between the different parts of the specification of a method. A first step into this direction is achieved by [Fensel & Groenboom, 1995] where proof rules are defined for languages like KARL and (ML)^2. Based on these proof rules, automated support by theorem provers is possible. As the description formalisms include logic over states like dynamic logic, we will investigate the possibility to use theorem provers like the Karlsruher Interactive Verifier KIV [Reif, 1995] developed for program verification based on dynamic logic.

(3) Methods and tools are necessary that support the cyclic development of appropriate PSMs. This includes a library with problem-solving methods schema indexed by their functionality, assumptions, and cost, and operations working on assumptions and deriving PSM instantiations. [Van de Velde, 1994] defines three components of a modelling library: Modelling components are structures useful for the construction of complete models. Generic models are frames representing a class of complete models. Modelling operators transform a model into another one. Substantiating these ideas seems to be a promising research direction.

Acknowledgments. We would like to thank Ameen Abu-Hanna, Kees de Koning, Guus Schreiber, Annette ten Teije, Peter Terpstra and Bob Wielinga for helpful discussions that enabled this paper. We would also like to thank Manfred Aben, Jürgen Angele, Richard Benjamins, Gertjan van Heijst, Rudi Studer and two anonymous referees for comments on earlier versions of the paper. We especially would like to thank Frank van Harmelen, for his contributions to earlier versions of the paper, and Joost Breuker, for discussions that stimulated most of the presented work.

---

7. This would require perfect rationality of the decision process that constructs the optimal problem solver with limited rationality.

References

[Akkermans et al., 1993] J. M. Akkermans, B. Wielinga, and A. TH. Schreiber: Steps in Constructing Problem-Solving Methods. In N. Aussenac et al. (eds.): *Knowledge-Acquisition for Knowledge-Based Systems*, Lecture Notes in AI, no 723, Springer-Verlag, Berlin, 1993.

[Benjamins, 1993] V. R. Benjamins: *Problem Solving Methods for Diagnosis*, PhD Thesis, University of Amsterdam, Amsterdam, The Netherlands, June 1993.

[Bredeweg, 1994] B. Bredeweg: Model-based diagnosis and prediction of behaviour. In [Breuker & Van de Velde, 1994], pp. 121—153.

[Breuker & Van de Velde, 1994] J. Breuker and W. Van de Velde (eds.): *The CommonKADS Library for Expertise Modelling*, IOS Press, Amsterdam, The Netherlands, 1994.

[Bylander, 1991] T. Bylander: Complexity Results for Planning. In *Proceedings of the 12th International Joint Conference on Artificial Intelligence (IJCAI-91)*, Sydney, Australia, August 1991.

[Bylander & Chandrasekaran, 1988] T. Bylander and B. Chandrasekaran: Generic Tasks in Knowledge-Based Reasoning. The Right Level of Abstraction for Knowledge Acquisition. In B. Gaines et al. (eds.): *Knowledge Acquisition for Knowledge-Based Systems*, vol I, pp. 65—77, Academic Press, London, 1988.

[Bylander et al., 1991] T. Bylander, D. Allemang, M. C. Tanner, and J. R. Josephson: The Computational Complexity of Abduction, *Artificial Intelligence*, 49, pages 25—60, 1991.

[Chandrasekaran et al., 1992] B. Chandrasekaran, T.R. Johnson, and J. W. Smith: Task Structure Analysis for Knowledge Modeling, *Communications of the ACM*, 35(9): 124—137, 1992.

[David et al., 1993] J.-M. David, J.-P. Krivine, and R. Simmons (eds.): *Second Generation Expert Systems*, Springer-Verlag, Berlin, 1993.

[de Kleer & Williams, 1987] J. H. de Kleer and B. C. Williams: Diagnosing Multiple Faults, *Artificial Intelligence*, 32():97—130, 1987.

[Fensel, 1995a] D. Fensel: Assumptions and Limitations of a Problem-Solving Method: A Case Study. In *Proceedings of the 9th Banff Knowledge Acquisition for Knowledge-Based System Workshop (KAW'95)*, Banff, Canada, February 26th - February 3th, 1995.

[Fensel, 1995b] D. Fensel: Formal Specification Languages in Knowledge and Software Engineering, *The Knowledge Engineering Review*, 10(4), 1995.

[Fensel & Groenboom, 1995] D. Fensel and R. Groenboom: A Formal Semantics for Specifying the Dynamic Reasoning of Knowledge-based Systems. In *Proceedings of the Knowledge Engineering: Methods and Languages Workshop (KEML'96)*, January 15-16, 1996.

[Fensel & van Harmelen, 1994] D. Fensel and F. van Harmelen: A Comparison of Languages which Operationalize and Formalize KADS Models of Expertise, *The Knowledge Engineering Review*, 9(2), 1994.

[Goel et al., 1987] A. Goel, N. Soundararajan, and B. Chandrasekaran: Complexity in Classificatory Reasoning. In *6th National Conference on Artificial Intelligence (AAAI'87)*, Seattle, Washington, July 13-17, 1987, pages 421—425.

[Kifer et al., 1995] M. Kifer, G. Lausen, and J. Wu: Logical Foundations of Object-Oriented and Frame-Based Languages, *Journal of the ACM*, 42:741-843, 1995.

[Kozen, 1990] D. Kozen: Logics of Programs. In J. v. Leeuwen (ed.), *Handbook of Theoretical Computer Science*, Elsevier Science Publ., B. V., Amsterdam, 1990.

[Landes & Studer, 1995] D. Landes and R. Studer: The Treatment of Non-Functional Requirements in MIKE. In *Proceedings of the 5th European Software Engineering Conference ESEC'95*, Barcelona, Spain, September 25-28, 1995.

[Levesque, 1984] H. J. Levesque: Foundations of a functional approach to knowledge representation, *Artificial Intelligence*, 23(2):155—212, 1984.

[Marcus, 1988] S. Marcus (ed.). *Automating Knowledge Acquisition for Experts Systems*, Kluwer Academic Publisher, Boston, 1988.

[Marcus et al., 1988] S. Marcus, J. Stout, and J. McDermott VT: An Expert Elevator Designer That Uses Knowledge-based Backtracking, *AI Magazine*, 9(1):95—111, 1988.

[Musen, 1992] M. A. Musen: Overcoming the Limitations of Role-Limiting Methods, *Knowledge Acquisition*, 4 (2): 165—170, 1992.

[Nebel, 1995] B. Nebel: Artificial intelligence: A Computational Perspective. To appear in G. Brewka (ed.), *Essentials in Knowledge Representation.*

[Poeck et al., 1996] K. Poeck, D. Fensel, D. Landes, and J. Angele: Combining KARL And CRLM For Designing Vertical Transportation Systems. In [Schreiber & Birmingham, 1996].

[Puppe, 1993] F. Puppe: *Systematic Introduction to Expert Systems: Knowledge Representation and Problem-Solving Methods*, Springer-Verlag, Berlin, 1993.

[Reif, 1995] W. Reif: The KIV Approach to Software Engineering. In M. Broy and S. Jähnichen (eds.): *Methods, Languages, and Tools for the Construction of Correct Software*, Lecture Notes in Computer Science (LNCS), no 1009, Springer-Verlag, Berlin, 1995.

[Rich & Knight, 1991] E. Rich and K. Knight: *Artificial Intelligence*, McGraw-Hill, New York, 2nd edition, 1991.

[Rouveirol & Albert, 1994] C. Rouveirol and P. Albert: Knowledge level model of a configurable learning system. In Lecture Notes in Aritificial Intelligence (LNAI), no 867 Springer-Verlag, Berlin, 1994.

[Schreiber & Birmingham, 1996] A. Th. Schreiber and B. Birmingham (eds.): *Special Issue on Sisyphus, The International Journal of Human-Computer Studies*, to appear, 1996.

[Schreiber et al., 1993] A. Th. Schreiber, B. J. Wielinga, and J. A. Breuker (eds.): *KADS: A Principled Approach to Knowledge-Based System Development, vol 11 of Knowledge-Based Systems Book Series*, Academic Press, London, 1993.

[Schreiber et al., 1994] A. TH. Schreiber, B. Wielinga, J. M. Akkermans, W. Van De Velde, and R. de Hoog: CommonKADS. A Comprehensive Methodology for KBS Development, *IEEE Expert*, 9(6):28—37, 1994.

[Steels, 1990] L. Steels: Components of Expertise, *AI Magazine*, 11(2), 1990.

[Straatman & Beys, 1995] R. Straatman and P. Beys: A Performance Model for Knowledge-based Systems. In M. Ayel and M. C. Rousset (eds.): *EUROVAV-95 European Symposium on the Validation and Verification of Knowledge Based Systems*, pages 253—263. ADEIRAS, Universite de Sovoie, Chambery, 26-28 June 1995.

[Tank, 1992] W. Tank: *Modellierung von Expertise über Konfigurationsaufgaben*, Infix, Sankt Augustin, Germany, 1992.

[ten Teije & van Harmelen, 1994] A. ten Teije and F. van Harmelen: An Extended Spectrum of Logical Definitions for Diagnostic Systems. In *Proceedings of DX-94 Fifth International Workshop on Principles of Diagnosis*, 1994.

[Terpstra et al., 1993] P. Terpstra, G. van Heijst, B. Wielinga, and N. Shadtbolt: Knowledge Acquisition Support Through Generalised Directive Models. In [David et al., 1993], pp. 428—455.

[Top & Akkermans, 1994] J. Top and H. Akkermans: Tasks and Ontologies in Engineering Modeling, *International Journal of Human-Computer Studies*, 41():585—617, 1994.

[van Harmelen & ten Teije, 1995] F. van Harmelen and A. ten Teije: Approximations in Diagnosis: Motivations and Techniques. In C. Bioch and Y.H. Tan (eds.), *Proceedings of the Dutch Conference on AI (NAIC'95)*, Rotterdam, June 1995.

[Van de Velde, 1994] W. Van de Velde: A Constructivist View on Knowledge Engineering. In *Proceedings of the 11th European Conference on Artificial Intelligence (ECAI'94)*, Amsterdam, August 1994.

[Wielinga & Schreiber, 1994] B. J. Wielinga and A. Th. Schreiber: Conceptual Modelling of Large Reusable Knowledge Bases. In K. von Luck and H. Marburger (eds.): *Management and Processing of Complex Data Structures*, Springer-Verlag, Lecture Notes in Computer Science, no 777, pages 181—200, Berlin, Germany, 1994.

[Wielinga et al., 1995] B. Wielinga, J. M. Akkermans, and A. TH. Schreiber: A Formal Analysis of Parametric Design Problem Solving. In B. R. Gaines and M. A. Musen (eds.): *Proceedings of the 8th Banff Knowledge Acquisition for Knowledge-Based Systems Workshop (KAW-95)*, vol II, pp. 31/1—37/15, Alberta, Canada, 1995.

The Thin End of the Wedge: Efficiency and the Generalised Directive Model Methodology

Kieron O'Hara and Nigel Shadbolt

Artificial Intelligence Group, Dept. of Psychology, University of Nottingham, University Park, Nottingham NG7 2RD, United Kingdom
{koh,nrs}@psyc.nott.ac.uk

Abstract. Problem-solving methods (PSMs) are often used as means to achieve efficient knowledge-based systems. However, depending on how 'efficiency' is characterized, different conceptions of PSMs are possible. The value of a particular view of efficiency in knowledge engineering is defended, and it is shown how such considerations lend support to the GDM methodology.

In this paper, we show how the Generalised Directive Model (GDM) methodology is addressing a problem in knowledge engineering first discussed by us in our (1993a). To an extent, this account can be seen as an end point to a long series of discussions about GDMs that have appeared in the literature (van Heijst et al 1992; Terpstra et al 1993; O'Hara 1993; O'Hara & Shadbolt 1993b; Motta et al 1994a; Motta et al 1994b; Major & O'Hara 1995; Motta et al 1996). On top of that, we hope to add a number of pertinent comments about problem-solving methods and their use in knowledge engineering frameworks; these comments will generally be organised around a discussion of very interesting recent work by Fensel & Straatman (1996). In particular, we claim that problem-solving methods can be seen as approaching the problem of efficient system development from a number of directions, and that how a problem-solving method is defined depends crucially on how one wants to address efficiency. We hope also to clarify the discussion over the relative merits of formal and informal methods.

1 Problem-Solving Methods as Routes to Efficiency

In their (1996), Fensel & Straatman (FS) are very keen to establish a role for problem-solving methods in knowledge engineering. The importance of this task should not be underestimated; in the various discussions about the content of models which have raged over the past few years, perhaps we in the knowledge acquisition field have lost sight of precisely why we argue over these things. FS are concerned to ground (or re-ground) such talk in tangible products. Their view is that a problem-solving method should improve efficiency.

Their argument is illustrated by an example using a PSM to produce a more efficient design system. They begin with a system they argue is conceptually clean (i.e. there is a 'precise and clear distinction of different conceptual types of knowledge and [it] defines the dynamic behavior of the problem-solving process in a highly understandable manner'), which works on the principle of generate-and-test. It generates all the solutions in the problem space, and then applies a metric to find a solution which is at least as good as any other. This method has a number of advantages, not least that it is very straightforward. Its conceptual cleanness comes from the fact that each different class of knowledge identified is used by one particular inference. For example, the class of knowledge about what constraints there are over the domain is used only as part of the testing inference when a design is verified as valid.

The obvious drawback with generate-and-test is that it is highly inefficient in any domain with even a moderately large problem space. Generating *all* designs is very expensive. The key point is to note that with dynamic feedback from previous attempts, the designer can prune many branches of the search tree. When the designer uses *this* method, the result is the well-known propose-and-revise structure. According to FS, this efficiency gain comes at a price. Of course, propose-and-revise is, all things being equal, far superior as a design method than generate-and-test, so there would be few who were not willing to pay this price.

Both the proposal and the revision steps collapse distinctions made by the generate-and-test method. In this way, we can see that, on their account, propose-and-revise is not merely a refinement of the simpler method. It is not that the classifications of knowledge get more fine-grained as the analysis of design continues (though this may happen as well). In fact, as we move from generate-and-test to propose-and-revise, some classifications get coarser-grained as those distinctions collapse. Hence the (mere) refinement of knowledge categories and relationships cannot (always) produce optimal or more efficient solutions. Put another way, efficiency gains are not only produced by local optimizations of inference structures, but also by global changes. We pause to note here that the GDM methodology is explicitly a refinement methodology committed to local change, and indeed in the GDM grammar (see Section 5 below) classifications of knowledge can apparently only get more fine-grained. Hence, FS's critique is implicitly inconsistent with the analysis of generic problem-solving underlying GDMs.

Of course, the cogency of this critique depends crucially on FS's view of what a PSM is and what it does. They see a PSM as fully described by four components.

- A functional specification. This is a declarative description of the desired IO behaviour.
- An operational specification. This is an account of how to realise that behaviour in an artificial system.
- A set of assumptions. These are, in effect, a set of conditions that the domain and context must satisfy for the PSM to be appropriate.
- A cost description. This specifies the resources that will be required for the operational specification to produce the desired IO behaviour in the domain.

These components fit together as in Figure 1.

Now we can see how such a PSM might aid knowledge engineering. We want to know if a particular method is suitable for our purposes. Then we need to verify that (i) the goal of our system matches the functional specification; (ii) that the assumptions on which the PSM is based hold in the domain; and (iii) that the cost of using the PSM is adequately bounded.

As the knowledge engineer moves from PSM to PSM, what he does is analyse the assumptions, and refines his view of the domain accordingly. Note that it is possible for assumptions to be refined — it is impossible for a knowledge engineer to *decrease* his knowledge of a domain (assuming that he writes everything down assiduously). But the refinement of assumptions does not necessarily lead to a refinement of PSMs, as the generate-and-test/propose-and-revise example is intended to show.

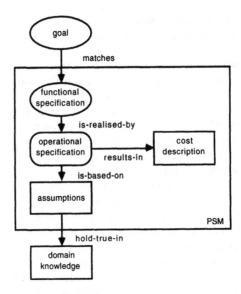

Fig. 1. The PSM and its environment

2 The Ambiguity of 'Efficiency'

We hope we have represented FS's argument correctly. As it stands, it is, as we pointed out, an attack on the ideas behind GDMs (or at least on the claim that GDMs are always sufficient to produce a solution). Strangely, though, we are quite happy to agree with much of their argument. It is the purpose of this section to show how such a circle can be squared.

We particularly applaud FS's focus on the purpose of PSMs, and on their advocacy of the yardstick of efficiency. However, knowledge engineering is a complex process, and consequently 'efficiency' is an ambiguous notion. FS do not address the issue of which sense of 'efficiency' PSMs are there to promote.

First of all, there are various types of efficiency measures that may or may not be appropriate in an application, and each of these measures determines a kind of efficiency. For example, there is the efficiency of the system in producing output in a certain time span, or with a certain limit to computational resources. Or the efficiency gains might be to do with ease of debugging, maintenance or extension of the system; a PSM might well produce a slower, more cumbersome system as the price of producing a system that an organization may use over long periods of time in radically differing contexts.

These types of efficiency would come under the rough heading of 'cost description'. FS should probably be taken to be referring to the production of output within limits of time and computational resources. In that case, their argument presupposes that those types of efficiency are the ones to be aimed for. Indeed, this is often the case, but not exclusively. Sometimes different cost descriptions are desirable.

A second kind of efficiency is efficiency within a PSM. Someone who advocated this sort of view of efficiency would take a PSM as providing the framework for a system; for example, he would want a system that performed, say, propose-and-revise as specified in some description of p-and-r. The PSM would then provide the knowledge categories that are needed, not only for the production of the system's output, but also for secondary tasks such as providing explanations for the user, or providing standard input and output forms. In that case, PSM analysis takes the PSM as given, and would not be concerned with moving through different types of PSM to find the best one. The aim of a knowledge engineering methodology would then be the selection of a PSM, followed by the maximization of efficiency within that type. FS's argument couldn't hold here, because the operational specifications, assumptions and cost descriptions would vary as the functional specification was held constant. The requirement to stick to a particular set of classes of knowledge would invalidate the inference that straightforward refinement could not deliver the optimal system.

Of course, such a type of system is pretty rare. But it does serve to show how a particular way of viewing the efficiency problem can lead to different pictures of what a PSM should provide for the knowledge engineer.

There is a third type of efficiency related to knowledge engineering, and this one is much more relevant. The efficiency sought is that of the *knowledge engineering process*. When the PSM provides efficiency in this direction, what it aims to do is to make the process of moving from user requirements to implementation as inexpensive as possible. A PSM designed to do this will not necessarily deliver the best final system in the sense assumed by FS; rather, the methodology would need to have built into it extra ways of facilitating efficient code. The gain for the organization commissioning the target system is in the production of a system grounded in a more accurate or congenial cognitive model, one that would facilitate KA. A likely result of this is that the system will be more easily understood and maintained by non-specialist staff, particularly if they are domain experts (though it is important to remember that merely producing a cognitively accurate model will not necessarily improve understanding and maintenance).

These different types of efficiency aimed for will lead to different conceptions of PSMs. But as conceptions of PSMs change, then so will the arguments surrounding them. For example, consider the generate-and-test/propose-and-revise example of FS. The crux of this example is that propose-and-revise is a development from generate-and-test (and not a refinement of it). But the fact that the two PSMs are in this development-of relationship is entirely dependent on the way they are described. They are described as they are by FS because they use the four component framework mentioned above. The process of applying a PSM involves matching a goal against a functional specification.

Consider an account of PSMs which saw the object to be modelled as an account of expert behaviour, as opposed to the logico-mathematical formalization of the expertise. Such an account, though it might include the generate-and-test and propose-and-revise PSMs, will not see propose-and-revise as an *extension* of generate-and-test in any way, since the behaviour of a domain expert could be described as one or the other but not both. *Either* the expert generates all solutions, *or* he does not. If the PSM is intended to describe the expert in this sort of way, as opposed to describing the IO relations of the task he is performing, then we can agree that propose-and-revise is not a *refinement* of generate-and-test, but equally is not an extension of it either. Hence the argument based on the particular account of PSMs that FS give breaks down. In particular, in the GDM grammar, a generate-and-test structure is built using a *different* route to a propose-and-revise structure; the decisions the knowledge engineer would be called upon to make by the GDM grammar would make the decision between generate-and-test and propose-and-revise at a fairly early stage in the modelling process.

Indeed, it is even possible to describe generate-and-test as an extension of propose-and-revise on this account. To do this, one would have to see the *propose* stage as the generation of a complete set of solutions, and the *revise* stage as a selection process involving the removal from this set of the non-optimal solutions. Of course, the result would be a very artificial and formalistic interpretation of the relevant terms, but the important point is that it would not be an inconsistent one.

So far, we have isolated a number of types of efficiency, and shown that FS's arguments only apply necessarily to one. In the next section, we will discuss the use of PSMs in knowledge engineering, to try to show that other types of efficiency can be of importance when it comes to the application of PSMs in a domain. We shall then go on to argue that the GDM methodology is more suited to the increase of other types of efficiency.

3 Problem-Solving Methods and Knowledge Level Primitives

Generally, the term 'PSM' has tended to apply to generic descriptions of problem-solving that yielded a functional account of how the problem-solving worked (see e.g. van de Velde 1988). Since most of the work in this field was 'coming from' the same direction — AI/expert systems — there was a reasonable measure of agreement in what a PSM should convey (Karbach et al 1990). In the first place, the PSM should contain some sort of account of what the problem-solving consisted in — how the problem-solving should be conceptualized. And secondly, it should contain a knowledge level specification of how to perform the task, in terms of the classes of knowledge, types of inference, control, etc..

This then results in a clear high level methodology. Look at the problem-solving; verify that it matches the conceptualization in the PSM; use the PSM as the basis of the application. In that event, merely by identifying the problem-solving as, say, propose-and-revise or systematic diagnosis or whatever, you get the inference and control structures for free.

However, as we pointed out in our (1993a), this type of methodology is not as clear cut as it may at first seem, because the two pieces of the PSM are actually pulling in different directions. Let us call the account of problem-solving the 'task', and let us call the functional specification a 'knowledge level primitive' or KLP. A PSM, then, yokes together a task and a KLP. Classifying problem-solving involves giving the problem-solving a task name. That immediately brings an associated KLP into play, which can be used as the basis for an efficient system. This is, of course, a great short cut in the production of efficient systems, as FS point out.

The problem arises because it is the classification of the problem-solving in terms of the task vocabulary that is problematic. Problem-solving is typically amenable to a number of radically different classifications, depending on one's point of view. We don't have the space here to discuss this in great detail, but the position is defended in (O'Hara & Shadbolt 1993a). A good demonstration of the non-determinacy of the classification of problem-solving in the Sisyphus I project can be found in (Gaines 1991). (O'Hara & Shadbolt 1993b) shows how each of the six generic tasks in Chandrasekaran's taxonomy can be fundamentally reinterpreted in terms of the others. (Clancey 1985) discusses how psychological issues and AI issues should be kept separate. Perhaps the most convincing case is made by (Allemang & Rothenfluh 1992), who show empirically, albeit on a rather small sample, that the same problem-solving can be conceptualized in terms of a suite of PSMs in different ways even within a group of people familiar with that suite (in their case, generic tasks).

And now the problem is clear. Given that we know that problem-solving can be classified in terms of tasks in a number of different ways, it follows that the systems built on the basis of the associated KLPs will have differing computational properties corresponding to the differences between the KLPs. And then they will differ in terms of efficiency. So it seems to follow that the best classification of the problem-solving in terms of the task is the one that is associated with the most efficient KLP (in that context). But that is precisely the fact that we cannot know when we start KA!

This is a very abbreviated and simplified version of a fairly complex argument. See (O'Hara & Shadbolt 1993a, 1993b) for more detailed discussion. Those papers discuss the problem in terms of psychology, but the issue arises even when a purely engineering view of AI is taken. Taking the problem as given, the question we must now address is whether FS manage to get around this problem, with their goal- and assumption-based approach.

4 Goals and Assumptions

One point to note is that the problem could be solved if the PSM-space in use was very attenuated. That is, if there were only a handful of PSMs that were being used by your methodology, you could then simply generate all solutions and test them all against the cost estimates, and choose an optimal solution. The drawback of this is that there would only be a handful of possible architectures for your expert systems. In that case, although you could certainly make sure that you had the most efficient of this limited range, you could not guarantee that you had a solution that was particularly efficient in general terms.

This, incidentally, is why the decompositional, refinement-based methodologies in knowledge engineering, such as GDMs, CommonKADS and the later task-analysis-based generic tasks developed; so that a wider range of task classifications were available for a finer-grained conceptual analysis of the problem-solving (O'Hara & Shadbolt forthcoming).

This is a potentially serious problem for FS. They cannot take the easy route of claiming that propose-and-revise is a monolithic PSM, which results in a particular type of system, because propose-and-revise can result in a wide range of systems, depending on the operational properties of the revision process. If the revision process is particularly chaotic, then an optimal solution may only be approached slowly. (Motta et al 1996, Section 4) discusses the considerable differences in efficiency for a final system given different control regimes for a basic propose-and-revise system in the context of Sisyphus II, and a detailed theoretical extension of this discussion can be found in (Zdrahal & Motta 1995). For example, within the general propose-and-revise method for parametric design, there are two obvious routes to go: (i) instantiate one parameter at a time, removing all the constraint violations before moving on; (ii) instantiate all the parameters at each revision cycle, and only then recalculate the constraint violations (of course, there are many other opportunistic and/or hybrid control structures that can be imposed upon the revision of a parametric design as well as these two). Depending on which control regime actually gets chosen, the efficiency considerations can vary quite dramatically. For instance, Motta et al were able to show that (ii) was more efficient than (i) if there is a high number of interdependencies between the constraints. This is the sort of efficiency result that makes it impossible to know how efficient a system is going to be *simply* on the assumption that one PSM rather than another (e.g. propose-and-revise as opposed to generate-and-test) will be used. The suite of PSMs must be very large if they are to be used as a basis of a claim that efficiency will be in any way *maximised*.

It is therefore essential that a PSM like propose-and-revise be seen as a class of methods, rather than a single monolithic one. When FS say 'The *operational specification* [of a PSM] consists of inferences and the data- and control-flow between them', they must be saying (given that they agree that propose-and-revise is a PSM in its own right) that data- and control-flow are variable to cope with circumstances — only this will have the effect of avoiding the monolithic approach. And indeed it is a very fair point that formalising such items does make it possible to manipulate their form (within limits), in order to fit the PSM to the peculiar context of a particular system. The effect of a family of methods is produced by matching the functional specification, and then having a variable operational specification.

The worry is that the choice of PSM in their example (propose-and-revise) is explicitly connected with the parametric design task (cf. Sisyphus II). Now, it is well known that propose-and-revise is a constructive method associated with design tasks. But note that this is an instance of the connection between task classification and KLPs that we discussed in Section 3.

FS define design formally as follows.

> A ... design problem can be defined by a problem space, requirements, constraints, and a preference ... . The *problem space* describes the space which contains all possible designs. The definition of the problem space is domain-specific knowledge. Further, a finite set of *requirements* is assumed to be given by the user. A design which fulfills all requirements is called a *desired design*. In addition to the case-specific user input, a finite set of *constraints* model additional conditions for a valid design. These constraints are domain knowledge describing the regularities in the domain in which the design is constructed. A design that fulfills all constraints is called a *valid design*. A design that is desired and valid is called a *solution*. The *preference* defines a preference function on the problem space and can be used to discriminate between different solutions. (FS 1996)

Parametric design is the special case where the design artifact can be described by a set of attribute-value pairs. This description is augmented by a definition in FOPC later.

Nevertheless, despite the impeccable logic, we have to say that the ambiguity of what a task is will of necessity rear its head. For, no matter how formal a task description can be, the reinterpretation of it in terms of some other task will always be possible.

For instance, we can even define a diagnostic task — i.e. an analytic task — that is absolutely isomorphic to the design task defined by FS.

A diagnosis problem can be defined by a classification space, symptoms, system model, and a preference ... . The *classification space* describes the space which contains all possible diagnoses. The definition of the classification space is domain-specific knowledge. Further, a finite set of *symptoms* is assumed to be given by the user. A diagnosis which explains all symptoms is called a *desired diagnosis*. In addition to the case-specific user input, a *system model* models additional conditions for a valid diagnosis over the domain. This model is domain knowledge describing the regularities in the domain in which the diagnosis is performed. A diagnosis which is validated by the system model is called a *valid diagnosis*. A diagnosis which is desired and valid is called a *solution*. The preference defines a preference function on the classification space and can be used to discriminate between several solutions (e.g. the most parsimonious diagnosis that is both desired and valid should be selected).

This definition can also be supplemented in the obvious way by an FOPC definition (and indeed a parametric analogue of the design task can be produced by insisting that the final classification be in the form of a set of attribute-value pairs). Clearly all and only that problem-solving which can be recognised as design on the first definition can be recognised as diagnosis on the second definition. But the two tasks will be associated typically with particular methods or PSMs (e.g. propose-and-revise for the former and heuristic classification for the latter). These will generally result in systems of varying efficiency. So the efficiency *will* depend on the 'correct' classification of the task in the first place. The only way to be *sure* that you have the most efficient solution — even in the formal case — is to generate *all* solutions.

The point is that the formal characteristics of a task are not necessarily the ones that will be activated when problem-solving is classified as one or another PSM. Often, a straightforward natural language description, or common sense description, of the expertise will be used in advance of any formal work. For instance, diagnosis is what a doctor does, and design is what a designer does. But as we see from our definition of diagnosis compared to FS's definition of design, in computational/formal terms the two might be doing something very similar.

In that event, then two systems intended to perform the same tasks should be very similar too. But if the one only uses PSMs 'suitable' for analytic tasks while the other only uses PSMs 'suitable' for constructive tasks, then it cannot be guaranteed that equally efficient systems are going to be built for the two domains. And if that is the case, then it seems clear that it is possible that a more efficient system for (at least) one of the systems could have been built given a different task classification.

The moral is the well-known one that moving from describing a task (conceptual modelling) to building a system (design/implementation) is not easy. PSMs can ease the problem, but not by as much as has been claimed.

There are, it seems to us, only three possible ways out of the difficulty. None of these three ways is problem-free; certainly none of them manages to guarantee that an optimal or near-optimal solution will definitely be found for an arbitrary problem. However, each one is a viable attempt at damage limitation.

- Restrict the stock of PSMs. As we suggested earlier, given a small number of PSMs, all of them can be generated and tested in a particular domain.

- Concentrate on the formal and computational characteristics of the domain. Obviously this would be FS's preferred solution. This method is likely to work best when the formal/computational characteristics of the domain are already well-known and documented. FS (1996) is one of the most complete and comprehensive attempts to flesh out this alternative.
- Concentrate on a good classification of the problem-solving. The third alternative is to move away from formal and characteristic accounts to discursive accounts in a natural language. The advantage here is that there will be a quick route from the expert to the task classification, especially when the expert is a non-technical soul. The aim will then be to break down the task into a number of more primitive inferences, whose implementation will be more straightforward, by virtue of their relative simplicity. In this way, refinement-based approaches, such as GDMs and generic task analyses can carve a niche for themselves despite the criticisms of FS.

In the next section, we show how the GDM methodology exploits this third approach to knowledge engineering.

5 GDMs

The advantage of a wide PSM library is that the models chosen are more likely to fit the problem-solving. However, if, in the library, the descriptive element of the PSM is too closely linked to the operational element, then the search for the best operational account of the problem-solving is likely to be hampered by the very size of the library. The formal route advocated by FS is one way of coping with the problem — although their claim to be able to maximize efficiency will fall foul of our arguments in the previous section. Let us make it clear now that we do not set up the GDM methodology as an exclusive alternative to the formal approach; sometimes a formal approach will be appropriate, sometimes an informal approach.

The essence of the GDM approach is a grammar of various elements. The primitives of the grammar are as follows.
- **Roles.** These are classes of domain knowledge, indexed according to the role that the knowledge plays in problem-solving. Graphically represented by rectangles.
- **Inferences.** These have formerly been known as inference steps; however, after discussions within the VITAL project partners, it was decided that the idea of each inference being a 'step' was rather misleading, given the rewritability of such inferences. These are classes of domain knowledge that enable knowledge which plays one role to 'create' knowledge which plays another. Graphically represented by ovals.
- **IO Relations.** These connect roles and inferences. Each inference has at least one role as an input and at least one role as an output. It is important to note that these are not arrows of control flow. In a sense, they are a conventional representation of the form of a (type of) inference; however the inference can be 'traversed' or used in either direction (in the same way in which an inference of the form 'if p then q' can be used, in the right circumstances, to derive p from q or q from p).

Graphically represented by arrows, from the input role(s) to the inference, and from the inference to the output role(s).

- **Rewrite rules.** These take an inference (possibly with some specification of context) as input, and produce a more complex, fine-grained version of the inference as output. Application of a rewrite rule to an inference results in a more detailed specification of that inference. The rewrite rules are arrayed in a **grammar**. The grammar in effect specifies an infinitely large model library.
- **GDMs.** A GDM is a connected graph made up of inferences and roles. The connections are made by having some roles be at once the output of one or more inferences and the input of one or more other inferences. The same role can be both the input and output of a particular inference. If a rewrite rule is applied to an inference which is a component of a GDM, we also say that the GDM has been rewritten.

This has all been pretty familiar stuff since (van Heijst et al 1992). The cyclic methodology too has been discussed in detail elsewhere (e.g. Motta et al 1996). GDMs drive KA in a cycle. First the current GDM is used to specify classes of knowledge to be acquired. After this knowledge is acquired it then provides pointers to the knowledge engineer about where the model needs a finer grain (in other words, the more knowledge that is acquired, the better he understands the problem-solving). At that point, the knowledge engineer can rewrite the current GDM on the basis of the grammar; this new GDM becomes the current GDM and the cycle starts again. The methodology is not monolithic, and in fact the knowledge engineer is best advised to use the resources of the GDM methodology opportunistically, rewriting or acquiring knowledge as he thinks fit. He can stop rewriting either when he runs out of applicable rewrite rules, or when the model is sufficient for his particular purposes.

One final aspect of the GDM methodology we should mention is the *least commitment strategy*. When a rewriting of the GDM takes place, the knowledge engineer should make sure that the rewriting is the minimal rewriting possible, and he should be very sure of his ground when he commits himself to a rewrite. The net result is that the GDM methodology allows the knowledge engineer to delay making important modelling decisions until he is sure of his ground — this contrasts with alternative modelling methodology, when far-reaching modelling decisions (e.g. commitment to a particular model) have to be made at an early stage in the KA process, when the amount of knowledge available on which he can base such a decision is necessarily low.

The GDM library is very wide both in terms of size and range. There are infinitely many models in the library, but it important to stress that these models aren't all trivial variants of a small group of models (although obviously the decompositional grammar does make the development of trivial variants highly possible). The range of models covers pretty much all of the standard types of model in the literature, both analytic models (O'Hara 1993) and synthetic models (Motta et al 1996). The latest version of the grammar, version 4.6, contains approximately 100 rules governing the positioning of some 60 primitive roles and inferences. So clearly the GDM grammar will allow the derivation of a very wide variety of inference structures, as well as allowing subtle deviations from standard models.

We won't bang on about the virtues of GDMs here. (O'Hara 1993) discusses the advantages of the approach. What is important here is that the form of the GDM grammar results in a refinement-based model structure of precisely the kind that FS criticise.

To address their criticism, we will briefly mention the major area of agreement between the GDM approach and FS's goal- and assumption-based approach. The GDM analysis proceeds on the basis of what FS call assumptions about the domain. The GDM term is 'conditions', which is perhaps a better piece of terminology, since these conditions are not *assumed* to be true, but *shown* to be true of the domain. In GDMs, a condition is attached to a rewrite; when the condition is demonstrated to hold, the rewrite can be applied.

The form of these conditions long vexed researchers in the VITAL project. The early papers from the ACKnowledge project (van Heijst et al 1992; Terpstra et al 1993) hint that the conditions could be formal conditions, but in fact do not go into any detail about this question. (O'Hara 1993) ducks the question entirely by restricting the discussion to the algebraic aspects of the GDM grammar. In the end, theoretical discussions such as (O'Hara & Shadbolt 1993a, 1993b) — summarized in Section 3 above — convinced us that a strictly formal approach would fail. This is not to say that there should be no content of a formal kind in GDMs. Committing to particular models may well carry with it a commitment to particular computational styles. This is the sort of knowledge that comes with pragmatic experience of knowledge engineering, and could be added to GDMs. The main point is that formal considerations cannot by themselves *determine* which GDM rewrites to use.

The resulting idea was that, associated with each rule, role and inference in the grammar, would be an informal, discursive, natural language description of the sort of phenomena one should expect to find in the domain problem-solving when the item in question is to be found in a GDM description of that problem-solving. The informality of the account meant that the knowledge engineer could not rely on any sort of algorithmic conception of 'applying a rewrite', for example.

The grammar provides an expressive language for the knowledge engineer to describe the problem-solving; this language should also be understandable by a domain expert in many cases. The whole process should be eased further by the knowledge engineer constructing a translation manual between the generic terms to be found in the GDM grammar and the domain-specific terms that the expert understands. In this way, the acquisition of knowledge, the verification of a model, and the early, conceptual part of the KBS development process are all aided by the provision of this language and its discursive semantics. The efficiency of the development process that is aided by such an approach is not the type of efficiency that FS aim for, but instead should increase the knowledge engineer's own efficiency.

We would also argue that the cost of this is not necessarily high, at least in some domains. Although the semantics of GDMs are indeterminate, we have seen that the determinate semantics of the more formal approaches cannot actually produce all the advantages that are claimed for them.

Because implementational considerations are kept relatively separate from the semantics of GDMs, the GDM approach cannot guarantee to produce the most efficient solution. But as we have argued, neither can the approach advocated by FS. The advantage of the GDM approach is that the language of the model, and the partitions of the code, should be readily understandable by people familiar with the domain. This should mean that a GDM-based system will, for example, provide more comprehensible explanations for the users, and be easier to debug, maintain and extend.

In the GDM tool that has been produced in the VITAL project (Figure 2), the cyclic nature of GDM development is embedded in the whole design. At any point during its use, there are a number of actions that a knowledge engineer can perform. The current GDM may be rewritten, if there are any rules applicable. Or a KA tool can be called up, and its output associated with particular roles or inferences in the current GDM.

So when some knowledge is acquired from the GDM tool using a particular KA tool, the KA action will be associated with an item in the current GDM ('components', say). A KA tool can only be called when a role or an inference is highlighted, and then the output of that particular session with the tool will be associated with the highlighted role or inference. When the GDM was rewritten to include the 'components' role, a partition was created in the knowledge base corresponding to that role. When a KA tool is called from the 'components' role, all the knowledge acquired during that session is stored in a file kept in the 'components' partition. The partitioning of the knowledge base is therefore a directory structure for the files containing the knowledge which together makes up the knowledge base.

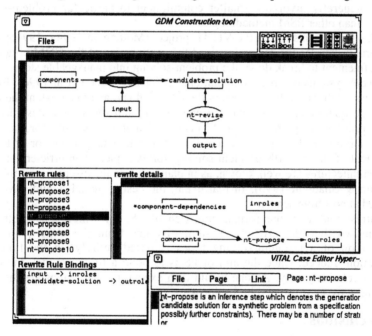

Fig. 2. The VITAL GDM Tool

This partitioning of the knowledge base, of course, aids efficiency in the event that the code is *also* structured like the GDM (i.e. when the PSM does *not* undergo wholesale global change as envisaged by FS). As we argued in Section 2, if the choice or development of the PSM is based on the expert's *behaviour*, as opposed to a functional description of the *task* he is carrying out, then the assumption that a PSM will not undergo such change looks more reasonable. In that event, the domain knowledge used in the KB will automatically be organised in such a way as to promote the efficiency of the final implementation, by radically cutting down search times in large knowledge bases.

Understanding of the items in the current GDM is facilitated by a hypertext help system (the window of which can be seen in the lower right of Figure 2), which calls up a small piece of text describing the knowledge that should go into any of the roles or inferences. In addition, the knowledge engineer should be able to use his experience of modelling expertise to suggest likely rewrites.

The upshot of a GDM approach to system development is that the conceptual modelling and knowledge acquisition should be relatively easier. Since there is no such thing as a free lunch, this means that the system design is correspondingly harder. But the way that the GDM methodology works in this respect is as 'the thin end of the wedge'. The GDM methodology should make the initial stages of KBS development easier, and as the process gets harder, the knowledge engineer's expertise should then click in. The aim of the GDM methodology is that it 'gets the project going'. Early modelling decisions are typically those with the greatest influence over the course of the KA process; GDM decisions, made on the least commitment strategy, generally involve a smaller commitment to particular problem-solving structures than other PSM methodologies.

In the experiments run in the VITAL project (Motta et al 1994a; 1994b; 1996), the general principles for design involved the continuation of the GDM principle of model refinement to break down the problem-solving into manageable steps, and the results were systems of great computational efficiency (Motta et al 1996). But this process has relatively little guidance in the methodology, and to an extent the results rely on the quality of the knowledge engineering and the system designer. One obvious problem in particular would occur when it is desirable for the KBS's problem-solving to diverge fairly deeply and fundamentally from (or at least be independent of) the expert's problem-solving, for example, when efficient problem-solving architectures are well-known, as in planning (see the discussion of this issue in Cottam & Shadbolt 1996). In that event, the design model would have to be developed almost from scratch.

Contrast that with the formal approach of FS, for which it is pretty well irrelevant whether the artificial system diverges from the expert, since the identification of a problem-solving types is based entirely on the functional specification. Indeed, since the aim of FS is to build a formal model, the design process is relatively easy. As one would then expect, the hard steps are the initial modelling steps, as we argued in Section 4.

6 Conclusions

The criticisms of GDMs made by FS do not find their target, as they mistakenly assume that GDMs are intended to serve the same purpose as their own formal PSMs. However, GDMs form a parallel type of method for approaching KBS development. GDMs are highly informal, and are intended to increase the efficiency of knowledge engineering and knowledge acquisition, whereas FS's PSMs are highly formal and are intended to increase the efficiency of the target system. What the best relationship between formal and informal methods is is an issue which has yet to be convincingly tackled; it may be that using the two in tandem in some way, perhaps allowing for redundancies in the knowledge base, may be possible. What FS have shown is that (a) the GDM approach cannot be formal, and (b) that the GDM approach cannot be used as a 'front end' to a formal design methodology, if the intention of the formalization is first and foremost to increase the efficiency of the target system.

We do not intend this paper to be taken as an attack on formal methods in any way. We believe that both formal and informal methods have their place, and that each has its advantages and disadvantages. To that extent, it is likely that we share much common ground with FS. For example, we can agree that it is sometimes the case that global changes to a PSM can be a route to efficiency (of come type), which would thereby rule out GDMs as a means of getting there. Equally, FS would probably agree that their formal methodology is likely to produce less of a cognitive model of the problem-solving. The argument between us is whether or not this is much of a drawback.

Our main point, though, is that one's KBS development style need not be formal to promote efficiency. As currently conceived, GDMs have little or no formal content, and yet they *do* promote certain types of efficiency. In particular, we have argued that the advantages of the informal GDM approach include: they can make the knowledge acquisition and knowledge engineering process understandable for domain experts; by following the structure of the expert problem-solving they make the provision of explanations for the users easier; similarly, they make debugging and maintenance easier; they make modelling easier (and more accurate), by making a large (indeed, infinite) number of models available with minimal memory costs; they guide or direct the acquisition of knowledge, allowing a sensible choice of KA tool and KB partition for the acquisition task to be made. As yet, formal approaches cannot make these claims.

Acknowledgments

James Cupit was largely responsible for the implementation of the GDM tool. Thanks to our partners on the VITAL project, particularly at the Open University, ONERA and Bull CEDIAG, for advice, help and comments on the development of the GDM grammar and methodology. Thanks also to the EKAW referees for their perspicuous comments on this paper, and for refusing to be convinced!

References

Dean Allemang & Thomas E. Rothenfluh (1992) 'Acquiring Knowledge of Knowledge Acquisition: A Self-Study of Generic Tasks' in Th. Wetter, K.-D. Althoff, J. Boose, B.R. Gaines, M. Linster & F. Schmalhofer (eds.) *Current Trends in Knowledge Acquisition — EKAW '92* (Springer, Berlin) pp.353-372

William J. Clancey (1985) 'Heuristic Classification' in *Artificial Intelligence* vol.27 pp.289-350

Hugh Cottam & Nigel Shadbolt (1996) 'Domain and System Influences in Problem Solving Models for Planning' in this volume.

Dieter Fensel & Remco Straatman (1996) 'The Essence of Problem-Solving Methods: Making Assumptions for Efficiency Reasons' in this volume.

B.R. Gaines (1991) 'The Sisyphus Problem Solving Example Through a Visual Language With KL-ONE-Like Knowledge Representation' in M. Linster (ed.) *Sisyphus Working Papers Part 2: Models of Problem Solving* (Arbeitspapiere der GMD 633, St Augustin)

W. Karbach, Marc Linster & Angi Voß (1990) 'Model-Based Approaches: One Label — One Idea?' in Bob Wielinga, John Boose, Brian Gaines, Guus Schreiber & Maarten van Someren (eds) *Current Trends in Knowledge Acquisition* (IOS Press, Amsterdam) pp.173-189

Nigel Major & Kieron O'Hara (1995) 'Grounding DTMs: An Interview Tool for Acquiring Meta-Strategic Teaching Knowledge' in J. Hallam (ed.) *Hybrid Problems, Hybrid Solutions* (IOS Press, Amsterdam) pp.145-155

Enrico Motta, Kieron O'Hara & Nigel Shadbolt (1994a) 'Grounding GDMs: A Structured Case Study' in *International Journal of Human-Computer Studies* vol.40 pp.315-347

Enrico Motta, Kieron O'Hara, Nigel Shadbolt, Arthur Stutt & Zdenek Zdrahal (1994b) 'A VITAL Solution to the Sisyphus II Elevator Design Problem' in *Proceedings of 8th Banff Knowledge Acquisition for Knowledge-Based Systems Workshop* (Calgary) vol.3 chapter 40

Enrico Motta, Kieron O'Hara, Nigel Shadbolt, Arthur Stutt & Zdenek Zdrahal (1996) 'Solving VT in VITAL: A Study in Model Construction and Knowledge Reuse' forthcoming in *International Journal of Human-Computer Studies*

Kieron O'Hara (1993) 'A Representation of KADS-I Interpretation Models Using a Decompositional Approach' in Christiane Löckenhoff, Dieter Fensel & Rudi Studer (eds.) *3rd KADS Meeting* (Siemens AG, Munich) pp.147-169

Kieron O'Hara & Nigel Shadbolt (1993a) 'AI Models as a Variety of Psychological Explanation' in *Proceedings of the 13th International Joint Conference on Artificial Intelligence* (Morgan Kaufmann, San Mateo, Calif.) vol.1 pp.188-193

Kieron O'Hara & Nigel Shadbolt (1993b) 'Locating Generic Tasks' in *Knowledge Acquisition* vol.5 pp.449-481

Kieron O'Hara & Nigel Shadbolt (forthcoming) 'Interpreting Generic Structures: Expert Systems, Expertise and Context' in Paul Feltovich, Ken Ford & Robert Hoffman (eds.) *Human and Machine Expertise in Context*

Peter Terpstra, Gertjan van Heijst, Nigel Shadbolt & Bob Wielinga (1993) 'Knowledge Acquisition Process Support Through Generalised Directive Models' in J.-M. David, J.-P. Krivine & R. Simmons (eds.) *Second Generation Expert Systems* (Springer-Verlag, Berlin) pp.428-454

Walter van de Velde (1988) 'Inference Structure as a Basis for Problem Solving' in *Proceedings of the 8th European Conference on Artificial Intelligence* (Pitman, London) pp.202-207

Gertjan van Heijst, Peter Terpstra, Bob Wielinga & Nigel Shadbolt (1992) 'Using Generalised Directive Models in Knowledge Acquisition' in Th. Wetter, K.-D. Althoff, J. Boose, B.R. Gaines, M. Linster & F. Schmalhofer (eds.) *Current Developments in Knowledge Acquisition — EKAW '92* (Springer-Verlag, Berlin) pp.112-132

Zdenek Zdrahal & Enrico Motta (1995) 'An In-depth Study of Propose & Revise Problem Solving' in *Proceedings of 9th Banff Knowledge Acquisition for Knowledge-Based Systems Workshop* (Calgary)

Principles for Libraries of Task Decomposition Methods – Conclusions from a Case-study

Klas Orsvärn

Swedish Institute of Computer Science
Box 1263, 164 28 Kista, Sweden
E-mail: klasorsv@sics.se, URL: http://www.sics.se/~klasorsv

Abstract. Chandrasekaran and Steels proposed several years ago that libraries of reusable problem solving methods, for use in model-driven knowledge acquisition, should be organized as hierarchies of task decomposition methods, rather than as collections of complete methods. One of the most comprehensive examples to date is Benjamins' library of methods for diagnosis tasks. In a case-study of using Benjamins' library, to model a specific diagnosis application, the most suitable model generated by the library had to be modified in several ways, despite the fact that the application is relatively simple and mainstream. This caused significant difficulties, both in identifying the modification requirements, and in creating the necessary adaptations. This paper proposes a set of general principles which libraries of task decomposition methods can be evaluated against, in order to prevent unnecessary adaptations. The principles concern method correctness, specialization of selection criteria, and method generality.

1 Introduction

At the end of the 1980's, Chandrasekaran and Steels [7, 8, 16, 17] more or less simultaneously proposed a kind of problem solving method that is here called task decomposition method, that was more modular than previous reusable problem solving methods used for model-driven knowledge acquisition (e.g. generic tasks [6], role-limiting methods [10], and interpretation models [5]); and they called for the development of libraries of task decomposition methods, organized in hierarchically, with a basic task such as diagnosis or design at the root.[1]

The proposals were well received by other researchers in the field of model-driven knowledge acquisition, and was adopted in several approaches [14, 18, 13, 4]. However, very few comprehensive libraries of task decomposition methods have to date been presented (a lot of research is still devoted to monolithic problem solving methods), and even fewer evaluations of such libraries have been made.

One of the most comprehensive libraries of task decomposition methods, that has been presented so far, is Benjamins' library of problem solving methods for

---

[1] Chandrasekaran used the term task structure [8].

diagnosis tasks [3, 2]. It covers a wide range of the state-of-the-art in model-based diagnosis in one hierarchical collection of task decomposition methods, and has been subjected to scientific reviewing.

This paper first recapitulates a case-study in knowledge modelling, using Benjamins' library to model an existing diagnosis application [11]. In the case-study, the best model that could be generated with the library was not quite suitable. Guidelines for adapting a selected interpretation model [12] were used to make the necessary modifications. However, identifying modification require-ments, and making correct adaptations, is still a significant difficulty. Moreover, the modification requirements were of a common character, which suggests that they could have been anticipated in the library. Libraries of task decomposi-tion methods are complex - they cannot be evaluated by testing alone (i.e. by case-studies like the one reported here). The main objective of this paper is to propose a set of general principles which libraries of task decomposition methods can be evaluated against, in order to prevent unnecessary adaptations.

The next section describes the relevant background. After that, the case-study is recapitulated, followed by a proposal of principles for preventing unnec-essary adaptations. The use of the principles is then illustrated by describing how to detect and eliminate some violations in methods of Benjamins' library, which would have prevented most of the need to make adaptations in the case-study. Finally, conclusions are drawn.

2 Background

The above mentioned proposals of Chandrasekaran and Steels were very simi-lar. The central idea is that a method decomposes a task into subtasks, which are themselves first class tasks, and which may be further decomposed by other methods, etc., until a level of decomposition is reached where the required knowl-edge is available in domain models. Associated to a method is control knowledge for combining the results of subtasks into the desired result of the method. Many methods may be applicable to the same task, and the selection in an application is guided by explicit selection criteria associated to each method. The representa-tional frameworks proposed by Chandrasekaran and Steels were quite different, but that is of little relevance to the topic of this paper.

Task decomposition methods can be used simply as a way to make complete problem solving methods more modular. But there is a potential for replacing a large set of complete methods for the same task of a generic nature, e.g. diag-nosis or design, which address different application features, with a hierarchical collection of task decomposition methods (but tasks and methods can occur in more than one place in the hierarchy). This is what is here called a *library of task decomposition methods*. Both authors called for the development of such libraries. This was based on the observation that many methods seem to share the same high level task decomposition, such as propose-critique-modify in de-sign methods. Chandrasekaran sketched such a library of design methods [7]. Both authors suggested that method selection is not only a concern in knowledge acquisition, but could also be done dynamically at run-time by a problem solver.

The main motivation for both proposals was to reduce the proliferation problem, i.e. that libraries of complete problem solving methods would have to contain too many overlapping methods in order to cover a wide range of applications. A similar motivation was to support scaling up of applications [15], i.e. to more easily adapt them to changing requirements.

2.1 Benjamins' Library

Benjamins' library of task decomposition methods for diagnosis tasks [3, Ch. 5] adheres to the notion of task decomposition described above, and is represented in a framework similar to that of the CommonKADS library [4]. Subtasks which are not further decomposed in the library are called primitive inferences. They should be accomplished directly using domain models, but that is beyond the scope of the library. Each task has a definition, describing the input, the output, and the goal (requirements on output). Each method has a set of suitability criteria – conditions that are used to select method in an application. The criteria are expressed in terms of properties of the environment, domain, and available knowledge, i.e. what is called task features in CommonKADS [4]. Suitability criteria of methods may be static or dynamic. The latter refer to the knowledge roles in the current state of problem solving, and so can be used to achieve flexible problem solving.

At the root of the hierarchy, there is (only) one method, the prime diagnostic method, which decomposes the diagnosis task into the following three subtasks:

Symptom detection takes an observation as input and determines whether it is normal or abnormal.

Hypothesis generation takes the set of initial observations, divided into normal and abnormal, and outputs a set of hypotheses that each explains the initial observations.

Hypothesis discrimination prunes the set of hypotheses by making additional observations.

Other methods decompose these tasks further (for an overview, see [2]). For most tasks, there is more than one method to choose from. By making method selections for each task, one finally gets a task structure where all the leaves are primitive inferences. This corresponds to a KADS-I interpretation model [5], except that it is more fine grained, and is hierarchically decomposed. The library is capable of generating very many different interpretation models.

2.2 Objectives of the case-study

Benjamins made no strong claims about the degree of support for knowledge modelling that the library provides for a knowledge engineer in practice. The main objective of the case-study was to gain knowledge about the practical limitations.

The target of knowledge modelling in the case-study was reverse engineering of an existing diagnosis application, henceforth called HP, which guides a service technician in the task of diagnosing a specific device, which is an electronic measuring instrument. HP is a consultation system that makes a sequence of requests for tests to be performed by the user, who inputs the results of each test to the system, which finally reports which part of the device is faulty. HP was developed and fielded in 1989 by Infologics and Swedish Telecom. Since domain modelling is beyond the scope of Benjamins' library, it was left out of the case-study. For this reason, the difference between reverse engineering and normal knowledge acquisition is not great. What really matters is the requirements on the application. No attempt was made to account for how the system was originally specified and structured.[2] Similarly, aspects of HPs behaviour that can be regarded as accidental, rather than due to requirements, were not accounted for. The goal was rather to create a model of a KBS with the functionality of HP, that addresses the task features that HP addresses. It can be argued that the functionality of HP is limited by the difficulty to achieve advanced functionality in a first-generation KBS development approach. However, the detected weaknesses in the library were not due to those limitations.

3 The Model Generated by the Library

This section will briefly describe the interpretation model generated by making method selections in the library according to the suitability criteria. In most cases, the suitability criteria of more than one method were applicable, and there was no guidance for deciding which one to choose in those cases. In those cases selections were made with the objective of generating the interpretation model that would have provided the best support for efficient development of a system with the functionality of HP (difficulties in the selection process are discussed in [11].) The task structure (task decomposition down to the level of primitive inferences) of the resulting model is illustrated in figure 1 (the corresponding inference structure is quite complex). The following description of the model also mentions some of the rationale for making these particular choices.

The first subtask of the Prime Diagnostic method, called symptom detection, is performed by lookup in a table of normal values, which is compared with the observed value. If they are different, the observation is abnormal.

Hypothesis generation is performed by the model-based method, i.e. based on a device model. It decomposes into three subtasks: (i) find the set of contributors to each abnormal observation, (ii) transform the contributor sets into a provi-

---

[2] HP was originally specified with a decision tree (with some extensions) and implemented as a rule-based system. The decision tree and the rules refer directly to specific parts, tests, and outcomes, so the problem solving strategy is not explicit.

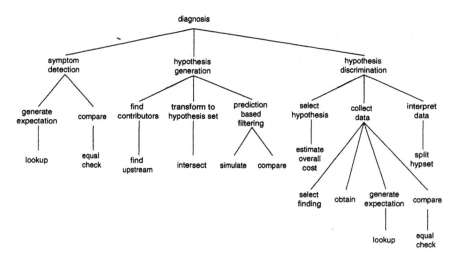

Fig. 1. The task structure generated with Benjamins' library for the HP application.
(NB. Some trivial inferences are not included.)

sional set of hypotheses[3] that each contributes to every abnormal observation,
(*iii*) filter out provisional hypotheses that can be ruled out using only initial observations (e.g. by prediction). For these three tasks, the following methods are
used. Find contributors is performed by the trace-back method, which simply
traces the network of connected components from the observed (abnormal) output upstream to the input(s), to identify the contributors to the observed output.
Based on a single-fault assumption, the contributor sets are transformed to a hypothesis set by set intersection. The corroboration method of prediction-based
filtering rejects hypotheses that contribute to normal observations.

Hypothesis discrimination is decomposed into three tasks: (*i*) select a hypothesis to test, (*ii*) make a new observation relevant to the selected hypothesis,
(*iii*) interpret the observation, i.e. update the set of hypotheses. This is iterated
until a final diagnosis is reached (e.g. only one hypothesis remains).

The smart select method of the select hypothesis task takes into account the
constraint to minimize the total cost of additional observations to reach a final
diagnosis. This is done by estimating for each hypothesis the total cost if that
hypothesis is tested next, including the number of observations and the cost of
each observation.

Given a selected hypothesis, an observation should be made, in order to
gather information that could reject the hypothesis. This is done by the probing
method, which means that the state and input of the device remains the same,
but a passive observation is made by probing the internal connections of the
device. Another alternative is the manipulation method, where the input to the
device is changed and the output observed. HP in fact uses either probing or

---

[3] If we assume there may be multiple faults (HP does not), the hypotheses may be
composite.

manipulation, depending on the situation, but the way the methods are represented in the library, there is no way to make the appropriate selection in each situation (approaches to model-based diagnosis are often geared towards only one kind of observation).

The hypothesis set is updated with the split-half method, which divides the set of hypothesis into two parts, one of which is rejected depending on whether the observation is normal or abnormal.

4 Evaluation of the Generated Model

The effort of trying to model the HP application using the model generated with Benjamins' library in section 3, revealed the following discrepancies between the model and the requirements in the application.

Cost estimation requires current observations The inference called estimate overall cost, assigns to each hypothesis an estimate of the total cost of additional observations required to reach a diagnosis. In HP, this inference would have to use the current set of observations as input, because HP sometimes selects the next observation by recognizing common symptoms which render some hypotheses more likely. However, in Benjamins' library, the current set of observations is not input in hypothesis discrimination.

No manipulation method The description of the generated model in section 3 mentioned that the manipulation method was not selected, since only one method of collect data could be selected. But HP uses manipulation observations as well.

User control of test selection HP allows the user to override the systems' recommendation for which observation to make next. This is not an option in Benjamins' library.

Redundancy between collect data and symptom detection As shown in figure 1, the decomposition of the collect data task uses the subtask of symptom detection for exactly the same purpose. This leads to structural redundancy in the model, which should be avoided.[4]

Corroboration based on trace-back The corroboration method of the prediction based filtering task eliminates those provisional hypotheses that contribute to a normal observation. Those contributors are identified by simulating the device. In HP, it is easier and more natural to identify them with the same method that is used to identify contributors to the abnormal observations in the find-contributors task, the trace-back method. [5]

Collect-data dependent on hypothesis selection The decomposition of the select hypothesis task has the purpose to minimize the total cost of making additional observations to reach a final diagnosis. This purpose can only

---

[4] It makes the model harder to understand, since one has to suspect that there is a subtle difference. Furthermore, modifications have to be made in two places.

[5] The trace-back method is based on strong assumptions, but those were introduced already in the initial model selection.

be achieved if hypothesis selection is based on an assumption about which observation will be made. However, the decision about which observation to make is made in the subsequent collect data task, more precisely in the inference called select finding (cf. figure 1). This dependence is easier to take into account if the inference called select finding belongs to the first subtask of the discrimination method.

5 Evaluation of Benjamins' Library

The case-study showed how the generated interpretation model could be modified in order to eliminate the discrepancies [11]. As reported there, the need to make the adaptations caused signficant difficulties, both in identifying the modification requirements, and in creating the necessary modifications. In addition to the need to adapt the generated model, a number of other difficulties were identified, in particular with respect to selecting and interpreting methods.

Although significant difficulties were encountered, one conclusion of the case-study was that Benjamins' library has important practical advantages over a collection of explicit interpretation models such as the KADS-I library [5], and is thus a big step forward towards truly comprehensive libraries. Furthermore, it seemed highly feasible to improve the library to prevent those difficulties in the future, e.g. by incorporating the adaptations back into the library. However, the application features that caused the adaptations in the case-study were of a quite common character, which suggests that the need to make those adaptations could have been anticipated. In this paper, the main issue is whether the need to make those improvements could have been detected without performing the case-study, by evaluating the library according to general principles for libraries of task decomposition methods.

6 Basic Requirements on Libraries of Task Decomposition Methods

All of the discrepancies above can be regarded as violations of three basic requirements, which will be described here. As mentioned in section 2 above, both Chandrasekaran and Steels proposed that task decomposition methods should have selection criteria, which guide the selection of methods in an application. Steels called these selection criteria task features, and made a distinction between conceptual and pragmatic features [16]. Conceptual features describe the nature of the input-output relation of the task, whereas pragmatic features describe constraints imposed by the environment or by limitations of the problem solving agent. This corresponds to Benjamins' distinction between task definition and suitability criteria. In the following, the term selection criteria will cover both of those constructs, since both have to be considered when selecting a method.

Model correctness requirement When a model is constructed according to selection criteria in a library of task decomposition methods, the generated model should satisfy the application requirements expressed in the selection criteria – otherwise there is something wrong with either the methods or their selection criteria. Note that this is based on the assumption that the subtasks at the lowest level of decomposition can be performed in the application.

Generality requirement For every task (or subtask) that the library has methods for, the set of methods should cover as many applications as possible.

Depth requirement An easy way to satisfy the generality requirement would be to have only very high level methods. This reveals the requirement that a library of task decomposition methods should provide as much as possible of the necessary task decomposition knowledge.

The generality and depth requirements are only partially satisfiable, i.e. they are ideals to strive for rather than states to be achieved.

7   Principles for Achieving the Basic Requirements

In the following, some more specific principles will be spelled out, which will enable us to systematically evaluate libraries of task decomposition methods, to detect violations against the basic requirements described in section 6.

7.1   Model Correctness Requirement

The modular nature of a library of task decomposition methods suggests a principled way to ensure that the model correctness requirement is satisfied. One of the approaches to model-driven knowledge modelling that has been inspired by the notion of task decomposition method is the ACKnowledge project, and their notion of Generalized Directive Models (GDM) [18]. GDMs are very similar to task decomposition methods, except they have no associated control structures – they only generate what CommonKADS calls function structures, a generalization of the notion of inference structure [4]. GDMs are based on an organization principle called the *compositionality principle*[18], which states (rephrased in the terminology used here) that *the input-output function achieved by a method depends only on the input-output functions of its subtasks, and the way the subtasks are composed together in the method.* This implies that methods with equal input-output functions can be exchanged, leaving the input-output function of the model as a whole unaffected. Without this principle, it is hard to see any systematic way to compose complete methods with specified properties out of a library of task decomposition methods, and it would then be unclear in which way the proliferation problem is reduced.

What was called selection criteria above, is what defines the correct input-output function of a method. The compositionality principle then directly suggests the following principle:

Method correctness principle: *A correct method will satisfy its selection criteria if its subtasks can be performed as specified.*

This principle implies that all assumptions imposed by a method on its subtasks, in order to satisfy its selection criteria, should be made explicit in the specification of those subtasks. Although this principle may seem obvious, it is not consistently adhered to in libraries of task decomposition methods, which is probably partly due to the fact that the principle is usually not made explicit.

This principle resembles analyses that have been made in the last few years regarding assumptions of certain reusable problem solving methods, such as cover-and-differentiate [1], and propose-and-revise (e.g. [19]), but the application here is to libraries of task decomposition methods.

The method correctness principle suggests a systematic way to evaluate the correctness of a library of task decomposition methods, by locally evaluating the correctness of each method. This is done by providing, for each method, an explicit argument for believing that the method will satisfy its selection criteria, assuming its subtasks can be performed. No assumption should be made about which methods will be applied at lower levels of decomposition. Availability of lower level methods is the topic of another principle (which will not be discussed here, since it is not motivated by the case-study).

The argument for method correctness does not have to be formal to be useful. With informal proofs, there is a danger that the proof is invalid. But it still facilitates the task of finding errors in a method, since we also have the option of showing that the proof is invalid. If the proof is found to be invalid, this will often indicate what is wrong with the method, e.g. tacit assumptions.

Consistent specialization of selection criteria It may seem that method correctness should be sufficient to guarantee model correctness, but it is not. The reason is that methods may introduce restricting assumptions, that further restrict the problem addressed by the model, compared to the selection criteria of higher level methods, and this may be done inconsistently.

In Benjamins' framework, a method that is applied to a task may have a more specific goal than that task. Benjamins calls this an *operationalization* of the goal. An example mentioned in section 3 is that the select hypothesis subtask of the discrimination method has the general goal to select one of the competing hypotheses, but the smart select method has the more specific goal to select that hypothesis which has the lowest associated cost. This is not just a matter of using a method that happens to be more specialized than necessary. It is part of a deliberate approach to increasing generality by allowing the higher level method, in this example the discrimination method, to abstract away from more specific task features, which can be handled at lower levels of decomposition, such as in this example minimization of observation cost. Specializing the *goal* of the method is not the only way to pursue this approach to increasing generality. Other selection criteria (Benjamins' suitability criteria) may also impose further restrictions. I will refer to this approach to library organization as based on *specialization of selection criteria*. It was a very important element in the proposals of Steels and Chandrasekaran. A drawback with this approach is that if the specialization addresses a task feature that also needs to be addressed in other subtasks as well, in order to achieve model correctness, this dependence between subtasks cannot be made explicit, since it occurs at a level of decomposition which abstracts away from that specific task feature. This was the cause of one of the discrepancies in the case-study – the tacit dependency between select hypothesis and collect data (cf. section 4).

In many cases, tacit dependencies of this kind, between subtasks of a method, can be eliminated by restructuring the method in such a way that the specialization only needs to be addressed in one subtask. Otherwise, the only principled solution is to extend the modelling framework of the library with a notion of *optional* selection criteria, which are assigned to the higher level method, in which the tacit dependency exists. This means that in addition to its explicit selection criteria, the method can optionally handle this optional selection criterion as well. Associated to this optional selection criterion of the method, is a set of additions that are needed in the descriptions of the subtasks, in order to satisfy method correctness with respect to the optional selection criterion as well.

When the selection criteria of a method (mandatory or optional) are more specific than the subtask of a higher level method that it is applied to, we may say that the method *introduces* a selection criterion. We can prevent tacit dependencies, which are due to inconsistent specializations of selection criteria, by imposing a requirement that *a method may introduce selection criteria only if those selection criteria can be satisfied locally in the subtask that the method is applied to*. But that is not enough. In the example of the smart select method, mentioned above, the introduced selection criterion is that the hypothesis with lowest associated (total) cost of observation be selected. This *can* be satisfied locally in the select hypothesis subtask. However, this selection criterion tacitly assumes a requirement which goes beyond selection of hypothesis, i.e. the requirement to minimize the total cost of observations in order to reach a diagnosis (this could have been an optional selection criterion of the discrimination method). When we choose the smart select method, this is the requirement we expect to be satisfied by the generated model. This leads to the following formulation of the principle:

Principle of local specialization: *A method may introduce selection criteria only if the corresponding task features of the higher level method can be satisfied locally in the subtask that the method is applied to.*[6]

---

[6] Instead of extending the scope of the principle to "the corresponding task feature of the higher level method", another approach would be to prohibit specialization of selection criteria, i.e. to require that selection criteria are never introduced at lower levels of decomposition, but always explicit as optional at higher levels. This is more straightforward, and probably better. But it is also more radical, which is why this approach was not pursued here.

7.2   Generality and Depth Requirements

To define more specific principles concerning the basic requirements of generality and depth, we need a more precise definition of generality of method. There are several relevant notions of generality. I will not attempt to cover all of them, but focus instead on one of them, which is wide enough to prevent the weaknesses that caused difficulties in the case-study. It states that a task decomposition method A is considered more general than B if the set of interpretation models that can be generated by B is a strict subset of the set of models that can be generated by A. The *set of interpretation models* that a task decomposition method can generate, includes the method itself, but also those interpretation models that can be generated by applying (available) lower level methods to the subtasks. Interpretation models that are equivalent may be regarded as equal in this comparison. For example, the decomposition structure can here be regarded as a way to decompose the control structure, and two interpretation models which differ only in the decomposition structure, can be regarded as equivalent if they have equivalent control structures.

An example, illustrated in figure 2, is that if we have a method MB that decomposes into five subtasks, $< a, b, c, d, e >$, we can increase its generality by replacing it with a method MA that decomposes into two higher level subtasks, $< x, y >$, which are then further decomposed by two lower level methods MX and MY into $< a, b >$ and $< c, d, e >$. The set of interpretation models that can be generated by MB contains only one element: $< a, b, c, d, e >$. The set that can be generated by MA is larger, and includes $< x, y >, < a, b, y >, < x, c, d, e >$, and $< a, b, c, d, e >$. Hence, MA is more general than MB.

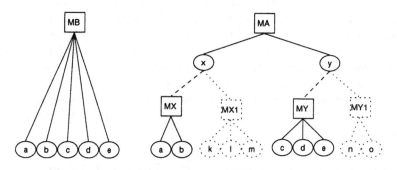

Fig. 2. Method MA is more general than method MB, i.e. MA can generate a superset of the interpretation models that MB can generate.

Principle of method generality: *A more general task decomposition method, in the above sense of generating a superset of interpretation models, should be prefered over a less general task decomposition method.*

Although MA is more coarse grained than MB, it does provide some decomposition, in applications where MB is not applicable. Moreover, in this kind of situation, it is usually the case that other decompositions of x and y will be immediately suggested, as will be shown in section 8. In figure 2, this is illustrated as the shaded methods $MX1$ and $MY1$. This side-effect of increased generality goes some way towards satisfying the depth requirement. For the purpose of preventing the discrepancies in the case-study, this effect is sufficient, and I will therefore not go into more detail about how to achieve the depth requirement.

If we can argue that some specific interpretation models are not desirable, e.g. because of conflicts with other requirements, we can, for the purpose of this comparison, exclude those from the set of interpretation models that can be generated. In such cases, we may be able to increase generality without introducing an intermediate level of decomposition, as in the example in figure 2, but rather with an alternative decomposition. An example of this will be given in section 8.

The evaluation of a method against the method generality principle is made by trying to provide an explicit argument for the claim that the method cannot, or should not, be made more general. This annotation is very useful information for the KBS developer using the library (and for someone who maintains the library). There is no well defined procedure for determining whether there is a more general method. A number of guidelines can be given, but space does not permit a description of those here.

Potential conflicts A task decomposition method is more general if it generates a superset of interpretation models. But there is of course a possiblity that the increased generality introduces conflicts with other principles. In such a case, a trade-off has to be made. In such cases, the generality principle usually loses. If no special care is taken, the more general method will often conflict with the method correctness principle, e.g. if the method is made more general by simply relaxing the definitions of its subtasks. But even with more general methods that can be shown to work correctly, there is still a possibility, at least in theory, that the additional interpretation models are not useful in practice (e.g. because their selection criteria are never satisfied in real applications). This would conflict with the direct opposite of the generality principle – a more specific method should be preferred, if it can be done without excluding any useful interpretation models.

8 Applying the Principles to Benjamins' Library

This section will show how the principles proposed above can be used to identify weaknesses in to the discrimination method in Benjamins' library, and to suggest modifications of the library that would have prevented some of the discrepancies in the case-study.

8.1 Local Specialization in Smart Select Method

Figure 3 illustrates the discrimination method and the smart select method that is applied to the first subtask, select hypothesis. As illustrated there, the select hypothesis subtask of the discrimination method has the goal to select one of the competing hypotheses, but the goal of the smart select method is more specific – to select that hypothesis which has the lowest cost. This means the method introduces a selection criterion, in this case a goal. We should then investigate whether this satisfies the principle of local specialization, i.e. that *a method may introduce selection criteria only if the corresponding task feature of the higher level method can be satisfied locally in the subtask that the method is applied to.*

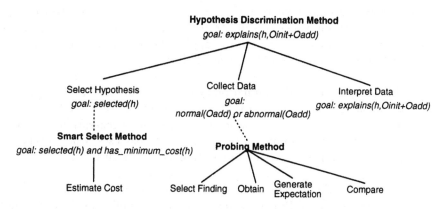

Fig. 3. The discrimination method, and the smart select method, with their goals, as defined by Benjamins.

The corresponding task feature of the higher level method, i.e. of the discrimination method, would be a constraint to minimize the overall cost of making additional observations to reach a final diagnosis. To investigate whether the principle is satisfied, we should try to provide an argument which shows that the constraint can be satisfied by the discrimination method, and see which assumptions are needed about the subtasks.

The specialized goal of the smart select method already suggests what we have to assume regarding the select hypothesis subtask – that the selected hypothesis is the one with lowest estimated cost. However, the collect data subtask is where the actual decision is made about how to test the selected hypothesis. We must therefore also assume that the best observation, with respect to cost minimization, is selected in the collect data subtask. This is not mentioned in the definition of the collect data task.[7] This means that the cost-minimization task feature cannot be handled locally in the select hypothesis tasks, and thus the principle is violated.

So, how to handle this violation? One way would be to introduce cost-minimization as an optional selection criterion of the discrimination method, associated with the added restrictions on select hypothesis and collect data to use only the cheapest observations. But the method of collect data would to a

---

[7] None of the methods of collect data address this constraint.

large extent have to redo the cost-estimating look-ahead that is already done in the smart select method. Such redundancy should be avoided if possible. If the discrimination method can be modified to avoid this redundancy, by creating a more general method, it can be done without sacrificing any desirable properties of the current method. This will be investigated next.

8.2   Generality of Discrimination Method

Let us now investigate whether there is a more general alternative to the discrimination method, which was illustrated in figure 3, according to the principle of method generality. The method is applied to the hypothesis discrimination task, which Benjamins' describes in the following way:

> "In the hypothesis discrimination task extra knowledge (additional observations) is gathered in order to discriminate between the hypotheses that survived the filtering phase of the hypothesis generation task. The output of the discrimination task is a set of diagnoses, where every diagnosis explains the initial and additional observations."

According to that description, the central operation is to request an observation, i.e. a transfer task. But this transfer task is not explicit in the discrimination method. The collect data task has a larger responsibility. It takes a hypothesis as input and outputs an observation classified as normal or abnormal. Moreover, the first operation in the discrimination method, to select a hypothesis, is not necessary. A decision about which observation to make can be based on only inspecting the set of competing hypotheses, without selecting one of them as the one to test. The current decomposition prevents this way to achieve the task.

What is necessary, is first to decide on an observation to make, then a transfer task to make this observation, and then update the set of hypotheses with respect to the new observation. Since the prime diagnostic method is based on the symptom detection task,[8] it is consistent to use the symptom detection task between the transfer task and the interpret data task. This yields the decomposition of the hypothesis discrimination method shown in figure 4.

In terms of the set of interpretation models that *can* be generated, this decomposition is, strictly speaking, not more general than the original one. The new decomposition requires an intermediate transfer task, called Obtain Data, which takes an observable as input, and outputs an observation. That might seem inherent to the discrimination method, but the user may want the transfer task to cover more than this obtain task does, e.g. in order to have options about which observations to make. One of Benjamins' methods of collect data does this. It is called the compiled test method, and it decomposes the collect data task into only one task, a transfer task called compiled-test, which asks the user to perform a test associated to a hypothesis, and report the result as normal

---

[8] According to the generality principle, symptom detection should not be in the prime diagnostic method, but that is another issue.

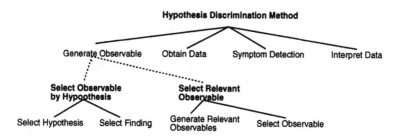

Fig. 4. The more general discrimination method, proposed here, and two methods for its first subtask.

or abnormal. Another way to describe this method is that the user performs part of the problem solving process, in this case makes the decision about which test to make, and interprets the result as normal or abnormal. This kind of method, where a transfer task performs what is in other methods regarded as part of the problem solving process, can be regarded as undesirable in a library of task decomposition methods. The library would have to include a much larger number of methods, if it would consistently include such alternatives too, and very little would be gained, since it is easy to make the necessary modifications in applications where such an alternative is prefered, by simply replacing ordinary subtasks with a transfer task. If we exclude those interpretation models that use a more coarse-grained transfer task, the new decomposition method is strictly more general than the original one, since it covers those desirable models that could be generated by the original method, and is also capable of generating some additional models, e.g. the one needed in HP.

The task called generate observable needs to be further decomposed. A method that is close to Benjamins' methods, would have select hypothesis as the first subtask, and then introduce select observable (of hypothesis) as the next. But it is also apparent that another alternative is to skip the intermediate hypothesis selection and select an observation by taking the complete set of competing hypotheses into account. This illustrates that more general decompositions suggest alternative refinements to the library developer, that were not obvious with the more specific decomposition.

9 Impacts on the HP application

In relation to the discrepancies in the case-study, described in section 4, the more general discrimination method proposed above would eliminate the discrepancies called "no manipulation method", "redundancy between collect data and symptom detection", and "collect-data dependent on hypothesis selection". In a similar way, the discrepancy called "cost estimation requires current observations" would be eliminated by making the prime diagnostic method more general, and the discrepancy called "corroboration based on trace-back" would have been prevented by making the corroboration method more general.

The only discrepancy left is the one called "user control of test selection". In the case-study, the chosen modification was to add an ask-user task as the last subtask of the generate-observable task, which enabled the user to override the test selection proposed by the KBS. As was argued in section 8.2, there are good reasons to not include such methods in the library, where a transfer task covers what is in other methods regarded as part of the problem solving process. It is better to handle them by adaptation.

10 Conclusions

The goal of this paper was to propose a set of general principles that libraries of task decomposition methods can be evaluated against, in order to avoid unnecessary adaptations, and which specifically could have prevented the need to make adaptations in the case-study described in sections 3, 4, and 5.

Three principles were proposed: method correctness, local specialization, and method generality. As discussed in section 9, all of the discrepancies detected in the case-study, with one exception, could have been prevented by explicitly applying the principles. These discrepancies would also occur in many other applications. There is reason to believe that there are many other violations in Benjamins' library and in other libraries. The conclusion is that the use of principles such as these could play an important role in making libraries of task decomposition methods provide stronger support in real applications.

11 Further Work

Although the principles proposed here are already useful, there is still a long way to go to reach a thorough understanding of how to prevent unnecessary adaptations in libraries of task decomposition methods. For example, if the different roles of selection criteria were clear, the method correctness principle could be expressed more precisely, and thus applied more easily (e.g., some selection criteria impose constraints that should be satisfied, whereas others express strong assumptions that are exploited to satisfy the constraints). The kinds of modularity issues discussed here have counterparts in other fields of software engineering and reuse, which indicates a potential for using results from those fields. Many of the issues discussed here could become more clear, if we had a modelling language for task decomposition methods that was better adapted to faciliating the use and evaluation of such methods. However, it is not clear what the requirements on such a language are. The proposals made here will serve as one set of initial requirements.

There are two ways to reduce the difficulties of making adaptations. One way is to facilitate adaptations, e.g. with guidelines for the adaptation process [12]. The other way, which has been pursued here, is to increase the coverage of the library, so that adaptations are avoided. But it is unlikely that all adaptations *can* be avoided. Moreover, a library with truly large scale coverage, which prevents the need for adaptation as much as possible, may lead to other difficulties, e.g. in method selection and library maintenance. For some kinds of adaptations, preventing them may cause greater difficultes than it eliminates. Section 8.2 pointed to one kind of adaptation with this property – introducing a transfer task to allow another agent (usually the user) to perform, or over-ride, part of the problem solving. It would be very valuable to identify other classes of variations between applications that are better to handle by adaptation than by reuse. The approach taken in Protégé-II is that adaptations should be confined to mapping relations from method ontology to application ontology [9]. There may also be other kinds of adaptations that cannot, or should not, be avoided. More research on this issue is needed.

The principles proposed here were deliberately focused on preventing adaptations, and specifically the kinds of discrepancies that occured in the case-study. To prevent other kinds of discrepancies, and other kinds of difficulties, other principles will be needed. The way that these principles have been derived, from basic requirements and examples of concrete weaknesses, clearly shows a way to identify other principles than those needed in the case-study. For example, there are relevant notions of method generality that are not covered by the principle of method generality. Similarly, other basic requirements could be identified, e.g. ease of method selection, maintenance, incremental addition of methods, reuse of subtasks accross basic task types. Some of those were discussed in the case-study recapitulated here [11], and some principles have been proposed by others to that end [15, 18, 3, 4]. But the principles underlying good libraries of task decomposition methods are still far from being well understood.

Acknowledgements Ameen Abu-Hanna, Richard Benjamins, Hesham A. Hassan, and Olle Olsson provided helpful comments on the case-study that is recapitulated here [11].

References

1. J. M. Akkermans, B. J. Wielinga, and A. Th. Schreiber. Steps in constructing problem-solving methods. In N. Aussenac, G. Boy, B. Gaines, M. Linster, J.-G. Ganascia, and Y. Kodratoff, editors, *Proc. of EKAW'93*, number 723 in Lecture Notes in Computer Science, pages 45–65. Springer-Verlag, 1993.
2. Richard Benjamins and Wouter Jansweijer. Towards a competence theory of diagnosis. *IEEE Expert*, 9(5), 1994.
3. V. R. Benjamins. *Problem Solving Methods for Diagnosis*. PhD thesis, University of Amsterdam, Amsterdam, The Netherlands, June 1993.
4. J. Breuker and W. Van de Velde, editors. *CommonKADS Library for Expertise Modelling: Reusable Problem Solving Components*. IOS-Press, Amsterdam, August 1994.
5. J. A. Breuker, editor. *Model Driven Knowledge Acquisition: Interpretation Models*. University of Amsterdam and STL Ltd, 1987. ESPRIT Project P1098, Deliverable D1 (task A1).
6. B. Chandrasekaran. Generic tasks in knowledge based reasoning: High level building blocks for expert system design. *IEEE Expert*, 1(3):23–30, 1986.

7. B. Chandrasekaran. Design problem solving: A task analysis. *AI Magazine*, 11:59–71, 1990.

8. B. Chandrasekaran, T. R. Johnson, and J. W. Smith. Task-structure analysis for knowledge modelling. *Communications of the ACM*, 35(9):124–137, 1992.

9. J. H. Gennari, R. B. Altman, and M. A. Musen. Reuse with Protégé-II: From elevators to ribosomes. Technical Report KSL-94-71, Stanford Knowledge Systems Lab, 1995.

10. J. McDermott. Preliminary steps towards a taxonomy of problem-solving methods. In S. Marcus, editor, *Automating Knowledge Acquisition for Expert Systems*, pages 225–255. Kluwer, Boston, 1988.

11. Klas Orsvärn. Case-study in knowledge modelling with Benjamins' library of diagnosis methods. In *Proc. Knowledge Engineering Forum '95*, number 903 in Arbeitspapiere der GMD, pages 83–94, Sankt Augustin, Germany, March 1995. GMD.

12. Klas Orsvärn, Olle Olsson, and Hesham A. Hassan. Guidelines for adapting an interpretation model in an application. In *Proc. Knowledge Engineering Forum '95*, number 903 in Arbeitspapiere der GMD, pages 95–106, Sankt Augustin, Germany, March 1995. GMD.

13. Karsten Poeck and Ute Gappa. Making role-limiting shells more flexible. In N. Aussenac, G. Boy, B. Gaines, M. Linster, J.-G. Ganascia, and Y. Kodratoff, editors, *Proc. of EKAW'93*, number 723 in Lecture Notes in Computer Science, pages 103–122. Springer-Verlag, 1993.

14. A.R. Puerta, J. Egar, S. Tu, and M. Musen. A multiple-method shell for the automatic generation of knowledge acquisition tools. *Knowledge Acquisition*, 4:171–196, 1992.

15. William F. Punch III. *A Diagnosis System Using A Task Integrated Problem Solver Architecture (TIPS), Including Causal Reasoning*. PhD thesis, Ohio State University, Ohio, 1989.

16. L. Steels. Components of expertise. *AI Magazine*, 11(2):29–49, Summer 1990.

17. L. Steels. The componential framework and its role in reusability. In Jean-Marc David, Jean-Paul Krivine, and Reid Simmons, editors, *Second Generation Expert Systems*, pages 273–298. Springer-Verlag, Berlin Heidelberg, Germany, 1993.

18. G. van Heijst, P. Terpstra, B. J. Wielinga, and N. Shadbolt. Using generalised directive models in knowledge acquisition. In Th. Wetter, K. D. Althoff, J. Boose, B. Gaines, M. Linster, and F. Schmalhofer, editors, *Current Developments in Knowledge Acquisition: EKAW-92*, Berlin, Germany, 1992. Springer-Verlag.

19. B. Wielinga, J. Akkermans, and A. Schreiber. A formal analysis of parametric design. In *Proc. 9th Banff Knowledge-Acquisition for Knowledge-Based Systems Workshop*, March 1995.

A Purpose Driven Method for Language Comparison

The REVISE project[1][2][*]

[1] SWI, University of Amsterdam Roetersstraat 15, 1018 WB Amsterdam, The Netherlands
[2] Faculty of Mathematics and Computer Science Vrije Universiteit De Boelelaan 1081a, 1081 HV Amsterdam, The Netherlands

Abstract. Current efforts to compare knowledge engineering (KE) modelling languages have been limited to either rather shallow comparisons on a broad-set of languages, or to detailed comparisons with limited applicability to a narrow set of languages. In this paper we propose a novel way of organising language comparisons. This method is based on an alternating decomposition of the goals that a language tries to achieve and the linguistic methods it employs to achieve these goals. This new method for comparing languages allows a general comparison at high levels of abstraction, while not preventing more precise comparisons whenever possible. One result of our comparison method is an insight in the different assumptions that underly the languages to be compared. Two further consequences follow from the proposed comparison method, namely (i) a measure for the degree of similarity between languages, and (ii) a method for translating between languages. After describing our method, we apply it to a pair of KE modelling languages, and show how it yields insights in the assumptions underlying the languages and how it can be used to produce a translation procedure between the languages.

1 Introduction

In this section we discuss the two main motivations for this paper: "Why do we need to compare languages?" and "Why do we need a new method for comparing languages?"

1.1 Why do we need to compare languages?

The field of KE has seen an increase of modelling languages in recent years [8, 2]. Such a large family of languages which all have roughly the same aim prompts the need to categorise and compare such languages, for the following reasons:

---

[*] This work has been (partially) funded by the Netherlands Computer Science Research Foundation with financial support from the Netherlands Organization for Scientific Research (NWO) within the REVISE-project, SION-project no. 612-322-316. The following members of the REVISE project contributed to this paper (listed in alphabetical order): Frances Brazier[2], Frank van Harmelen[2], Remco Straatman[1], Jan Treur[2], Niek Wijngaards[2], Mark Willems[2]

- To enable *choosing* the appropriate language for a particular application. Different properties of the languages make them suitable for different uses (e.g. for different types of applications, for different stages in the development process, etc). A comparison and categorisation helps to choose the appropriate language given a set of desired properties for a given purpose.
- To make it possible to *translate* a model from on language into another. Such translations are necessary to facilitate engineering in application projects, to increase re-usability of knowledge models between projects, and to enable use of different languages in different stages of a single project.

An important aspect in both these points is that each language embodies different assumptions about the objects and processes to be modelled, and about how the modelling primitives in a language should be used. These assumptions are often made implicitly, but both for choosing among and translating between languages it is essential that these different underlying assumptions are made explicit.

1.2   Why do we need a new method for comparing languages?

In the past few years, a number of attempts have been made to compare and classify KE modelling languages. These can be found in [3, 4, 5, 8, 2]. We will discuss the deficiencies of each of these attempts. Two parameters can be used to characterise all of these comparison attempts, namely the degree of similarity among the languages that were compared, and the amount of details that was studied in the comparison.

One of the first attempts at a broad comparison of KE modelling languages was the Sisyphus-I project [3, 4]. A number of languages was used to model the same simple task. The family of languages that was involved was very broad: Generic Tasks, KARL, OMOS, KADS. and others. As a result, the models that were constructed varied considerably, and only general properties of the languages could be studied. No final comparison paper appeared in the literature.

The VT-effort [5] also aimed at comparing a broad scope of modelling languages by modelling the same task in many languages. The problem of too little similarity among the set of languages was partly avoided by concentrating mainly on modelling domain and inference knowledge, and leaving control issues out of the comparison effort.

A third comparison effort was made at the ECAI'92 workshop on formal modelling languages for knowledge-based systems [8]. This effort again aimed at comparing a very broad set of languages $((ML)^2, MC, AIDE, KARL, DESIRE, OBJ3, MILORD, K_{BS}SF)$. Again, as a result, only rather general conclusions could be drawn.

Almost the opposite choice was made in [2]. This effort compared a family of closely related languages (OMOS, MODEL-K, MoMo, FORKADS, KARL, $(ML)^2$, QIL, $K_{BS}SF$, all aimed at KADS expertise models, and all being sufficiently precise for either formalisation or operationalisation). As a result, this study differed from the previous three in the greater amount of detail to which the languages could be compared. The obvious limitation of this study was of course the restricted applicability.

All of this can be summarised as follows: often the underlying assumptions and aims of the languages were so different that they prevented a meaningful comparison, while in other cases the applicability of a meaningful comparison was limited to languages based on very strong and therefore limiting assumptions. In other words: current comparison efforts have been limited to either rather shallow comparisons on a broad-set of languages, or to detailed comparisons with a limited applicability to a narrow set of languages. The purpose of this paper is to propose a novel way of organising language comparisons. This new method for comparing languages will enable us to perform a comparison of languages at varying degrees of detail, allowing us a general comparison at high levels of abstraction, while not preventing more precise comparisons whenever possible. An explicit result of our comparison method will be insight in the different assumptions that underly the languages to be compared. Our method will enable us to detect when these assumptions correspond or differ, and, as a result, we can we can extend our comparison to the maximum level of detail permitted by the shared assumptions.

2 Comparison Method

The essence of the approach to language comparison that we advocate in this paper is that we begin by explicitly formulating the goals that each of the languages tries to achieve. Strange as it may seem, we do *not* take either the syntax or the semantics of the languages as a starting point for the comparison, but we concentrate instead on the *goals* that the language designers tried to achieve.

In itself, such a goal oriented approach to language comparison is not new: [8] already speaks about a "purpose-driven" comparison, and distinguishes formalisation and operationalisation as two distinct goals of separate sets of languages. The same distinction was made in [2] to divide the languages that are compared. However, after such a distinction based on language goals, both these papers subsequently concentrated on syntactic and semantic issues within each group.

The novelty of our approach lies in the fact that we use such language goals not only as a first division criterion, but that we use it as the sole basis for the entire comparison. In other words: our approach could justly be called a "purpose-driven" comparison method.

In somewhat more detail, our comparison method proceeds as follows: We first distinguish high level *goals* that the language designers have tried to achieve. In general, these will be quite abstract concepts such as "expressive power", "executability", "reusability", "formal precision" etc. Notice that these are the types of distinctions also used in [8] and [2]. In our approach we then proceed to analyse which *methods* the language designers have employed to achieve these goals. These methods will be somewhat more concrete than the corresponding goals, and could be terms such as "compositionality", "information hiding", "separation of control", etc. Each of these methods to achieve an abstract goal can itself be regarded as a somewhat more concrete goal, for which we can discern even more concrete methods, and so on recursively. At the lowest levels of this recursively alternating goal/method decomposition, we will arrive at very specific syntactic or semantic properties of the languages in question such as subprocedure constructs, global state representations, use of formal constructions, etc.

A crucial point is that such detailed language constructs appear in this goal/method decomposition tree *according to the reason why they were included in the language*, and not simply on the basis of a superficial or semantic similarity.

We will now discuss two important consequences that follow from such a goal-oriented comparison method, namely: - a measure for the degree of similarity between languages, and - a method for translating between languages

A measure for the degree of similarity between languages First of all, our comparison method gives us insight in the degree of similarity of the languages involved. When descending through the goal/method decomposition tree, languages that had corresponding high-level goals may well realise these goals in different ways, and therefore have different low-level goals. The level at which the languages begin to differ while descending through the goal/method tree is a measure for the similarity of the languages.

Notice that this measure of similarity cannot be derived by looking at the syntactic structure of the language: languages with very similar goals on quite concrete levels in the tree may well make different syntactic choices at the very lowest level, and therefore look superficially very different, even though they are in fact quite similar. Conversely, languages which have similar syntactic or semantic constructions may in fact be radically different when we look at how these constructions are mean to be used (ie. why the were included in the language).

A method for translating between languages A second consequence of our proposal for organising a language comparison is that it yields a translation method between the languages involved. This procedure works as follows: whenever we want to translate a construct c from language L_1 into language L_2, we look up the construct in the goal/method tree for L_1. We then traverse the tree upwards until we reach a node g which also occurs in the tree for L_2. This means that apparently the construct c is used in both L_1 and L_2 for reason (goal, purpose) g. We then descend downwards from g into the tree for L_2 to find language constructs which are used in L_2 to realise goal g, and into which construct c should therefore be translated.

Notice that if construct c appears both in L_1 and L_2, this does not mean that c from L_1 should also be translated as c in L_2. After all, c may feature in L_1 for entirely different reasons than in L_2. Instead, c from L_1 must be translated into a construct which is included in L_2 for the same reasons for which c was include L_1.

A further point to notice is that the effectiveness of this translation procedure is directly dependent on the degree of similarity between the two languages. If L_1 and L_2 are very different in their goals and in the methods they use to achieve these goals, then for many constructs c in L_1, we will have to traverse up to quit high in the tree before hitting a node shared with the tree for L_2. For such a high node (= an abstract goal), there will in general be very many constructions which contribute to realising that goal, which would render the method ineffective. This is of course exactly as expected, since translation mechanisms between two closely related languages will be more effective than those between distant languages.

Predictions From the above two consequences from our comparison method (a measure for language-similarity and a procedure for language-translation), we can derive two predictions that can be used to test the validity of our proposal.

1. If we take two related KE modelling languages, and we construct their goal/method decomposition trees, then these trees should coincide at the highest levels, and should begin to diverge at the lower levels in the hierarchy. Furthermore, the levels where the trees begin to differ should correspond to our intuitions on how similar the languages are and on the nature of their differences.
2. If we take a model expressed in one of the two languages, and apply the translation procedure described above, we should end up with a more or less natural description of the same model in the other language, or, alternatively, we should be able to explain precisely why certain constructs could not be translated in a natural way, in terms of missing correspondences between the goal/method trees for the two languages.

In the following sections, we will perform exactly these two experiments for two modelling languages for knowledge-based systems.

3 Goal graph

The design of (formal) specification languages and frameworks is, in general, based on a number of assumptions with respect to the goals the languages/frameworks pursue. A number of frameworks have been designed for modelling and specifying complex tasks in which reasoning plays an essential role, a number of which are mentioned above. The assumptions behind the design of two of these frameworks/languages, namely ML^2/KADS and DESIRE have been compared. The comparison has shown that the goals of the languages/frameworks are quite similar.

3.1 High level goals

At the top level five goals have been distinguished (the numbering refers to the graphs shown in figure 5).

H1 transparency: the structure of a system's architecture should be transparent: specifications should be comprehensible;

H2 reusability: specifications and architectures should be easily adapted to changing requirements, new knowledge, etc., to allow for reusability of specifications in different applications and/or tasks ;

H3 expressive power: a framework and specification language must be expressive: sufficient means must be available to model and specify the types of knowledge and interaction required;

H4 establishing properties: specification languages must allow for verification of system behaviour;

H5 realizability: specifications should provide sufficient detail to allow for implementation.

3.2   Lower level goals

Languages/frameworks may differ in the way in which the goals above can be pursued. To achieve these goals, lower level goals such as compositionality, play an important role. These lower level (sub)goals make the corresponding goals more concrete: they can be considered means to reach the higher level goals. Below each of the lower level goals distinguished will be described together with the relation to the more abstract goals with which they are directly associated. These goals are characteristic for the languages/frameworks considered and have been grouped together in a graph within which levels indicate levels of abstraction.

L0 Compositionality Modularisation is a generally accepted means to structure systems and specifications in both software and knowledge engineering: a means which is in line with the five main goals. Both ML^2 and DESIRE have been designed on the basis of this concept: complex reasoning systems are viewed as compositional systems within which complex tasks are modelled and specified as interacting subtasks and different types of knowledge are manipulated. This principle, compositionality, is essential to both frameworks. Together with the five goals characteristics, compositionality is one of the most important elements in the design of complex (reasoning) systems. Compositionality can be seen a central goal, and many of the other lower level goals are related to it. These other lower level goals are: (1) separation of knowledge types, (2) formal semantics, (3) partial specification, (4) operationalisation, (5) interactivity, (6) reflection and (7) partial reasoning, as described below. The relations among these lower level goals (as well as with the main goals described above) is also depicted in figure 5. The numbering refers to this figure.

L1 Separation of knowledge types Distinctions between the different types of knowledge involved, is one of the basic goals of compositional approaches to system design. The function of the knowledge involved is the basis for distinctions, and explicit separation of knowledge in system specifications.

The lower-level goals on which such distinctions are based are:

L1a case-specific/case-independent: Case-independent knowledge is used to reason about specific situations on the basis of additional information specifically related to the specific situations - case-specific information. For example, in a medical domain, information on a specific patient can be distinguished from general knowledge expressing relations between symptoms and diseases in the domain of medicine.

L1b separation of control Knowledge of control is explicitly distinguished from other knowledge involved. The interference of control knowledge with other knowledge may lead to systems that are not transparent and difficult to maintain. Separation of control knowledge, as part of the compositionality of a system can contribute to high level goals such as transparency and reusability. Also the high level goal of being able to establish properties of a specification is supported by separation of control knowledge.

L1c primitive components One of the principles on which compositional systems are based, is the principle that tasks can be decomposed and that a lowest level of decomposition can be assumed.

L1d layers Not only are different types of knowledge distinguished: different characteristics are often distinguished on the basis of which layers of knowledge are distinguished. The KADS three layer model distinguishes domain layer, inference layer and task layer. In DESIRE a knowledge dimension and a task dimension are distinguished.

L2 Formal semantics One of the guiding goals of both languages is that in order to establish properties of a system, it is necessary to formally express functionality, structure and behaviour.

L2a formal semantics of static aspects of reasoning For complex (reasoning) systems declarative, logic-based specifications are formulated with well-defined formal semantics. The goal of monotonicity for primitive subprocesses is a lower-level related goal.

L2b formal semantics of dynamic aspects of reasoning In many applications essential requirements are imposed on the dynamics of the system to be developed. During modelling, dynamic aspects are considered intensively. Therefore informal and formal semantics for dynamics are important. To this end temporal logic (for DESIRE) and dynamic logic (for ML^2) are used. Lower level goals behind the formal semantics of dynamic behaviour include persistency, controlled inference and directed reasoning.

L3 Partial specification During modelling, partial specification is often useful: reuse of existing specifications is supported by existing partial specifications. Related lower-level goals are:

L3a information hiding Compositionality allows for information hiding, which in turn supports partial specification. Components can be developed independently from each other. Essential in this approach is that information in one component is hidden from other components. Information to be shared with other components is specified in the interface of a component. A lower level goal is translation of elements of lexicons between components.

L3b generic (task) models Generic models are another means of using partial specifications. The specification is an abstract, domain-independent description of a task which can be specialised and instantiated.

L4 operationalisation One way to check whether the formal specifications of a system suffice is to implement a prototype on the basis of the specifications and to examine the behaviour. For some formal languages/frameworks operationalisation is a high-level goal, for which software environments support execution.

L5 interactivity Within complex interactive systems, interaction between systems and users should be explicitly modelled and specified. In the first place the lower-level goal of distinguishing agents is essential. For example, this can be fulfilled by defining separate components that model the different agents and that include knowledge of how to interact with each other.

L6 reflection In many problem solving processes explicit representation of reflective reasoning/meta-reasoning is of importance; e.g., to inspect and analyse in detail the current state of the process. To this end modelling techniques are required to be able to reflect on specific information and knowledge states of the system but also on task control.

L7 partial reasoning Reasoning is a dynamic process in which partial processes can be distinguished. To specify such reasoning compositionality is used (to separate or hide reasoning in one component from that in other components). The lower-level goal of controlled inference is of importance here.

L7a controlled inference In many complex situations exhaustive reasoning seldom occurs. Often reasoning processes proceed (a following task is begun) on the basis of a limited number of conclusions: either because a limited number suffice or because sufficient effort has been invested. Such factors are also explicitly modelled. The lower level goal of controlled inference is directed reasoning.

4 Using the comparison method to translate between languages

As mentioned in section 2, one of the expected results our comparison method would be the ability to perform translations between the compared languages. When translating between languages, it makes sense to translate parts of the source language playing a certain role (e.g. control knowledge) to the part of the target language that plays the same role. Our comparison method identifies which parts of the language are responsible for achieving a certain goal in the respective languages. Because of this we expect the comparison to be helpful in translating between languages.

The comparison-lattice describes, for each of the languages, which language elements are responsible for reaching a higher-level goal. If we want to translate a language element in the source language, we need to identify the language element(s) in the target language it must map onto. The appropriate element(s) can be found by tracing in the lattice which elements in the target language have the same parent goal as the source language element. It may both be the case that multiple elements map onto a single element and that multiple elements map onto a single element.

We will try to translate a specific, simple, DESIRE specification into a corresponding $(ML)^2$ specification. This experiment has two goals: (1) to evaluate whether the lattice helps in translating between languages, and (2) to try to gain insight in the relation between DESIRE and $(ML)^2$. Because of the second goal, we will also try to translate parts which are not described in the lattice (by using additional knowledge).

The next sections will describe the results of a case study in translating a DESIRE specification into a $(ML)^2$ specification. We start by describing the DESIRE model used for the translation experiment. Because of the two goals underlying the experiment, we will split our evaluation in two parts. First we will describe the approach followed and the problems experienced in translating DESIRE into $(ML)^2$. Next, we will discuss to what extent the comparison lattice was helpful in translating the specification.

4.1 The case: translating a DESIRE specification to $(ML)^2$

The DESIRE specification used is that of a simple system for car diagnosis. We will only briefly describe the specification here ([6] contains the complete DESIRE specification and [7] the underlying motivation). The system uses *hypothetical reasoning* to come to a diagnosis. Hypothetical reasoning consists of determining a hypothesis, followed by the evaluation of this hypothesis. This continues until an acceptable hypothesis is found. Evaluating a hypothesis is done by determining which observations are consistent with the hypothesis, and comparing the actual observation with the expected observation. If a mismatch between these is found, the hypothesis can be rejected immediately. A hypothesis is confirmed when all observations match. The order in which hypotheses are tried, is predetermined. Which observations to test for a given hypothesis is determined by a causal network, that links hypothesis to observations.

4.2 Translating DESIRE specifications to $(ML)^2$

This section describes the specific lessons learned with respect to the translation between DESIRE and $(ML)^2$. This section will be fairly detailed and some parts require knowledge of both languages.

Functional decomposition The DESIRE decomposition of complex components in subcomponents can be translated into the task decomposition of $(ML)^2$. Primitive components can be translated into primitive tasks and their associated primitive inferences in $(ML)^2$. As stated in the graph (see figure 5) the component that models communication with the user (such as *obtain-observation-results*) can be modeled as a transfer task in $(\text{ML})^2$.

Primitive components When translating DESIRE primitive components into $(\text{ML})^2$, one has to consider different parts of the graph. First of all, the graph states that case independent knowledge is present in static roles in $(\text{ML})^2$ and in the knowledge base of primitive components in DESIRE. Second, $(\text{ML})^2$ also discerns domain dependent (domain layer) and domain independent knowledge (inference layer). The connection between these two layers is provided by static roles which redefine the domain knowledge in terms of the role it plays at the inference layer (for instance a disease at the domain layer is lifted to a hypothesis at the inference layer). So the knowledge-base of a DESIRE primitive component must be split into a domain-dependent part (which will be placed in a domain theory and is lifted to an inference layer static role) and a domain independent part (which will be placed in the inference body). An example of this translation is the knowledge base of *hypothesis-determination*. This knowledge base contains knowledge about preference between hypotheses, and knowledge on how to select the most prefered hypothesis that has not been selected yet.

```
knowledge base Hypothesis_Determination-kernel-kb
    better_hypothesis_than( broken_headlights, empty_battery );
    better_hypothesis_than( empty_battery, broken_starting_motor );
    if not rejected( broken_headlights )
       then selected( broken_headlights ) ;
    if not rejected( H: Hypothesis )
       and rejected( Hrej: Hypothesis )
       and better_hypothesis_than( Hrej: Hypothesis, H: Hypothesis )
       then selected( H: Hypothesis ) ;
end knowledge base Hypothesis_Determination-kernel-kb
```

Fig. 1. Hypothesis Determination knowledge base in DESIRE

It should be clear that the first type of knowledge ends up at the domain-layer in $(\text{ML})^2$, and the second type in the inference body. Also note that since DESIRE does not make this distinction, human interpretation of the knowledge base is necessary to make this selection. Also additional vocabulary must be added for the static roles and/or the domain theory. Figure 2 depicts the translation.

A difference that is not stated in the graph is that in DESIRE primitive component can have multiple target sets. In $(\text{ML})^2$ this would correspond to an inference which has more than one goal, which is not allowed. The DESIRE component with multiple targets (*hypothesis-evaluation* with targets *evaluate-to-confirm* and *evaluate-to-reject*) is modeled as two independent inferences in $(\text{ML})^2$, one for each target. The data flow was adapted accordingly (since not all inputs were needed for both goals) which resulted in a less complex data flow.

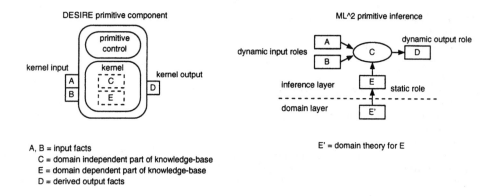

A, B = input facts
  C = domain independent part of knowledge-base
  E = domain dependent part of knowledge-base
  D = derived output facts

E' = domain theory for E

Fig. 2. Translating primitive components

Control over components As specified in the comparison graph, the task control knowledge-base in DESIRE and the task body in $(ML)^2$ are both responsible for the ordering of reasoning steps. In DESIRE control over the ordering of reasoning steps is specified by rules, whereas in $(ML)^2$ it is specified in procedural expressions based on QDL. However, since we know both representations are meant to provide the same function, we can easily translate between these representations. To this end, we first made control flow diagrams for the DESIRE task control database. Then, we constructed procedural programs that resulted in the same ordering of subtasks.

During task control translation, a difference between the languages emerged that was not described in the comparison graph. In DESIRE an explicit method for dealing with failing reasoning steps is present. In DESIRE, failure of a subcomponent to produce its target can be detected afterwards by the parent component by means of the `evaluation(<component>,<target set>,failed)` test, available in the task-control vocabulary. A complex component can also signal its failure by the `own-state(failed)`. In $(ML)^2$ this feature is missing, and one can only test *beforehand* whether a primitive inference will succeed for a given input (by means of the `has-solution_<pia-name>(<input>,<output>)` test). If a primitive inference is called in $(ML)^2$ and it fails, the entire system will fail. For a task no language elements are available to deal with failure of subtasks, or to denote its own failure.

Our solution to this problem was to adapt all tasks such that, in case of failure, they would return a special output value to denote failure. For primitive inferences we used the definition of primitive tasks (which in $(ML)^2$ are tasks that do nothing but call a certain inference) to mimic the behaviour of DESIRE primitive components. The body of the primitive task is defined such that it will test whether a primitive inference will fail (in which case the special output value is returned), and otherwise return the normal output of the primitive inference. Figure 3 shows a (part of) a $(ML)^2$ primitive task created this way.

ps–task–module hypothesis–determination
  import
    hypothesis–determination ,
    definitions ;
  input
    Eval–Hypos : evaluated–hypothesis set ;
  output
    Sel–Hypo : hypothesis ;
  signature
    programs
      hypothesis–determination : evaluated–hypothesis set ×hypothesis ;
  task–structures
  ∀ Eval–Hypos : evaluated–hypothesis set
  ∀ Sel–Hypo : hypothesis
    (hypothesis–determination (Eval–Hypos , Sel–Hypo) ≡
      IF more–solutions–hypothesis–determination (Eval–Hypos , Sel–Hypo) THEN

        give–solution–hypothesis–determination (Eval–Hypos , Sel–Hypo)
      ELSE
        (Sel–Hypo := ∅)
      FI);
end–ps–task–module

Fig. 3. Communicating failure of primitive inferences

Data flow between components When trying to translate the DESIRE data flow, the graph suggests that input and output roles in $(ML)^2$ have the same function as the input and output of components in DESIRE. Translation of information is done by translation of vocabulary and truth values by transformations in DESIRE, and by passing the info in roles in $(ML)^2$.

Data flow can be translated into $(ML)^2$ by "merging" inputs and outputs of components into intermediate roles. In fact, this difference between the languages stems from a difference in creation process. Aben [1] describes that during the construction of the inference layer *role ontology mappings* are necessary in order to be able to connect inferences which are selected from the library. These mappings ensure that the input roles roles of the consuming inference are compatible with the output roles of the producing inferences. So, whereas in DESIRE these mappings are part of the specification, in $(ML)^2$ they are part of the *process* of creating the specification. Figure 4 tries to clarify this distinction.

A further difference between the transformations in DESIRE and role ontology mappings in $(ML)^2$ is that DESIRE distinguishes object-meta(-meta-...,) relations between knowledge. In $(ML)^2$ this distinction is not present. In the translation, the object-meta distinction between knowledge is lost.

In the DESIRE specification a number of predicates were used to indicate where a particular input fact came from. Examples of this are the `selected` and `candidate` predicates for observations. In $(ML)^2$ these identifying predicates are not strictly necessary, since the source of inputs is identified by the input predicates in the primitive inferences. In order to stay close to the original DESIRE

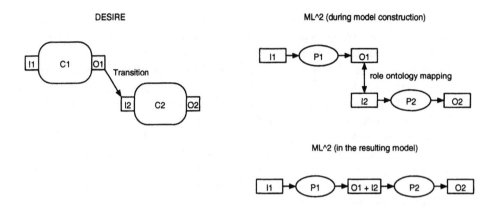

Fig. 4. Translating data flow between components

specification we included the identifying predicates, even though they perform no function in $(\text{ML})^2$.

Finally, unlike DESIRE, the $(\text{ML})^2$ data-flow does not strictly follow the decomposition. Communication between inferences is done strictly by means of the roles at the inference layer, leaving an unclear role for the input and output variables of tasks.

4.3 Translating using the comparison graph

This section describes lessons learned regarding the use of the comparison graph in the translation process. It will use language specific examples only to illustrate what was learned.

In general, the graph was successful in identifying sources and targets for the translation tasks, and we were able to find suitable translations for the concepts we could identify counterparts in the other languages for. For instance, the comparison graph correctly identified that DESIRE task control knowledge bases should be translated into $(\text{ML})^2$ task bodies. After this the actual translation between these elements was straightforward, despite the difference in representation.

On the negative side, we experienced a number of problems using the graph. These could be classified as: lack of guidance, errors in the graph, lack of detail, and concepts without counterpart. Of these, the first one is the most serious problem, the second and third problem are mainly problems of creating the comparison graph. The last one is a general problem for which no translation method can provide an answer.

- **Lack of guidance** The comparison graph does not give enough guidance in the ordering of the translation tasks. We first started out by picking some leaf of the graph and trying to translate that concept in DESIRE to the associated concept(s) in $(\text{ML})^2$. After a few concepts were tried in this way, it became clear that translation could not be done in this arbitrary order. Because of the strong dependence of the various parts of an $(ML)^2$ specification certain translation tasks need to be performed before others. For instance, one cannot write down the task layer completely before the types of roles at the inference layer are known. Since there is no way to derive an ordering from the comparison graph, we used additional information here. In [1] guidelines for translating informal KADS specifications into $(ML)^2$ are given. These guidelines also prescribe an ordering on this translation. In the DESIRE to $(ML)^2$ translation process we used this ordering, using the comparison graph to select appropriate DESIRE concepts for the $(ML)^2$ concept at hand. The ordering gave considerable guidance to the translation process and solved the above mentioned problem.

- **Errors in the comparison graph** Some errors in the original graph (that are now corrected) also confused the translation process. For example, the comparison graph indicates that both languages use "layers" as a way to distinguish between different types of knowledge. The graph then states that DESIRE uses object-meta distinctions for this purpose, and $(ML)^2$ uses a distinction between domain and inference layer for this purpose. Translation between these concepts in the respective languages is not possible though, since these are different distinctions between knowledge types. In fact, the comparison graph is not specific enough at this node and it should have contained sub-nodes. One sub-node for the distinction "domain-specific vs. domain independent" and one for the distinction "object-meta knowledge". The same can be said for the nodes under "information hiding" which also deal with dissimilar concepts. In general, one should take care that children of a node really describe methods for the same goal.
- **Lack of detail** In general the graph in its current state lacks detail. A lot of language primitives are not present in the graph, which makes translation difficult. In our experience, the graph should contain all the language primitives to maximize its usefulness for translation.
- **Concepts without counterpart** Other problems in translating between the languages mainly consisted of concepts for which no counterpart exists in the other language. Clear examples for this are the above mentioned distinctions between "domain-specific vs. domain independent knowledge" (present in $(ML)^2$, but not in DESIRE) and "object-meta knowledge" (present in DESIRE, but not in $(ML)^2$). Translation between these concepts requires human creativity to, respectively, create and destroy the extra distinctions. However as stated in the introduction of this section this was to be expected.

5 Conclusions

For our conclusions, we will distinguish between the three different possibles ways in which the combined goal-subgoal tree for two languages can be used, namely as a comparison method, as a distance measure, and as a translation method.

As a comparison method, our approach has distinct advantages over existing approaches. It allows a combination of both high-level and detailed comparison of the languages, whereas previous comparisons have always done either one or the other. Furthermore, our method encourages to abstract from syntactic differences between the languages, and focuses on the goals and motivations that are embodied in the languages to explain the differences between the languages.

Concerning the use of our method as a difference measure, after our experiment we would not claim that our method provides a very precise notion of "difference" between two languages, but it is nevertheless useful as a general indication. The higher the level in the tree where two languages begin to differ, the further apart the two languages are. Furthermore, our difference measure differentiates between different aspects of a language: $(ML)^22$ and DESIRE differ early on in the tree concerning the operationalisation of the language, but are quite similar in other respects.

Regarding the use of our method as an aid in the translation process, we do not think that our goal-subgoal tree will ever lead to an automated translation process. Nevertheless, the general impression after the translation experiment was that the graph helped in decomposing the translation task by grouping related parts of the specification together. This lead to clearly delimited subtasks in the translation process. On the negative side, we found that the graph gives no guidance with respect to the order in which the translation should be carried out (since no dependencies between the various fragments of a language are taken into account) and that the original graph lacked detail and was incorrect in places.

We are not in a position to compare the amount of work saved during our translation experiment with the amount of work it took to construct our graph. Further experiments would be required for such an analysis. Such future work should also indicate the applicability of this work to other languages, both inside and outside the field of knowledge modelling.

Acknowledgments

We thank the two anonymous referees for their helpful comments.

References

1. M. Aben. *Formal Methods in Knowledge Engineering*. PhD thesis, University of Amsterdam, Faculty of Psychology, February 1995. ISBN 90-5470-028-9.
2. D. Fensel and F. van Harmelen. A comparison of languages which operationalise and formalise KADS models of expertise. *The Knowledge Engineering Review*, 9:105–146, 1994.
3. M. Linster. Sisyphus'91 part 2: Models of problem-solving. statement of the sample problem. In D. Smeed, M. Linster, J. H. Boose, and B. R. Gaines, editors, *Proceedings of EKAW91*, Glasgow, 1991. University of Strathclyde.
4. M. Linster. Sisyphus'91/92: Models of problem solving. *Int. J. of Human Computer Studies*, 40(3), 1994. Editorial special issue.

81

5. A. Th. Schreiber and W. P. Birmingham. The Sisyphus-VT initiative. *International Journal of Human-Computer Studies*, 1996. Editorial special issue.

6. R. Straatman, F. Brazier, F. van Harmelen, J. Treur, N. Wijngaards, and M. Willems. A purpose driven method for language comparison. Revise project, University of Amsterdam and Free University of Amsterdam, 1995.

7. J. Treur. Heuristic reasoning and relative incompleteness. *International Journal of Approximate Reasoning*, 8:51–87, 1993.

8. J. Treur and Th. Wetter, editors. *Formal Specification of Complex Reasoning Systems*, Workshop Series. Ellis Horwood, 1993.

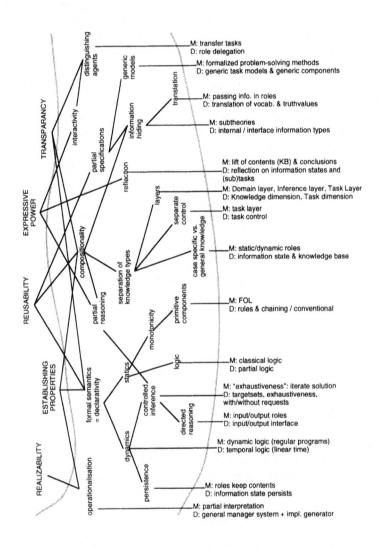

]

Fig. 5. The goals and subgoals of $(ML)^2$ and DESIRE

A Conceptual and Formal Model of a Diagnostic Reasoner

Richard Benjamins[1] and Manfred Aben[2]

[1] SWI, University of Amsterdam, Roetersstraat 15, NL-1018 WB Amsterdam, the Netherlands, richard@swi.psy.uva.nl***

[2] Unilever Research Laboratories, Olivier van Noortlaan 120, NL-3133 AT Vlaardingen, the Netherlands, Manfred.Aben@2488taux.urlnl.sprint.com

Abstract. The knowledge acquisition process can be supported by distinguishing different models in the development process of knowledge-based systems, where each model is dedicated to a specific phase. Two of these models are the conceptual model and the formal model. Conceptual models of knowledge-based systems facilitate initial system specification because they are easy to understand and construct. However, such models are often ambiguous and inconsistent, and contain hidden assumptions. The use of formal methods is a way to overcome these problems, and formalization becomes essential when we have to guarantee that system specifications are met, such as in safety critical systems. This paper presents a conceptual model and a formal model of a diagnostic reasoner, and includes a proof which shows that the high-level specification of our reasoner is ensured by the formal model presented.

1 Introduction and motivation

Conceptual modeling is a widely recognized activity in the process of knowledge-based system (KBS) development. A conceptual model (CM) is an informal, though highly structured, model for initial system specification [14]. In a CM, one specifies the required functionality of the system at a high level, without loosing oneself in details concerned with design or implementation. Conceptual models in Knowledge Engineering share the same motivation as the structured models in Object-Oriented Modeling [12] and Structured Analysis [20]. Due to its high-level, on the one hand, a CM facilitates initial system development but, on the other hand, leaves room for ambiguities and inconsistencies (e.g., inferences can be interpreted in more than one way [3]). A CM is only a first step in the development process of a knowledge-based system, and a long way is still to go before it can be implemented.

Current knowledge engineering approaches acknowledge this gap between a conceptual model and its implementation, and, to bridge it, they view KBS development as an incremental (though nonlinear) process, in which subsequently more detailed models are constructed. Several knowledge engineering approaches such as KADS [14], MIKE [2] and Vital [16] advocate the use of the following, increasingly more detailed, models: conceptual model (informal, but structured), formal model (language with a mathematically defined syntax and semantics), design model (specifies the system architecture, and the data structures), and

*** Richard Benjamins is supported by the Netherlands Computer Science Research Foundation with financial support from the Netherlands Organisation for Scientific Research (NWO). The work has partly been supported by the HCM program, financed by the CEC.

implementation model (implementation of data structures in a computer language). The formal model is an essential model in this process when we deal with safety-critical systems, because it enables consistency checking and correctness proving of the models [13].

Formal models are a means to get rid of the ambiguities and inconsistencies in conceptual models. However, constructing formal models is difficult and time consuming. Recently, both in software and in knowledge engineering, several efforts have been made to connect the conceptual model with the formal model [15, 11, 18].

Diagnostic systems often operate under safety-critical conditions, for example in airplanes or in chemical process industries, where finding the right causes of symptoms is crucial. Diagnosis is a complex task for which many approaches and techniques have been put forward. It is therefore not easy to develop diagnostic knowledge-based systems for a particular application. Recently we have presented a conceptual analysis of diagnosis [4] which integrates many approaches and diagnostic systems in a uniform way. The analysis identifies the relevant goals (tasks) in diagnosis, and the way in which these goals can be achieved (by problem-solving methods). We showed how the analysis can be used to semi-automatically generate conceptual models of diagnostic strategies [5].

The aim of this paper has to be seen in the context of integrating conceptual and formal models. We will show how to construct a conceptual and a formal model of a diagnostic reasoner (a hypothesis generator). During the formalization process, we have to be precise about what we exactly mean with the conceptual model.

The structure of the paper is as follows. In Section 2, we present the conceptual model of our diagnostic reasoner. In Section 3, we describe its formalization, and prove that our model indeed describes the intended behavior. Section 4 discusses the formalization, and puts it in a broader perspective. Finally, Section 5 concludes the paper.

2 Conceptual modeling

In this section, we briefly explicate the ingredients of our analysis, and then present the conceptual model of our diagnostic reasoner, which is a hypothesis generator.

2.1 Conceptual analysis

Task A task has a goal and is characterized by the type of input it receives and the type of output it produces. A task is a specification of *what* needs to be achieved. For example, the goal of diagnosis is to find a solution that is consistent with all observations. A task can be decomposed into subtasks (by a problem-solving method).

Problem-Solving method A problem-solving method (or method, PSM) describes *how* the goal of a task can be achieved. It has inputs and outputs and decomposes a task into subtasks and/or primitive inferences. In addition, a method specifies the data flow between its constituents in terms of the input and output types. Control knowledge determines the execution order and iterations of the subtasks and inferences of a PSM.

Primitive inference A primitive inference (or inference) defines a reasoning step, with its inputs and outputs, that can be carried out using domain knowledge to achieve a goal. Inferences form the actual building blocks of a problem solver. When all tasks are decomposed, through PSMs, into inferences, and we connect inferences based on shared inputs and outputs, the corresponding

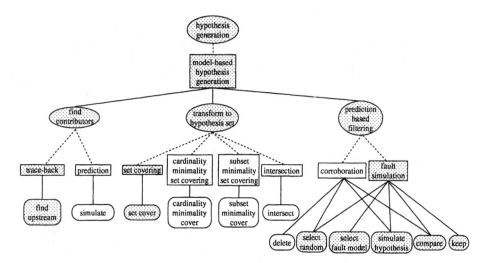

Fig. 1. The relations between tasks (ellipses), methods (rectangles), and inferences (rounded rectangles) illustrated in diagnosis. Dashed lines denote that methods are alternatives for realizing tasks. Solid lines decompose a method into subtasks and/or inferences.

data-flow structure forms an **inference structure** [14]. An inference structure represents all possible reasoning paths, and does not restrict itself to a specific strategy. Control knowledge needs to be imposed on an inference structure to get a particular strategy.

Task-method structure Fig. 1 illustrates the relations between tasks (ellipses), PSMs (rectangles), and inferences (rounded rectangles). The figure represents part of the PSMs for diagnosis from [4]. A task may be realized by several methods (dashed lines), each of which consists of subtasks and/or inferences (solid lines). Fig. 1 is a tangled hierarchy because the same inferences, tasks, and methods can appear at several places (e.g., the compare inference in Fig. 1; in other words, they are reusable).

Domain knowledge Domain knowledge describes the declarative, domain specific knowledge of an application, independently of its use in problem solving (e.g., the 3-multiplier, 2-adder circuit in [7]).

2.2 The conceptual model of the diagnostic reasoner

Commonly, diagnosis is divided into three subtasks: symptom detection, hypothesis generation and hypothesis discrimination [5, 7, 8]. To keep our presentation manageable, we focus in this paper on hypothesis generation. The inputs of our hypothesis generator are normality and abnormality observations (symptoms) and a simple device model, and the output is a hypothesis set (terminology is adopted from [6]). The status of observations (abnormal, normal) is determined by the symptom detection task. Our hypothesis generator exploits fault models, which describe the behavior of components when they are broken. A component may have several fault models, each of them describing a particular way in which a component may behave incorrectly.

The goal of our hypothesis generator is to find hypotheses which cover the symptoms or abnormality observations (O_{ab}), while being consistent with the normality observation ($O_{\neg ab}$).

The greyed-out part of Fig. 1 shows the task-method structure of our hypothesis generator, which is the result of selecting the methods *trace-back* method, *set-covering* method, and *fault-simulation* method. As explained in Section 2, we can connect inferences based on shared inputs and outputs, to get an inference structure. An inference structure only specifies data dependencies and not control dependencies. Control is specified separately. The inference structure is shown in Fig. 2. Control knowledge of the inference structure can be specified in

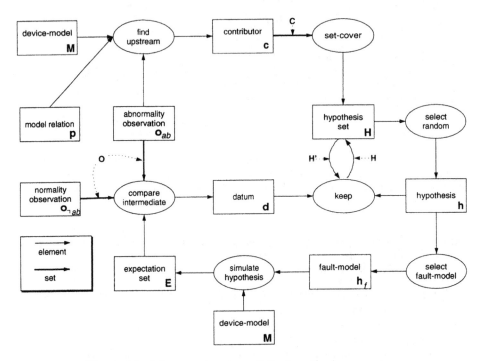

Fig. 2. The inference structure of the hypothesis generator.

many ways, each leading to a different strategy to generate hypotheses. In this paper we will, however, not formalize control knowledge, because formalizing the dynamics of a KBS is still an open issue. Moreover, control knowledge can only restrict the problem-solving behavior, but not extend it.

3 Formalization of the hypothesis generator

At a high level we can formally specify the functionality of our hypothesis generator as: $(H \cup M \vdash O_{ab}) \land (H \cup O_{\neg ab} \cup M \not\vdash \bot)$, where H are the hypotheses, O_{ab} the abnormality observations, $O_{\neg ab}$ normality observations, and M the device model. This should be read as the conjunction of (1) all hypotheses cover the abnormality observations (i.e., the union of the device model and the hypotheses entail the abnormality observations), and (2) the union of the hypotheses, the normality observations and the device model is not inconsistent.

In this section, we briefly introduce the formal language used, then, we present the domain terms and the formalization of the individual inferences that make up the conceptual model, and, finally, we will prove that the combination of the inferences in the inference structure (Fig. 2) meets the requirements given above.

3.1 The formal language used

In our formalization, inferences are formalized as predicates in order sorted first order predicate logic (as in (ML)² [19]). We distinguish explicitly between the input and output arguments of these predicates, which represent the input and output types of the inference. The inference layer is a meta-layer to the domain layer, and we presume a trivial naming relation between terms at the inference layer and expressions at the domain layer.

3.2 The constituents of an inference

Inferences define the relation between inputs and outputs. To define inferences precisely, we distinguish various constituents of an inference according to the distinct roles that they play. As a simple example, consider the select inference that takes as input a set of integers (instances) and a selection criterion largest, and produces as output a particular integer.

Preconditions. The preconditions of an inference define the properties that must hold on the inputs ($\imath$) of the inference: $pre(\imath)$[4]. In our example, the preconditions could require that the input set is not empty, and that the selection criterion is a partial order on the elements of the input set.

Inference Body. The body of an inference specifies the relation between the inputs and the outputs (o): $body(\imath; o)$. In our example, the body would describe that the output instance is a member of the input set, and that the selected instance satisfies the selection criterion (i.e., is the largest integer in the input set).

Postconditions. The postcondition of an inference defines the properties that must hold for the resulting outputs, with respect to the inputs of the inference: $post(\imath; o)$. In our example, we could conclude as a postcondition that the output integer is unique and never undefined, because the set is non-empty and by definition contains no duplicates, and, in a (finite and nonempty) set of integers there is always a largest integer. In theory, the postcondition could consist of all consequences of the precondition and the body (and thus be logically redundant). However, in knowledge engineering practice, the postcondition should consist of only those consequences that might be useful to choose the inferences.

3.3 Formalization of the domain

The domain terms that are used by the inferences are illustrated in Fig. 3 for a very simple device model (of a car). The basic elements are components (fuel tank, battery, etc.). Components can contribute to (ab)normality observations, and contributors are combined to get hypotheses. A contributor is interpreted disjunctively: at least one component in a contributor is faulty. A hypothesis is interpreted conjunctively: all components are faulty. In the figure, {comp1, comp5, comp3} is a hypothesis based on the contributors {comp1, comp2, comp3}, {comp3, comp5} and {comp3, comp4}. {comp3} is a single fault hypothesis. Domain terms are formalized as sorts [1] as illustrated in Table 1. In the definitions of *fault model* and *behavior model*, "input" and "output" are functions

---

[4] Preconditions, in our approach, are inspired by the preconditions in the tradition of Hoare [10] and Dijkstra [9].

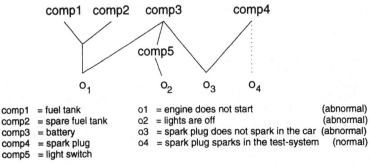

Fig. 3. Illustration of the domain terms: component, contributor, hypothesis, and (ab)normality observation.

Symbol	Explanation	Sort/Type	Example
$comp$	component	*instance*	battery
o_{ab}	abnormality observation	*expression denoting wrong value of component attribute*	voltage(battery) $= 0$
$o_{\neg ab}$	normality observation	*expression denoting correct value of component attribute*	voltage(battery) $= 12$
c	contributor	*set of comp*	{switch, battery}
h	hypothesis	*set of comp*	{battery}
H	hypothesis set	*set of h*	{ {battery}, {battery, fuel tank} }
h_f	fault model	$\{< input(comp), output(comp) > \|comp \in h\}$	{high-voltage(spark plug), no-spark(spark plug)}
$Comp$	device components	*set of comp*	{fuel tank, spare fuel tank, battery, spark plug, switch}
S	structural model	$\{connected-to(comp_i, comp_j)\| comp_{i,j} \in Comp\}$	connected-to(battery, switch)
B	behavioral model	$\{< input(comp), output(comp) > \|comp \in Comp\}$	{high-voltage(spark plug), spark(spark plug)}
M	device model	$M = B \cup S$	

Table 1. Domain terms used in this paper.

over *comp*, and thus have a value. Note that we distinguish correct behavior (B) from fault behavior (h_f) by the set to which they belong (output of the symptom detection task). Whether a behavior is correct or faulty, is not visible from the behavior description itself, but is a modality attributed to that behavior description.

3.4 Formalization of the inferences

find-upstream find-upstream traverses a model of the physical device. The type of the model (functional, structural or otherwise) is not relevant, the only requirement being that there exist directed relations between the components in the device model. In this paper, we take the structural **connected-to** relation, as defined in the device model M. find-upstream now traces back through the device model to find the contributor (set of components) to an abnormality observation o_{ab}. It does so, by first selecting the component in the abnormality observation (by looking at the corresponding fault model (h_f)), and then tracing back through the **connected-to** relations to find components that could have caused the observed component to display faulty behavior. The directed relation is denoted by p. The find-upstream inference applies p to the other arguments:

$$
\begin{aligned}
& o_{ab} : abnormality\ observation && (1) \\
& \text{p} : relation && (2) \\
& c : contributor && (3) \\
& M : model && (4) \\
& \text{find-upstream}(o_{ab}, \text{p}, M; c) \triangleq && (5) \\
& \quad M \vdash \text{p}(o_{ab}, c). && (6)
\end{aligned}
$$

Using p, this inference selects a set of instances (namely the set of components that constitutes the contributor c) from a structure (the model M). Its postcondition requires that c contributes to o_{ab}:

$$
\text{contributes-to}(c, o_{ab}), \qquad (7)
$$

which only follows from the body of the inference, if the **contributes-to** relation holds whenever $\text{p}(o_{ab}, c)$ holds.

set-cover The body of the set-cover inference states that no hypothesis can have an empty intersection with any of the contributors.

$$
\begin{aligned}
& C : contributor\ set && (8) \\
& H : hypothesis\ set && (9) \\
& \text{set-cover}(C; H) \triangleq && (10) \\
& \quad \forall\ h \in H && (11) \\
& \quad \forall\ c \in C && (12) \\
& \quad\quad h \cap c \neq \emptyset. && (13)
\end{aligned}
$$

select-random This inference randomly selects a hypothesis from the hypothesis set.

$$
\begin{aligned}
& H : hypothesis\ set && (14) \\
& h : hypothesis && (15) \\
& \text{select-random}(H; h) \triangleq && (16) \\
& \quad h \in H. && (17)
\end{aligned}
$$

select-fault-model A fault model describes the fault-behavior of the components corresponding to the hypothesis. This inference selects a fault model for a hypothesis, and requires that there is at least one fault model for each hypothesis.

$$
\begin{aligned}
& h : hypothesis && (18) \\
& h_f : fault\ model && (19) \\
& comp : component && (20) \\
& \text{select-fault-model}(h; h_f) \triangleq && (21) \\
& \quad \forall\ comp && (22) \\
& \quad\quad < input(comp), output(comp) > \in h_f \rightarrow && (23) \\
& \quad\quad\quad comp \in h\ \wedge && (24) \\
& \quad\quad comp \in h \rightarrow && (25) \\
& \quad\quad\quad \exists\ < input(comp), output(comp) > && (26) \\
& \quad\quad\quad\quad < input(comp), output(comp) > \in h_f. && (27)
\end{aligned}
$$

simulate-hypothesis The fault models are used by simulate-hypothesis to derive observations that one would expect if the components belonging to the hypothesis were indeed faulty. The derivation is modeled with entailment: the union of the device model M and the fault model h_f entail the expectations E, where the sets (M, E) and the union ($\cup$) are interpreted as conjunctions.

$$h_f : fault\ model \tag{28}$$
$$M : model \tag{29}$$
$$E : expectation\ set \tag{30}$$
$$\text{simulate-hypothesis}(h_f, M; E) \triangleq \tag{31}$$
$$M \cup h_f \vdash E. \tag{32}$$

compare-intermediate This inference compares the set of expectations E to the abnormality O_{ab} and normality observations $O_{\neg ab}$. The sets are considered equal if all abnormality observations are as expected, while the normality observations are not contradicted by the expectations. In other words, E covers O_{ab} ($O_{ab} \subseteq E$) and is consistent with $O_{\neg ab}$, and thus also with $O_{\neg ab} \cup O_{ab} = O$ (because consistency is a weaker requirement than covering). Assuming equal to be identity, we can formalize it as:

$$O_{ab}, O_{\neg ab} : observation\ set \tag{33}$$
$$E : expectation\ set \tag{34}$$
$$d : datum \tag{35}$$
$$\text{compare-intermediate}(O_{ab}, O_{\neg ab}, E; d) \triangleq \tag{36}$$
$$O_{ab} \subseteq E \wedge \tag{37}$$
$$O = O_{ab} \cup O_{\neg ab} \wedge \tag{38}$$
$$((\forall e \in E \tag{39}$$
$$\neg e \notin O \wedge d = equal) \vee \tag{40}$$
$$(\exists e \in E \tag{41}$$
$$\neg e \in O \wedge d = \neg equal)). \tag{42}$$

Thus, if for each o_{ab} there is an e that covers it, and there is no e that contradicts O, then d is equal, otherwise it is $\neg$equal.

keep The keep inference takes a hypothesis and a set of hypotheses and conditionally produces a set of hypotheses that contains all input hypotheses.

$$d : datum \tag{43}$$
$$H, H' : hypothesis\ set \tag{44}$$
$$h : hypothesis \tag{45}$$
$$\text{keep}(d, H, h; H') \triangleq \tag{46}$$
$$(d = equal \wedge H' = H) \vee \tag{47}$$
$$(d \neq equal \wedge H' = H \setminus \{h\}). \tag{48}$$

3.5 Combining the inferences

In this section, we prove that the combination of the individual inferences (see Fig. 2) formalized in Section 3.4 meets the high-level specification of our hypothesis generator. First we show that the inference structure is compatible, i.e., that each inference implies the preconditions of the inferences that consume its output [1]. Next, we present the conjunctive composition of the inference structure, and simplify it. Finally, we prove that the resulting formula implies the original specification.

Compatibility We have the following preconditions of the individual inferences.

find-upstream. The relation p must be transitive:

$$\forall\ o : observation \tag{49}$$
$$\forall\ c, c' : contributor \tag{50}$$
$$p(o, c) \wedge \texttt{fed-by}(c, c') \rightarrow p(o, c'). \tag{51}$$

fed-by is a transitive relation and is defined on contributors, connected-to is defined on components:

$$fed - by(c, c') \triangleq \tag{52}$$
$$\forall\ comp \in c \tag{53}$$
$$\exists\ comp' \tag{54}$$
$$connected - to(comp', comp) \wedge \tag{55}$$
$$comp \in c'. \tag{56}$$

set-cover. We have not yet specified a precondition of this inference, but here we require that the input set of contributors is not empty:

$$C \neq \emptyset. \tag{57}$$

select-random. Similarly, here we require that the input hypothesis set is not empty:

$$H \neq \emptyset. \tag{58}$$

select-fault-model. We require that the input hypothesis is not empty:

$$h \neq \emptyset. \tag{59}$$

simulate-hypothesis. Here, we require that the selected fault-model is not empty:

$$h_f \neq \emptyset. \tag{60}$$

compare-intermediate. We require that there are normal and abnormal observations, and that simulate-hypothesis indeed produces expectations:

$$O_{ab} \neq \emptyset\ \wedge \tag{61}$$
$$O_{\neg ab} \neq \emptyset\ \wedge \tag{62}$$
$$E \neq \emptyset. \tag{63}$$

keep. We require that the input hypothesis h is indeed an element of the input hypothesis set H. Moreover, because keep contains a test on the datum d, we require that d is either equal or $\neg$equal:

$$h \in H\ \wedge \tag{64}$$
$$d \in \{equal, \neg equal\}. \tag{65}$$

We briefly show how each precondition is ensured by the preceding inferences. We leave out the proofs, as they are relatively straightforward.

⟨find-upstream, set-cover⟩. The definition of find-upstream is not enough to ensure the precondition of set-cover. The latter precondition can be satisfied, if we ensure that the model M contains a contributor for each abnormality observation. We do not want to withdraw the precondition of set-cover, so we have to strengthen the precondition of find-upstream:

$$\forall \, o : observation \tag{66}$$
$$\forall \, c, c' : contributor \tag{67}$$
$$p(o, c) \land \texttt{fed-by}(c, c') \rightarrow p(o, c') \land \tag{68}$$
$$\forall \, o_{ab} \in O_{ab} \tag{69}$$
$$\exists \, c \tag{70}$$
$$M \vdash p(o_{ab}, c). \tag{71}$$

O_{ab}, p and M are not produced by any inference, so we cannot prove this precondition from the inference structure itself. This precondition, therefore, is a proof obligation for the environment. In this case the environment would be the domain knowledge (for the relation p and the model M) and (the inference structure of) the symptom-detection task (which is not dealt with in this paper).

⟨set-cover, select-random⟩. The precondition and the body of set-cover ensure that the precondition of select-random holds.

⟨select-random, select-fault-model⟩. The precondition and body of select-random ensure that there is a h, but this h could in principle be empty. However, the body of set-cover ensures that H contains no empty hypotheses. So the precondition of select-fault-model can be proved from the two predecessor inferences of select-fault-model.

⟨select-fault-model, simulate-hypothesis⟩. The body of select-fault-model (18–27) ensures that there is a fault model for each component that corresponds to the hypothesis. Thus, h_f can never be empty, and the precondition of simulate-hypothesis is fulfilled.

⟨select-random, keep⟩, ⟨set-cover, keep⟩, ⟨compare-intermediate, keep⟩. The definition of select-random (17) is identical to the first precondition of keep (64), which is also part of the body of set-cover (11). Thus this precondition is fulfilled. The second precondition of keep is $d \in \{equal, \neg equal\}$ (65). This precondition is guaranteed by the body of compare-intermediate in (40) and (42).

⟨simulate-hypothesis, compare-intermediate⟩. The precondition and body of simulate-hypothesis ensure that $E \neq \emptyset$ (63). The precondition that the abnormal and normal observations are not empty cannot be proven from the inference structure, since they are not produced by any inference. Hence, the environment (symptom-detection) should ensure that the precondition holds.

⟨keep, select-random⟩. The precondition of select-random (58) is $H \neq \emptyset$. keep can delete an element from this set, and thus threatens the precondition. We can ensure compatibility by adding to (48) of the body of keep: $H' \neq \emptyset$. We prevent thus the output hypothesis set from being empty. This makes sense because if it were empty, then find-upstream would not have generated all contributors, which we assume to be impossible.

Summarizing, given the above (strengthenings of the) preconditions of the inferences and their bodies as presented above, we can derive that their combination satisfies the compatibility requirement. However, we still have to prove that the preconditions on the initial inputs are satisfied by the environment (not dealt with in this paper).

Composition Now, we apply the conjunctive composition[5] of the inferences:

---

[5] During the composition process, we also include the quantifiers and group them. In the original formalizations they had a local scope.

$$
\begin{array}{ll}
H : \textit{hypothesis set} & (72) \\
O_{ab}, O_{\neg ab} : \textit{observation set} & (73) \\
M : \textit{model} & (74) \\
\quad \textbf{model-based-hypothesis-generation}(O_{ab}, O_{\neg ab}, M; H) \triangleq & (75) \\
\quad\quad \forall\, h : \textit{hypothesis} & (76) \\
\quad\quad \forall\, d : \textit{datum} & (77) \\
\quad\quad\quad \exists\, C : \textit{contributor set} & (78) \\
\quad\quad\quad \exists\, p : \textit{relation} & (79) \\
\quad\quad\quad \exists\, o_{ab} : \textit{observation} & (80) \\
\quad\quad\quad \exists\, h_f : \textit{fault model} & (81) \\
\quad\quad\quad \exists\, H' : \textit{hypothesis set} & (82) \\
\quad\quad\quad \exists\, E : \textit{expectation set} & (83) \\
\quad\quad\quad C = \{c | o_{ab} \in O_{ab} \wedge \textsf{find-upstream}(o_{ab}, p, M; c)\} \wedge & (84) \\
\quad\quad\quad \textsf{set-cover}(C; H') \wedge & (85) \\
\quad\quad\quad \textsf{select-random}(H'; h) \wedge & \\
\quad\quad\quad \textsf{select-fault-model}(h; h_f) \wedge & (86) \\
\quad\quad\quad \textsf{simulate-hypothesis}(h_f, M; E) \wedge & (87) \\
\quad\quad\quad \textsf{compare-intermediate}(O_{\neg ab}, O_{ab}, E; d) \wedge & (88) \\
\quad\quad\quad \textsf{keep}(d, H', h; H). & (89) \\
& (90)
\end{array}
$$

The order of the conjuncts suggests a top-to-bottom order of evaluation, but this is not assumed. The only dependence between the conjuncts is determined by the shared variables, and by the compatibility requirement.

Simplification The keep inference, and the distinction of the intermediate H' from the final H have a control flavor. Instead of explicitly keeping hypotheses that satisfy the compare-intermediate inference, we can state that all hypotheses that remain in H satisfy compare-intermediate. So we quantify h over H (95), and specify that for each such h compare-intermediate holds (108). Furthermore, we replace select-random and set-cover with their bodies. We now get a *reformulation* that removes the control flavor, but does not affect the semantics.

$$
\begin{array}{ll}
H : \textit{hypothesis set} & \\
O_{ab}, O_{\neg ab} : \textit{observation set} & (91) \\
M : \textit{model} & (92) \\
\quad \textbf{model-based-hypothesis-generation}(O_{ab}, O_{\neg ab}, M; H) \triangleq & (93) \\
\quad\quad \boxed{\forall h \in H} \qquad\qquad (76) & (94) \\
& (95) \\
\quad\quad\quad \exists\, o_{ab} : \textit{observation} & (96) \\
\quad\quad\quad \exists\, h_f : \textit{fault model} & (97) \\
\quad\quad\quad \exists\, C : \textit{contributor set} & (98) \\
\quad\quad\quad \exists\, p : \textit{relation} & (99) \\
\quad\quad\quad \exists\, E : \textit{expectation set} & (100) \\
\quad\quad\quad C = \{c | o_{ab} \in O_{ab} \wedge \textsf{find-upstream}(o_{ab}, p, M; c)\} \wedge & (101) \\
\quad\quad\quad \boxed{\begin{array}{l} \forall\, c \in C \\ \forall\, h' \in H \\ \quad h' \cap c \ne \emptyset \wedge \end{array}} \qquad \textsf{set-cover} & (102) \\
& (103) \\
& (104) \\
\quad\quad\quad \boxed{h \in H \wedge} \qquad\qquad \textsf{select-random} & (105) \\
\quad\quad\quad \textsf{select-fault-model}(h; h_f) \wedge & (106) \\
\quad\quad\quad \textsf{simulate-hypothesis}(h_f, M; E) \wedge & (107) \\
\quad\quad\quad \boxed{\textsf{compare-intermediate}(O_{\neg ab}, O_{ab}, E; equal).} \quad (89\text{--}90) & (108)
\end{array}
$$

The relation p and the domain model M are defined in the domain knowledge. If we have a particular relation p that realizes the find-upstream inference, then we can replace the application of the relation p by its domain knowledge definition (unfolding). The body then refers, through p, to domain specific knowledge. If we unfold all inferences in this way, we obtain a specification for diagnosis in domain specific terms. However, if we abstract from the exact definition of the domain relation, and the postcondition does not refer to that relation, then we can remove the references to the domain-specific knowledge by substituting the inference by its postcondition. This is obviously a weakening of the inference. Find-upstream had as a postcondition contributes-to(c, o_{ab}) (7). (105) is redundant with respect to (95), so it can be removed. As we have seen in (18–22) and (28–32), select-fault-model and simulate-hypothesis produce in combination the expectations that can be derived from h using a fault-model h_f (106–107). If we replace both inferences by this relation, we get:

$$
\begin{array}{ll}
H : hypothesis\ set & (109) \\
O_{ab}, O_{\neg ab} : observation\ set & (110) \\
M : model & (111) \\
\textbf{model-based-hypothesis-generation}(O_{ab}, O_{\neg ab}, M; H) \triangleq & (112) \\
\quad \forall\, h \in H & (113) \\
\qquad \exists\, C : contributor\ set & (114) \\
\qquad \exists\, h_f : fault\ model & (115) \\
\qquad \exists\, E : expectation\ set & (116) \\
\end{array}
$$

$$
\boxed{\begin{array}{l}
\forall\, o_{ab} \in O_{ab} \\
\quad \exists\, c \in C \\
\qquad \text{contributes-to}(c, o_{ab}) \wedge
\end{array}} \quad (101)
\begin{array}{l}
(117) \\
(118) \\
(119)
\end{array}
$$

$$
\begin{array}{ll}
\forall\, c \in C & (120) \\
\forall\, h' \in H & (121) \\
\quad h' \cap c \neq \emptyset \wedge & (122)
\end{array}
$$

$$
\boxed{M \cup h_f \vdash E \wedge} \quad (106\text{--}107)
\begin{array}{l}
(123)
\end{array}
$$

$$
\text{compare-intermediate}(O_{ab}, O_{\neg ab}, E; equal). \quad (124)
$$

The contributes-to relation is to be proven with respect to some model M. This can be written explicitly by stating that the relation tuples need to be a member of M or that the relation instance be provable (in the domain knowledge) using M. We replace compare-intermediate (124) with the part of its body that is concerned with $d = equal$ (37–40), and reformulate (121–122) such that we avoid the intermediate variable h':

$$
\begin{array}{ll}
H : hypothesis\ set & (125) \\
O, O_{ab}, O_{\neg ab} : observation\ set & (126) \\
M : model & (127) \\
\textbf{model-based-hypothesis-generation}(O_{ab}, O_{\neg ab}, M; H) \triangleq & (128) \\
\quad \forall\, h \in H & (129) \\
\quad \forall\, o \in O_{ab} & (130) \\
\qquad \exists\, C : contributor\ set & (131) \\
\qquad \exists\, h_f : fault\ model & (132) \\
\qquad \exists\, E : expectation\ set & (133) \\
\qquad \forall\, c \in C & (134) \\
\qquad\quad \text{contributes-to}(c, o_{ab}) \wedge & (135)
\end{array}
$$

$$
\boxed{h \cap c \neq \emptyset \wedge} \quad (121\text{--}122)
\begin{array}{l}
(136)
\end{array}
$$

$$
M \cup h_f \vdash E \wedge \quad (137)
$$

$$
\boxed{\begin{array}{l}
O_{ab} \subseteq E \wedge \\
O = O_{ab} \cup O_{\neg ab} \wedge \\
\forall\, e \in E \\
\quad \neg e \notin O.
\end{array}} \quad (124)
\begin{array}{l}
(138) \\
(139) \\
(140) \\
(141)
\end{array}
$$

Proof In order to prove that the composition of inferences implies the goal specification of our hypothesis generator: $(H \cup M \vdash O_{ab}) \wedge (H \cup O_{\neg ab} \cup M \not\vdash \bot)$, we require an exact definition of `contributes-to` (135). We will assume it to be equivalent to entailment in the context of the device model M, thus: $C \cup M \vdash O_{ab}$ (147). Furthermore, each contributor c is a disjunction of components. Each h is a conjunction of components (each of which is an element of some c). Consequently, the requirement that each h in H has a non-empty intersection with each c in C (136) can be rephrased as "Each h entails each c" and therefore the conjunction of h's entails the conjunction of c's: $H \vdash C$ (148). Finally, we define: $H_f = \{h_f | h \in H\}$ (150), and we get:

$$
\begin{array}{ll}
H : hypothesis\ set & (142)\\
O_{ab}, O_{\neg ab} : observation\ set & (143)\\
M : model & (144)\\
\textbf{model-based-hypothesis-generation}(O_{ab}, O_{\neg ab}, M; H) \triangleq & (145)\\
\quad \exists\ C : contributor\ set & (146)\\
\quad\quad C \cup M \vdash O_{ab}\ \wedge & (147)\\
\quad\quad H \vdash C\ \wedge & (148)\\
\quad \exists\ E : expectation\ set & (149)\\
\quad\quad M \cup H_f \vdash E\ \wedge & (150)\\
\quad\quad O_{ab} \subseteq E\ \wedge & (151)\\
\quad\quad O = O_{ab} \cup O_{\neg ab}\ \wedge & (152)\\
\quad\quad \forall\ e \in E & (153)\\
\quad\quad\quad \neg e \notin O. & (154)
\end{array}
$$

We will now show that this conjunction implies $(H \cup M \vdash O_{ab}) \wedge (H \cup O_{\neg ab} \cup M \not\vdash \bot)$. The first part of the conjunction $(H \cup M \vdash O_{ab})$ follows immediately from (147–148) and the transitivity of entailment.

To prove that $H \cup O_{\neg ab} \cup M \not\vdash \bot$, assume the following:

1. H is consistent,
2. O is consistent,
3. M is correct,
4. H is a weakening of H_f, and
5. E is the set of *all* observables (expectations) that follow from H (i.e., simulate-hypothesis and the fault-models are complete with respect to H).

The first assumption is reasonable because we do not want to derive inconsistent hypotheses. The second assumption is called the *non-intermittency assumption* that states that devices behave consistently (during a diagnostic session), that is, the observations do not change their status. The third assumption states that the device model is a correct description of the device. The fourth assumption holds because H_f is a strengthening of H: H states that components are faulty, while H_f describes *how* they are faulty. Thus, we can substitute H_f (150) by H. The fifth assumption requires that we strengthen (150) to:

$$\forall e\ \ M \cup H \vdash e \rightarrow e \in E. \qquad (155)$$

Now assume that $H \cup O_{\neg ab} \cup M \vdash \bot$. Then:

$$\exists e\ \ M \cup H \vdash e \wedge \neg e \in O_{\neg ab}. \qquad (156)$$

As a consequence of our assumption (5) and (155), $e \in E$. Due to (153–154), $\neg e \notin O$. From (152) $O = O_{\neg ab} \cup O_{ab}$, we get $O_{\neg ab} \subset O$ and hence, $\neg e \notin O_{\neg ab}$, which contradicts our premise $\neg e \in O_{\neg ab}$ in (156). Summarizing, giving the above assumptions (1–5), we can prove that the combination of inferences satisfies the specification of our hypothesis generator.

4 Discussion

Assumptions We have presented a proof, that shows how an inference structure constructed from a set of inferences, satisfies the task it was aimed to model, namely to generate hypotheses that cover the abnormality observations while being consistent with the normality observations. However, we have to note the following points:

1. In the process of simplifying the conjunctive composition formula for the inference structure, we have applied some weakening, such as replacing inferences by their postcondition.
2. We have interpreted the relation contributes-to as entailment. Clearly, this is a strong assumption, but in order to guarantee the proof, we cannot interpret it weaker than the relation in the high-level specification of the hypothesis generator.

Other specifications of diagnostic systems In this paper we were concerned with a hypothesis generator whose specification is: $(H \cup M \vdash O_{ab}) \wedge (H \cup O_{\neg ab} \cup M \not\vdash \bot)$. As described in [6, 17], the following scale of increasingly weaker specifications can be distinguished:

1. **cover** $\triangleq H \cup M \vdash O$,
2. **intermediate** $\triangleq (H \cup M \vdash O_{ab}) \wedge (H \cup O_{\neg ab} \cup M \not\vdash \bot)$,
3. **consistent** $\triangleq H \cup O \cup M \not\vdash \bot$.

Given that $O = O_{ab} \cup O_{\neg ab}$, (1) implies (2), and (2) implies (3). When we can prove that some specification is implied, then we can certainly prove it for the weaker variants.

The determining factor for generating covering, intermediate, or consistent hypotheses, is the type of *comparison* between, on the one hand, the sets of abnormality and normality observations, and, on the other hand, the set of expectations corresponding to a fault model. In our formalization we have used the compare-intermediate inference, whose name already suggests that it leads to the intermediate specification (as we have proved). The formalization of compare-intermediate can be found in (33–42). Similar proofs could be given using alternative formalizations of compare, which are shown below:

compare-covers$(O_{ab}, O_{\neg ab}, E; d) \triangleq$
$O = O_{ab} \cup O_{\neg ab} \wedge$
$((O \subseteq E \wedge d = equal) \vee$
$(\exists o \in O$
$o \notin E \wedge d = \neg equal)).$

compare-consistent$(O_{ab}, O_{\neg ab}, E; d) \triangleq$
$O = O_{ab} \cup O_{\neg ab} \wedge$
$((\forall e \in E$
$\neg e \notin O \wedge d = equal) \vee$
$(\exists e \in E$
$\neg e \in O \wedge d = \neg equal)).$

compare-covers says that if the observations are a subset of the expectations (i.e., for each observation there is an expectation that covers it), then the two sets are considered equal. compare-consistent considers the two sets equal if the negation of an expectation cannot be observed.

Outcome of formalization process Based on the formal analysis performed here, we have been able to interpret our inference structure in a unique manner. In particular, the formal analysis has proven to be essential in identifying hidden assumptions (such as that contributes-to has to be interpreted as "entailment"), detecting inconsistencies, and making explicit unspecified I/O dependencies.

5 Conclusions

In this paper we have presented a conceptual and formal model of a hypothesis generator for diagnosis. By means of the formal model we have been able to prove that our conceptual model, under some assumptions, meets its specification.

The strong point of conceptual models is that they are easy understandable, and therefore, are a good starting point for developing KBSs. Such models give a better insight in what diagnostic systems do, than descriptions of the implemented algorithms. However, their weak point is that they allow for ambiguities and inconsistencies. Formal models are difficult to build, but they are important if we want to ensure that systems do what they are supposed to do, that is, that they meet their specifications. This is especially important in the case of safety critical systems, which is often the case with diagnostic systems.

For clarity reasons, we demonstrated our approach with a hypothesis generator that makes some simplifying assumptions about the device model. For example, the device model does not contain feedback loops (otherwise find-upstream encounters problems). If such assumptions do not hold, a more complex reasoner is required, implying a more complex formalization.

Formal models are difficult to build, and currently work has been started to integrate conceptual models with formal models to support this process [15, 11, 18]. One way of support is to select skeletal formal schemata from a library and to refine these general schemata. A library of formal schemata of inferences is described in [1], and we have used some of such schemata. For example, select-random for selecting a hypothesis (14–17) is an instantiation of the general schema shown below. Currently we are investigating how the refinement process can be supported.

$$
\begin{aligned}
&S : instance\ set &&(157)\\
&\iota : instance &&(158)\\
&\mathsf{select}(S;\iota) \triangleq &&(159)\\
&\quad \iota \in S. &&(160)
\end{aligned}
$$

Another type of support is to semi-automatically generate the formal model, based on the structure of the conceptual model. This is possible when the conceptual and formal model have a similar structure which can be exploited in the transformation process [18]. Such support typically covers the "administrative detail" inherent to formal specifications, such as type declarations and import relations. The most difficult and interesting part of the formal model can however not be generated automatically, and needs dedication of the knowledge engineer.

Ideally, these kinds of support (library selection and transformation) should be part of an integrated knowledge acquisition tool (e.g. Kadstool, VOID). Constructing the proof itself can in principle also be supported, but requires further investigation.

References

1. M. Aben. *Formal Methods in Knowledge Engineering*. PhD thesis, University of Amsterdam, Amsterdam, 1995.

2. J. Angele, D. Fensel, S. Neubert, and R Studer. Model-based and incremental knowledge engineering: The MIKE approach. In J. Cuena, editor, *Knowledge Oreinted Software Design*, volume A-27 of *IFIP Transactions*, pages 139–168. Elsevier, Amsterdam, 1993.

3. C. Bauer and W. Karbach, editors. *Proceedings Second KADS User Meeting*, ZFE BT SE 21, Otto-Hahn Ring 6, D-8000 Munich 83, 17–18 February 1992. Siemens AG.

4. V. R. Benjamins. *Problem Solving Methods for Diagnosis*. PhD thesis, SWI, University of Amsterdam, Amsterdam, The Netherlands, June 1993.

5. V. R. Benjamins. Problem-solving methods for diagnosis and their role in knowledge acquisition. *International Journal of Expert Systems: Research and Applications*, 8(2):93–120, 1995.

6. L. Console and P. Torasso. Integrating models of the correct behaviour into abductive diagnosis. In L. C. Aiello, editor, *Proc. ECAI-90*, pages 160–166, London, 1990. ECCAI, Pitman.

7. R. Davis and W. C. Hamscher. Model-based reasoning: Troubleshooting. In H. E. Shrobe, editor, *Exploring Artificial Intelligence*, pages 297–346. Morgan Kaufmann, San Mateo, California, 1988.

8. J. H. de Kleer and B. C. Williams. Diagnosing multiple faults. *Artificial Intelligence*, 32:97–130, 1987.

9. E. W. Dijkstra. *A Discipline of Programming*. Prentice-Hall, Englewood Cliffs, New Jersey, 1976.

10. C. A. R. Hoare. The axiomatic basis of computer programming. *Communications of the ACM*, 12(10):567–583, October 1969.

11. P. G. Larsen, N. Plat, and H. Toetenel. A formal semantics of data flow diagrams. *Formal Aspects od Computing*, 3, 1993.

12. J. Rumbaugh, M. Blaha, W. Premerlani, F. Eddy, and W. Lorensen. *Object-Oriented Modelling and Design*. Prentice Hall, Englewood Cliffs, New Jersey, 1991.

13. J. Rushby. Formal methods and their role in the certification of critical systems. Technical Report CSL-95-1, SRI, 1995.

14. A. Th. Schreiber, B. J. Wielinga, and J. A. Breuker. *KADS: A Principled Approach to Knowledge-Based System Development*. Academic Press, London, 1993.

15. L. T. Semmens, R.. B. France, and T. W. G. Docker. Integrated structured analysis and formal specification. *The Computer Journal*, 35(6):600–610, 1992.

16. N. R. Shadbolt, E. Motta, and A. Rouge. Constructing knowledge based systems. *IEEE Software*, 1993.

17. A. ten Teije and F. van Harmelen. An extended spectrum of logical definitions for diagnostic systems. In *Proceedings of DX-94 Fifth International Workshop on Principles of Diagnosis*, 1994.

18. F. van Harmelen and M. Aben. Structure preserving specification languages for knowledge-based systems. *International Journal of Human-Computer Studies*, 44(2), 1996.

19. F. van Harmelen and J. R. Balder. $(ML)^2$: a formal language for KADS models of expertise. *Knowledge Acquisition*, 4(1), 1992. Special issue: 'The KADS approach to knowledge engineering'.

20. E. Yourdon. *Modern Structured Analysis*. Prentice Hall, Englewood Cliffs, New Jersey, 1989.

Ontology Construction for Technical Domains*

Jan Benjamin[1] Pim Borst[2] Hans Akkermans[2] Bob Wielinga[1]

[1] University of Amsterdam, Social Science Informatics
Roetersstraat 15, NL-1018 WB Amsterdam, The Netherlands
E-mail: {benjamin, wielinga}@swi.psy.uva.nl
[2] University of Twente
Information Systems Department INF/IS
P.O. Box 217, NL-7500 AE, The Netherlands
E-mail: {borst, akkerman}@cs.utwente.nl

Abstract. An important recent idea to facilitate knowledge sharing is to provide libraries of reusable components (models, ontologies) to end users. However, when libraries become large, finding the right library components is a knowledge demanding task in itself. Our suggestion therefore is that methods will be needed that help the user to gradually *construct* such knowledge. This paper describes a framework how to do this for reasoning in technical domains. We then show how an application ontology can be incrementally constructed with our framework, for the domain of heat exchangers.

1 Introduction

An important recent idea to support knowledge acquisition is to provide libraries of reusable knowledge components (ontologies). We find such an approach in very diverse projects such as CommonKADS (expertise models (Wielinga *et al.*, 1993)), the ARPA Knowledge Sharing Initiative (sharable ontologies (Gruber, 1993)), GAMES (medical ontologies (van Heijst *et al.*, 1995)), OLMECO (mechatronic design components (Akkermans *et al.*, 1995)), and KACTUS (technical domain ontologies (Schreiber *et al.*, 1995)).

Although we believe that libraries of reusable components will prove to be a viable and highly useful approach to effective knowledge engineering, new problems arise with the advent of such libraries: their sheer size will cause problems related to structuring, retrieval, applicability, assessment and maintenance of the knowledge archived. One of these problems has been called the indexing problem (Klinker *et al.*, 1990): how can library elements be supplied with indices that provide helpful hooks for retrieval and

* This work has been supported in part by the Commission of the European Communities as Esprit-III projects P6521 OLMECO (Open Library for Models of MEchatronic COmponents), and P8145 KACTUS (modelling Knowledge About Complex Technical systems for multiple USe). The partners in the OLMECO project are PSA Peugeot-Citroën (F), BIM (B), Fagor (Sp), Ikerlan (Sp), Imagine (F), University of Twente (NL) and ECN (NL). The partners in the KACTUS project are: Labein (Sp), Lloyd's Register (UK), ISL (UK), Statoil (N), Cap Programmator (S), University of Amsterdam (NL), University of Karlsruhe (D), Iberdrola (Sp), Delos (I), Fincantieri (I) and Sintef (N). This article expresses the opinions of the authors and not necessarily those of the consortia.

composition? This already is not an easy problem, since it involves a lot of domain-specific knowledge that must be strongly condensed and highly structured for easy user access. Taxonomies that are used for indexing libraries tend to become rather complicated themselves as soon as the library becomes large — as, for example, shown by our experiences with the OLMECO design library which currently contains about 500 simulation model components.

However, even when the indexing problem would have been adequately solved, other issues arise related to shareability. A library will most probably contain several ontologies related to the same part of the world. Each of these ontologies may represent a different viewpoint, a different level of abstraction or may concern different aspects of the same object or phenomenon. For example, the Ontolingua library of ontologies contains an extensive set of concepts related to thermal systems, but it is difficult to decide which of these concepts are relevant in a particular context. The problem is that deciding which ontologies are relevant to solve a particular problem, requires knowledge of the relevance of certain distinctions that may only become available during the knowledge acquisition process itself.

Hence, when libraries become large, finding the right library components is a knowledge-intensive task in itself. Our suggestion therefore is that methods will be needed that help the user to incrementally *construct* such knowledge: by starting from relatively commonsense information, and expanding this into the right technical concepts and choices, through the step by step addition of new ontological distinctions. This is the approach that we will elaborate in this paper. We describe a generic framework how to construct ontologies for reasoning in technical domains in an incremental manner. We then show how an application ontology can be constructed with our framework for the domain of heat exchangers.

We begin with an intuitive explanation of our example technical domain, viz., that of heat exchangers, and sketch what kind of considerations and ontologies play a role in gaining a step-by-step understanding of the functioning of such engineering systems (Sec. 2). Sec. 3 outlines our general framework for ontologies and stepwise ontology construction through mapping rules and other construction operators. This framework is then applied to the example of the heat exchanger in Sec. 4, showing how application ontologies can be constructed in a stepwise manner. Sec. 5 contains related work and a concluding discussion is given in Sec. 6.

2 An Example: Heat Exchangers

A heat exchanger is a device that transfers heat from one fluid to another without mixing the fluids. These devices are widely used in space heating and air-conditioning, power production, waste heat recovery and chemical processing. Various types of man-made heat exchangers are depicted in Figure 1. One of the world's most efficient heat exchangers, however, is found in the blood-vessel system of the legs of wading birds such as herons and penguins (Scholander, 1958). This is why they can walk on ice without having their legs frozen.

Heat exchangers basically consist of two fluids separated by a solid wall. When one of the fluids has a higher temperature than the other, heat will flow from the hot fluid,

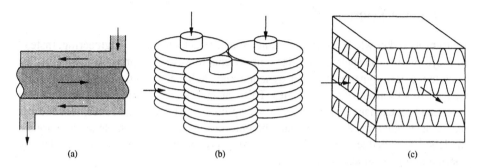

Fig. 1. Heat exchangers. Different types, from left to right: *(a)* Concentric tube counter flow device; *(b)* Fin-tube heat exchanger; *(c)* Plate-fin heat exchanger. The arrows indicate the direction of the fluid flows.

through the wall, to the cold fluid. This heat flow will cause the temperature of the cold fluid to rise and the temperature of the hot fluid to drop. To keep this process of heat exchange going, the temperature of the hot water will be kept high by pumping in new hot water on one side to replace the water that has lost its heat. On the other side of the device the cold water that has been heated is pumped out of the heat exchanger to other devices and is then replaced by new cold water.

The various types of heat exchangers only differ in their geometric structure and flow arrangement, as illustrated in Figure 1. The geometry and flow arrangement characteristics determine the operating conditions of heat exchangers and their efficiency.

If we want to understand the behaviour of a heat exchanger, we need to consider the underlying dynamic physical processes. Engineering textbooks mention three main categories of thermodynamic processes causing heat exchange: (i) *conduction*; (ii) *convection*; (iii) *radiation*. Heat transfer by radiation is well known from sunny days, but at the standard operating temperatures, radiation is not very significant within heat exchangers. Convection is heat transport by displacing the matter that carries the heat. In heat exchangers this occurs *within* each of the two fluids separately, by pumping in new water and removing the old water. Conduction is heat transport caused by passing on heat from one part of the heat-carrying matter to neighbouring parts. This is what happens *between* the two fluids of a heat exchanger: the hot fluid first passes the heat to the separating wall, which on its turn transfers it to the cold fluid. For conduction the fluid itself does not need to move, and this is what makes it different from convection.

In predicting behaviour or designing heat exchangers we need to model the physical processes in more detail. This is done by specifying and assembling the appropriate laws and rules of physics. These laws provide the mathematical relations that give the formal, quantitative description of a process. Flow arrangement and geometric characteristics are typically reflected in the shape and/or the parameters of the equations. The collected equations can then be run by a simulator to study and optimize the behaviour of the heat exchanger.

3 General Framework

Reusability of knowledge is an important issue in recent knowledge engineering. Instead of recycling off the shelf knowledge components however, we propose to *construct* a knowledge base dynamically. Our dynamic knowledge construction approach lets the user fill in a framework of ontologies. This framework can describe a technical device such as a heat exchanger from different viewpoints. It explicates the conceptual choices made, or in other words it represents the ontological commitments. Hence, previously modelled knowledge is reused, not by using preassembled specific models, but by specializing general knowledge.

Although a ready-to-use model seems far more easy to apply, it does not suffice completely. A model or ontology can contain some knowledge objects that are present in several domains, but it can not represent all objects in a specific domain. According to Van Heijst (van Heijst, 1995), (medical) subdomains have domain-specific concepts that are often specializations of the basic (medical) concepts. In many application domains there are additional ontological distinctions that are specific for that domain. So, it must be possible to differentiate the general toplevel categories, according to the demands of a certain domain.

This section discusses the general framework for our dynamic knowledge construction approach. First, the building blocks of the framework are described. These are ontologies of two different types: primary ontologies modelling actual objects within a domain and secondary ontologies describing relevant dimensions, typologies or theories that can be applied to the primary objects. The second part of this section discusses the construction principles of the framework. The notion of ontological mapping is introduced and a number of mapping types are distinguished. A small example illustrates the mapping process.

3.1 Building blocks

Two types of building blocks constitute the general framework. These are primary knowledge objects, which represent relevant elements in a certain domain, and secondary distinctions, which can be applied to the primary objects dynamically. The primary knowledge objects as well as the distinctions are modelled as *generic ontologies*. A generic ontology is a general, meta-level viewpoint on a set of domain theories (Schreiber *et al.*, 1995).

Primary ontologies Primary ontologies represent distinguished parts of the (concrete or abstract) world. They model general viewpoints on a domain, such as physical, functional or behavioural aspects. Primary ontologies consist of concepts and relations that are considered important and relevant items concerning a technical domain. An example of a primary ontology is a *physical entity ontology*, which describes physical items in the world. It models physical objects, natural objects, artefacts and substances. A *process ontology* is another type of primary ontology, which contains knowledge about physical processes. A primary conceptualization can also describe objects like functions, goals, tasks and actions. This *functional entity ontology* models a teleological viewpoint. The final example is an ontology describing physical phenomena, which are naive, commonsense descriptions of processes (see also Sec. refappl-ontology).

Secondary ontologies Secondary ontologies introduce additional distinctions, typologies or theories that can be applied to objects of primary ontologies. Or actually, they serve as 'meta-models' for conceptual decisions. A secondary ontology implements a particular dimension from which one can approach a domain. In KACTUS three types of secondary ontologies are considered. The first type is an ontology, that models simple distinctions or properties, for example abstractness, intentionality and origin. The *origin ontology* differentiates between man-made, natural and mental entities. The second type of ontology describes taxonomies or typologies of primary objects. Examples are a *function typology*, that consists of various types of functions, and a *physical domain typology*, including physical domains such as hydraulics, thermodynamics and electronics. The last type of a secondary ontology is a conceptualization of complex theories, like geometry, mereology, topology and material science. A *mereological ontology* for instance represents a structural viewpoint on a domain. It contains multiple types of *part-of* relations between concepts, which are abstracted to *m-individuals*. Using a notion such as m-individual makes it possible to express a generic relation, because there are less constraints on the types of the arguments.

The difference between primary and secondary concepts is not absolute. There remains a choice in which type of ontology a certain predicate is represented. It is possible to *reify* secondary concepts into primary concepts. For example, the property *red* can be regarded as the concept *redness*. The type of domain and application determine which concepts are primary and which secondary. See also (Benjamin, 1995) for a number of ontologies of the KACTUS library.

3.2 Ontological mappings

The process of dynamic knowledge construction is implemented by a number of ontological mappings. A mapping can combine a primary ontology and a secondary ontology. A secondary ontology describes a point of view from which one can approach a primary conceptualization. So by actually looking at a primary ontology from that particular viewpoint a new ontology is formed. An ontological mapping creates a new model, that originates from the primary ontology and that is specified according to the secondary ontology.

There are various types of ontological mappings. Without pretending to present the complete set, we distinguish two basic types of mappings: a mapping as a 'relation' between ontologies and a mapping as an 'ontology construction instrument'.

An ontological mapping can represent an equivalence relation between the objects of two ontologies. The objects can be identical, but playing different roles in different domains. Examples are the notion of a shoe in a shoe production and a shoe shop domain (Wiederhold, 1994) and the notion of a breaker in various electrical applications. Two objects can also play the same role in different domains, like a heat exchanger and a electrical transformer. Both are devices which transform a kind of stuff by an interaction process. Finally, two objects can be similar, but at different levels of abstraction, like a transformation-through-interaction component and a heat exchanger. The relevance to ontology construction is that equivalence relations show the reusable elements of ontologies and give hints how a (new) concept can be named or renamed.

An ontological mapping is also used as an instrument to construct new ontologies or new elements of ontologies. There are basic, elementary operations and additional mappings, which are more complex. Currently, we consider four types of basic mappings:

- *rename mapping*
  This mapping generates a new concept based on an existing (primary) concept. For example, *man-made physical object* $\longmapsto$ *artefact*.
- *attribution mapping*
  An attribution mapping adds or deletes a property of a concept or relation. It can also fix the value of an object. Consider for example the generic concept substance, that has a property temperature. A specific domain might need the notion of enthalpy. Then this property must be assigned to the concept substance.
- *role mapping*
  A role mapping maps a relevant theory onto a primary object. The operation determines which role an object plays in a certain theory. For example, the mapping *m-individual* $\longmapsto$ *substance* describes a mereological viewpoint on substances.
- *reification mapping*
  A secondary concept can be reified into a primary concept or vice versa. For example, *gaseous* $\longmapsto$ *gas*.

The basic ontological mappings can be combined to form additional, more complex mapping operations. The compound mappings are used to construct new (elements of) conceptualizations. Three examples of complex mappings are:

- *differentiation*
  A distinction or dimension is mapped onto a primary object. This operation differentiates the primary entity according to the secondary ontology. For example, the mapping *object cardinality* $\longmapsto$ *physical phenomenon* can result in single object phenomena such as flow or multiple object phenomena such as interaction. The differentiation mapping consists of a rename mapping and an attribution mapping.
- *typology mapping*
  The elements of a secondary typological ontology are mapped onto a primary concept. An example is the operation between a *functional typology* and a *component*. The typology mapping consists of a number of differentiation operations.
- *theory application mapping*
  A secondary ontology, that models a complex theory, is mapped onto a primary ontology. Or in other words, the secondary theory is applied to the primary concepts and relations. An example is the mapping between a *topological ontology* and a *component ontology*. The mapping process creates a topological viewpoint on a set of components, describing the connections between the objects. The individual mappings, where T denotes topology, are:

$$\text{node} \xmapsto{T} \text{process component},$$
$$\text{node} \xmapsto{T} \text{managing component},$$

$$\text{edge} \xmapsto{T} \text{connecting component,}$$
$$\text{connects} \xmapsto{T} \text{component.}$$

The last operation maps the relation *connects* onto the concept *component*. This results in a component-specific *connects* relation. The theory application mapping consists of rename mappings and role mappings.

There is no unique sequence in which a number of mappings must be applied. If one is only interested in the final result of the mapping process, it is less important which mapping is executed first. But if it is necessary not only to consider the final result, but also the intermediate concepts then the order does matter. Hence, the tree of construction has no unique structure.

In theory it is possible to map all secondary dimensions on all primary ontologies. But by doing so, a lot of mappings construct ontological elements that are meaningless in most domains. When the *mereological ontology* is mapped onto the concept *substance* for example, a conceptualization is created that deals with the parts of substances. Only when one is interested in molecules and atoms this can be a useful ontology. Therefore, secondary ontologies have certain constraints, that determine when these can play a role in an ontological mapping. A system can only be examined from a mereological viewpoint if it has a fixed structure. For the topological ontology to be useful, there has to be a type of interaction between the objects in a domain.

3.3 Example in the heat exchange domain

Heat exchangers are typically classified according to *flow arrangement* and *type of construction* (Incropera & DeWitt, 1988). Different types of heat exchangers only differ in structure (geometrical and topological properties) and arrangement of flow. Engineering textbooks differentiate between the construction type of the primary flow and the secondary flow. Hence, this gives three relevant properties: *construction type of primary flow*, *construction type of secondary flow* and *flow arrangement*. The primary fluid can move in a *tube* or along a *plate*. The construction type of the secondary fluid can also be a *tube*. Then, the heat exchanger has a *double-pipe* construction. The primary pipe is located inside the secondary pipe. Other types of construction are *fin* and *shell*. In a *parrallel* flow arrangement, the primary and secondary fluids enter at the same end, flow in the same direction, and leave at the same end. In the *counterflow* arrangement, the fluids enter at opposite ends and flow in the opposite directions. Alternatively, the fluids may move in *cross flow* (perpendicular to each other).

The three relevant properties can be used to construct a hierarchy of heat exchangers. Although the construction type of the primary flow and the construction type of the secondary flow are presented as independent distinctions, there are certain dependencies that exclude possible combinations. Generating a tree results either in figure 2 *(a)* (see also (Walker, 1982)) or in figure 2 *(b)*. The construction approach enables the user to build different hierarchies. Hence, there is no unique taxonomy of heat exchangers. The distinctions however are uniquely determined.

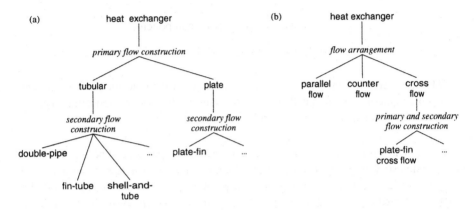

Fig. 2. Different taxonomies of heat exchangers. See Sec. 2 for a detailed description of the various types

4 Application of framework for ontology construction

This section presents a scenario how the framework of the previous section is filled in for the heat exchanger example as discussed in Section 2.

4.1 Overview

The scenario consists of a number of ontology construction steps. Each step introduces a new ontological theory linked to previous theories. Hence, we can view ontologies as a network. The network describes a technical device and which explicates the ontological choices made when modelling the device. The set of linked ontologies can be used to derive the relevant distinctions concerning a taxonomy of a heat exchanger. The network of ontologies 'formalizes' or 'theoretizes' the taxonomy.

Figure 3 gives a general overview of the scenario. The nodes are ontologies, which describe viewpoints on a domain. The links between ontologies are dependencies between ontological elements. The large double arrows model ontological mappings and the small horizontal arrows denote additional knowledge to execute the mapping. First, we try to model the physical phenomena and physical processes concerning a heat exchanger. The abstract notion of component establishes the link between processes and physical objects. However, the sequence of steps is not unique; it will vary with the task. Our objective is to derive the discriminating properties, which underlie a taxonomy of heat exchangers. The first two steps of the scenario are worked out in detail. The rest of the steps require a complex description of physical processes, which is beyond the scope of this paper.

4.2 Initial information

The input to the ontology construction process consists of knowledge about heat exchangers, which is contained in a textbook. This is a common approach in knowledge

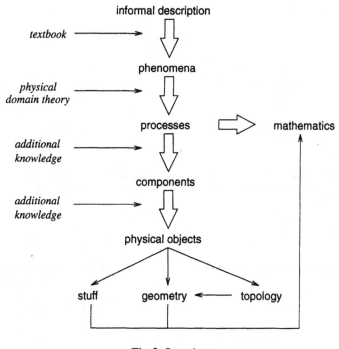

Fig. 3. Overview

acquisition. The chapter on heat exchangers of an engineering textbook has the following introduction (Incropera & DeWitt, 1988):

> "The process of heat exchange between two fluids that are at different temperatures and separated by a solid wall occurs in many engineering applications. The device used to implement this exchange is termed a *heat exchanger*, and specific applications may be found in space heating and air-conditioning, power production, waste heat recovery, and chemical processing..."

4.3 Phenomena

To go from an informal description of a textbook to a physical process ontology, we introduce the notion of a physical phenomenon. Phenomena are things that can be observed in a physical system. One can think of a phenomenon as a naive description of a process. Physical phenomena give hints about what processes determine the behaviour of a technical device. Three dimensions are important for phenomena. These are the type of object, that a phenomenon is about, the type of process with which it deals and the physical domain in which it takes place. A phenomenon can refer to one object or to multiple objects. The process can be discrete, continuous or static. Examples of a physical domain are the hydraulic domain, the thermodynamic domain or the electrical domain. The mapping process between the general notion of phenomenon and the three relevant dimensions results in a taxonomy of phenomena (Fig. 4).

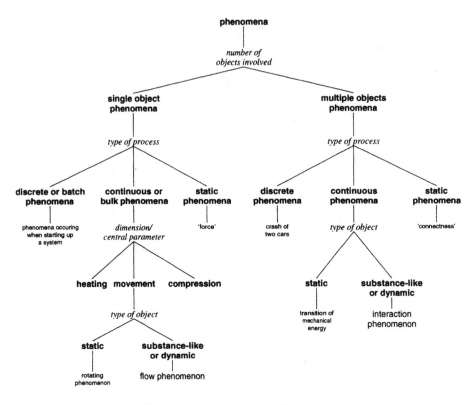

Fig. 4. A possible hierarchy of phenomena

The general description of a heat exchanger in the textbook indicates two important phenomena. First, the textbook mentions "... two fluids ... separated by a solid wall...". The observation that a heat exchanger has in and out flows suggests that two *flow phenomena* are occuring. A flow phenomenon can be classified as a single object, continuous phenomenon, related to the parameter location and to substances. Furthermore, the text tells that there is a process of heat exchange between the two fluids. This can be observed as the influence of the temperature of one fluid on the temperature of the other. When the first temperature is high, the temperature of the second fluid will increase in time. This is what is called an *interaction phenomenon* which is a phenomenon that concerns multiple entities (the fluids), is continuous and is substance-like.

4.4 Processes

The second step in the scenario depicted in Figure 3 leads from phenomena to physical processes. Basically, this comprises the mapping from commonsense concepts concerning physical systems to the scientific concepts of formal physics. Ontological mappings such as these can only be carried out by invoking a significant body of support theory (the small horizontal arrows in Figure 3). Here, we have three major components of support theory:

T_1 General theory of physical processes. Physical processes appear to have remark-able similarities across many different domains, including mechanics, electromag-netism, hydraulics, and thermodynamics. There is a finite set of primitive physical mechanisms out of which more complex physical processes can be constructed. A formalization of the associated ontology is found in the process-theory part of the PhysSys ontology of Borst *et al.* (Borst *et al.*, 1995).

T_2 Domain-specific physical theory. Specializing to a domain gives an additional source of relevant concepts. In the present case, the domain-specific theory used is ther-modynamics (Incropera & DeWitt, 1988). It provides us with notions such as convection, radiation and conduction, outlined in Sec. 2.

T_3 Logical consequences of situation-specific empirical and context information. In considering specific applications, there are usually additional case-dependent data. Such information is important because it can be employed to generate *constraints* on possible ontological mappings. An example here is the given that we are dealing with two fluids separated by a solid wall. This rules out the possibility that the (commonsense concept of) thermal interaction between the two fluids is mapped onto the (physical science concept) of convection, because no displacement of fluid is possible across a solid wall.

We now sketch, for our example of the heat exchanger, what kind of ontological mappings occur in moving from the *phenomena* or commonsense physical viewpoint – shown in Figure 4 – to the *process* viewpoint expressed in terms of scientific physical concepts. First, we note that there are two liquids which are both viewed as heat-containing matter. In the process part of the PhysSys ontology, there is an elementary concept called a *storage mechanism* that formalizes the physics notion that objects can be seen as stores of various kinds of physical *stuff*. In this case, heat is stored. The latter fact is used to map onto the proper domain of formal physics, i.e. thermodynamics. Then, a first part of the ontological mapping between 'phenomena' and 'physical processes' is:

$$\text{liquid}_1 \xoverset{T_{1,2,3}}{\longmapsto} \text{heat store}_1,$$
$$\text{liquid}_2 \xoverset{T_{1,2,3}}{\longmapsto} \text{heat store}_2.$$

The concept of store has a number of attributes, such as the carrier of what is stored (here, the liquid), its physical domain (here, thermodynamics: this determines what type of material is stored) and it may have a number of I/O ports. These are the points that enable interaction with the outer world.

The next step is to consider the mapping related to the notion of interaction. In the phenomena ontology we already have the commonsense concept of *thermal interaction*. Under the above-mentioned theory T_2, it follows that the possible range of the corresponding ontological mapping is: {*convection, conduction, radiation*} . Theory T_3 delivers some further constraints on this mapping. In this case, convection is ruled out as a candidate for the thermal interaction between the two fluids (no flow and mixing possible). Also, we can conclude that radiation is a highly unlikely candidate, because of the typical operating temperature. Thus, a mapping rule related to the concept of thermal interaction is:

$$\text{thermal interaction} \xmapsto{T_{2,3}} \text{conduction}$$

This mapping can be completed by invoking theory T_1 to formalize the notion of conduction. In the process part of the PhysSys ontology, there is another elementary concept called a 'dissipator mechanism' that expresses the notion that one way of physical interaction with the outer world is loss of stored stuff (heat) by dissipation. The simplest mapping possible for conduction is to view it as a dissipator in the thermodynamics domain: as a *thermal resistor* object. This determines the nature of the thermal interaction. Theory T_1 also tells us that the interaction concept in addition needs a connection structure (technically called a junction structure), that expresses the way the various objects (here, two stores and one dissipator object) are connected when interacting. Thus, an additional ontological mapping rule is: conduction $\xmapsto{T_1}$ thermal dissipator $\times$ interaction connection. Combining this with the mapping rule above, we obtain:

$$\text{thermal interaction} \xmapsto{T_{1,2,3}} \text{thermal resistor} \times \text{interaction connection structure.}$$

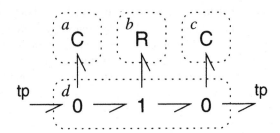

Fig. 5. Graphical representation of the result of the ontological mapping between commonsense phenomena and formal physical processes, for the heat exchanger example.

In Figure 5, the end result of the mapping between the composite concept 'thermal interaction between two separated fluids' from the phenomena ontology, and the formal ontology of physical processes, is graphically displayed. Here, a and c represent the two liquids formalized as heat stores (C for container), b stands for the conduction interaction object as a heat dissipator (R), and d is the object formally representing the interaction connection structure. The arrows represent the mentioned I/O ports, zeros and ones the two different ways they can be connected (this is specified in theory T_1), and tp is the attribute indicating the type of an I/O port through which physical interaction can take place (tp=thermal).

In sum, we see that ontological mappings can be incrementally constructed, but it is noted that they are very knowledge-intensive as well as theory-loaded.

4.5 Mathematics

The next step to find out the characteristics of a heat exchanger that influence its behaviour is to describe the processes mathematically. This yields a set of differential equations in which the dynamic variables are fully determined by the set of equations and parameters. To find the relevant equations an ontological mapping is executed between the process ontology on the one hand and a general mathematical ontology on the other. A mathematical theory like the EngMath ontology (Borst *et al.*, 1995) is applied to the process description of a heat exchanger. A part of the mathematical ontology is selected, which is 'filled in' according to the process ontology. This results in a set of differential equations with the important parameters. With T_4 representing a general theory of engineering mathematics the mapping can be represented as follows:

$$\text{process ontology (thermal resistor and structure)} \xmapsto{T_4} \text{set of differential equations.}$$

4.6 Components

The component ontology is the first step to relate parameters to heat exchanger characteristics. Components are subsystems with a limited interaction with other subsystems. Interaction between components is established with connections. When two components are connected, it means that they are able to exchange energy. A heat exchanger for instance has terminals where water can flow into or out of the device. In terms of energy flows, a heat exchanger exchanges hydraulic and thermal energy with its environment at these terminals. The component ontology further specifies that components can be decomposed into smaller components. The atomic components, i.e. components that cannot be further decomposed, are the carriers of the physical processes.

The ontological mapping from processes to components requires additional knowledge. A general theory about abstract components is required (T_5) as well as a topological ontology, that can represent possible configurations (T_6). The theory application mapping from the process ontology to the component ontology can be described as follows:

$$\text{process ontology (thermal resistor and structure)} \xmapsto{T_{5,6}}$$
$$\text{ontology of heat exchanging components.}$$

In (Top *et al.*, 1995), Top *et al.* have defined a set of generic components which play an important role in thermodynamic systems. For each component they specify which processes these components can be a carrier of. The components important for the heat exchanger example are the *pipe with external conduction* and *heat conductor*. For the heat exchanger, a suitable component configuration can be found by combining generic components and checking whether the system as a whole can have the processes found in the previous paragraph as in the process description. Figure 6 shows the result. This strategy can also be used when it would not have been possible to fully determine energy flows between the processes.

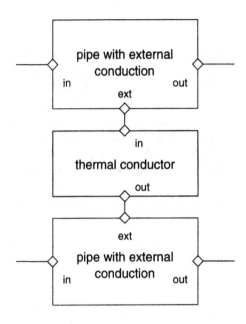

Fig. 6. The components of a heat exchanger

4.7 Physical objects

A physical object is an object in the real world, which has a certain shape and which is made out of a certain material. Components consist of physical objects. Vice versa, for each component, there may be different groups of physical objects that form the component. For instance, a pipe can be made from one cylindrical steel object, or it can be made out of four rectangular steel plates welded together.

The physical object ontology has three different viewpoints on physical objects: topology, geometry and material. The topological viewpoint deals with the placement of objects relative to eachother, i.e. whether one object touches another object. This is important because the connections on the component level impose restrictions on the topology of physical objects. For an electrical connection under normal circumstances, two objects must touch. The geometric part of the ontology defines the concepts required to reason about the location and shape of objects. The cylinder and plate shapes mentioned above are examples of these concepts. Naturally, the topological and geometrical ontologies are not independent. The fact that two objects touch can be derived from geometrical knowledge. Other important aspects of physical objects are related to the materials the objects can be made of. For heat flow through an object, the material it is made of must be a thermal conductor. In this case the thermal resistance is determined by the material and the shape of the object. So, the type of component puts restrictions on the materials that can be used.

For a heat exchanger, there are many configurations of objects that are compliant with the component configuration. For the moment it is not necessary to determine all possibilities, but it suffices to realize that they differ in geometry or in the materials they are made of. This is important because in the next paragraph it will be made clear that geometry is one of the aspects of a heat exchanger that determines the effectivity of these devices.

4.8 Mathematics revisited

Physical objects have characteristics that are determined by their geometry and the material they are made of. An example related to heat exchanger is the thermal resistance of an object. These characteristics are exactly the parameters in the mathematical description of the physical processes. If a mathematical relation for such a characteristic is known, it can easily be determined which shapes or which materials influence the performance of a heat exchanger positively.

The mathematical relations for our heat exchanger example show that differences in geometry lead to different characteristics of the objects, the heat exchangers consist of. These characteristics influence the performance of the device. Because the performance is one of the most important differentiating factors between heat exchangers, it is a good idea to classify heat exchangers by the geometry of their construction. The construction type is one distinction that helps building a taxonomy of heat exchangers.

5 Related work

Gruber was one of the first to introduce the word *ontology* in knowledge engineering as a formalism to communicate and reuse knowledge (Gruber, 1993). He proposes a definition of the term that relies heavily on the notion of 'conceptualization'. A body of formally represented knowledge is based on the objects, concepts and other entities that are presumed to exist in some area of interest and the relationships that hold among them. A conceptualization is an abstract, simplified view of the world that one wishes to represent for some purpose. An ontology is defined as an explicit specification of a conceptualization.

The ontology experiments of Gruber and his research group at the Knowledge Systems Laboratory of Stanford University have resulted in a set of ontologies in a formalism called Ontolingua, which can be reused to a certain extent. Especially the ontologies related to component modelling and those involved with engineering mathematics are relevant for technical domains. It is not intuitive however how to adjust an ontology to the specific demands of a domain or application. The conceptualizations are static components of knowledge.

Reuse of knowledge through dynamic construction on the other hand enables the user to build a situation-specific ontology out of relatively independent building blocks. Differentiation of generic objects by applying discriminating properties is not new. The Greek philosopher Aristotle used differentiae like animateness and substantiality to construct a hierarchy of entities. Our approach however places the philosophical ideas in a more computational context.

Sowa gives an overview of the ideas about Firstness, Secondness as well as Thirdness (Sowa, 1995). The philosopher Peirce was the first to actually mention the terms, being influenced by Kant and Aristotle. Firstness relates to the object itself, Secondness represents the role of the object and Thirdness models its context. A woman is an example of Firstness, the roles mother or attorney are examples of Secondness and parenthood or the legal system are Third. At the moment we only mention primary and secondary objects explicitly. The additional knowledge that is required to execute an ontological mapping can be considered as tertiary ontologies. They contain general theories, constraints and context information. The philosophical notion of Secondness and our secondary ontologies differ in the sense that the latter ones not only model simple distinctions like animateness or intentionality, but also complex theories like topology. Theory application is a new type of ontological mapping.

Guarino *et al.* describe in (Guarino *et al.*, 1994) a distinction that appears to correspond to the difference between primary and secondary concepts. According to Guarino, a sortal predicate (like *apple*) 'supplies a principle for distinguishing and counting individual particulars which it collects', while a non-sortal predicate (like *red*) 'supplies such a principle only for particulars already distinguished, or distinguishable, in accordance with some antecedent principle or method'.

6   Conclusions

In this paper we have pointed to issues in knowledge sharing that go beyond making available libraries of reusable components and the associated indexing problem. Retrieval and assembly from large libraries is itself a knowledge-intensive task. So, a relevant question becomes how we can guide the user in gradually building up the needed knowledge.

This papers discussed an approach to solving this problem by regarding the generative aspects of sharable ontologies. Our main conclusions are:

- Any application ontology seems to be built out of multiple but, on the other hand, rather general and separate ontologies. By considering the technical domain of heat exchangers, we have shown how such an application domain can be described in terms of a *web* of generic ontologies regarding, e.g., mereology, topology, geometry, and physical process theory. These generic ontologies represent different aspects of or viewpoints taken on the domain at hand.
- Concerning the construction process, we have described how this can be facilitated by gradually adding new 'dimensions' of conceptual distinctions. The explicit dimensions can help the user to overcome difficulties with library use, such as the indexing problem. In a way the user creates his own indexes. Goal and context knowledge thereby provide filters, to throw away unneeded concepts and distinctions as early as possible.
- Ontology mappings appear to be important construction operators in generating an application ontology from small generic ontologies. Import and renaming alone are insufficient to achieve this.

Although our work has only given some tentative directions, we feel that finding satisfactory answers to the considered question of knowledge and ontology construction is needed, in order to widen the circle of end users that can really profit from available libraries for knowledge sharing and reuse.

References

AKKERMANS, J. M., BORST, P., POS, A., & TOP, J. (1995). Experiences in conceptual modelling for a mechatronic design library. In Gaines, B. & Musen, M., editors, *Proceedings of the ninth international knowledge acquisition workshop KAW'95*, pages volume 2, pages 39.1–39.15. University of Calgary, SRDG Publications.

BENJAMIN, J. (1995). Towards generic ontologies.

BORST, P., AKKERMANS, H., POS, A., & TOP, J. (1995). The physsys ontology for physical systems. In *Working papers of the ninth international workshop on qualitative reasoning*, pages 11–21. Department of Social Science Informatics (SWI), University of Amsterdam.

GRUBER, T. R. (1993). A translation approach to portable ontology specifications. *Knowledge Acquisition*, 5:199–220.

GUARINO, N., CARRARA, M., & GIARETTA, P. (1994). An ontology of meta-level categories. In Doyle, J., Sandewall, E., & Torasso, P., editors, *Principles of knowledge representation and reasoning: proceedings of the fourth international conference (KR94)*, San Mateo, California. Morgan Kaufmann.

INCROPERA, F. P. & DEWITT, D. P. (1988). *Fundamentals of heat and mass transfer*. New York, Wiley.

KLINKER, G., BHOLA, C., DALLEMAGNE, G., MARQUES, D., & MCDERMOTT, J. (1990). Usable and reusable programming constructs. In *Proceedings 5th AAAI-sponsored Knowledge Acquisition for Knowledge Based Systems Workshop*, pages 14-1–14-20, Banff, Canada. SRDG Publications, University of Calgary.

SCHOLANDER, P. (1958). Counter current exchange, a princple of biology. Collected reprints Contribution No. 983, Woods hole oceanographic institute.

SCHREIBER, A. T., WIELINGA, B. J., & JANSWEIJER, W. H. J. (1995). The KACTUS view on the 'O' word. In *IJCAI Workshop on Basic Ontological Issues in Knowledge Sharing*. Also in: J. C. Bioch and Y.-H. Tan (eds.). *Proceedings 7th Dutch National Conference on Artificial Intelligence NAIC'95*, EURIDIS, Erasmus University Rotterdam, The Netherlands, pp. 159–168, 1995.

SOWA, J. (1995). Top-level ontological categories. *Int. J. of Human Computer Studies*, 43:669–685.

TOP, J., BORST, P., & AKKERMANS, H. (1995). Reusable thermodynamic model components for design. OLMECO deliverable, ESPRIT project 6521 OLMECO/WP2T45/ECN/01/4.0, ECN and University of Twente.

VAN HEIJST, G. (1995). *The role of ontologies in knowledge engineering*. PhD thesis, University of Amsterdam, SWI.

VAN HEIJST, G., FALASCONI, S., ABU-HANNA, A., SCHREIBER, A. T., & STEFANELLI, M. (1995). A case study in ontology library construction. *Artificial Intelligence in Medicine*, 7(5):227–255.

WALKER, G. (1982). *Industrial heat exchangers — a basic guide*. Hemisphere Publishing Corporation.

WIEDERHOLD, G. (1994). An algebra for ontology composition. Technical report, ARPA & Stanford University.

WIELINGA, B. J., SCHREIBER, A. T., & BREUKER, J. A. (1993). Modelling expertise. In Schreiber, A. T., Wielinga, B. J., & Breuker, J. A., editors, *KADS: A Principled Approach to Knowledge-Based System Development*, pages 21–46. London, Academic Press.

Text Clustering to Help Knowledge Acquisition from Documents*

Stéphane Lapalut

Projet ACACIA, INRIA Sophia Antipolis, BP 93,
06 902 Sophia Antipolis Cédex, France
Stephane.Lapalut@sophia.inria.fr
phone: 33-9365-7645, fax: 33-9365-7783

Abstract. At the earlier stage of the knowledge acquisition process, interviews of experts produce a large amount of rich but ill-structured texts. Knowledge engineers need some tool to help them in the exploitation of all these texts. We propose the use of a statistical method, the top-down hierarchical classification and a new interpretation of its results. The initial statistical analysis proposed by M. Reinert [16, 17] gives two kinds of results: first a segmentation of texts that reflects their "semantic contexts" that we use to raise structures of texts, and second, classes of significant terms belonging to these contexts, which can be related to the experts or to these specialities. In this paper, we describe the method, its empirical validity and a comparison with similar approaches, its uses with examples and results. We conclude with some research directions to extend the exploitation of the analysis results.

1 Introduction

In case of domain without established theory, such as complex accident analysis, the only way to obtain a significant and useful amount of data is to observe and interview experts working on various selected cases. This produces ill-structured text interviews. When reading all these interviews, the knowledge engineer lacks guidelines to model the domain, to distinguish and characterize the different approaches of the experts and to produce useful knowledge bases.

Given a huge corpus of expert's interviews, we propose the use of a statistical method called "top-down hierarchical classification", to handle both self contained texts and sets of chosen texts. It detects groups of terms of the corpus (a set of one or more texts) strongly distinguishable, according to the statistical occurrence of meaningful terms or pairs of them in small text units, such as sentences. These groups are called classes and have been identified as relevant semantic contexts [1, 16]. They lead to a partition of the corpus that reflects its structure. After interpreting each class with the help of related terms, the

---

* All examples come from a research supported by the French "Ministère de la Recherche et de l'Espace" under contract n.92 C 0757 and the French "Ministère de l'Equipement, des Transports et du Tourisme" under contract n. 93.0003.

knowledge engineer knows the subject of each part of the structure of the corpus. With these results, he is able to select parts of given expert's interviews relevant to his purpose and to focus his work.

In this paper, we first start with a precise description of the method and the associated statistical analysis. The second part introduces the bases of the tool and method established by Max Reinert, and the way we propose to extend it for the purpose of knowledge acquisition. The third part deals with examples from the domain of road safety expertise and shows the validity of both the text clustering approach and our method. The two last parts deal with related work, conclude on the realized work and propose some ideas for further research.

2 The Top-down Hierarchical Classification Method and its Extension

This section describes the statistical classification method with theoretical and practical details. This method has been developed by Max Reinert since 1984 and implemented in a tool called ALCESTE [17]. This tool presently processes only French texts, even if an English extension is planned. The current version is a commercial one. The purpose of Reinert was to use semantics contexts to help psychologists in their analysis and research of models. Given the statistical analysis results, we have found text clustering as another application.

2.1 Principles

The initial objective addressed was to discover semantic contexts characterized by groups of terms from a given corpus. A principle derived from the Huyghens decomposition formula is used: "to find a partition of a set that minimizes the intra-class variance, it is sufficient to find dichotomies that maximize the inter-class variance".

Texts to be analysed are put into a corpus, which may be organized into UCI (initial contextual units) that characterize each texts (see figure 2) or relevant parts of texts (such as chapters in a book). These first roughly distinguished pieces of the corpus are called ICU (initial contextual units). Then an automated process cuts each ICU into regular elementary contextual units (ECU). The classification, called top-down hierarchical classification is done on this set of ECU with the help of the set of words from the corpus. The result consists of a set of classes, defined by exclusive sets of ECU and sets of preponderant words appearing in them. Automated steps use statistical criteria as described in the next sections.

We refine the initial cycle [16] to adapt it for our purpose of discovering the structure of a corpus. We have found a correlation between natural articulations of the corpus and the structure given by the classes. We can sketch our method as shown in figure 1. The classes give a structure that is refined by the user with the help of class interpretations. Formally, we can consider the expert's

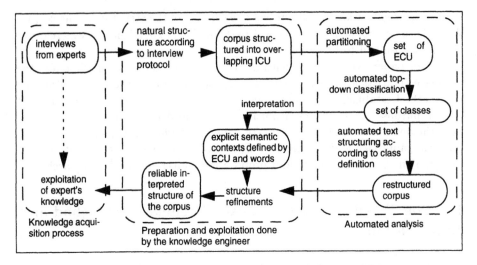

Fig. 1. Our extension of the method towards knowledge acquisition process.

documents processing as the research of correspondences between sets from a triplet U_1, S, TU_1 where:

U_1 is the elementary segmentation of the corpus (the set of ECU),

TU_1 the objective clustering of U_1 into classes (found by the top-down classification) and

S the implicit organization of the corpus according to the interrelated topics in interviews; this organization is to be discovered.

The whole analysis permits the clarification of S, which is the correspondence between the corpus viewed as a sequence of ECU and the semantics contexts defined by classes in TU_1.

Now, let us describe in detail the main point of the Reinert's method: the top-down classification algorithm. Firstly we explain the format of the inputs, secondly the theory that underlies the algorithm and thirdly the outputs relevant for our method.

2.2 Input Data

In this section we highlight the data format and the way they are extracted from the initial corpus. ALCESTE takes two inputs: the corpus, which can be composed of one or more texts, and a set of parameters, called the analysis plan, which the user gives to conduct the analysis. The corpus is organized by the user as a sequence of ICU (figure 2). These units delimit the different texts in the corpus or the natural articulations of a unique text, like a chapter in a book. In the case of single expert interview, the text interview is mostly a unique ICU. For each ICU, a label (like "*yve-int" in figure 2) and a number of special markers, (keywords starting with "*"), are used to type each ICU. By these keywords, the user specifies the kind of information each ICU is supposed to contain according to the protocol followed to obtain texts. The same keywords can be used in several ICU, such as "*INT" to type each ICU obtained from interviews of one expert. This feature is very useful when we treat several texts from several experts.

```
Example of a corpus composed of ten texts that define ten ICU with the keyword codes:

the first keywords name the ICU with the name of the text file it contains
the following keywords describe the types with the codes:

*Y states the name of the expert Yve      *INT means interview
*P    "              "         Pie         *DUO means case study by two experts
*M    "              "         Man         *TRIO means case study by three experts
*J    "        :     "         Jlo         *SOLO means case study by a single expert
*F    "              "         Fra
                                           *002 *003 *24 are the index numbers of the
   corpus                                      studied cases

        *yve_int *Y *INT
                    "ASCII text from interview of the expert Yve."
        *pie_int *P *INT
                    "interview of the expert Pie."
        *man_int *M *INT
                     " interview of the expert Man."
        *jlo_int *J *INT
                    "interview of the expert Jlo."
        *fra_int *F *INT
                    "interview of the expert Fra."
        *dan_man_002 *D *M *DUO *002
                    "conversation between Dan and Man during case 002 resolution."
        *dan_jlo_24 *D *J *DUO *24
                    "conversation between Dan and Jlo during case 24 resolution."
        *dom_fra_24 *E *F *DUO *24
                    " conversation between Dom and Fra during case 24 resolution."
        *man_pie_jlo_003 *M *J *P *TRIO *003
                    "conversation between Man, Jlo, Pie during case 003 resolution."
        *man_003 *M *SOLO *003
                    "discourse of Man during his case 003 resolution."
```

Fig. 2. Headers of the ten ICU in a corpus composed by ten expert's texts.

After ICU typing, the user sets the analysis plan parameters (ECU length, maximum number of classes) and starts the automated analysis. Before the main algorithm processing, the statistical analysis called "top-down hierarchical classification", a morphological reduction of the terms of the corpus is done. Two lists are then extracted from the corpus: one contains all the words from the corpus in alphabetical order, the other one contains the sequence of ECU that composed the corpus in the order they appear in the corpus. Some words, called toolwords (noisy words), such as prepositions or pronouns are recognized and typed according to dictionaries. Other words, such as nouns, verbs, adjectives, are considered as meaningful terms and called plain-words (non-noisy words). An ECU is a word sequence that integrates a fixed number of plain-words, as specified by the user in the analysis plan. ECU useful length ranges from 10 to 20 plain-words. ECU can be sketched as sentences from the corpus. The segmentation is performed according to the punctuation with a priority order of the signs (. >? >! >; >:>, > space). The fixed length is needed to validate the statistical algorithm and is not a strong constraint for the purposed context identification.

The mostly used analysis plan allows a double classification with ECU of two different lengths. It permits an adjustment of this length to obtain a better classification. The cross between the two hierarchies of classes found according to a χ^2 criteria determines a stable classification.

The program uses the two above lists as rows and columns of a double entry boolean table. The presence of a term in ECU is noted with 1 and its absence with 0 (figure 3). The completed table, which is a sparse matrix, is used as the input of the main algorithm. We describe it in the next section.

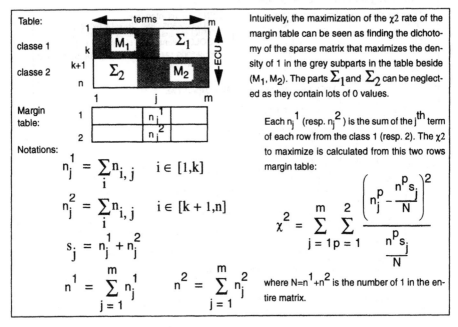

Fig. 3. Principle of the sparse matrix dichotomy using a χ^2 distance criteria.

2.3 The Algorithm

The applicability of the underlying statistical theory used by this algorithm was proven in [1, 11, 16]. In this section we expose the key points of the algorithm to have an overview of the whole process. Given the boolean table, which use terms as column entries and ECU as row entries ($m_{ij} = 1$ means that the ith term belongs to the jth ECU), we define classes as particular sets of rows; a given row belongs to a single class. The final set of classes is an incomplete partition of the initial set of ECU. To distinguish classes, the algorithm uses a χ^2 distance between the margins of two given sub-tables, determined by successive dichotomy as describes in figure 3. A margin is a row vector formed by the sum of all values in each column. At each step of the algorithm, the dichotomy that maximizes the χ^2 rate of the margin tables is found. In a simpler form, it can be stated as:

First step: find the dichotomy that maximizes the χ^2 association rate between the margins of the two determined classes.

Other steps: until the specified number of classes is reached, do:

    - pick the class with the greatest number of rows,

    - among all row combination, find the dichotomy that splits this class into two subtables and maximizes the χ^2 of their margins,

    - replace the picked class with the two found classes.

An example for a four terminal classes partitioning is drawn on figure 4. At the end of this process, each class is defined by an exclusive set of ECU and a set of terms; some terms can be found in several classes. Then for each class, two steps enable to determine the sets of the best correlated ECU and terms according to a χ^2 rate. Those results are used to draw the segmentation in our method.

The length of ECU in the corpus determines the quality of the found hierarchy of classes. The quality of a hierarchy refers to the partitioning of the corpus and to the related sets of terms that defined each class. The higher the ratio of terms that mostly belongs to the same class (occurrence number of a term in the ECU of the same class against the total number of his occurrence in all ECU), the better the classification. To improve this ratio and obtain a good hierarchy, we have to choose the appropriate length for ECU. The tool gives a percentage of terms that mostly appear in a single class to estimate the classification correctness, the average ranges from 50% to 70%.

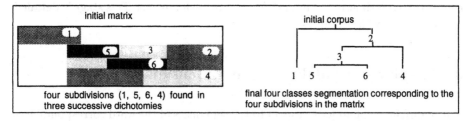

Fig. 4. An example of a classification ending with four terminal classes.

2.4 Statistical Analysis Outputs

Many productions result from the automated analysis. About ten times the size of the corpus distributed into fourteen files is generated. A lot of information about the corpus can be obtained with appropriate interpretations. We focused our effort on a small but relevant part of these outputs for our purpose. We briefly describe the format of files we have used, the interpretation and the results they lead to.

The first result we exploit is the double classification and the selected stable classes. The corpus structured as in figure 2 gives the hierarchies in figure 5. In this example, the analysis plan asks for 12 classes and the comparison between the two classifications enlightens 11 stable classes. For each of them, the number of correlated ECU is given with χ^2 rates. The rate of correctness of 54% empiricaly validates the choice of the ECU lengths made (12 and 14 plain-words per ECU).

To be useful, a meaning must be attached to each class. This work is the burden of the user as the classification is not supervised nor guided with a pre-determined lexicon. Each class is characterized by the list of its ECU and four files of correlated terms. These files permit the class labelling and for each class, consist of two lists of terms and two lists of couples of terms. For both couples of lists, one list concerns the best correlated terms to the class (profile) and the other the less correlated terms (anti-profile). An excerpt from a term profile is shown on figure 6. As few words are preponderant in profiles for each class, different readers are led to the same semantics context interpretations. These interpretations require some domain knowledge and lead to terminological choices. For each class, the user cross-checks the correctness of his four interpretations. In most cases, no contradiction occurs and one expression results to characterize each class. These class tags are used to guide the user in the next step, the labelling of each part of the corpus structure.

The outcome of our method arises in this last stage, the structure refinement. The set of preponderant ECU attached to the classes permits the clustering of the initial set of ECU, e.g. the corpus. With the help of a graphic distribution of ECU from the corpus for each class according to their χ^2 association rate, the codification is able to locate the small corpus parts (less than a page) that contain articulations of the implicit structure of the corpus. This stage is detailed in section 3.2 with examples.

3 Results and Validity of our Extension

The algorithm is blind with respect to the semantics of the word correspondences it makes. It only gives us an abstract result of all word associations that the reader can outline from the text. Of course, these associations reflect a feature of natural language, called semantic context. We describe here the way to interpret the analysis results and all the information given about the corpus. As six kinds of different analysis plan are relevant for common kinds of corpus and user's purposes, we focus on the most useful plan that is performed on both dialogues and book texts. This plan performs a cross between two hierarchies built with different lengths of ECU given by the user.

Our method addresses two goals, firstly to retrieve the natural articulations and the structure of the corpus, which is the main goal when the corpus contains only one text, and secondly to have qualitative information about differences and similarities between components of the corpus, especially in the case of corpus composed of several texts that come from different experts [13]. First we describe class interpretation, which is common to all kinds of analysis, then the relations

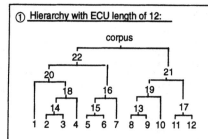

① Hierarchy with ECU length of 12:

② Hierarchy with ECU length of 14:

Stable classification in 11 classes obtained by the crossing of the two hierarchies:

classes	crosses ① ②	χ2
1	1 and 1	3923
2	12 and 9	3930
3	3 and 3	1853
4	11 and 8	4127
5	6 and 4	911
6	8 and 12	2369
7	5 and 7	1149
8	9 and 11	3285
9	10 and 10	3820
10	2 and 6	685
11	4 and 5	1265

Crosses between classes (from 1 to 12) and intermediate classes (from 13 to 22) of above hierarchies ① and ② determine 11 stable classes (classes 7 from ① and 2 from ② give no significante crossing).

For each pair of class (C1, C2) with C1 belonging to hierarchy ① and C2 to ②, the program calculates χ2 distance between margins of their associated submatrix. Pairs with higher χ2 are retained and determined stable classes. Results reported in the table reports come from the cross of the two above hierarchies. Class numbers with associated pairs and χ2 are given.

Fig. 5. An example of a stable classification resulting from the crossing between two hierarchies of classes obtained from the corpus sketched in figure 2, with two different ECU lengths (correctness of 54.08%).

between classes and corpus, considering a single text corpus. All examples used from now are translated from french.

3.1 Class Interpretation

Class Description Each class is characterized by four lists of terms. Two lists concern the most representative terms and pair of terms, the two others represent the less significant terms and pair of terms for the considered class. In all these lists, each term is characterized by five characteristics (listed in the order they appear in figure 6):

1. the place number in the dictionary of terms built from the corpus;
2. the number of occurrences in the ECU of the class;
3. the number of occurrences in the whole ECU;
4. ratio of ECU in the corpus in which the term appears;
5. χ^2 association rate between the term and the class;
6. the term in its reduced form with an optional mark.

The lists are sorted from the greater χ^2 rate to the lower one; keywords are treated apart (figure 6). Terms with low χ^2 rate and a 100% belonging rate are

①	②	③	④	⑤		⑥
409	50.	75.	66.67	1057.00	X	mesur+
72	25.	30.	83.33	667.29		grip+
122	20.	25.	80.00	510.39		characteris+
88	17.	20.	85.00	462.62		equipment+
57	13.	13.	100.00	420.22	0	join+
134	24.	51.	47.06	342.56		road+
593	12.	14.	85.71	329.12		surface+
121	5.	7.	71.43	112.47		countr+
247	5.	8.	62.50	97.20		light+
368	7.	19.	36.84	74.82		itinerar+
475	6.	15.	40.00	70.56		tyre+
934	*	91.	448.	20.31	503.27 *	*fra-ent
945	*	91.	996.	9.14	158.69 *	*F
944	*	150.	2653.	5.65	130.33 *	*ENT

List of terms correlated to the class 7 in the previous classification, with χ2 superior to the average χ2 (62.96):

The tagging of this class has been stated as: "interview of Fra dealing with grip of tyre on roads".

Fig. 6. Example of a class tag, according to one of its profile.

as representative as the one with the highest χ^2 rate (such a term exclusively belongs to one class). The list of terms from class 7 of the previous classification and its interpretation are given in figure 6.

Class Interpretation For each list, the user tags all classes with an expression constituted by preponderant terms, such as "the kinematics analysis process" or "the grip of tyre on road under various conditions", according to the terms with the highest χ^2 rates and percentages. For each class, two expressions say what the class is and two others say what the class is not. One can think that such a tag is a subjective task that will lead to different results with different konwledge engineers. It is not the case, as there are not so many terms to decide the right description, i.e. terms with the highest χ^2. Tags attach two expressions describing what a class is about and two additional expressions relating what the class is not about. So, four pieces of information are sufficient to check the rightness of the whole class description and then, to give a unique meaningful expression.

In this process, useful data that help the knowledge engineer are the explicit domains to which the subdomains evoked in the corpus belong (such as kinematics calculus, which is a subdomain of kinematics analysis). We use them as sorts to type each expression. They allow a simple way to check the coherence of the four expressions that describe classes. Comparisons between classes seem to be easier too with the help of these sorts. As we have experimented this way, it is only useful to improve the coherence between all class interpretations.

In the example of figure 7, a single text corpus results in five classes. In the car accident analysis field, there are two important stages in the diagnosis: collecting all the relevant informations after the car crash (noted C) and analyzing every documents to search all kinds of the needed data (noted A). The experts currently make another distinction, between three specialities: analysis of the infratructure in the car crash area (noted I), analysis of the driver's behavior (noted D) and analysis of kinematics aspects (noted K). Types C and A are exclusive since these are two distincts phases in the expert's activity. For the sake of the analysis, we consider that types I, D, K are exclusive, according to the focus of expert's analysis in regard of there own specialities. We remark that a link exists between types A and K.

For each class, the comparisons between tags related to both term lists and pair of term lists for class profiles and anti-profiles result directly in a single expression. If for a class, the profile leads to A and the anti-profile to A, there is a misleading interpretation for this class. Then the knowledge engineer has to revise his tags according to profiles and anti-profiles.

classes	profile	anti-profile	Typing of five classes from a "single text" corpus to crosscheck coherence of profiles according to anti-profiles ("crash" belongs to type A). Types are consistent w.r.t. profile and anti-profiles for each class (dealing with crash belongs to kinematics analysis).
1	A	I or C	
2	C	A	
3	crash	I, C	
4	I or D	A, C	
5	car1 crash	C	

Fig. 7. Example of a class interpretation crosschecking.

3.2 Single Text Analysis

In this part, we detail the results of a single text corpus study, the text entitled "*dan-jlo-24" in figure 2. Two experts, Dan and Jlo, of the same specialities (kinematics), are dealing with the case 24, which was unknow to them, with lots of comments about their activities according to a thinking aloud protocol. The text analysis leads to five classes. We use their related sets of ECU determined by ALCESTE to retrieve the implicit structure of the conversation between the experts during this case study.

From Classes to Text Structure Each set of ECU related to classes contains ECU with their χ^2 rate association and with the class they belong to. Each ECU is indexed with a number according to the order in which they appear in the corpus. These two kinds of information are used as cartesian coordinates to build the graphical correlation between all ECU and each class. Figure 8 represents graphics built with results from the previous single text corpus. Each graph relate ECU distribution (X axis) according to their χ^2 distance to this class (Y axis). ECU range from 1 to 1340. The five graphs comprise the final splitting (vertical dotted lines) refined by the user. For each graph, each bar above the X axis relates the χ^2 rate for one ECU of the related class. Bars under the X axis relates χ^2 of ECU from the four others classes (that does not means that these χ^2 are negative, but these oppositions allow a good visual appreciation of relative importance of each class). This is a simple visualization of ECU distribution according to classes. We observe that for a given class, the distribution is not a random one. Clusters of ECU appear and the hypothesis we made is that they reflect subjects dealt with in distinguishable parts of the corpus, in this case, one text. The gaps between clusters intend to be parts of the text where we can find articulations and swaps between one subject to another. Articulation locations give the final splitting drawn by dotted lines in figure 8.

To test this hypothesis, we submitted texts to a reader. His goal was to locate parts and transitions between them. For a 60 pages long conversation between two experts, the reader was able to recognize parts after three or four readings, without having certitude of their relevancy. In the same time, we analyzed the text with our method and we found a partitioning. The two results are compared in figure 8. According to precise locations of transitions in the pages of the text, the match between the program and the reader sounds accurate. For 12 parts suggested by the analysis, only four conflicts occur. In the next section, we investigate in depth the differences between the qualitative and quantitative information given by the reader in respect of the data provided by the analysis.

Exploitation and Refinements In the few experiments we have done, the structure suggested at the end of the analysis was always relevant. The resolution of conflicts concerning text splitting shows us that the reader tends to be too precise or to miss some articulations he was able to retrieve with a careful reading (in figure 8, see conflicts 1, 2 and 4 due to excessive preciseness, and conflict 3 due to insufficient preciseness). These two phenomena depend on the text, with at least one of them observed in all comparisons between the reader and the program. Another type of conflict occurs when comparing the reader's type attributions and class types for each part. The program is not intended to give the right ones, but the class types it provides are useful to help the human interpretation or to check them. For each of the four conflicts noticed, we have read again the related parts with possible types in mind. Three of them are not true discrepancies as the part subject interpretations are ambiguous. The other one is a conflict and the reader has given the right meaning. So, we can say that program class types lack precision. But in most cases, the program gives the right classe type and the conflicts point out ambiguous parts of the text. Anyway, the knowledge engineer has to read the text at least one time to make precise the articulations between the parts and the subject of each part. The same work without the help of the statistical analysis is somehow dull, takes a long time and it is difficult and time-consuming to check it.

Conclusion As regards our experiments and tests, the usefulness of the analysis is at least the guidance of the reader in the research of articulations in the structure of a single text corpus. Another aspect of its usefulness is to check the title that the reader gives to each part. According to the type of classes, we can type the clusters, in fact parts of the text. In our experiments, the reader was sometimes misled in this task. He gave titles that were not in accordance with the ones related by classes. For each conflict, a deeper reading of the incriminated parts of the text revealed that the class types from program were mostly the

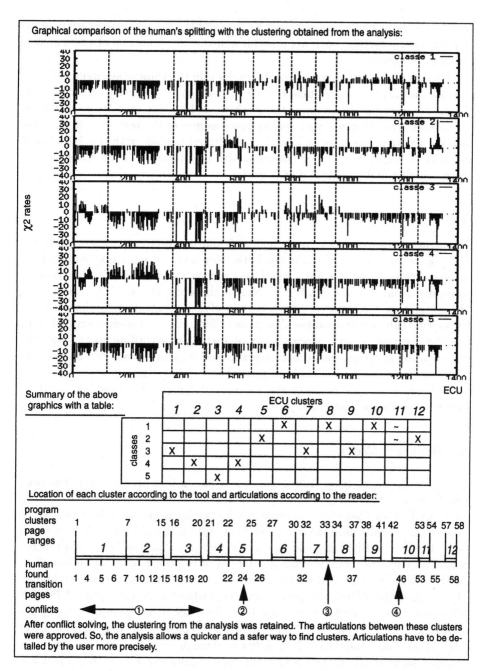

Fig. 8. Example of a text clustering and the comparison between the reader's and the program results.

right ones. In some cases, the reader's types and the program types are different but do not conflicting: both are possible and the interpretation of these sorts of parts is ambiguous.

To sum up, the statistical analysis results help the knowledge engineer to find the relevant parts from a single text corpus and to locate articulations between them. He only has to prepare the analysis and to interpret its results, then he specifies the structure with one or two readings of the text. It is a safer and quicker way than the same task conducted without the help of the analysis, which requires at least three or four readings, with no guarantee of the correctness of both splitting and meaning of each part.

3.3 Conclusion

From the analysis of both single text and multiple text corpora we conducted [12, 13], we get two results. Firstly, both inter-text and intra-text comparisons are possible and secondly, for a single text corpus, we obtain its precise (refined) structure. Above a given number of different kinds of text, e.g. ICU in the corpus, the overall text differences are given back by classes. Texts strongly characterized by specific subjects lead to peculiar classes. Side effect phenomena reveal some specific features of very precise parts of texts. So, according to the way the classification is carried out, different grains and structure levels can be reached. The main remaining problem is to put relevant texts together within a corpus to highlight a level of detail or some desired differences between texts and so, expert's knowledge particularities.

4 Related Work

Statistical approach is far from being a new one in text processing. It has been widely used in text categorization[9, 15], as well as in language analysis [19, 3]. Some applications have been made to the knowledge acquisition field. Statistical methods are mostly used to strengthen a conceptual method [15, 6, 9]. Tools such as NLDB [9] and SKIS [15] combine both conceptual and statistical approaches within a hybrid system. Most applications tend to provide a set of tools such as NLDB, which is a "set of statistical method", or to offer an assistant to a human expert, like INLEN [10] that "performed a sophisticated data analysis", KITTEN [18] where "the knowledge acquired is being feedback to facilitate the intelligence of people", MOCA [6] that "helps analysts to cope with large quantities of intelligence data" and SADC [14]. A few of them pretend to perform automated analysis, such as NLDB and SKIS, but they require the user to build lexicons (NLDB) or well defined sets of criteria (keyword↔category correspondences in SKIS) adapted to the knowledge engineer purpose and to the considered domain.

Texts in natural language format serve as entries in KITTEN, NLDB, SADC and SKIS. Corpora are used in various ways, from "a set of entities that are sentences whose features are words they contain" (IMS project, [7]) to sequences of keywords (SKIS). The ALCESTE segmentation method is close to the one used in KITTEN, but with the constraint of the ECU fixed length. Statistical treatments mostly use term weighing. Some algorithms, such as TEXAN in KITTEN or the "similarity measuring component" in SKIS implement a distance measurement too. The only algorithm with a pure distance measurement is TEXAN. But it is a "simple distance-in-text measure" that lacks to take into account the whole corpus. ALCESTE process the whole corpus, by the way of the crossed entries of non-noisy words and ECU in the matrix (see section 2.3), which allows a measurement distance based on a χ^2 criteria. It meets the requirements proposed in MOCA, as "it does not need to input the number of clusters desired", it allows "overlapping cluster" on non-noisy words and it analyses the corpus as a whole to produce clusters.

The intended results of discovering the corpus structure can be compared to the one of the text logical structure as in SADC method, despite that this latter uses a purely conceptual approach. The work of Hearst [8] adresses this goal too. We must take into consideration this latter approach as its goal is nearly the same as ours, but with some differences, both in the used method and in the obtained results. Her goal was to "partition expository texts into coherent multi-paragraph discourse units which reflect the subtopic structure of the text". This is the first difference with our method, as expository texts are a bit more structured than texts from expert interviews. She uses a "texttiling" algorithm based on similarity determination. She processes a corpus segmentation into "token-sequences" of a fixed length. A token-sequence includes a predetermined number of consecutive tokens ($\tilde{2}0$) and it is similar to ECU in our method. Then she uses a window including a fixed number of token-sequence (6) to perform "comparison of adjacent pairs". So this algorithm performs a *local* analysis of the corpus. It only gives similarity indications without any other detail than the token occurrence frequency. She does not seem to use the pre-existent structure of the corpus.

The algorithm we presented in this paper performs an *overall* analysis and a correspondence between text units. We think it is more suitable for ill-structured text, such as interviews, than Hearst's texttiling algorithm. With our method, we obtain more than the overall corpus structure. For instance, detailed indications about term distribution and correlation enable us to tag the structure and can be used later for other purposes, such as ontology building.

To conclude, the presented method and algorithm meet previous work. They are candidate to be a "more sophisticated text analysis technique" [18], but till now with a human assistance. The corpus organization (ICU), its segmentation (ECU) and the clustering algorithm (cf. section 2.2) contribute to enhance and refine the set of statistical tools and methods commonly used; then the overall extension reaches a useful feature to help the knowledge acquisition process. We detail further possible extensions in the next section.

5   Conclusion and Further Research

In this paper we have detailed the basis of the method to enlighten both the structures of corpora and the subjects of their parts. The first remark is about the typing of classes and the parts of the structure. The knowledge engineer can perhaps be helped in the determination of a type grid, but it is not an advantage. As the experts' conversations and interviews are very spontaneous, a too constraining tool can lead to bad results. Anyway, the knowledge engineer must have to read those texts and to understand them. Our method results in a spare of time and facilitates management of a huge amount of expertise texts. As the class typing is only a means to check the class analysis correctness and to guide the knowledge engineer in his reading, no refinement such as the use of a predefined nomenclature seems to be useful to improve this method. With the help of a statistical learning method [3], we can expect to gain some automated extension to perform the class tagging.

To identify specific vocabulary, terminologies of domains and subdomains, our method can be useful. The tool already allows the research of terms related to a given one, without class consideration. Combined with the multiple text corpus analysis, we hope to find a way to help knowledge engineers to establish terminologies from a given domain or expert. The use of decision tree algorithms as in CART [6] can be a way to help exploitation of the big amount of produced data. Another interesting track are the (semi)automated indexation tools. A lot of results using various implemented methods have been achieved in this domain. Probabilistic frameworks such as PASSAT and Leximappe [4] are worth to be related. An interesting work was made by D. Bourigault with the help of the tool LEXTER [2], a terminology extraction software. It mainly produces an hypertext version of the discovered domain ontology. As it uses a morpho-syntactical analysis to build a grammatical network of term relevant to the domain, it is a conceptual approach, opposed to the statistic one. In the same way, we should mentioned the ACTIA approach [5], which proceeds to a careful linguistical analysis and leads to conceptual clusters. Both these approachs and ours may be worth to be combined in the same framework.

So, the use of term correspondence analysis by the means of the top-down hierarchical classification provides useful results to help the management of roughly structured texts. Implicit structures of single texts and differences inside a set of texts can be discovered. It guides the reader in his work, which becomes quicker and safer than reading without help. The method to exploit a single text is well established and the multiple text corpus exploitation is promising [13]. The knowledge engineer gaines a clear overview and understanding of the expertise documents. Then he is able to organise the knowledge base building, to pick up the relevant part of text to anwer modelling choices, to draw hypothesis and test them. But we are far to have fully exploited the richness of the results provided by the statistical analysis.

References

1. J.P. Benzecri. *L'analyse des Données*. Dunod, Paris, 1973.
2. D. Bourigault. Lexter, a terminology extraction software for knowledge acquisition from texts. In *Proceedings of the 9th Knowledge Acquisition for Knowledge Based Systems Workshop*, Banff, Canada, 1995.
3. E. Charniak. *Statistical language learning*. Bradford books. The MIT Press, Cambridge, Mass., 1993.
4. J. Chaumier and M. Dejean. L'indexation assistée par ordinateur, principes et méthodes. *Documentaliste - Sciences de l'information*, 29(1):3-6, 1992.
5. C. Desjardins, C. Riccardi-Rigault, P. Plante, L. Dumas, and F. Henri. ACTIA. In F. Maurer, editor, *2nd Knowledge Engineering Forum*, number SFB 501 Bericht 01/96, Kaiserslautern University, Germany, 1996.
6. S.K. Fall, T.C. Crawford, S.L. Souders, and M.J. Rabin. Automated knowledge acquisition technics for intelligence analysts. AAI, 1095 of SPIE:66-77, 1989.
7. B.R. Gaines and M.L.G. Shaw. Using knowledge acquisition and representation tools to support scientific communities. In *Proceedings of the Twelve National Conference on Artificial Intelligence*, volume 1, pages 707-712. AAAI Press, 1994.
8. M.A. Hearst. Multi-paragraph segmentation of expository text. In *Proceedings of the 32nd Annual Meeting of the ACL*, Las Cruces, NM, June 1994.
9. P.S. Jacobs. Using statistical methods to improve knowledge-based news categorization. *IEEE Expert*, 8(2):13-23, April 1993.
10. K.A. Kaufman, R.S. Michalsky, and L. Kershberg. Knowledge extraction from database: design principles of the INLEN system. In *Proceedings of the 6th International Symposium on Methodology for Intelligent Systems*, number 542 in LNCS, pages 152-161, Berlin, 1991. Springer-Verlag.
11. M. Kendall and A. Stuart. *Inference and Relationship*, volume 2 of *The advanced Theory of Statistics*. Charles Griffin and Co Ltd, 1979.
12. S. Lapalut. Text clustering to support knowledge acquisition from documents. Technical Report RR-2639, INRIA U.R. de Sophia Antipolis, BP 93, 06902 Sophia Antipolis Cedex, 1995. ftp://ftp.inria.fr/INRIA/publication/RR/RR-2639.ps.gz.
13. S. Lapalut. How to handle multiple expertise from several experts: a general text clustering approach. In F. Maurer, editor, *2nd Knowledge Engineering Forum*, number SFB 501 Bericht 01/96, Kaiserslautern University, Germany, 1996.
14. B. Moulin and D. Rousseau. Automated knowledge acquisition from regulatory texts. *IEEE Expert*, 7(5):27-35, October 1992.
15. M.S. Register and N. Kannan. A hybrid architecture for text classification. In *Fourth International conference on Tools with Artificial Intelligence, TAI'92*, pages 286-92, Arlington, VA, USA, 1992. IEEE Compu. Soc. Press.
16. M. Reinert. *Classification descendante hiérarchique pour l'analyse de contenu et traitement statistique de corpus*. PhD thesis, Université Paris 6, Paris, 1979.
17. M. Reinert. *Notice du logiciel ALCESTE, version 2.0*, 1992.
18. M.L.G. Shaw and B.R. Gaines. KITTEN: Knowledge initiation and transfert tools for experts and novices. *Int. J. Man-Machine Studies*, 27:251-280, 1987.
19. Z.B. Wu, L.S. Hsu, and C.L Tan. A survey on statistical approaches to natural language processing. technical report TRA4/92, Departement of Information Systems and Computer Science, National University of Singapore, Kent Ridge, Singapore 0511, April 1992.

A Quality-Based Terminological Reasoning Model for Text Knowledge Acquisition

Udo Hahn, Manfred Klenner & Klemens Schnattinger

Freiburg University
⟨Œᶠ⟩ Computational Linguistics Group
Europaplatz 1, D-79085 Freiburg, Germany
{hahn,klenner,schnattinger}@coling.uni-freiburg.de

Abstract We introduce a methodology for knowledge acquisition and concept learning from texts that relies upon a quality-based model of terminological reasoning. Concept hypotheses which have been derived in the course of the text understanding process are assigned specific "quality labels" (indicating their significance, reliability, strength). Quality assessment of these hypotheses accounts for conceptual criteria referring to their given knowledge base context as well as linguistic indicators (grammatical constructions, discourse patterns), which led to their generation. We advocate a metareasoning approach which allows for the quality-based evaluation and a bootstrapping-style selection of alternative concept hypotheses as text understanding incrementally proceeds.

1 Introduction

The work reported in this paper is part of a large-scale project aiming at the development of a German-language text knowledge acquisition system for two real-world application domains — test reports on information technology products (current corpus size: approximately 100 documents with 10^5 words) and medical findings reports (current corpus size: approximately 120,000 documents with 10^7 words). The concept acquisition problem we face is two-fold. In the information technology domain lexical *growth* occurs at dramatic rates – new products, technologies, companies and people continuously enter the scene such that any attempt at keeping track of these lexical innovations by hand-coding is clearly precluded. Compared with these dynamics, the medical domain is lexically more stable but the sheer *size* of its sublanguage (conservative estimates range about 10^6 lexical items/concepts) also cannot reasonably be coded by humans in advance. Therefore, the designers of text understanding systems for such challenging applications have to find ways to automate lexical/concept learning as a prerequisite and, at the same time, as a constituent part of the text knowledge acquisition process. Unlike the current mainstream with its focus on statistically based learning methodologies (Lewis, 1991; Resnik, 1992; Sekine et al., 1992), we advocate a symbolically rooted learning approach in order to break the concept acquisition bottleneck, one which is based on expressively rich (terminological) knowledge representation models of the underlying domain (Hahn et al., 1996b; Hastings, 1996).

We consider the problem of natural language based knowledge acquisition and concept learning from a new methodological perspective, *viz.* one based on metareasoning about statements expressed in a terminological knowledge representation language. Reasoning is about *structural linguistic* properties of phrasal patterns or discourse contexts in which unknown words occur (assuming that the type of grammatical construction exercises a particular interpretative force on the unknown lexical item), or it is about *conceptual properties* of particular concept hypotheses as they are generated and continuously refined by the ongoing text understanding process (e.g., consistency relative to already given knowledge, independent justification from several sources). Each of these grammatical, discourse or conceptual indicators is assigned a particular "quality" label. The application of quality macro operators, taken from a "qualification calculus" (Schnattinger & Hahn, 1996), to these atomic quality labels finally determines which out of several alternative hypotheses actually hold(s).

The decision for a metareasoning approach is motivated by requirements which emerged from our work in the overlapping fields of natural language parsing and learning from texts. Both tasks are characterized by the common need to evaluate alternative representation structures, either reflecting parsing ambiguities or multiple concept hypotheses. For instance, in the course of concept learning from texts, various and often conflicting concept hypotheses for a single item are formed as the learning environment usually provides only inconclusive evidence for exactly determining the properties of the concept to be learned. Moreover, in "realistic" natural language understanding systems working with large text corpora, the underdetermination of results can often not only be attributed to incomplete knowledge provided for that concept in the data (source texts), but it may also be due to imperfect parsing results (originating from lacking lexical, grammatical, conceptual specifications, or ungrammatical input). Therefore, competing hypotheses at different levels of validity and reliability are the rule rather than the exception and, thus, require appropriate formal treatment. Accordingly, we view the problem of choosing from among several alternatives as a *quality-based decision task* which can be decomposed into three constituent parts: the continuous generation of quality labels for single hypotheses (reflecting the *reasons* for their formation and their significance in the light of other hypotheses), the estimation of the overall *credibility* of single hypotheses (taking the available set of quality labels for each hypothesis into account), and the computation of a *preference order* for the entire set of competing hypotheses, which is based on these accumulated quality judgments.

2 Architecture for Quality-Based Knowledge Acquisition

The knowledge acquisition and concept learning methodology we propose is heavily based on the representation and reasoning facilities provided by terminological knowledge representation languages. As the representation of alternative hypotheses and their subsequent evaluation turn out to be major requirements of that approach, provisions have to be made to reflect these design decisions by an

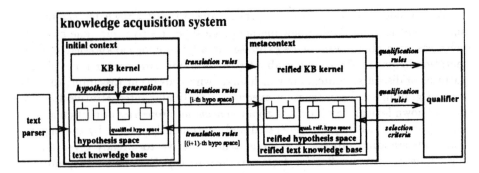

Figure1. Architecture for Text Knowledge Acquisition

appropriate system architecture of the knowledge acquisition device (cf. Fig. 1). In particular, mechanisms should be provided for:

- Expressing *quality-based assertions* about propositions in a terminological language; these metastatements capture the ascription of belief to these propositions, the reasons why they came into existence, the support/weakening they may have received from other propositions, etc.
- *Metareasoning* in a terminological knowledge base about characteristic properties and relations between certain propositions; the corresponding *second-order expressions* refer to factual propositions (ABox elements) as well as concept and role definitions (TBox elements).

The notion of context we use as a formal foundation for terminological meta-knowledge and metareasoning is based on McCarthy's context model (McCarthy, 1993). We here distinguish two types of contexts, *viz.* the initial context and the metacontext. The *initial context* contains the original terminological knowledge base *(KB kernel)* and the *text knowledge base,* a representation layer for the knowledge acquired from the underlying text by the text parser (Hahn et al., 1994). Knowledge in the initial context is represented without any explicit qualifications, attachments, provisos, etc. Note that in the course of text understanding – due to the working of the basic *hypothesis generation* rules (cf. Section 4) – a hypothesis space is created which contains alternative subspaces for each concept to be learned, each one holding different or further specialized concept hypotheses. Various truth-preserving *translation rules* map the description of the initial context to the *metacontext* which consists of the reified knowledge of the initial context (cf. Section 3). By *reification,* we mean a common reflective mechanism (Friedman & Wand, 1984), which splits up a predicative expression into its constituent parts and introduces a unique anchor term, the *reificator,* on which *reasoning about* this expression, e.g., the annotation by qualifying assertions, can be based. Among the reified structures in the metacontext there is a subcontext embedded, the *reified hypothesis space,* the elements of which carry several qualifications, e.g., reasons to believe a proposition, indications of consistency, type and strength of support, etc. These quality labels result from incremental hypothesis evaluation and subsequent hypothesis selection, and, thus, reflect the operation of several second-order *qualification rules* in the *qualifier* (*quality*-based *classifier*). The derived labels are the basis for the selection of those representation structures that are assigned a high degree of credibility – only those *qualified hypotheses* will be remapped to the hypothesis space of the initial context by way of (inverse) translation rules. Thus, we come full circle. In particular, at the end of each quality-based reasoning cycle the entire original i-th hypothesis space is replaced by its $(i+1)$-th successor in order to reflect the qualifications computed in the metacontext. The $(i+1)$-th hypothesis space is then the input of the next quality assessment round.

3 Formal Framework of Quality-Based Reasoning

Description Logics. We use a standard concept description language, referred to as $\mathcal{CDL}$, which has several constructors combining *atomic* concepts, roles and individuals to define the terminological theory of a domain (for a subset, see Table 1; Woods & Schmolze (1992) give a survey of terminological languages).

Concepts are unary predicates, *roles* are binary predicates over a domain Δ, with *individuals* being the elements of Δ. We assume a common set-theoretical semantics for $\mathcal{CDL}$ – an interpretation $\mathcal{I}$ is a function that assigns to each concept symbol (the set $\mathbf{A}$) a subset of the domain Δ, $\mathcal{I} : \mathbf{A} \to 2^\Delta$, to each role symbol (the set $\mathbf{P}$) a binary relation of Δ, $\mathcal{I} : \mathbf{P} \to 2^{\Delta \times \Delta}$, and to each individual symbol (the set $\mathbf{I}$) an element of Δ, $\mathcal{I} : \mathbf{I} \to \Delta$. *Concept terms* and *role terms* are defined inductively. Table 1 contains corresponding constructors and their semantics, where C and D denote concept terms, while R and S denote roles. $R^\mathcal{I}(d)$ represents the set of role fillers of the individual d, i.e., the set of individuals e with $(d, e) \in R^\mathcal{I}$.

By means of *terminological axioms* (for a subset, see Table 2) a symbolic name can be introduced for each concept. It is possible to define necessary and sufficient constraints (using $\doteq$) or only necessary constraints (using $\sqsubseteq$). A finite set of such axioms is called the *terminology* or *TBox*. Concepts and roles are associated with concrete individuals by *assertional axioms* (see Table 2; a, b denote individuals). A finite set of such axioms is called the *world description* or *ABox*. An *interpretation* $\mathcal{I}$ is a model of an ABox with regard to a TBox, iff $\mathcal{I}$ satisfies the assertional and terminological axioms. Terminology and world description together constitute the *terminological theory* for a given domain.

Syntax	Semantics
C_{atom}	$\{d \in C^\mathcal{I}_{atom} \mid C_{atom} \text{ is atomic}\}$
$C \sqcap D$	$C^\mathcal{I} \cap D^\mathcal{I}$
$C \sqcup D$	$C^\mathcal{I} \cup D^\mathcal{I}$
$\exists R.C$	$\{d \in \Delta^\mathcal{I} \mid R^\mathcal{I}(d) \cap C^\mathcal{I} \neq \emptyset\}$
$\forall R.C$	$\{d \in \Delta^\mathcal{I} \mid R^\mathcal{I}(d) \subseteq C^\mathcal{I}\}$
R_{atom}	$\{(d, e) \in R^\mathcal{I}_{atom} \mid R_{atom} \text{ is atomic}\}$
$R \sqcap S$	$R^\mathcal{I} \cap S^\mathcal{I}$

Table1. Syntax and Semantics for a Subset of $\mathcal{CDL}$

Terminological Axioms	
Axiom	Semantics
$A \doteq C$	$A^\mathcal{I} = C^\mathcal{I}$
$A \sqsubseteq C$	$A^\mathcal{I} \subseteq C^\mathcal{I}$
Assertional Axioms	
Axiom	Semantics
$a : C$	$a^\mathcal{I} \in C^\mathcal{I}$
$a \, R \, b$	$(a^\mathcal{I}, b^\mathcal{I}) \in R^\mathcal{I}$

Table2. $\mathcal{CDL}$ Axioms

$\Re(a:C) = r : \text{REIF} \sqcap r \text{ BINARY-REL INST-OF} \sqcap r \text{ DOMAIN } a \sqcap r \text{ RANGE } C \sqcap r \text{ HYPO } H$
$\Re(a \; R \; b) = r : \text{REIF} \sqcap r \text{ BINARY-REL } R \sqcap r \text{ DOMAIN } a \sqcap r \text{ RANGE } b \sqcap r \text{ HYPO } H$

Table3. Sketch of the Reification Function $\Re$

Reification. Let us assume that any hypothesis space H contains a characteristic terminological theory. In order to reason about that theory we split up the complex terminological terms by means of reification. We here define the (bijective) *reification* function $\Re(t.term_H) = r.term$, where $t.term_H$ is a terminological term known to be true in the hypothesis space H and $r.term$ is its corresponding reified term, which is composed of the reificator (an instance of the concept class REIF), the type of binary relation involved (including INST-OF and ISA), the relation's domain and range, and the identifier of the hypothesis space in which the term holds. Table 3 gives two definitions for $\Re$, more complex ones are provided in Schnattinger et al. (1995). By analogy, we may also define the function $\Re^{-1}$ with the corresponding inverse mapping.

Given the set $\mathcal{R}$ which denotes all $\Re(x \; R \; y)$ and the set $\mathcal{P}$ of all instances p of the class REIF (i.e., $p : \text{REIF}$), we supply the function $\pi : \mathcal{R} \mapsto \mathcal{P}$, which maps each reified term to the corresponding instance of REIF, i.e., the reificator:

$$\pi \left(\Re \left(x \; R \; y \right) \right) \equiv \pi \left(p : \text{REIF} \sqcap p \text{ BINARY-REL } R \sqcap \right.$$
$$\left. p \text{ DOMAIN } x \sqcap p \text{ RANGE } y \sqcap p \text{ HYPO } H \right) = \quad p$$

Translation between Contexts. *Translation rules* are syntactic transformations which derive sentences in the metacontext that are equivalent to sentences in the initial context. A translation rule from context κ to context κ' is any axiom of the form $\text{ist}(\kappa, \phi) \leftrightarrow \text{ist}(\kappa', \phi')$, with ϕ and ϕ' being formulas. These translation rules are lifting rules in the sense of McCarthy (1993), as they also relate the truth in one context to the truth in another one.

Instead of supplying a translation rule for each conceptual role from the set $\mathbf{P}$, for brevity, we state a single second-order axiom such that the initial context be translatable to the metacontext under truth-preserving conditions:

$$\forall R : R \in \mathbf{P} \; \rightarrow \; (\forall d, r \; \exists p, q : \text{ist}(initial, \; d \; R \; r) \leftrightarrow$$
$$\text{ist}(meta, \; \pi(\Re(d \; R \; r)) = p \sqcap p \text{ QUALIFIED } q))$$

In the metacontext, qualifications can now be expressed instantiating the specific role QUALIFIED by a qualifying assertion with respect to some reificator.

In a similar way, we may construct a translation scheme which (re)translates the metacontext to the initial context. This rule incorporates the quality of some reified element p, which must exceed a specific threshold criterion (cf. Sec. 5).

4 Hypothesis Generation

In the architecture we propose, text parsing and concept acquisition from texts are tightly coupled. For instance, whenever two nominals or a nominal and a verb are supposed to be syntactically related the semantic interpreter simultaneously evaluates the conceptual compatibility of the items involved. Since these reasoning processes are fully embedded into a terminological knowledge representation system, checks are being made whether a concept denoted by one of these objects can fill a role of the other one or is an instance of this concept. If one of the items involved is unknown, i.e., a lexical or conceptual gap is encountered, this interpretation mode generates initial concept hypotheses about the class membership of the unknown object, and, as a consequence of inheritance mechanisms, provides conceptual role information for the unknown item.

Besides these conceptually rooted computations, the hypothesis generation process also assigns labels which indicate the type of syntactic construction under analysis. These labels convey information about the language-specific provenance of the hypotheses and their individual strength. This idea is based on the observation that syntactic constructions differ in their potential to limit the degrees of freedom for conceptually interpreting an unknown lexical item and thus to constrain the range of plausible inferences that can be drawn to properly locate its associated concept in the domain's concept hierarchy. For example, an apposition like "the operating system OS/2" doubtlessly determines the superclass of "OS/2" (here considered as an unknown item) to be "operating system", while "IBM's OS/2" at best allows to infer that "OS/2" is one of the products of IBM (e.g., a computer or a piece of software). Thus we may stipulate that hypotheses derived from appositions are more reliable ("certain") than those derived from genitival phrases only, independent of the conceptual properties being assigned.

The general form of a parser query (cf. also Fig. 1) triggering the generation of hypotheses is: $\texttt{query-type}(target, base, label)$, with $target$ being the unknown lexical item, $base$ a given knowledge base concept, and $label$ being the type of syntactic construction which relates $base$ and $target$. In the following, we will concentrate on two particular instances of query types, $viz.$ those addressing permitted role fillers and instance-of relations, respectively.

The basic assumption behind the permitted role filler rule, $PermHypo$ (Table 4), is that the target concept fills (exactly) one of the n roles of the base concept (only those roles are considered which admit nonnumerical role fillers and are "non-closed", i.e., still may accept additional role fillers). Since it cannot be decided on the correct role yet, n alternative hypotheses are opened (unless additional constraints apply) and the target concept is assigned as a potential filler of the i-th role in its corresponding hypothesis space. As a result, the classifier is able to derive a suitable concept hypothesis by specializing the target concept (initial status "unknown") according to the value restriction of the base concept's i-th role. Additionally, $PermHypo$ assigns a syntactic quality label to each i-th hypothesis indicating the type of syntactic construction in which the (lexical counterparts of the) target and base concept co-occur in the text. These qualifying assertions are expressed at the terminological level by linking the reificator of a terminological term via a role QUALIFIED to a qualifying proposition.

In the syntactic qualification rules described in Tables 4 and 5 the symbol $\Longrightarrow$ separates the condition part (starting from the operator **EXISTS**) from the action part (containing the **TELL** operator). The procedural semantics of the operators **FORALL** and **EXISTS** should be intuitively clear; the operator **TELL** is used to initiate the assertion of terminological terms. Furthermore, $target \in \mathbf{I}$, $base \in \mathbf{I}$ and $label \in PermSynLabel = \{$PP-ATTRIBUTION,GENITIVE-

---

IF parser queries: `permitted-role-filler`$(target, base, label)$
THEN
FORALL $i \in [1..n]$ **DO** {n being the number of admitted roles}
  generate($base$ ROLE$_i$ $target$)
  EXISTS q_i :
  $\pi(\Re(base \text{ ROLE}_i target))$ QUALIFIED q_i $\Longrightarrow$
  TELL q_i : $label$

Table4. Qualification Rule *PermHypo*

ATTRIBUTION, CASE-FRAME-ASSIGNMENT}, which is a subset of the syntactic quality labels.[1] **generate** is a function that – in the initial context – either retrieves an already existing hypothesis space containing a particular terminological assertion, or, if no such hypothesis space exists, creates or specializes a hypothesis space and asserts a particular terminological term in this newly constructed hypothesis space. A transformation rule immediately maps this terminological assertion to its reified form in the metacontext.

As an example how *PermHypo* might work, consider the occurrence of a base and a target concept in a sentence fragment such as "a computer with OS/2", and let "OS/2" be the target concept. The base concept COMPUTER has multiple attributes encoded in the domain's knowledge base, e.g., relating it to conceptual representations of a motherboard, hard disks, a monitor, and software. Each of these roles must be taken into account as a provisionally valid hypothesis for the correct integration of "OS/2". We thus get at least four initial hypotheses: OS/2 INST-OF MOTHERBOARD, OS/2 INST-OF HARDDISK, OS/2 INST-OF MONITOR, OS/2 INST-OF SOFTWARE. Additionally, any of these hypotheses receives the syntactic quality label PP-ATTRIBUTION.

The second qualification rule, *SubHypo* (Table 5), is triggered if a target has been encountered in an exemplification phrase ("operating systems like OS/2"), as part of a composite noun ("the WORM technology") or occurs in an apposition ("the operating system OS/2"). As a consequence, an instance-of relation between the target and the base item is hypothesized and, in addition, that syntactic quality label is asserted which indicates the language-specific construction figuring as the structural source for that hypothesis. In the expression below, $target \in \mathbf{I}$, $base \in \mathbf{A}$ and $label \in SubSynLabel = \{$EXEMPLIFICATION-NP, NOUN-DECOMPOSITION, APPOSITION-ASSIGNMENT}, which is another subset of the syntactic quality labels.

Hypothesis generation is not limited to the initial parser queries and immediate actions taken in the text knowledge base, but also occurs as a result of incremental terminological reasoning (classification) and semantic interpretation processes (e.g, verb interpretation). For instance, upon the generation or the retrieval of a hypothesis space the classifier consequently either forms a new

---

[1] Note that variants of the *PermHypo* rule exist which allow the base and the target object to be elements of the T-Box (i.e., $target \in \mathbf{A}$, $base \in \mathbf{A}$) rather than being elements of the A-Box, as stipulated for rule *PermHypo*. This accounts for the fact that, e.g., the referents of plural terms (e.g., "computers with PCI-boards") denote *classes* of objects (i.e., concepts) rather than *individuals* (i.e., instances).

> **IF** **parser queries: instance-of**$(target, base, label)$
> **THEN**
>   **generate**$(target : base)$
>   **EXISTS** q :
> $\pi(\Re(target : base))$ QUALIFIED q $\implies$
>   **TELL** q : $label$

Table5. Qualification Rule *SubHypo*

initial hypothesis on the target object, or it refines, confirms or rejects previously derived hypotheses. In all these cases corresponding quality labels are asserted which mirror the reasons on which the corresponding operations were based. Similarily, as a consequence of the completion of the case frame assignment process, verb interpretation rules are triggered which relate the arguments of the concept denoted by the verb to each other so that new conceptual relations emerge (for a fully worked out example, cf. Section 6).

5 Quality-based Reasoning

We here focus on additional mechanisms for the generation of quality labels for concept hypotheses (based on conceptual criteria holding at the knowledge representation level only), the continuous assessment of their credibility and the selection of the most credible concept hypotheses at the end of text analysis.

Concept-Based Generation of Quality Labels. In order to further constrain the hypotheses derived during the hypothesis generation phase, we supply second-order conceptual qualification rules (sketched below; for a detailed formal treatment, cf. Hahn et al. (1996b)). These are used to reason about the properties of (first-order) terminological descriptions available from the parser or the hypothesis generator and to derive purely conceptually-based quality labels for various concept hypotheses:

I: The *very positive* quality label MULTIPLY-DEDUCED is generated whenever the same role filler has been multiply derived in different hypothesis spaces.

II: The conceptual proximity of role fillers of a (non-ACTION) concept, which share a common concept class leads to the *positive* quality label SUPPORTED.

III: The inherent symmetry between two instances mutually related via two quasi-inverse relations (figuring as "inverted" role fillers of each other) is expressed by the *positive* quality label CROSS-SUPPORTED.

IV: The negative assessment for any attempt to fill the same mandatory case role of an ACTION concept more than once by different role fillers is expressed by the *negative* quality label ADDITIONAL-ROLE-FILLER.

Assessment of Quality Labels. During each learning step several qualification rules may fire and thus generate various quality labels. In order to select the most credible hypotheses from each cycle, we take the direction (positive/negative) and the individual 'strength' of each label into account by formulating the following *Threshold Criterion*:

> Select all hypothesis spaces that do not contain any quality label INCON-SISTENT-HYPO. Additionally, at least one APPOSITION-ASSIGNMENT label or the maximum number of CASE-FRAME-ASSIGNMENT labels (which lead to the firing of verb interpretation rules (cf. Section 6)) is required. If several of these hypothesis spaces exist, the one(s) with the least number of ADDITIONAL-ROLE-FILLER labels is (are) chosen.

Ranking of Hypotheses. Only those hypotheses that continuously reach the credibility threshold after each quality assessment cycle are transferred from the metacontext back to the initial context. At the end of the text analysis a final ranking of those concept hypotheses is produced that have repeatedly passed the *Threshold Criterion* by applying the following *Ranked Prediction Criterion*:

> Select all hypothesis spaces with the maximum number of MULTIPLY-DEDUCED labels. If there are more than one, rank these spaces in decreasing order according to the number of SUPPORTED labels they contain. If there are more than one with the same maximum number of MULTIPLY-DEDUCED and SUPPORTED labels, rank these spaces in decreasing order according to the number of CROSS-SUPPORTED labels.

6 A Concept Acquisition Example

We will now exemplify quality-based terminological reasoning by considering a concept acquisition task in the domain of information technology. As a result of applying syntactic and conceptual qualification rules different degrees of credibility are assigned to concept hypotheses and, finally, one hypothesis is selected as the most credible one. Let us assume the following terminological axioms:

PRODUCT $\doteq$ PHYSICAL-OBJECT $\sqcap$ $\forall$HAS-DEVELOPER.PRODUCER
HARDWARE $\doteq$ PRODUCT $\sqcap$ $\forall$HAS-WEIGHT.WEIGHT
NOTEBOOK $\doteq$ HARDWARE $\sqcap$ $\forall$HAS-DISPLAY.LCD-DISPLAY
ACCU $\doteq$ HARDWARE $\sqcap$ $\forall$ENERGY-FOR.NOTEBOOK
COMPANY $\doteq$ PHYSICAL-OBJECT $\sqcap$ $\forall$PRODUCES.PRODUCT
PRODUCER $\doteq$ COMPANY $\sqcap$ $\forall$PRODUCES.HARDWARE
NOTEBOOK-PRODUCER $\doteq$ PRODUCER $\sqcap$ $\exists$PRODUCES.(NOTEBOOK $\sqcup$ ACCU)
OFFER $\sqsubseteq$ ACTION $\sqcap$ $\forall$AGENT.PRODUCER $\sqcap$ $\forall$PATIENT.PRODUCT
DEVELOP $\sqsubseteq$ ACTION $\sqcap$ $\forall$AGENT.PRODUCER $\sqcap$ $\forall$PATIENT.HARDWARE

In addition, the following reified assertional axioms are stipulated (cf. Sec. 3):

$p_1 = \pi(\Re(Compaq : \text{NOTEBOOK-PRODUCER})) \sqcap p_1 \text{ QUALIFIED } q_1$
$p_2 = \pi(\Re(Compaq : \text{PRODUCER})) \sqcap p_2 \text{ QUALIFIED } q_2$
$p_3 = \pi(\Re(Compaq : \text{COMPANY})) \sqcap p_3 \text{ QUALIFIED } q_3$
$p_4 = \pi(\Re(Compaq : \text{PHYSICAL-OBJECT})) \sqcap p_4 \text{ QUALIFIED } q_4$
$p_5 = \pi(\Re(Compaq \text{ PRODUCES } LTE\text{-}Lite)) \sqcap p_5 \text{ QUALIFIED } q_5$
$p_6 = \pi(\Re(LTE\text{-}Lite \text{ HAS-DEVELOPER } Compaq)) \sqcap p_6 \text{ QUALIFIED } q_6$
$p_7 = \pi(\Re(LTE\text{-}Lite : \text{NOTEBOOK})) \sqcap p_7 \text{ QUALIFIED } q_7$
$p_8 = \pi(\Re(LTE\text{-}Lite : \text{HARDWARE})) \sqcap p_8 \text{ QUALIFIED } q_8$
$p_9 = \pi(\Re(LTE\text{-}Lite : \text{PRODUCT})) \sqcap p_9 \text{ QUALIFIED } q_9$

$p_{10} = \pi(\Re(LTE\text{-}Lite : \text{Physical-Object}))$ $\sqcap$ p_{10} QUALIFIED q_{10}

$p_{11} = \pi(\Re(NiMH\text{-}Accu \text{ ENERGY-FOR } LTE\text{-}Lite))$ $\sqcap$ p_{11} QUALIFIED q_{11}

$p_{12} = \pi(\Re(NiMH\text{-}Accu : \text{Accu}))$ $\sqcap$ p_{12} QUALIFIED q_{12}

$p_{13} = \pi(\Re(NiMH\text{-}Accu : \text{Hardware}))$ $\sqcap$ p_{13} QUALIFIED q_{13}

$p_{14} = \pi(\Re(NiMH\text{-}Accu : \text{Product}))$ $\sqcap$ p_{14} QUALIFIED q_{14}

$p_{15} = \pi(\Re(NiMH\text{-}Accu : \text{Physical-Object}))$ $\sqcap$ p_{15} QUALIFIED q_{15}

Finally, two (simplified) verb interpretation rules are supplied mapping lexical items onto "conceptually entailed" propositions of the text knowledge base:

EXISTS v, a, p: v : DEVELOP $\sqcap$ v AGENT a $\sqcap$ v PATIENT p $\Longrightarrow$
TELL p HAS-DEVELOPER a

EXISTS v, a, p: v : OFFER $\sqcap$ v AGENT a $\sqcap$ v PATIENT p $\Longrightarrow$
TELL a PRODUCES p

Consider the phrase "Marktanalytiker bestätigen, daß **Compaq** seit Jahren erfolgreich **LTE-Lites anbietet** und seit kurzem auch *Venturas*." Assuming *Venturas* to be the target concept, two ambiguities arise (these are rephrased in English terms): (1) "Market analysts say that Compaq has been successfully offering LTE-Lites for many years and *Venturas* [AGENT] has recently begun to do so as well." *vs.* (2) "Market analysts say that Compaq has been successfully offering LTE-Lites for many years and has recently begun to offer *Venturas* [PATIENT] as well.". For the first part of the sentence (up to "anbietet" *(offer)*), the parser incrementally generates a new instance of OFFER, assigns *Compaq* as AGENT and *LTE-Lite* as PATIENT of that instance (it has not yet encountered the unknown item *Venturas*). Thus, we get:

$p_{16} = \pi(\Re(offer\text{-}01 : \text{Offer}))$ $\sqcap$ p_{16} QUALIFIED q_{16}

$p_{17} = \pi(\Re(offer\text{-}01 \text{ AGENT } Compaq))$ $\sqcap$ p_{17} QUALIFIED q_{17}

$p_{18} = \pi(\Re(offer\text{-}01 \text{ PATIENT } LTE\text{-}Lite))$ $\sqcap$ p_{18} QUALIFIED q_{18}

The verb interpretation rule for OFFER has no effects, since $\langle Compaq$ PRODUCES $LTE\text{-}Lite\rangle$ is already true (p_5).

As already mentioned, the unknown item *Venturas* can either be related to *LTE-Lite* via the AGENT role or to *Compaq* via the PATIENT role of OFFER. This is achieved by the application of the hypothesis generation rule *PermHypo* (Table 4) that opens two hypothesis subspaces, **H1** and **H2**, for each interpretation of *Venturas*. Their reified counterparts, $\mathbf{H_r 1}$ and $\mathbf{H_r 2}$, are assigned the syntactic quality label CASE-FRAME-ASSIGNMENT (for the ease of readability, we will defer the consideration of syntactic quality labels in the formal descriptions of the current example until they contribute to the discrimination between different hypotheses in later stages of the sample analysis).

The creation of p_{19} (together with p_{17}) triggers the generation of two quality labels ADDITIONAL-ROLE-FILLER according to rule IV from Section 5 (note that for *both* spaces the propositions p_1 to p_{18} are assumed to hold). p_{19}, p_{18} and p_{16} cause the verb interpretation rule for OFFER to fire yielding p_{20}. Applying the terminological axioms for OFFER leads to the deduction of p_{21} (the AGENT role of

OFFER restricts any of its fillers to PRODUCER and its taxonomic superconcepts, viz. COMPANY (p_{22}) and PHYSICAL-OBJECT (p_{23}), by way of transitive closure). In particular, H_r1, which covers the AGENT interpretation contains the following assertions (p_{19} to p_{23}):

$$p_{19} = \pi(\Re(offer\text{-}01 \text{ AGENT } Venturas)) \sqcap p_{19} \text{ QUALIFIED } q_{19} \sqcap$$
$$q_{19} : \text{ADDITIONAL-ROLE-FILLER} \sqcap q_{17} : \text{ADDITIONAL-ROLE-FILLER}$$
$$p_{20} = \pi(\Re(Venturas \text{ PRODUCES } LTE\text{-}Lite)) \sqcap p_{20} \text{ QUALIFIED } q_{20}$$
$$p_{21} = \pi(\Re(Venturas : \text{PRODUCER})) \sqcap p_{21} \text{ QUALIFIED } q_{21}$$
$$p_{22} = \pi(\Re(Venturas : \text{COMPANY})) \sqcap p_{22} \text{ QUALIFIED } q_{22}$$
$$p_{23} = \pi(\Re(Venturas : \text{PHYSICAL-OBJECT})) \sqcap p_{23} \text{ QUALIFIED } q_{23} \sqcap$$
$$q_{23} : \text{MULTIPLY-DEDUCED}$$

On the other hand, H_r2 (p_{24} to p_{28}) covers the PATIENT interpretation:

$$p_{24} = \pi(\Re(offer\text{-}01 \text{ PATIENT } Venturas)) \sqcap p_{24} \text{ QUALIFIED } q_{24} \sqcap$$
$$q_{24} : \text{ADDITIONAL-ROLE-FILLER} \sqcap q_{18} : \text{ADDITIONAL-ROLE-FILLER}$$
$$p_{25} = \pi(\Re(Compaq \text{ PRODUCES } Venturas)) \sqcap p_{25} \text{ QUALIFIED } q_{25}$$
$$p_{26} = \pi(\Re(Venturas : \text{PRODUCT})) \sqcap p_{26} \text{ QUALIFIED } q_{26} \sqcap$$
$$q_{26} : \text{SUPPORTED}$$
$$p_{27} = \pi(\Re(Venturas : \text{PHYSICAL-OBJECT})) \sqcap p_{27} \text{ QUALIFIED } q_{27} \sqcap$$
$$q_{27} : \text{SUPPORTED} \sqcap q_{27} : \text{MULTIPLY-DEDUCED}$$
$$p_{28} = \pi(\Re(Venturas : \text{HARDWARE})) \sqcap p_{28} \text{ QUALIFIED } q_{28} \sqcap$$
$$q_{28} \text{ SUPPORTED}$$

In H_r2 all hypotheses generated for $Venturas$ (p_{26} to p_{28}) receive the quality label SUPPORTED, in H_r1 none. This support (cf. rule II from Section 5) is due to the conceptual proximity p_5 and p_9 have relative to p_{25} and p_{26}, respectively. Since both hypothesis spaces, H1 and H2, imply that $Venturas$ is at least a PHYSICAL-OBJECT the label MULTIPLY-DEDUCED (rule I from Section 5) is derived in the corresponding reified spaces, H_r1 and H_r2. Rule IV also triggers in H_r1 and H_r2, so it does not contribute to any further discrimination.[2]

H2 and thus H_r2, however, can further be refined. According to the terminological axioms, $Compaq$ – a NOTEBOOK-PRODUCER (p_1) – produces NOTE-BOOKs or ACCUs. Thus, $Venturas$, the filler of the PRODUCES role of $Compaq$ (p_{25}) must either be a NOTEBOOK (H_r2_1)

$$p_{29} = \pi(\Re(Venturas : \text{NOTEBOOK})) \sqcap p_{29} \text{ QUALIFIED } q_{29} \sqcap$$
$$q_{29} : \text{SUPPORTED}$$

or an ACCU (H_r2_2)

$$p_{30} = \pi(\Re(Venturas : \text{ACCU})) \sqcap p_{30} \text{ QUALIFIED } q_{30}$$

According to this distinction (cf. rule II), H_r2_1 (but not H_r2_2) is supported by $\langle Compaq$ PRODUCES $LTE\text{-}Lite \rangle$, $\langle LTE\text{-}Lite : \text{NOTEBOOK} \rangle$ and $\langle Compaq$ PRODUCES $Venturas \rangle$.

Since we operate with a partial parser, the linguistic analyses may remain incomplete due to extra- or ungrammatical input. Assume such a scenario as in:

---

[2] We only consider the derivation of quality labels referring to the target concept and leave away those labels that support propositions already contained in the *a priori* knowledge of the KB kernel.

"... **Venturas** ... **entwickelt** ... **Compaq**."[3] The parser triggers the hypothesis generation rule *PermHypo* on a presumed case frame assignment for the verb "entwickelt" *(develop)*. As a result, the newly generated (reified) hypotheses receive the same syntactic quality label, *viz.* CASE-FRAME-ASSIGNMENT. Due to the value restrictions that hold for DEVELOP, *Compaq* (*a priori* known to be a PRODUCER) may only fill the AGENT role. Correspondingly, in $\mathbf{H}_r 1$ and $\mathbf{H}_r 2$ the following reified propositions hold:

$$p_{31} = \pi(\Re(develop\text{-}02 : \text{DEVELOP})) \sqcap p_{31} \text{ QUALIFIED } q_{31} \sqcap$$
$$p_{32} = \pi(\Re(develop\text{-}02 \text{ AGENT } Compaq)) \sqcap p_{32} \text{ QUALIFIED } q_{32}$$

In **H1**, where *Venturas* is assumed to be a PRODUCER, *Venturas* (additionally to *Compaq*) may fill the AGENT role of DEVELOP, leading to $\mathbf{H}_r 1$:

$$p_{33} = \pi(\Re(develop\text{-}02 \text{ AGENT } Venturas)) \sqcap p_{33} \text{ QUALIFIED } q_{33} \sqcap$$
$$q_{33} : \text{ADDITIONAL-ROLE-FILLER} \sqcap q_{32} : \text{ADDITIONAL-ROLE-FILLER}$$

In **H2** and the spaces it subsumes, *viz.* $\mathbf{H2}_1$ and $\mathbf{H2}_2$, *Venturas* may only fill the PATIENT role. Given the occurrences of p_{31}, p_{32} and p_{34}, the verb interpretation rule for DEVELOP fires and produces p_{35}. This immediately leads to the generation of a CROSS-SUPPORTED label (rule III from Section 5) relative to proposition (p_{25}):

$$p_{34} = \pi(\Re(develop\text{-}02 \text{ PATIENT } Venturas)) \sqcap p_{34} \text{ QUALIFIED } q_{34} \sqcap$$
$$p_{35} = \pi(\Re(Venturas \text{ HAS-DEVELOPER } Compaq)) \sqcap p_{35} \text{ QUALIFIED } q_{35} \sqcap$$
$$q_{35} : \text{CROSS-SUPPORTED} \sqcap q_{25} : \text{CROSS-SUPPORTED}$$

Next, one of the interpretations of an ambiguous phrase such as "Die **NiMH-Akkus** von **Venturas** ..."[4] invalidates context $\mathbf{H2}_2$ (ACCU hypothesis) leading to the generation of the (entirely negative) quality label INCONSISTENT-HYPO in $\mathbf{H}_r 2_2$. The inconsistency is due to the fact that an accumulator cannot be part of another accumulator. For the hypothesis space $\mathbf{H}_r 1$ we get

$$p_{36} = \pi(\Re(Venturas \text{ PRODUCES } NiMH\text{-}Accu)) \sqcap p_{36} \text{ QUALIFIED } q_{36}$$

and for $\mathbf{H}_r 2_1$ we derive

$$p_{37} = \pi(\Re(NiMH\text{-}Accu \text{ ENERGY-FOR } Venturas)) \sqcap p_{37} \text{ QUALIFIED } q_{37} \sqcap$$
$$q_{29} : \text{SUPPORTED} \sqcap q_{28} : \text{SUPPORTED} \sqcap q_{26} : \text{SUPPORTED} \sqcap$$
$$q_{27} : \text{SUPPORTED}$$

As a consequence of the application of the rule *PermHypo*, the learner assigns to each reified hypothesis a syntactic label indicating that a prepositional phrase containing the target was attached to the base item (label PP-ATTRIBUTION).

Finally, consider the globally ambiguous sentence "Kein Wunder, daß der **Notebook Venturas** auf der Messe prämiert wurde.". Again, two readings are possible: (1) "There was no surprise at all that the Venturas notebook had been awarded at the fare" and (2) "There was no surprise at all that the notebook from [the manufacturer] Venturas had been awarded at the fare". Considering

---

[3] "... **Venturas** ... develops ... **Compaq**."

[4] "The **NiMH** accus as part of the **Venturas**..." provokes an inconsistency; this reading is opposed to "The **NiMH** accus supplied by **Venturas**..."

the first reading which implies VENTURAS to be a notebook, the *SubHypo* qualification rule (cf. Table 5) is triggered and assigns the (strong) syntactic label APPOSITION-ASSIGNMENT to proposition p_{29} from hypothesis space $\mathbf{H_r 2_1}$.

$$p_{29} = \pi(\Re(\textit{Venturas} : \text{NOTEBOOK})) \sqcap p_{29} \text{ QUALIFIED } q_{29} \sqcap$$
$$q_{29} : \text{APPOSITION-ASSIGNMENT}$$

On the other hand, the second reading (genitive phrase attachment) invokes the *PermHypo* rule and the assignment of the (weaker) syntactic label GENITIVE-ATTRIBUTION to proposition p_{38}. Note that the referent of "der Notebook Venturas" (*the notebook from Venturas*) has been resolved to *LTE-Lite* by the anaphor resolution component of our parser (Strube & Hahn (1995)). This reference resolution process is legitimated by hypothesis p_{20} of $\mathbf{H_r 1}$, *viz.* (*Venturas* PRODUCES *LTE-Lite*). Thus, we get for $\mathbf{H_r 1}$:

$$p_{38} = \pi(\Re(\textit{LTE-Lite} \text{ HAS-DEVELOPER } \textit{Venturas})) \sqcap p_{38} \text{ QUALIFIED } q_{38} \sqcap$$
$$q_{38} : \text{GENITIVE-ATTRIBUTION} \sqcap q_{21} : \text{SUPPORTED} \sqcap q_{22} : \text{SUPPORTED} \sqcap$$
$$q_{23} : \text{SUPPORTED} \sqcap q_{38} : \text{CROSS-SUPPORTED} \sqcap q_{20} : \text{CROSS-SUPPORTED}$$

Note that in our example we now encounter for the first time two *different* syntactic labels as derived from the *same* verbal input. This is due to the global ambiguity of the sentence. Up to this point, all reified hypothesis spaces have received the same type and number of syntactic quality labels (i.e., CASE-FRAME-ASSIGNMENT (2) and PP-ATTRIBUTION (1), respectively). Hence, considering only syntactic evaluation criteria, a ranking of hypotheses based on the *syntactic* quality labels would prefer $\mathbf{H2_1}$ over $\mathbf{H1}$, since the label APPOSITION-ASSIGNMENT (from $\mathbf{H_r 2_1}$) is stronger than the label GENITIVE-ATTRIBUTION (from $\mathbf{H_r 1}$), all other labels being equal.

Considering the collection of *conceptual* quality labels we have derived, this preliminary preference is further supported. The most promising hypothesis space is $\mathbf{H2_1}$ (covering the NOTEBOOK reading for *Venturas*) whose reified counterpart holds 10 positive labels: MULTIPLY-DEDUCED (1), SUPPORTED (8), CROSS-SUPPORTED (1),[5] but only one negative label (ADDITIONAL-ROLE-FILLER). In contrast, $\mathbf{H2_2}$ is ruled out, since an inconsistency has been detected by the classifier. Finally, $\mathbf{H_r 1}$ (holding the PRODUCER interpretation for *Venturas*) has received a weaker level of confirmation — MULTIPLY-DEDUCED (1), SUPPORTED (3), CROSS-SUPPORTED (1), and ADDITIONAL-ROLE-FILLER (2) — and $\mathbf{H1}$ is, therefore, less plausible than $\mathbf{H2_1}$ (cf. also the Ranked Prediction Criterion in Section 5). Summarizing our sample analysis, we, finally, have strong indications for choosing hypothesis $\mathbf{H2_1}$ over $\mathbf{H1}$ based on conceptual and syntactic assessment criteria, since they both point into the same direction (which, of course, needs not always be the case).

The preference aggregation scheme we have just sketched is based on a solid formal decision procedure which outweighs the contributions of different types

---

[5] Only those quality labels are considered which refer to the concept hypotheses under consideration. Quality labels which relate to *a priori* known concepts are simply discarded (namely, q_{17}, q_{18}, q_{32} : ADDITIONAL-ROLE-FILLER and q_{25}, q_{38} : CROSS-SUPPORTED).

and numbers of quality labels (Schnattinger & Hahn, 1996). A preliminary empirical test of our approach produced favorable results (Hahn et al., 1996a), but still suffers from the lack of sufficiently sized knowledge bases (the current test site contains approximately 650 concepts and 350 roles).

7 Related Work

Our approach bears a close relationship to the work of Mooney (1987), Martin (1992), and Hastings & Lytinen (1994), who aim at the automated learning of *word meanings* and their underlying concepts from context. But there is a main difference between their work and ours – the need to cope with *several competing* concept hypotheses is not an issue in these studies. Considering, however, the apparent limitations almost any parser available for realistic text understanding tasks currently suffers from (finally leading to the generation of partial parses only), usually more than one concept hypothesis can be derived from a given natural language input. Therefore, we stress the need for a hypothesis generation and evaluation component as an integral part of any robust natural language system that learns in tandem with such coverage-restricted devices.

Other systems aiming at text knowledge acquisition differ from our approach in that they either rely on hand-coded input (Skuce et al., 1985) or use overly simplistic keyword-based content analysis techniques (Agarwal & Tanniru, 1991), are restricted to a deductive learning mode (Handa & Ishizaki, 1989), use quantitative measures for uncertainty to evaluate the confidence of learned concept descriptions (as the WIT system, cf. Reimer (1990)), or lack the continuous refinement property of pursuing alternative hypotheses (as the SNOWY system, cf. Gomez & Segami (1990)). Nevertheless, WIT and SNOWY are closest to our approach, at least with respect to the text understanding methodologies being used, namely, the processing of realistic texts and the acquisition of taxonomic knowledge structures with the aid of a terminological representation system. The processing of written texts can, in general, be considered a major step towards the automation of knowledge acquisition (Virkar & Roach, 1989) which, so far, has been entirely dominated by interactive modes in a dialogue setting, e.g., KALEX (Schmidt & Wetter, 1989) or AKE (Gao & Salveter, 1991).

8 Conclusion

We have introduced a methodology for knowledge acquisition and concept learning from texts that relies upon terminological (meta)reasoning. Concept hypotheses which have been derived in the course of the text understanding process are assigned specific "quality labels" (indicating their significance, reliability, strength). Quality assessment of hypotheses accounts for conceptual criteria referring to their given knowledge base context as well as linguistic indicators (grammatical constructions, discourse patterns), which led to their generation.

Metareasoning, as we conceive it, is based on the reification of terminological expressions, the assignment of qualifications to these reified structures, and the reasoning about degrees of credibility these qualifications give rise to based on the evaluation of second-order qualification rules. Thus, the metareasoning approach we advocate allows for the quality-based evaluation and a bootstrapping-style selection of alternative concept hypotheses as text understanding incrementally proceeds. A major constraint underlying our work is that this kind of quality-based metareasoning is completely embedded in the homogeneous framework of standard (first-order) terminological reasoning systems using multiple contexts, so that we may profit from their full-blown classification mechanisms.

The applicability of this terminological metareasoning framework has been shown for a concept acquisition task in the framework of realistic text understanding. We are currently focusing on the formulation of additional qualification rules and query types, the formalization of a qualification calculus which captures the evaluation logic of multiple quality labels within a terminological framework (Schnattinger & Hahn, 1996), and an in-depth empirical evaluation of our approach based on a large corpus of texts (Hahn et al., 1996a). The knowledge acquisition and learning system described in this paper has been fully implemented in LOOM (MacGregor, 1994).

Acknowledgments. This work was supported by a grant from DFG under the account Ha 2097/2-1. We like to thank the members of our group for fruitful discussions. We also gratefully acknowledge the provision of the LOOM system from USC/ISI.

References

Agarwal, R. & M. Tanniru (1991). Knowledge extraction using content analysis. *Knowledge Acquisition*, 3(4):421–441.

Friedman, D. & M. Wand (1984). Reification: reflection without metaphysics. In *Proc. of the 1984 ACM Symposium on Lisp and Functional Programming*, pp. 348–355. Austin, Texas, August 1984.

Gao, Y. & S. Salveter (1991). The Automated Knowledge Engineer: natural language knowledge acquisition for expert systems. In *Proc. 6th Knowledge Acquisition for Knowledge-Based Systems Workshop*, pp. 8.1–8.16. Banff, Canada.

Gomez, F. & C. Segami (1990). Knowledge acquisition from natural language for expert systems based on classification problem-solving methods. *Knowledge Acquisition*, 2(2):107–128.

Hahn, U., M. Klenner & K. Schnattinger (1996a). Automatic concept acquisition from real-world texts. In *Proc. of the AAAI Spring Symposium on 'Machine Learning in Information Access'*. Stanford, Cal., March 1996. San Mateo, CA: AAAI Press.

Hahn, U., M. Klenner & K. Schnattinger (1996b). Learning from texts: a terminological metareasoning perspective. In S. Wermter, E. Riloff & G. Scheler (Eds.), *Connectionist, Statistical and Symbolic Approaches to Learning in Natural Language Processing*, pp. 453–468. Berlin: Springer.

Hahn, U., S. Schacht & N. Bröker (1994). Concurrent, object-oriented dependency parsing: the PARSETALK model. *International Journal of Human-Computer Studies*, 41(1-2):179–222.

Handa, K. & S. Ishizaki (1989). Acquiring knowledge about a relation between concepts. In *EKAW'89 - Proc. Europ. Knowledge Acquisition Workshop*, pp. 380–390.

Hastings, P. (1996). Implications of an automatic lexical acquisition system. In S. Wermter, E. Riloff & G. Scheler (Eds.), *Connectionist, Statistical and Symbolic Approaches to Learning in Natural Language Processing*, pp. 261–274. Springer.

Hastings, P. & S. Lytinen (1994). The ups and downs of lexical acquisition. In *AAAI'94 - Proc. of the 12th National Conf. on Artificial Intelligence. Vol. 2*, pp. 754–759. Seattle, Wash., July/August 1994. Menlo Park: AAAI Press/MIT Press.

Lewis, D. (1991). Learning in intelligent information retrieval. In L. Birnbaum & G. Collins (Eds.), *Machine Learning: Proc. of the 8th Intl. Workshop*, pp. 235–239. Chicago, Ill., June 1991. San Mateo, CA: Morgan Kaufmann.

MacGregor, R. (1994). A description classifier for the predicate calculus. In *AAAI'94 - Proc. of the 12th National Conf. on Artificial Intelligence. Vol. 1*, pp. 213–220. Seattle, Wash., July/August 1994. Menlo Park: AAAI Press/MIT Press.

Martin, W. (1992). Concept-oriented parsing of definitions. In *COLING'92 - Proc. 15th Intl. Conf. on Computational Linguistics*, pp. 988–992. Nantes, France.

McCarthy, J. (1993). Notes on formalizing context. In *IJCAI'93 - Proc. of the 13th Intl. Joint Conf. on Artificial Intelligence. Vol. 1*, pp. 555–560. Chambery, France, August/September 1993. San Mateo, CA: Morgan Kaufmann.

Mooney, R. (1987). Integrated learning of words and their underlying concepts. In *Proc. of the 9th Annual Conf. of the Cognitive Science Society*, pp. 974–978. Seattle, Wash., July 1987. Hillsdale, NJ: L. Erlbaum.

Reimer, U. (1990). Automatic knowledge aquisition from texts: learning terminological knowledge via text understanding and inductive generalization. In *Proc. 5th Knowledge Acquisition for Knowledge-Based Systems Workshop*, pp. 27.1–27.16. Banff, Canada.

Resnik, P. (1992). A class-based approach to lexical discovery. In *Proc. of the 30th Annual Meeting of the Association for Computational Linguistics*, pp. 327–329. Newark, Delaware, USA, June/July 1992.

Schmidt, G. & T. Wetter (1989). Towards knowledge acquisition in natural language dialogue. In *EKAW'89 - Proc. Europ. Knowl. Acquisition Workshop*, pp. 239–252.

Schnattinger, K. & U. Hahn (1996). A sketch of a qualification calculus. In *FLAIRS'96 - Proc. of the 9th Florida AI Research Symposium*. Key West, Florida, May 1996.

Schnattinger, K., U. Hahn & M. Klenner (1995). Terminological meta-reasoning by reification and multiple contexts. In *Progress in Artificial Intelligence. EPIA'95 - Proc. of the 7th Portuguese Conf. on Artificial Intelligence*, pp. 1–16. Funchal, Madeira Island, Portugal, October 1995. Berlin: Springer.

Sekine, S., J. Carroll, S. Ananiadou & J. Tsujii (1992). Automatic learning for semantic collocation. In *Proc. of the 3rd Conf. on Applied Natural Language Processing*, pp. 104–110. Trento, Italy, March/April 1992.

Skuce, D., S. Matwin, B. Tauzovich, F. Oppacher & S. Szpakowicz (1985). A logic-based knowledge source system for natural language documents. *Data & Knowledge Engineering*, 1(3):201–231.

Strube, M. & U. Hahn (1995). PARSETALK about sentence- and text-level anaphora. In *EACL'95 - Proc. of the 7th Conf. of the European Chapter of the Association for Computational Linguistics*, pp. 237–244. Dublin, Ireland, March 1995.

Virkar, R. & J. Roach (1989). Direct assimilation of expert-level knowledge by automatically parsing research paper abstracts. *International Journal of Expert Systems1*, 1(4):281–305.

Woods, W. & J. Schmolze (1992). The KL-ONE family. *Computers & Mathematics with Applications*, 23(2-5):133–177.

Extracting Conceptual Knowledge from Text Using Explicit Relation Markers

Paul R. Bowden, Peter Halstead, and Tony G. Rose

Department of Computing
Nottingham Trent University
Nottingham, England

This paper describes a method for extracting knowledge from large corpora using conceptual relations such as definition and exemplification. The two major steps in this process are the identification of specific relations using positive and negative triggering, and the extraction of the conceptual information by combinatorial pattern-matching. Validation of extracted candidate text is performed by analysis of part-of-speech tag patterns. The algorithms are embodied in a robust program which is capable of attempting extraction even in the absence of part-of-speech tags in the input text. Unlike many knowledge extraction systems, the KEP program is designed to be non domain specific. Intended applications described include knowledge acquisition for automatic examination question setting and marking , and knowledge acquisition for the creation and updating of semantic nets used in a hypermedia-based tutoring system.

Introduction

It is often assumed that Knowledge Acquisition (KA) for expert systems and other knowledge-based programs must involve comprehensive interactive sessions with human experts. However there is now a growing awareness that a vast amount of human knowledge has already been extracted and codified, in the form of printed text in dictionaries, thesauri, user manuals, encyclopaedias, reference guides and expository texts. More and more of such text is becoming available in machine readable form and with this growth there has been a corresponding rise of interest in Message Understanding (MU) and Knowledge Extraction (KE) systems. These do not of course eliminate human input, but attempt to relegate it to a post processing phase, reducing the intellectual load on humans as far as possible whilst making good use of existing hard-won knowledge resources.

In this paper we discuss a novel KE system currently under development which has as its goal the extraction from text of items of knowledge to be used in Computer Aided Learning (CAL) systems. The KEP system extracts conceptual information from sentences. For example, given the text in *Figure 1a.*, the extractions shown in *Figure 1b.* are output.

We define a sorting routine to be a function which orders a list of items according to some criterion. An example of a sorting criterion is alphabetical order. The bubble sort and the quick sort are well-known examples of sorting routines. The four elements of a sorting routine are the input list, the output list, the sorting criterion, and the sorting algorithm.

Figure 1a. Example text for processing

Concept: sorting criterion
Example_0: alphabetical order

Concept: sorting routines
Example_0: bubble sort
Example_1: quick sort

Concept: sorting routine
Definition: a function which orders a list of items according to some criterion

Concept: sorting routine
Part_0: input list
Part_1: output list
Part_2: sorting criterion
Part_3: sorting algorithm

Figure 1b. KEP output for text in Figure 1a.

Domain Specificity

One of the greatest stumbling blocks to successful Knowledge Extraction has been the perceived need for full syntactic, semantic and pragmatic analysis of the input text. However, these requirements have recently been challenged by many Natural Language Processing (NLP) researchers who see the goals of robustness and large-scale processing as paramount [e.g. Jacobs (1992), Stede (1992)]. The ever-increasing quantities of machine readable text available to the computer on the desk demand fast, easy to use and helpful intelligent text processing systems. Early KE systems have invariably been domain specific, attempting to extract information from sources such as newspaper reports [e.g. Rau and Jacobs (1988), Hobbs et al. (1992)] and banking telexes [e.g.Young and Hayes (1985), Lytinen and Gershman (1986)]. These message understanding applications have often been very successful due to their ability to limit vocabulary and domain knowledge to small well-defined fields. However, KE systems which attempt to escape from the domain specific paradigm are still few and far between. This is unfortunate because it is just such programs which will be required for the generalised intelligent extraction systems of the future.

Clearly, a KE system which attempts to use world knowledge to be non domain specific is currently not feasible on practical grounds. A different approach must be taken to achieve generality. Since factors external to the text are impractical, devices within text must be used. One way is to use knowledge about *how* information is encoded within a piece of writing. The study of textual discourse structure provides insights into such devices. Specifically, the structures variously known as *conceptual relations, coherence relations,* or *semantic relations* are available. The preferred term in this paper will be conceptual relation, since the various instances all involve a concept which is elucidated in some fashion.

Conceptual Relations

One example of a conceptual relation is the *definition* relation, where there is a concept (the item being defined) and its elucidation (the actual definition of the concept). However, the term coherence relation also carries some weight since these textual structures tend to make a text coherent and, via anaphoric links and other mechanisms, cohesive. [Morris and Hirst (1991)] have pointed out that the terms *coherence* and *cohesion* are often (incorrectly) used interchangeably. Whereas cohesive links are all about the sticking-together of words in a text, coherence is concerned with relations among sentences and clauses, such as *elaboration, cause,* and *exemplification.* Furthermore, whereas cohesion lends itself to computational identification, there does not exist a general computationally feasible mechanism for identifying coherence relations. The KEP program represents an attempt to rectify this omission, albeit by looking for specific types of relation.

Many researchers have attempted to categorise the various conceptual relations, or to examine a particular relation in some depth. For example, [Vander Linden and Martin (1995)] have made a study of the forms of the *purpose* relation as used in instruction manuals, from a Natural Language Generation (NLG) perspective. [Ahmad and Fulford [1992]] used both manual lookup and corpus-based methods to compile lists of lexical forms used in the *synonym, hyponym, partitive, causal* and *material* relations. Broad studies include that of [Cruse (1986)], who considers taxonomies (hyponymy), meronomies (parts and pieces), opposites (including antonyms) and synonyms. [Lyons (1977)] considers conceptual relations as part of a wider treatise on semantics, where the term *formulae* is used to describe lexical patterns used to evince conceptual relations. Attempts have also been made to standardise terminology for particular applications, such as the British Standard Guide to the Establishment and Development of Monolingual Thesauri [BSI, (1987)] which considers hierarchical relationships (generic, whole-part, and instance), and the associative relationship (the *related term* relationship, for example as between "birds" and "ornithology").

Definition, Exemplification, and Partition

The three conceptual relations presently handled by the KEP system are definition, exemplification and partition. These three relation types were chosen because it was felt that they were likely to occur in expository texts, particularly in the domain of computer science. Although the aim of the system is to be domain independent, the chosen test corpora and the first application lie in this subject area. For the purposes of the system described in this paper, the following are the definitions of the three selected relation types:

> **A definition** is a description of a concept in such a way and to such a depth that it presents the essential features of that concept.

Definitions play a crucial role in subjects requiring specific technical terms, such as engineering, mathematics and law. Thus the word "technical" is used in the sense of *expert jargon* here, rather than in the narrower sense of "engineering or scientific". Note also that the word "essential" within the definition is being used in the sense of *captures the essence of.*

> **An exemplification** is an elaboration of a concept using a specific instance (or instances) of that concept.

Examples are a valuable tool in instructional text and their roles in pedagogical applications have been much studied [see e.g. Mittal and Paris (1983)]. Almost all expository texts make use of exemplifications, this paper being no exception.

> **A partition** is an elaboration of a concept using a list (or partial list) of its component parts.

The partition relation is signalled by keyphrases such as *is made up of three parts, comprises, has the following components* etc. It is not to be confused with the material relation, which describes the substance from which a concept (usually a physical object) is made.

Relation Detection

For systems which detect and process *definition* relations from dictionaries and thesauri, the act of relation *detection* is straightforward, for each book entry is certain to be a candidate. Such systems, for example [Alshawi (1987), Gang Zhu and Shadbolt (1994)] tend to concentrate on the extraction of the various semantic parts of the definition into some useful data structure. The aim of the KEP program is to extract entire word strings rather than to dissect extracted concepts into their semantic parts. However, the detection of definitions within running text is not as straightforward as the simple location of definitions in a dictionary. Consider sentences **a** through **d** below, which are intended to represent sentences taken at random from some body of text.

a A marsupial is defined as an animal with a pouch for its young.
b A byte is a contiguous group of eight bits.
c A television set is a modern marvel.
d There is a way to do this.

Clearly, **a** and **b** are definitions, whereas **c** is not (it is merely a statement about televisions in general). Sentence **d** is clearly not useful as a standalone. Note that **a** contains the trigger phrase *is defined as* but **b** through **d** contain only the very general phrase *is a*. It is difficult to pin down what makes **b** a definition but **c** not. We shall return to this later.

The initial stage of the KEP program reads plain text from a file into memory. The user indicates whether the text is already in one-sentence-per-line format, and whether the text is part-of-speech tagged. The sentence structure of the text is then extracted, so that each detected conceptual relation instance may be referenced by sentence number and position within the sentence. Miscellaneous tidying tasks are also performed at this stage, such as the identification of possible headings (which are treated as separate sentences).

Positive and negative trigger phrases are then used to locate possible instances of conceptual relations. The character string *define* is sufficient to catch sentence **a**. The negative trigger string *cannot be defined* can then be used to rule out some sentences containing the characters *define* in the wrong sense. Each relation type processed by KEP has two trigger data files associated with it, one each for positive and negative trigger lists. These lists have been found to be very short (up to twenty or so trigger patterns in each) but no formal exhaustive search for trigger patterns has been yet performed; see [Ahmad and Fulford (1992)] or [Hearst (1992)] for possible systematic approaches to this task. It is found that roughly one in fifty positively triggered sentences are subsequently de-triggered due to the presence of an overlapping negative trigger.

We now return to the *is a* problem. Since relation instances are detected in the simple manner described above, a decision has to made as to whether to include *is a* as a trigger or not. The solution adopted is to include it, but try to filter out non-definitions so triggered at a later stage. This will be described later. The negative trigger *there is a* is also employed, and this de-triggers sentence **d** above.

Conceptual Extraction

The KEP program uses an essentially pattern-driven approach to relation extraction. After the triggering stage, a list of triggered sentences is held for each of the three relations handled. Two stages of pattern matching are then performed on each triggered sentence for each relation type: the first is entirely non-syntactic, but the second relies upon part-of-speech tags provided by an external tagger (although useful output may be produced even for untagged input). The tagger currently used is an experimental tagger service available via email from the Corpus Linguistics Group (CLG) at the University of Birmingham (UK).

Pattern-matching techniques have proved successful in various robust parsing and extraction systems, such as that of [Alshawi (1987)] and of [Hayes and Mouradian (1981)]. [Hearst (1992)] has also described a pattern-based system for extracting hyponym relations (having a very limited single specific syntax) from free text. What these systems have in common is the use of part-of-speech information to aid in the template matching. Where KEP differs from this approach is to perform an initial set of largely non-syntactic template matching operations to cut a sentence up into sections, but reserve syntactic information for the subsequent validation of each of the possible segmentations of the triggered sentence.

The KEP program looks for single-sentence relations, with the exception that endophoric links may start within a sentence but end in a different one. The triggered sentence is segmented in a number of ways according to a tokenisation string generated combinatorially. An example demonstrates this. Consider the sentence *An example of a high-level language is PASCAL*. This sentence contains an instance of the *exemplification* relation. Each relation type in KEP has an associated list of single-character tokens, such as e for the word string *An example of*, and = for the word string *is*. Punctuation characters are tokenised to themselves and each is regarded as a word in the sentence. Word strings with no specific tokens are represented by the token X. The combinatorial algorithm tokenises the triggered sentence in all possible ways, i.e. for one, two, three etc uses of non-overlapping tokens. For the above sentence, this gives the following tokenisations:

eX=X. eX=X eX. eX X=X. X=X X. X

Note that the X-token is allowed to cover words which are part of other tokens when those other tokens are not being used as part of the current tokenisation. Tokens may be re-used for several similar word strings without compromising the generation of distinct tokenisations. For example, the token 'e' may be used for *example, examples, an example, an example of* etc. The generated tokenisations might look identical but the word strings associated with each token would not be the same in these cases.

Also associated with each relation is a file of templates against which tokenisations are to be matched. One such template for the exemplification relation takes the form eC=0. . This is deemed to match the tokenisation eX=X. above, where the first X corresponds to C in the template, and the second to 0 in the template. The C in the template stands for Concept, and the 0 in the template stands for the first example (up to ten, 0 through 9, may be present in the template).

The tokenisation process associates a word string with each token. For the tokenisation eX=X. , the associated word strings and corresponding template tokens are given in *Table 1*. This gives the extraction **Concept**: a high-level language **Example_0**: PASCAL. Since the input sentence may be tokenised in many ways (just over a thousand for a sentence containing ten non-X tokens) a large set of tokenisations must be matched against each template in the relevant template file. This results in a list of zero or more candidate extractions such as that extraction given above, because different tokenisations may match different templates. The list of candidate extractions is then passed on to the second stage of the extraction process.

Tokenisation	Word string	Template token
e	An example of	e
X	a high-level language	C
=	is	=
X	PASCAL	0
.	.	.

Table 1. Example tokenisation for sentence *An example of a high-level language is PASCAL.*

Note that this first stage of the extraction process is almost entirely non-syntactic. The effect is to cut the triggered sentence into sections delimited by key relation phrases and punctuation. Since parsing is not performed, some of the candidate segmentations will match templates designed to catch other word-patterns in the sentence, giving rise to instances where the concept/example are swapped or where too-long or too-short word phrases are indicated. The "correct" extraction is usually one of the candidate extractions so the task of the second stage is to provide a decision procedure to obtain the "best" candidate.

Syntactic Candidate Validation

In this stage, text fragments from the first stage of extraction are examined syntactically. This presently relies upon the input text being correctly tagged for parts of speech. Many of the candidate extractions are thereby disqualified. Again, the approach is based upon pattern-matching techniques. Files of allowed tag patterns are maintained for each relation type and for each part of the relation (concept, or elucidation parts). These tag template files are also dependent on the specific tagset used. The patterns in the files are non-recursive, so that templates such as those given in *Figure 2.* occur.

```
NN
NN NN
ADJ NN
ADJ NN NN
ADJ ADJ NN NN
ADJ NN XX XX XX
```

Figure 2. Example tag patterns for syntactic validation.

In this figure, an imaginary tagset uses NN to mean any singular or plural noun, and ADJ for adjectives (including comparatives and superlatives). Valid extracted concepts often occur as simple noun phrases, although prepositional phrases and other constructs modifying the head do occur. The mechanism also allows for an XX tag to match any single tag in the text being validated.

The input sentence under consideration is tag-stripped and the string of tags corresponding to the word string in the fragment being tested is compared against all tag patterns in the relevant file. If a single match occurs, the fragment is deemed syntactically correct. The tag files are continuously being augmented so as to validate good syntaxes detected in trials. Currently only a handful of tag patterns are implemented in each case, but it is hoped to make the mechanism more flexible in the near future by implementing a recursive nomenclature.

It was mentioned earlier that non-tagged input may be used. In this case, the validation stage described above is not available and so the entire candidate set is passed on to the amalgamation stage. This stage takes the remaining (non-invalidated) candidates and reduces them to a single "best choice". Note that even for tagged input, there may be more than one syntactically validated candidate. At the moment the amalgamation algorithm amounts to picking the first valid candidate for tagged input, and presenting all candidates otherwise.

Anaphora

Endophoric relationships within text bind it into a cohesive and coherent whole. They are the answer to the question "What makes a text a text?". [Halliday and Hasan (1976)] have extensively categorised the types of cohesive relation involved, including anaphora, cataphora, ellipsis and substitution. The resolution of coreferential links within text has been a large area for research in its own right, and sophisticated suites of programs have been developed to tackle this complex problem [see e.g. Carter (1987)]. Anaphoric links do not necessarily start in one sentence and end in another. They can link clauses within the same sentence, as in: *As for personal computers, these usually comprise keyboard, VDU and processor box.* Thus even a program which processes single sentences must provide mechanisms for handling such occurrences.

It is frequently the case that syntactically validated fragments from the extraction stage described in the previous section are found to be anaphoric (pointing to previous text), cataphoric (pointing forwards in the text) and even semi-exophoric (pointing out of the text to some other entity on the page, such as a figure or a table). Simple anaphoric fragments include *this, these* etc. More complex constructs include phrases like *such devices, this type of <noun>, given in Figure. 5.7* etc. The simpler demonstratives are validated before syntax-checking, but the more complex phrases are handled in a function designed specifically to detect endophoric links.

Links which point to tables and figures within the text cannot be simply resolved, and where such a pointer is detected the output is therefore set to text such as *<given in*

an accompanying diagram>. The set of phrases indicating such links is small and so is hardcoded into the detection function.

Links within the text proper do at least terminate on other phrases, and so some attempt could be made to follow them back (or forward) to the relevant concept (or example etc). For phrases like *such a device* in the sentence *An example of such a device is the laser printer* it is likely that the linked concept lies in the immediately preceding sentence, usually as the head. This is an area within KEP which is presently being worked on; currently the detection code is being implemented (using a file to hold trigger text patterns such as those given above). However, it is already evident that only simple target concepts will be extractable. Anaphoric links may point back to intangible concepts described by the whole of a preceding paragraph (or even larger textual unit). No simple syntax-based extraction method would ever succeed in resolving such links; systems incorporating semantic and pragmatic knowledge will be required.

Performance Remarks

The current version of the KEP system is written in the 'C' programming language, and is compiled and run on a Hyundai Sparc10 compatible machine. Initial tests were performed on a pre-tagged text size of 2,925 lines (168,203 characters as 20,5378 words). This test text contained 977 sentences on elementary computer science.

The speed at which processing proceeds is dependent upon the amount of processing required on each input sentence. Untriggered sentences are processed at about ten per second. Triggered sentences have processing times which depend upon the number of word-pattern tokens present in the sentence (this increasing exponentially with the number of tokens) and upon the number of sentence tokenisations so-produced which happen to match a template-file pattern. The latter is dependent on the contents of the token and template files, but processing of triggered sentences through to extraction currently takes between 1 and 20 seconds.

Two metrics have been applied to test results: *precision* and *recall*. Precision is calculated as the number of extractions the system gets right divided by the number of extractions the system gives. Thus it answers the question "what fraction of the given answers were correct?". Precision says nothing about the coverage of a system, and so it is possible for a program to have a very high precision and yet extract very little of the available knowledge. The recall metric resolves this omission. Defined as the number of extractions the system gets right divided by the number of possible extractions, recall shows how comprehensively knowledge is vacuumed from the text.

In the initial tests for the exemplification relation the system gave 5 extractions of which 5 were deemed to be correct, giving a precision of 100%. The 5 correct extractions came from a pool of 21 possible extractions (this excluding multi-sentence occurrences, false triggerings, and other extractions outside the scope of the program), giving a recall of 24%. All figures are for post-training runs (see comments later). The results for all three relations are summarised in *Table 2*. below.

Relation	Precision (%)	Recall (%)
Exemplification	100	24
Definition	100	33
Partition	100	66

Table 2. Extraction results summary

Note that the figures given are for single-sentence relations only. These are sentences which completely contain the relation. KEP does not yet have the code to tackle two-sentence relations, or greater aggregates. However, we take these single-sentence instances to include sentences with one or two endophoric links to other sentences. At present, if the link is recognised as such, we count the sentence as correctly extracted. Clearly, this is not satisfactory in the long run and future development will attempt to extract the true concept (see the earlier section on anaphora).

Because triggering is essentially keyword driven, the number of false triggerings is high (18 for the exemplification test). Numerically, the dominant reason for the high false triggering rate is the presence of sentences *describing* relations given elsewhere, but not actually containing instances of relations themselves. A sentence such as *the example above is not a very good one* illustrates this phenomenon. We dub these sentences *relation references*. All the false triggerings in the exemplification test were caused by relation references.

However, there are other ways in which a false triggering can occur. For example, the phrase *sets a good example* causes a false triggering for exemplification due to the presence of the word *example*. The false triggering rate is reduced somewhat by the negative triggering facility, but the simple negative triggering mechanism currently employed is not capable of catching this case unless the whole phrase is added to the list; similar phrases such as *sets a bad example* would also be required. There is therefore a case for developing triggering methods (positive and negative) employing some syntactic knowledge and which can recognise idioms.

It sometimes arises that a good example of a relation is not extracted because the relevant patterns (tokenisation, syntax) are not stored in the data files. This is a problem of lack of exposure to large amounts of text and the consequent manual augmentation of the pattern files. Once the new patterns have been added, the extraction occurs correctly, usually without an increase in false extractions arising from the introduction of the new forms. There is also one technical reason which explains some failures to extract: a 10-token limit has been placed on the tokenisation routine so as to limit the number of tried tokenisations to a sensible value. There is no reason why this limit should not be raised, save speed of processing. However, it is to be noted that the number of possible tokenisations increases from n to $2n+2$ when the maximum number of tokens allowed in a sentence is incremented by one. Thus triggered sentence processing times would increase approximately exponentially with the number of tokens permitted.

Occasionally, non-extraction is caused by errors in the tags attached to the input words. Since these are created by a program external to KEP, it is reasonable to correct these tags manually prior to a second pass. However, there are some sentences which refuse to yield the required extraction because of their form. An example of such a sentence for the definition relation is:

> Defined as *a function which orders a list of items a sorting routine* is a common function in large programs.

The problem here is that no sensible tokenisation scheme can split the italicised part of the sentence, which appears as an X-token in all attempts. It is interesting to note that the above sentence does not scan easily for a human reader, and that if a comma is placed after the word *items,* not only does the sentence become easier to read for a human, but also a template can now be constructed to successfully extract the concept and its definition. The majority of the failed extractions in the test trials arose due to such examples, so clearly this is a priority area for future research. A tokenisation scheme which examined the X-spans for their substructure would be required to resolve the original comma-less sentence. Since this would mean identifying sentential components such as noun phrases, verbs, etc then syntactic knowledge would have to be applied at the tokenisation stage. Thus X could represent any noun phrase, Y any prepositional phrase, and so on. This approach would blur the distinction between pattern matching and parsing.

There is a fundamental problem concerning the calculation of recall. This is the difficulty in assigning a figure to the number of relations present in a text. Preliminary reader trials using short texts (c. 2000 words) have shown that there is not often a consensus on what constitutes the relation set. For example, some people would regard the sentence *ROM can only be read from, not written to* as a definition of ROM, whereas to others it is merely a statement *about* ROM. However, if the sentence is rephrased as *ROM is memory which can be read from but not written to,* it looks much more like a definition. To some extent this problem arises because definition may not be a "true" conceptual relation, since it can encompass other relations such as partition. Another example involves the naming of concepts: we would regard *a byte is a contiguous group of eight bits* as a definition, but *a contiguous group of eight bits is called a byte* as an instance of the *nomination* relation. Similar instances can be found for the exemplification and partition relations.

Thus the denominator in the recall calculation turns out to be very difficult to assign. Tighter ways of identifying instances of specific relations would help, but as discussed earlier, there is little consensus as to the names of the various relations, let alone their forms. Indeed, attempts to come up with lists of relations rarely even identify the same set, notwithstanding the use of synonyms. All that can be done at present is to state how the particular study assigned the denominator in the recall calculation. In our case, the denominator counts were provided by ourselves.

Since the current system does not follow anaphoric links or process multi-sentence relations, it mostly avoids problems with complex intangible concepts not explicit in the text. Such concepts are not easily extractable from functional parts of sentences, such as the head. They derive from complex understandings of situations described within preceding text, and require considerable processing of these structures in order to answer the question "what is being exemplified?" Such extractions are outside the scope of the current system. As discussed in the Introduction, nearly all current message understanding systems which are capable of tackling knowledge extraction from texts as a whole are domain specific, having concept slots more or less built-in by the designers. It is our opinion that successful extraction of complex "constructed" concepts in a non domain specific manner will require systems having scope equal to or greater than that of the Conceptual Dependency (CD) model [Schank and Abelson (1977)].

There is one other point relating to complex concepts which has emerged from the work done so far. This is that even though we only attempt to extract single-sentence instances we often extract a relation, such as an exemplification, which is quite meaningless outside of the context in which it was embedded. For example:

Concept: use of loops
Example_0: bill program in Chapter 1

Examples such as this serve to demonstrate the dangers of trying to extract knowledge from text without attempting to completely understand the whole text.

We will conclude this section with a few remarks concerning the degree of domain independence achieved. Since no domain-specific knowledge is encoded in the program, we claim complete domain independence. Instead of being *domain* dependent, this approach is *conceptual relation* dependent. In order to add a new domain to a domain-dependent system, knowledge of that domain (including lexical knowledge) must be added. Often, a domain-dependent system has not been designed to cope with more than one domain at a time. The addition of the new domain conflicts with the existing domain, or it may require extra processing (e.g. to perform topic analysis so that the domain of the presented text is initially identified). Since KEP is a conceptual relation dependent system, the addition of a new relation requires the addition of new pattern files for that relation. However, KEP *has* been designed to cope with more than one relation at a time. In fact, the idea is to allow the addition of as many relations as may be desired.

Two queries are thereby raised. The first concerns potential conflicts between relations. For example, there may be a conflict between the nomination relation and the definition relation, as described above. However, the real question here is whether there are any quite distinct relations which share one or more lexical patterns. With only three relations coded so far, the only instance encountered is that of *is a*. When used in *A cat is a carnivore* it signifies class membership, whereas in *A carnivore is a meat eater* it signals a definition. But note that this problem certainly isn't confined to any particular domain (zoology, computer science etc). Thus there may be a way of tackling it, based upon the tag patterns in the part to the right of *is a*, or perhaps based upon the stored output of a previous run of KEP (in which the carnivore concept was defined explicitly). For example, if the concept *carnivore* existed in a semantic net maintained by KEP, then it might be easier to assign a sentence such as *A cat is a carnivore* to the correct relation. Of course, stored knowledge about the concept *carnivore* could be described as domain knowledge, and therefore one might then argue that KEP was no longer domain independent. But such knowledge would have been knowledge obtained by KEP itself, and not programmed in by a human. Furthermore, KEP would not restrict its learning to any particular domain. Thus we can continue to assert that KEP is domain independent.

The second query concerns the *generality* of relation syntaxes. It might be argued that certain word patterns occur only in certain domains (we are thinking about legal documents and so forth here). By adding the relevant templates to the template files, are we not in a sense making the program domain specific? The answer is no. What we are doing here is making the program *less* specific. The program is still able to process all the other domains it has encountered for the conceptual relation under consideration. The addition of extra patterns, although possibly slightly slowing the execution for existing texts, does not result in a significant increase in false extractions from these previous texts.

Further Research

We have already mentioned several areas for future research, including amalgamation of candidate extractions and anaphor resolution. A progression from sub-syntactic towards pragmatic levels is beginning to emerge. Each stage performs processing on the output of the previous lower stage, but there is at present no feedback between these levels. This is another possible area for research, since it might be the case that semantic information is required at the lowest level. On a less advanced level, we intend to increase the repertoire of relations handled from the present three. Obvious candidates include the *causation* relation and the *composition* relation (sometimes called the material relation).

An intended application for the KEP program lies in the CAL arena. An existing examination marker [Allott et al (1994)], which attempts to mark as correct or incorrect a single-sentence answer to a displayed question, will take as its input lexical strings output by KEP. The Allott system uses an activation-passing network (APN) to achieve its binary decision based upon text fragments present or absent in the student's answer, together with other information such as the order of such fragments and various multi-level activations. As such it would mesh well with KEP, which produces textual output in a format easily written to the desired APN input format. Since the APN system works on *textual* input, it would not be necessary for KEP to perform deeper analyses on the word strings it obtains.

The aim of this research would be to demonstrate a system which uses automatically-acquired knowledge to mark examination questions set by humans. For example, the question might be *What is a high-level language?* Although this question will have been input by a person, the various answers generally accepted to be correct would have been obtained automatically from large amounts of machine-readable text in the computer science domain. Ultimately, it might even be possible to autogenerate the questions themselves. The sorts of question involved might be: *Give three examples of output devices*; *Define a database management system*; *Name the constituent parts of a PC* etc. Such a program would demonstrate for the first time a text-based intelligent system capable of reading about a subject, setting an examination on it, running the examination, and then marking it. However, the authors of this paper are not expecting to be replaced by such a system in the near future. Clearly, any knowledge placed in the APN by a system such as this will have to be examined very carefully by humans.

This is also true of a second intended application, the creation or updating of the semantic net used by a hypertext-based tutoring system currently under development [Edwards et al. (1995)]. This system provides a windows-based interface incorporating query input and answer generation in a sub-language of English [Long et al. (1995)]. Conceptual relations such as the hyponym relation and the exemplification relation map very well onto the semantic net model. The former utilises the *is a type of* link to indicate classes within classes, and the latter is embodied as the *instance* link. The partition relation maps perfectly to the *has part* link and numerous other mappings can be thought of.

We have already mentioned the use of semantic nets as part of a potential learning mechanism for KEP. The net would act as a repository for knowledge gleaned during past runs of the program, this knowledge being used in the current run to disambiguate the relation type (see discussion on *is a* in the previous section). However, the automatic updating of semantic nets is no sinecure, as has been pointed out by [Hearst (1992)]. In addition, since lexical strings lifted straight from text would not be sufficient for this application, some extra processing would be required on the extracted elements so as to obtain the required degree of understanding. In the case of definitions, which often define the concept by way of its attributes and abilities, some form of attribute/property extraction processing, such as that of [Gang Zhu and Shadbolt (1994)], might be useful.

On a simpler level, it is often the case that a concept is extracted in both its singular and plural forms (see *sorting routine(s)* in *Figure 1b*). The identicality of two such concepts can be recognised using a string comparison algorithm to identify possible cases, plus a method of reducing one form to the other. We have therefore developed a self-contained routine which provides the singular forms of English plural nouns [Bowden, Halstead and Rose (1996)]. This is a straightforward task for about 95% of plural forms but the existence of the irregular 5% means that various exception lists must be provided. The developed routine provides correct singulars in more than 999 distinct cases out of 1000, and will be incorporated into the candidate extraction amalgamation program discussed earlier.

Conclusion

We have demonstrated that an approach to extraction of conceptual relation information, from large machine-readable corpora, based on word-pattern matching and syntactic checking is feasible. Future areas of research must consider improved triggering methods, the resolution of anaphors at least to a modest level, and of greater degrees of knowledge extraction from the lexical strings cut from the source texts. Two possible applications, the acquisition of knowledge suitable for simple examination question setting, and the automatic updating of semantic nets for tutoring systems, have been described. Long-term developments will almost certainly require higher-level treatments, bringing in both semantic and world knowledge.

References

Ahmad, K. and Fulford, H. *Semantic Relations and their Use in Elaborating Terminology* Computing Sciences Report CS-92-07, Univ. Surrey, England (1992).

Allott, N., Fazackerley, P. and Halstead, P. *Automated Assessment: Evaluating a Knowledge Architecture for Natural Language Processing* Procs EXPERT SYSTEMS '94 (Cambridge, England (1994)

Alshawi, H. *Processing Dictionary Definitions with Phrasal Pattern Hierarchies* Computational Linguistics **13** 3-4 (1987)

BSI (British Standards Institution) *British Standard Guide to Establishment and Development of Monolingual Thesauri BS 5723:1987, ISO 2788-1986* (1987)

Bowden, P., Halstead, P. and Rose, T. *Dictionaryless English Plural Noun Singularisation Using A Corpus-Based List of Irregular Forms* (paper to be presented at ICAME '96, Univ. Stockholm, Sweden) (1996)

Carter, D. *Interpreting Anaphors in Natural Language Texts* Ellis Horwood (1987)

Cruse, D. A. *Lexical Semantics* Cambridge University Press (1986)

Edwards, M. A., Powell. H., and Palmer-Brown, D. *A Hypermedia-based Tutoring and Knowledge Engineering System* In Procs. ED-MEDIA '95 Graz, Austria (1995)

Gang Zhu and Shadbolt, N. *Mining Knowledge: The Partial Parsing of Texts* Departmental paper, AI Research Group, Dept. Psychology, Univ. Nottingham (UK).

Halliday, M. A. K. and Ruqaiya Hasan *Cohesion in English* Longman (1976)

Hayes, P. J. and Mouradian, G. V. *Flexible Parsing* American Journal of Computational Linguistics **7** 4 (1981)

Hearst, M. A. *Automatic Acquisition of Hyponyms from Large Text Corpora* Procs. COLING-92, Nantes, France (1992)

Hobbs, J. R. et al. *Robust Parsing of Real-World Natural-Language Texts.* In *Text-Based Intelligent Systems* Lawrence Erlbaum Associates (1992)

Jacobs, P. S. *Text Power and Intelligent Systems.* In *Text-Based Intelligent Systems* Lawrence Erlbaum Associates (1992)

Long, G., Powell. H., and Palmer-Brown, D. *A Syntax-free NLP Interface for an Intelligent Tutoring Environment* In Procs. CSNLP 95 (4th Int. Conf. on the Cognitive Science of Natural Language Processing, Dublin City Univ., Ireland) (1995)

Lyons, J. *Semantics* Cambridge University Press (1977)

Lytinen, S. L. and Gershman, A. *ATRANS: Automatic Processing of Money Transfer Messages* In Procs. 5th Nat. Conf. on Artificial Intelligence, Philadelphia (1986)

Mittal, V. O. and Paris, C. L. *Categorizing Example Types in Instructional Texts: the need to consider context* Procs. AI-ED 93 (Edinburgh, 23 - 27 Aug. 1993)

Morris, J. and Hirst, G. *Lexical Cohesion Computed by Thesaural Relations as an Indicator of the Structure of Text* Computational Linguistics **17** 1 (1991)

Rau, L. F. and Jacobs, P. S. *Integrating Top-down and Bottom-up Strategies in a Text Processing System* In Procs. 2nd Conf. on Applied Natural Language Processing, Morristown, NJ, USA (1988).

Schank, R. and Abelson, R. *Scripts Plans Goals and Understanding* Lawrence Erlbaum Associates (1977)

Stede, M. *The Search for Robustness in Natural Language Understanding* Artificial Intelligence Review **6** (1992)

Vander Linden, K. and Martin, H. *Expressing Rhetorical Relations in Instructional Text: A Case Study of The Purpose Relation* Computational Linguistics **21** 1 (1995)

Young, S. R. and Hayes, P. J. *Automatic Classification and Summarization of Banking Telexes* In Procs. 2nd Conf. on AI Applications, IEEE Comp. Soc. (1985)

Structuring Information in a Distributed Hypermedia System

Célia Ghedini Ralha*

Division of Artificial Intelligence
School of Computer Studies
University of Leeds, Leeds LS2 9JT, England
E-mail: ghedini@scs.leeds.ac.uk

Abstract. This paper addresses some particular issues pertaining to the problem of automatically structuring informal knowledge available on the Internet through a distributed hypermedia system like the World-Wide Web (WWW). It presents a new approach to the integration of hypertext and hypermedia technology with Knowledge Acquisition (KA) which deals with knowledge before the process of formalization. This approach coordinates aspects of automatic computation of nodes in hyperspace through dynamic linking with intelligent mapping of the domain material by the application of qualitative spatial reasoning. This article reports results of multi-disciplinary research that involves cognitive aspects of human memory recovery and association, automatic linking of knowledge from a wide variety of sources (expressed in multiple formats), and an adequate visual interface to display large maps of supporting material.

1 Introduction

KA mixes various types of activities, including deciding what knowledge should be brought to bear on a problem, how to extract (i.e. knowledge elicitation), interpret, organize, model (i.e. represent) and encode it in a knowledge-based system.

Normally, the KA process involves a major data collection activity that commences with largely informal knowledge from a wide variety of sources, in order to focus on more structured knowledge elicitation from key knowledge sources. Finally it leads to the transformation of what is elicited into formal knowledge structures that form the basis of a computational knowledge base. The management of this data collection activity and the, often very large, corpus of material resulting, has been a major candidate for support through KA tools based on hypermedia technology [8].

* Supported by a scholarship from CNPq of the Brazilian Government and leave of absence from CEF. I gratefully acknowledge the help from Dr. Anthony G. Cohn (and EPSRC grant GR/H/78955) without whom this work would not have been possible.

Conventionally, KA interface design has been based on the teletype approach. As a result, the man-machine channel of communication has been constrained to some extent. Hypertext and hypermedia technology provide an ideal approach to the development of knowledge-based systems by enlarging the man-machine communication channel. Knowledge bases may be considered as a kind of hypermedia and hypertext system, that consist of nodes (concepts, facts, texts, graphics, sounds) interconnected with static and dynamic links (relations, rules). The techniques and tools for hypermedia and hypertext systems are gradually improving and are emphasizing the capabilities of a knowledge-based system in communication and structuring of domain knowledge [25].

This work focuses on the elicitation and structuring of semi-formal knowledge supported by hypertext and hypermedia technologies. The intention is to work with knowledge before the formalization process, hence our usage of the term 'semi-formal knowledge' above previously used by [8]. The approach involves an automated way to structure documents described by a set of attributes in a web-based model through the building of hyperspace maps [22, 21].

Since the Internet is posing an increasing demand on interactive task automation, many services might be offered and diverse intelligent assistants created. Larger bodies of knowledge, as extensive knowledge-based systems, will need to be acquired and maintained as artificial intelligent systems are scaled up and applied to real-world problems through the Internet. Although the Internet technology allows for easier exchange and reuse of knowledge descriptions on a large scale, conventional distributed hypermedia systems suffer from a number of problems which have only just started to be tackled. These problems have a substantial impact on automated KA efforts and may be thus analysed:

- *Disorientation* [6] is the most frequent cited problem in hypermedia systems. Either the user or the KA tool will have to face the problem of having to know where to get related material throughout the Internet.
- *Formal Specifications* of the documents content are necessary to index and retrieve hypermedia objects through a reasoning process.
- *Absence of a Classification Scheme* - Navigation across the Internet may be an arduous task because of the absence of an effective classification scheme for the enormous amount of information available through billions of interlinked Uniform Resource Locators - URL (http://www.w3.org/pub/WWW/Addressing/URL/Overview.html).
- *Low Level of Abstraction* - The relationship between documents (i.e. hyperlinks) are modeled on a very low level of abstraction, what prevents knowledge reuse, is liable to redundancies and is costly to maintain.
- *Real Automated KA through the Internet* - The problem of automated KA is not restricted to dynamic structuring of semi-formal knowledge. The problem is much more complex as it involves the transformation of semi-formal knowledge to formal domain knowledge-bases, where specification of ontologies, inference knowledge, task knowledge and problem solving methods should be included.

In Sect. 2 we describe a model which intends to present solutions to some of the problems just mentioned, without attempting to be a complete tool to perform automated KA through the Internet. The model resembles cognitive aspects of human memory recovery and association, making use of dynamic linking and qualitative spatial reasoning. In Sect. 3 we find an overview of a prototype system called HyperMap, which implements the model presented in Sect. 2. The practical use of HyperMap is illustrated in Sect. 4 by two examples related to the Sisyphus III problem (for more information on the Sisyphus III see http://www.psyc.nott.ac.uk/aigr/research/ka/ka.html) on the geological domain. Some related works and final comments are included in Sect. 5.

2   An Overview of the Approach

Integrating hypertext/hypermedia technology with KA as a data collection activity involves finding ways to link the large amount of informal knowledge that may be expressed in many different formats. Our approach to this problem is two fold. First we build a method of dynamic linking; secondly, we model the topology of the hyperspace with qualitative spatial relations based on a primitive concept of 'connection' between spatial regions.

2.1   Dynamic Linking

Dynamic linking is a method for the automatic computation of "relatedness" between nodes in hypertext where conceptual connectivity or semantic proximity is considered. This method is specially important in our approach as it deals with large hypertext/hypermedia systems where the activation of a node (a fragment of text, a frame, a screen) will automatically indicate to the user the most relevant nodes without the need for the link between the two nodes ever to have been explicitly coded.

In our approach, the use of dynamic linking to build the hyperspace map is based on a modified version of the computer model of human memory proposed by Hintzman [11]. Since the computer model used is a metaphor for the theory, it is appropriate to summarize the theoretical ideas that the model is intended to represent.

As Hintzman points out, his model originated from Richard Semon's Theory [27] which assumed that each learning experience leaves behind its own memory trace or "engram". Semon argued that the contents of consciousness are produced by a kind of resonant state (i.e. homophony) in which the common properties of the traces stand out and their distinctive properties are marked, so that what appears in consciousness is an abstraction, rather than the content of a particular memory trace.

Hintzman's contribution has been to cast this theory into the form of a computer model [10]. The simulation model of episodic memory, dubbed Minerva 2, was applied to the learning of concepts, as represented by the schema-abstraction task. Only the schema-abstraction aspects of this work will be covered here.

In a Hintzman model a memory trace is a record of an experience or episode which is represented as a trace or vector, an ordered list of features or **attributes**. Every conscious experience gives rise to its own memory trace, no matter how similar it may be of an earlier one. Thus, phenomena that are repeated but nevertheless command attention will be represented in memory over and over again. A **probe** is an active representation of an experience, in *primary memory*[2] which is communicated in parallel to all traces in *secondary memory*[3]. Each trace is assumed to be activated according to its similarity to the probe. Thus, traces sharing many properties with the probe are activated strongly, whereas traces that overlap little with the probe are activated hardly at all.

Hintzman's simulation model of human memory was used since it offers an approach to the problem of content-addressable retrieval from a large information base. One difference in the representation of attributes is that Hintzman uses n-tuples of +1's, -1's and 0's for each memory trace and probe to represent the features present, not present , or indeterminate. Hintzman was partly concerned with the phenomenon of loss of memory elements so he used a three-state attribute system whereas we represent simply the set of those present. Our representation makes it easier to delete or add attributes to frames, although it fails to distinguish between properties being not present and not known to be present. However, we have not needed to make this distinction in our applications.

We use Hintzman's model in the following way[4]. An information base is composed of a set of frames[5] (e.g. pages of information). Associated with each frame is an open set of attributes. The constituent of a frame and its attributes constitutes a memory trace in Hintzman's model. A probe consists of a set of attributes which are then matched against all traces. The matching traces constitutes the set of dynamic links for the probe. These matching traces can be classified according to the degree of match. For the process of trace retrieval, an index of similarity is computed between the probe and each trace. Each trace is associated with a frame of information, such as a paragraph, a page or a complete text depending on granularity specifications.

Figure 1 shows the process of trace activation. Attributes are $A_1^i, A_2^i, \ldots, A_{n_i}^i$ and memory traces/frames are shown from top to bottom. Allied to each frame is the URL address, the link name and a set of attributes (which are not all presented in the diagram for reasons of clarity). Figure 6 shows memory traces/frames related to the first example of Sect. 4. For a better idea of the set of attributes that constitute each frame of this information base see Appendix A.

We now turn to the problem of measuring the degree of activation of a

---

[2] We have adopted James's [12] terminology of primary memory as the active representation of the current experience.

[3] Secondary memory is the vast pool of largely dormant memory traces.

[4] This idea is related to the work of a group at The Scottish HCI Centre. They have developed StrathTutor system, described as approaching intelligent hypertext in [13].

[5] The frame associated with each memory trace is intended to represent on-line documentation on a specific domain of knowledge expressed through **HyperText Markup Language** (HTML). The HTML format is used in the WWW initiative.

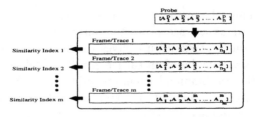

Fig. 1. Trace Activation.

trace since the usefulness of a model (similarly to human memory) for patterned information depends on its ability for selective recall of the desired items. Thus, associative recall ought to consider some form of the concept of similarity [14]. We use the Tanimoto Similarity (S) measure following [13]. If x and y are the set of attributes of the probe and memory trace respectively, then this similarity equation has the form $S = |x \cap y|/|x \cup y|$. This function is independent of the length of the attribute sets and we have adopted it as one basic measure of frame activation. Note that $0 \leq S \leq 1$ and the degree of similarity grows directly with the value of S (e.g. $S = 0.4$ represents higher similarity than $S = 0$). Also note that this similarity measure does not take account of the number of attributes in $|x| \cup |y|$ compared to the total number of attributes in the domain space. For example, if $|x \cap y|$ and $|x \cup y|$ are 2 and 8 respectively, then the same similarity is computed as in the case when these figures are 200 and 800. If the total attribute space is 1000 one might argue that one has more confidence in the latter computation of 0.25 than the former. One could take account of this aspect on the similarity computation, but we do not do this here.

In our similarity algorithm for each frame retrieval, an index of similarity is computed between the set of attributes from the probe and each frame. In this way, the set of activated frames constitutes the set of dynamic links associated with a particular probe. The user can set a local **similarity threshold**, below which frames are regarded as not activated. We might notice that the whole activation process is highly context-specific: how a concept emerges will vary according to which episodic or memory traces have been activated by the probe.

The actual similarity algorithm works only on the content (i.e. presence or absence of particular topics in the information base), but in principle there is no reason why it shouldn't be extended to include intensity (i.e. a weighted measure of the importance or frequency of the topics) as well. Though it is clear that the simple similarity calculation used alone does not respect the importance of different features. Thus, a weighted function which takes into consideration both content and intensity should be further evaluated. This could be done by giving each attribute a value, relating to its importance in the present frame or the current probe. Also more sophisticated methods might permit the current probe to influence the similarity calculations.

2.2 Qualitative Spatial Relations

We now turn to the problem of intelligent mapping of the domain material already created by dynamic linking which is done through the application of spatial reasoning. This navigation aid is intended to give a bird's-eye view of the content of a large multi-dimensional information space. This bird's-eye view is intended to direct users to gather information relevant during the early stages of the development of knowledge-based systems.

When computing the similarity index between attributes (list of features) of a frame and the probe set, operations are carried out which can be used to induce a topological structure on the information space. A set of spatial relations are used based on the theory[6] of space and time presented in [24][7].

The basic part of the theory assumes a primitive dyadic relation: $C(x, y)$ read as 'x connects with y' which is defined on regions. Two axioms are used to specify that C is reflexive and symmetric. In terms of points incident in regions, $C(x, y)$ holds when the topological closure of the regions x and y share a common point. With the relation $C(x, y)$, eight jointly exhaustive and pairwise disjoint dyadic relations are defined. These relations describe differing degrees of connection between regions from being externally connected to sharing mutual parts and being identical.

In our application (as in [15]) we currently use just five basic **spatial relations**[8] formed by disjoining certain pairs of the eight mentioned above. Given the set of attributes from an activated frame (x) and the set of attributes from the probe (y) we may say that the two sets either coincide $EQ(x, y)$, overlap $PO(x, y)$, have proper containment $PP(x, y)$, as PP is asymmetric supports an inverse $PPi(x, y)$, or are disjoint $DR(x, y)$ (empty intersection).

These five predicates can be formally defined as below, where P and O are auxiliary predicates used to define the others:

$$DR(x, y) \equiv_{def} \neg C(x, y)$$
$$PP(x, y) \equiv_{def} P(x, y) \wedge \neg P(y, x)$$
$$EQ(x, y) \equiv_{def} P(x, y) \wedge P(y, x)$$
$$PO(x, y) \equiv_{def} O(x, y) \wedge \neg P(x, y) \wedge \neg P(y, x)$$

$$P(x, y) \equiv_{def} \forall z[C(z, x) \rightarrow C(z, y)]$$
$$PPi(x, y) \equiv_{def} PP(y, x)$$
$$O(x, y) \equiv_{def} \exists z[P(z, x) \wedge P(z, y)]$$

The qualitative closeness between the set of attributes from activated frames (x) and the set of attributes from the probe (y) corresponds to the left-to-right order in Fig. 2. Although, all relations may provide information to the user we may say that to have an empty intersection $DR(x, y)$ is worst, to overlap $PO(x, y)$ is better, to have proper containment $PP(x, y)$ is still better, and to coincide $x = y$ is perfection. Proper containment PP and its inverse PPi are incomparable[9].

---

[6] The word 'theory' means a set of formal axioms which specifies the property and relations of a collection of entities.

[7] Publications of the Qualitative Spatial Reasoning group at leeds University can be found at http://www.scs.leeds.ac.uk/spacenet/publications.html.

[8] Strictly speaking, these five relations define a mereological system [28].

[9] See Fig. 4 of [15] for examples.

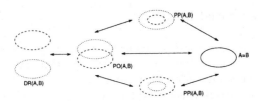

Fig. 2. This figure depicts the possible transitions between the five binary spatial relations, assuming a notion of continuity [15].

2.3 Integrating Dynamic Linking and Spatial Relations

The use of Hintzman's simulation model of human memory in a hypermedia environment can be integrated nicely with the above spatial reasoning techniques, thus giving further descriptive power. The idea of 'relatedness' expressed by dynamic linking of frames of information can be viewed as implementing a conceptual 'connection' between them, and thus providing an interpretation for the $C(x, y)$ relationship. Thus rather than simply being able to describe whether two frames are similar/connected, we can express their spatial/mereological relationship with their 'attribute space'. For example if all frames that are similar to x are also similar to y, then we may infer that x is 'part of' y (i.e. $P(x, y)$).

Up to now we have considered a probe as an external new region with attributes itself (see Fig. 1). But we can change our view slightly if we consider **contextual probes** instead, as show in Fig. 3. Thus if a particular frame 'Frame/Trace 2' is of interest at some time, we may want to know what other frames are related to it. In this case the attributes of 'Frame/Trace 2' are the probe. A variant of this is that we might want to apply a 'filter' - i.e. ignore some of the attributes or perhaps weight some more strongly than others.

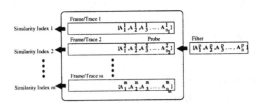

Fig. 3. Contextual Probe Alliance.

The Tanimoto similarity measure with thresholding give us a way to compute which frames are related (and how strongly) to a probe (or to each other) and the spatial predicates then allow further structure to be placed on the information space by classifying links as one of PP, PPi, PO or EQ. Furthermore we can use the similarity measure S, (which can be used directly to give a strength measure to $C(x, y)$) to induce a strength measure on the other spatial relations. In the case of PP, PPi, and PO this is straightforward (here we will just use the S

value directly, though there are other possibilities based on the formal definitions of these relations). However, we might want to impose further structure on the information space. Consider, in particular the case of a set of frames $F_1...F_n$ all of which are unattached (DR) to each other. Can we impose any structure on these frames? We could define a proximity measure which tell us how 'unattached' they are. One way of doing this would be to compute the shortest path between two frames as measured by $C(x,y)$, but to normalize the weight as a value between 0 and 1 we take its reciprocal[10].

$$N(x,y) = \frac{1}{min \ \{n : \exists(x_1,...,x_n) \ [x = x_1 \ \wedge \ y = x_n \ \wedge \ \forall \ 1 \leq i < n \ C(x_i, x_{i+1})]\}} \tag{1}$$

Note that when $C(x,y)$ then $N(x,y) = 1$. A more sophisticated measure would take account the similarity index as well as the path length. Thus we could define:

$$N'(x,y) = max\{(\prod_{i=1}^{i=n} S(x_i, x_{i+1}))N(x,y)\} \tag{2}$$

Figure 4 illustrates an example of the use of 1 and 2. There are four frames $(F1, F2, F3, F4)$ where each relation $C(x,y)$ has its own similarity measure. Applying 1 $N(F1, F3) = 0.5$, $N(F1, F4) = 0.5$ and $N(F1, F2) = 1$, so the higher the value of $N(x,y)$ the closer the frames are. Applying 2: $N'(F1, F2) = 0.3$, $N'(F1, F3) = 0.09$ and $N'(F1, F4) = 0.105$ which shows that although $N(F1, F3) = N(F1, F4)$, $N'(F1, F3) < N'(F1, F4)$. This means that $F1$ is more proximal to frame $F4$ than to $F3$ using N' whereas they were equidistant under the N measure.

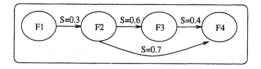

Fig. 4. Use of proximity measure.

3 The HyperMap System

The main idea behind HyperMap is to build the spatial cognitive maps of the hyperspaces influenced by the human cognitive mapping process. For this purpose HyperMap first learns the internal lexicon of the material stored at the specific site. The internal lexicon is considered people's long-term memory for words and there is evidence to suggest that this is constructed as a network of

---

[10] Different measures could be applied to normalize this function, but we have simply used the reciprocal here.

associations, which provides semantic information [9]. This network of associations is the resulting hyperspace built through the use of the dynamic linking method already described. Secondly, HyperMap reasons over the hyperspace to build the spatial relations which will result in the spatial cognitive map.

The learning of the internal lexicon is achieved through the automatic extraction of attributes or key words[11] from the homepage of a specific site, as well as its hyperlinks. Simple linguistic processing techniques are presently being used for this purpose based on the frequency of content words. Words are selected by first gathering every distinct word that occurred over the training set, extracting the common words, then ranking the resulting words according to their frequency of occurrence, and finally choosing the words which appeared more than once. A 'stopping list' of function words, such as 'the', 'and' and 'of', is used to avoid very common words. However, the approach used is very naive since linguistic context does not contain semantic information alone, it also contains syntactic and grammatical structure.

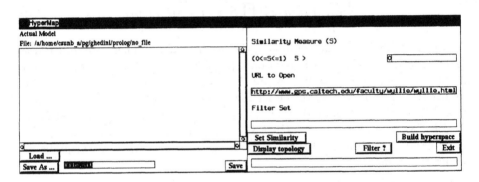

Fig. 5. HyperMap window.

Figure 5 shows the main window of HyperMap. In summary, HyperMap[12] works as follows. Suppose the URL address is given as input without any similarity threshold. Assume that the granularity level adopted is sub-sections of the homepage file. HyperMap extracts attributes (as listed in Appendix A) and builds the frames as seen in Fig. 6. Notice that there were no pre-defined links in the material and that dynamic linking techniques are used to build the hyperlinks for each sub-section. After the hyperlinks are defined, spatial relations can be applied to map the hyperspace, through conceptual connectivity and spatial (semantic) relationships, and subsequently displayed graphically in the format of, for example, Venn diagrams [29] (see Fig. 8).

---

[11] A program written in Snobol language was developed for the automatic extraction of lexicons. See Appendix A for examples of list of lexicons.

[12] HyperMap's main implementation has been done using SICStus Prolog 2.1#9 under the X Windows environment on a Sun/Sparc Station. The libWWW-perl is used to recover a HTML file via Internet from any URL address.

```
Frame/Trace 1
  '/home/csun/.../complete.html' ,'experimental igneous petrology',[set of attributes of w in Appendix]
Frame/Trace 2
  '/home/csun/.../node1.html','tonalites and trondhjemites',[set of attributes of x in Appendix]
Frame/Trace 3
  '/home/csun/.../node2.html','silicate and carbonate melts',[set of attributes of y in Appendix]
Frame/Trace 4
  '/home/csun/.../node3.html','publications',[set of attributes of z in Appendix]
```

Fig. 6. Frames related to Professor Wyllie's site.

The above scenario describes a typical interaction with the current HyperMap with the first example used in Sect. 4. The actual system needs to be extended in several ways. For example, HyperMap should provide an option to set the granularity level according to the user's wish, so that frames would represent different degrees of information, such as paragraphs, sub-sections, whole pages or cluster of sites depending on the intention of the search. It should also be possible to build higher level of links between sites, as for example one link between the first and second site examples of Sect. 4.

Other very important future work includes refining the actual method of automatic extraction of attributes and references from texts. Better techniques and more intelligent ones should be applied to incorporate domain knowledge to the statistical regularity of 'content words' (they vary their occurrence frequency within specific domains as compared to general language). Thus multi-word term lists to the representation of texts may use a framework able to incorporate different sorts of information. The possibility of using semantic information via classification tags present in on-line dictionaries, or via the semantic information available in WordNet [17] should be investigated and evaluated. Also the possibility of using phrases instead of single words as attributes should be taken into consideration. Ultimately corpus based parsing applying statistical methods may be evaluated as a possible solution.

4 Some Examples using HyperMap

This section uses two different examples related to the Sisyphus III (Rocky III) problem. As a first contact with the geological domain, non-specialists might use HyperMap to acquire a very basic level of geological competence through the Internet access of WWW sites of experts around the world. At present, the user is responsible for manually finding such sites - HyperMap does not assist in this. In addition, the simplistic attribute collection techniques place a severe limit on this competence.

In order to illustrate the system in the Sisyphus III context, two different geology expert sites were used which include material on terrestrial and lunar igneous rocks. Figure 7 shows these examples (using data as at 14/11/95).

Consider Fig. 5 where Prof. Wyllie's URL address is input to the system. The

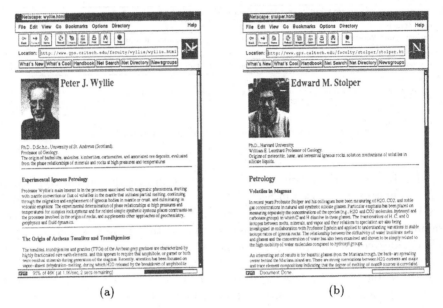

(a) (b)

Fig. 7. Web Sites on Geology.

adopted granularity level creates a frame for each different topic or sub-section, so each section of text in Fig. 7(a), headed by a bold-face title, will give rise to a frame in the HyperMap model. Thus 'Experimental Igneous Petrology' is an example of a frame in Fig. 6. Suppose that after the user has clicked on the 'build hyperspace' option he wants to see the map of the hyperspace through the option 'display topology'. This part is still under development but Fig. 8 shows the kind of maps that could result from this option using Venn diagram and taking into consideration the similarity measure between the linked material. In Fig. 8(a) we have four classes or frames represented where w, x, y and z correspond respectively to 'Experimental Igneous Petrology', 'The Origin of Archean Tonalites and Trondhjemites', 'Immiscibity between Silicate and Carbonate Melts' and 'Selected Publications'.

In Fig. 8(a) we can see a diagrammatic representation of spatial relations between specific classes or frames w, x, y and z. The set of relations created in this example include only two spatial relations, overlap (PO) and disjoint (DR): PO(x, y), PO(x, z), PO(x, w), PO(y, x), PO(y, z), PO(y, w), PO(z, x), PO(z, y), DR(z, w), PO(w, x), PO(w, y) and DR(w, z). Notice that each overlapped area varies in size. This corresponds to the similarity closeness on proximity measures: classes x and y are the closest ones ($S = 0.17$), followed by y and w ($S = 0.08$), x and w ($S = 0.05$), y and z ($S = 0.03$) and the least connected ones are x and z ($S = 0.01$). Also we can easily see that there is no connection between classes w and z.

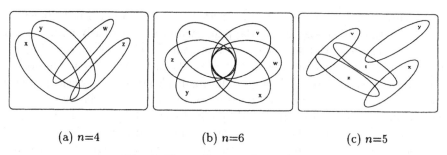

(a) $n=4$ (b) $n=6$ (c) $n=5$

Fig. 8. Venn diagram for n classes.

The diagrams in Fig. 8 were drawn by hand. It would be nice if such Venn diagrams could be drawn automatically. Figure 9 shows an extension to Venn diagrams for 'n' classes [1, 2], which can be used in the automatization drawing process, trough the techniques presented in [23] (though without accounting for overlap degree varying with S).

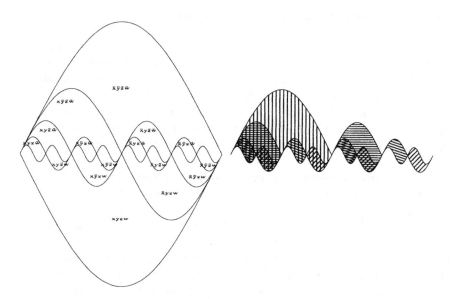

Fig. 9. Venn-type diagram for four classes.

Figure 7(b) includes material related to Prof. Stolper's work. The created frames are 'Volatiles in Magmas', 'Melt Densities at High Pressures', 'Thermodynamics of Geological Materials', 'Melting of the Earth's Mantle', 'Hydrogen Isotopes in Martian (?) Meteorites' and 'Selected Publications'. Figure 8(b) shows the resulting map using a Venn diagram with six classes where t, v, w, x, y

and z correspond respectively to the created frames mentioned just above.

Notice that all classes are overlapping each other apparently with the same degree of closeness. But we could also represent the same example of Fig. 8(b) through Fig. 8(c) where a threshold of $S \geq 0.05$ on the C relation is imposed to reinforce the strength of overlapping. This figure also takes into consideration the similarity closeness on proximity measures so we notice that classes v and z are the closest ones $(S = 0.13)$, followed by v and t $(S = 0.09)$, x and t $(S = 0.08)$, x and z $(S = 0.07)$ and the weakest overlapping y and t $(S = 0.06)$.

For a more general examination over both sites above imagine that we change the granularity specifications from topics or sub-sections, inside a specific site, to the complete sites of Professors Wyllie and Stolper. Then a rough analysis would be that Prof. Wyllie's site includes material more closely related as a whole, since the strongest link was created between frames x and y $(S = 0.17)$, even though his site is 1 Kbyte bigger than Prof. Stolper's one. The strongest relation in Prof. Stolper's material is between v and z with a lower similarity index $(S = 0.13)$. These are some of the possibilities using HyperMap's approach to reason over material's content through the Internet.

5 Related Work and Final Comments

Although the model presented in Sect. 2 cannot be considered as a complete approach to perform automated KA through the Internet, it introduces some possible solutions to the problems referred in Sect. 1. In the traditional kinds of hyperspace indexing tools, or even in the intelligent ones[13], the ability to build semantic maps of hyperspace automatically is missing. The possibility of reasoning over degrees of strength of content between related material, expressed through formal specifications, would be very helpful for the disorientation problem.

There is research on designing general classification frameworks for arbitrary documents making use of AI techniques, for example through a fuzzy object-comparison [20] perspective, or based on the reuse methodology developed in the SOUR project [18] which aims to build a useful tool for the classification, storing and retrieval of Internet information.

More formal work involving the writing of formal specifications to reason about multimedia material content using set theory and mereology has been done [30]. This research focuses on the re-examination of the roles of mereology and set theory in knowledge representation where a multimedia indexing system can be viewed as a particular SetNM theory.

Even though it does not claim to be a complete approach to perform automated KA through the Internet, the approach presented here has still some problems to be solved. The Venn diagrams for 'n' classes presented in the previous section (or indeed other diagrammatic techniques) may become inadequate

---

[13] Either the normal automated web wanderers, spiders and robots such as WebCrawler, JumpStation, Aliweb, WWWWorm, or the intelligent knowledge-based or interactive learning approaches, such as WebWatcher and Letizia.

on realistically sized knowledge-based systems. Techniques such as clustering or multidimensional scaling may be applicable to represent many dimensions of the hyperspace on the computer screen. Visualization techniques are still an open research issue, since finding appropriate methods to present a mass of data on a limited screen size is not an easy problem to be solved. Also a visualization tool, which focuses on the integration of WWW systems, should not only enable the structure of the hyperspace to be displayed comprehensively (perhaps at variable grain sizes), but also should readily allow the user to access the different parts of the hyperspace and the information to be found there. Another very hard problem, which is subject of many research projects, is how to deal with non-textual information such as the automatic extraction of attributes from graphics, sound and video frames.

Perhaps more elaborated spatial metaphors for KA should be searched for in the light of information systems where the intention is not only to help alleviate problems of disorientation in cyberspace, but actually acquire knowledge available through the Internet. Recently, there has been strong interest in the application of spatial metaphors and three-dimensional interaction to information systems, but no similar interest seems to have manifested itself in the KA community. Works from SemNet [7][14] through to a fully-integrated 3D viewer [3] implemented as part of the Harmony browser for the Hyper-G distributed hypermedia information system [4, 5][15] should be reviewed in the light of the possibility of integrating hypermedia distributed systems with KA.

Finally, automated KA is the next natural progression of the KA task. Whether automated methods might be more competent than humans for acquiring or fine-tuning certain kinds of knowledge or even might significantly reduce the heavy load and high cost in human resources are topics not specifically treated here. But, certainly future work on real automated KA through the Internet should involve a more complex approach in order to make possible the reuse of domain knowledge bases. Ontologies, inference knowledge, task knowledge and problem solving methods must certainly be contemplated by such approaches, and maybe by the use of CommonKADS Conceptual Modeling Language [26] or other formal modeling languages. This article reports on work still under evaluation. Although a proof-of-concept prototype has been implemented, clearly further work is required before a definitive tool can be built. However we believe that these ideas may prove to be a useful approach to the challenging task of automatically structuring of knowledge.

---

[14] An exploratory system where knowledge bases can be visualized through directed graphs in three dimensions. Nodes or labeled rectangles are connected by lines or arcs, which do not intersect each other because of the 3D model. Techniques like random, multidimensional scaling, clustering, fisheye views, heuristics and manual editing were explored for positioning nodes.

[15] A system that provides a three-dimensional graphical overview map of the information space, which is a dynamic representation of the Hyper-G information space mapped out onto a plane with the third dimension used to encode document size. Here users can "fly" over the hyperspace landscape looking for salient features and access documents by double-clicking their 3D representations.

References

1. D. E. Anderson and F. L. Cleaver. "Venn-Type Diagrams for arguments of n terms", *Journal of Symbolic Logic*, vol. 30, number 2, June 1965.

2. D. E. Anderson and R. B. Angell. "Venn diagrams for n classes", *Journal of Symbolic Logic*, vol. 31 (Abstracts of Papers), 1966.

3. K. Andrews and M. Pichler. "Hooking up 3-space: three-dimensional models as fully-fledged hypermedia documents". *Proceedings of MHVR'94*, Moscow, September 1994.

4. K. Andrews and F. Kappe. "Soaring through hyperspace: a snapshot of Hyper-G and its Harmony client". *Proc. of Eurographics Symposium on Multimedia/Hypermedia in Open Distributed Environments*. Graz, Austria, June 1994.

5. K. Andrews, F. Kappe and J. Schipflinger. "Harmony: a tool for navigating through deep hyperspace". *Proc. of ED-MEDIA 94*, Vancouver, Canada, June 1994.

6. E. J. Conklin. "Hypertext: an introduction and survey". *IEEE Computer*, 20(9), 1987.

7. K. M. Fairchild, S. E. Poltrock, and G. W. Furnas. "SemNet: three-dimensional representations of large knowledge bases". In R. Guindon, editor, *Cognitive Science and its Applications for Human-Computer Interaction*, Lawrence Erlbaum, Hillsdale, NJ, pp. 201-233, 1988.

8. B. R. Gaines and M. L. G. Shaw. "Integrated Knowledge Acquisition Architectures". *Journal of Intelligent Information Systems*, 1(1):9-34, 1992.

9. K. Hapeshi. "Simulating the Development of the Language Lexicon". *AISB Quarterly*, Winter 1994/95 No. 90, 1995.

10. D. L. Hintzman. "MINERVA 2: A simulation model of human memory". *Behaviour Research Methods, Instruments and Computers*, 16:96-101, 1984.

11. D. L. Hintzman. "Schema abstraction" in a multiple-trace memory model. *Psychological Review*, 93:411-28, 1986.

12. W. James. *The Principles of Psychology*. New York: Holt, 1890.

13. M. R. Kibby and T. Mayes. "Towards Intelligent Hypertext". In R. McAllese (ed.), *Hypertext: Theory into Practice*, Intellect Ltd, Oxford, England, pp. 138–144, 1993.

14. T. Kohonen. *Content-addressable memories*. Springer-Verlag. New York, 1987.

15. F. Lehmann and A. G. Cohn. "The EGG/YOLK Reliability Hierarchy: Data Translation and Model Integration Using Ordered Sorts with Prototypes". In *Proc. 3rd Int. Conf. on Knowledge Management (CIKM94)*. ACM Press, Gaithersburg, Maryland, 1994.

16. H. Maurer. "Why Hypermedia Systems are Important". In *Proc. 4th Int. Conf. on Computer Assisted Learning*. Springer-Verlag, 1992.

17. G. A. Miller, R. Beckwith, C. Fellbaum, D. Gross and K. Miller. *Introduction to WordNet: an On-line Lexical Database*, (WordNet documentation), 1993.

18. F. L. Neves and J. N. Oliveira. "Classifying Internet Objects". In *Proc. of the WWW National Conference Internet Multimedia Information – IMI'95.*. Braga, Portugal, July 1995.

19. Hyacinth S. Nwana, R. C. Paton, T. J. M. Bench-Capon, and M. J. R. Shave. "Facilitating the development of knowledge based systems". *The European Journal on Artificial Intelligence*, 4(2/3):60-73, 1991.

20. J. N. Oliveira. "Fuzzy Object Comparison and Its Application to a Self-Adaptable Query Mechanism". *Invited Paper, 6th Int. Fuzzy Systems Association World Congress.*, 1995.

21. Célia G. Ralha. "Towards an Intelligent Hyper-Media Environment for Knowledge Acquisition". In *Proc. 2nd Groningen Int. Information Technology - GRONICS'95 (http://www.cs.rug.nl/~tino/gronics/CeliaRalha.ps.gz).* Groningen, The Netherlands, February 1995.

22. Célia G. Ralha and A. G. Cohn. "Building Maps of Hyperspace". In *Proc. of the WWW National Conference Internet Multimedia Information - IMI'95 (http://www.di.uminho.pt/cdrom/tmp/papers/p5/5.ps).* Braga, Portugal, July 1995.

23. Célia G. Ralha. *Venn Diagram for 'n' classes - Design Report*, October 1995. (Not published).

24. D. A. Randell, Z. Cui and A. G. Cohn. "A Spatial Logic based on Regions and Connection". In *Proc. 3rd Int. Conf. on Knowledge Representation and Reasoning*, Morgan Kaufmann, San Mateo, pp. 165-176, 1992.

25. J. A. Rantanen. "Hypermedia in knowledge acquisition and specification of user interface for KBS: an approach and a case study". *Knowledge Acquisition*, 2(3):259-278, 1990.

26. G. Schreiber, B. Wielinga, H. Akkermans, W.Van de Velde and A. Anjewierden. "CML: The Common KADS Conceptual Modeling Language". In Luc Steels, Guus Schreiber and Walter Van de Velde (eds), *A Future for Knowledge Acquisition - Proc. of EKAW'94*, Springer-Verlag, Belgium, pp. 1-25, 1994.

27. R. Semon. *Mnemic Psychology.* (B. Duffy, Trans.) London: George Allen & Unwin, 1923. (Original work published 1909).

28. P. Simons. *Parts: A Study in Ontology.* Clarendon Press, Oxford, 1987.

29. John Venn. *Symbolic Logic*, London, 1881.

30. W. Zadrozny and M. Kim. "Computational Mereology: A Study of Part-of Relations for Multimedia Indexing". In C. Eschenbach, Ch. Habel and B. Smith (eds), *Topological Foundations of Cognitive Science - Papers from the Workshop at the FISI-CS*, NY, July 1994.

A   Appendix

The following lists show the key-words used to encode the set of attributes of frames or classes (w, x, y and z) related to the URL address of Prof. Wyllie in Sect. 4.

Experimental Igneous Petrology (w): temperatures, phase, relationships, systems, pressures, associated, professor, rocks, igneous, experimental, processes, high, origin, mantle.

The Origin of Archean Tonalites and Trondhjemites (x): Lee, carbonate-rich, melt, primary, glass, lee, during, igneous, rocks, carbonatites, Woh-jer, basalt, experimental, related, liquid, defined, minerals, boundary, subduction, between, liquids, carbonate, phase, silicate, Experimental, Nuk, Figure, determine, depth, positions, results, field, function, generation, tonalites, requires, pressures, contours, lower, fig, match, laan, der, fields, terms, h, van, nuk, approach, area, temperatures, trondhjemite, 1, content, contents, surface, pressure, temperature, 2, garnet, figure, amphibole, boundaries, magmas, h2o, residual, liquidus

Immiscibity between Silicate and Carbonate Melts (y): phase, h2o, residual, minerals, liquidus, petrological, evidence, alkaline, igneous rocks, carbonatites, crystalline, products, conjugate, immiscible, liquids, experimental, studies, miscibility, gaps, variety, silicate, carbonate, range, pressures, conditions, controls, _A-enriched, magma, precipitates, minerals, evolution, _A, differentiates, residual, carbonate-rich, melt, yields, phase, Woh-jer Lee, related, problems, lithosphere, crust, boundary, minerals, primary, carbonates, factor, liquid paths, igneous rocks, two-liquid,phase boundaries, pressure, Na/(Ca+Mg+Fe), Ca/(Mg+Fe), results, metasomatism, carbonatic, fluids, subduction, carbonatites, deposits

Selected Publications (z): Van, Geol, Petrol, Laan, Wyllie, metasomatism, petrol, applications, laan, der, 1993, wolf, van, melting, geol, implications, kbar, r, s, 1992, m, b, wyllie, p, j

Diagrammatic Knowledge Acquisition: Elicitation, Analysis and Issues

Peter C-H. Cheng

ESRC Centre for Research in Development, Instruction and Training,
Department of Psychology, University of Nottingham, Nottingham, NG7 2RD.
email: peter.cheng@nottingham.ac.uk

Abstract. This paper considers the acquisition of knowledge that experts would naturally express in the form of diagrams — diagrammatic knowledge acquisition, DKA. The implications for DKA of previous research on diagrammatic representations and reasoning are considered. Examples of knowledge elicitation and knowledge analysis, with two different diagrammatic representations, are given. They demonstrate the feasibility of DKA. Issues raised by the analysis of the examples are discussed and consideration is given to the development of DKA tools and methodologies. DKA is distinguished from knowledge visualization, which attempts to design effective visual presentations of given information that is already expressed as propositions.

1 Introduction

What are the potential roles for diagrammatic knowledge representations in knowledge acquisition (KA)? What are the problems to be addressed when attempting to use diagrams in eliciting and analysing expert knowledge for use in knowledge based systems, KBSs? The desire of experts to draw diagrams whilst solving problems or explaining some aspect of their specialist domain will be a familiar phenomenon to knowledge engineers. Similarly, figures, charts, flow diagrams and a host of other diagrammatic forms are found in the documents of most domains, such as text books, instruction manuals, working sketches. However, use of diagrammatic representations for KA has been rather neglected in this field. By overlooking diagrams we may not only be missing important knowledge and powerful problem solving methods, in some domains, but also missing efficient methods for eliciting, analysing and implementing knowledge.

Diagrammatic representations have an established place in knowledge engineering, but this has mainly been in the form of data visualization aids, rather than in processes to acquire knowledge (see Jones, 1988 for a review). In cognitive science much is known about how humans reason with particular diagrams and what makes effective diagrammatic representations. Several AI systems have demonstrated the feasibility and benefits of using diagrammatic representations, which could be potentially incorporated into KBSs.

Diagrammatic representations are being considered rather than *visual representations*. Diagrammatic representations are a subset of all visually perceived representations, and are graphical notational systems that involve artificial, symbolic or simplified visual depiction, which are not organised in the form of a linear verbalisable or propositional structures (Kulpa, 1994). In this view, most KA techniques are not diagrammatic, although some exploit visual features, including some implementations of repertory grids and concept laddering. The graphical aspects of these techniques aids the visualization of the information rather than deeply encoding the knowledge. *Propositional representations* will to refer to conventional knowledge representational formalisms, such a logic, semantic networks and frames/schema.

Shaw and Woodward (1990) present a framework describing knowledge acquisition as modelling expert knowledge. The adequacy of their model will not be discussed here, but it is merely adopted as a framework that provides a convenient context and consistent terminology, for the purposes of the present analysis. Central to the framework are the processes involved in the production of (i) intermediate knowledge bases and (ii) computer knowledge bases from (a) mental models, (b) conceptual models and (c) semi-formal conceptual models[1]. A computer knowledge base is essentially a KBS and intermediate knowledge base is an organized and refined, but unimplemented, body of knowledge. Mental models are internal to experts and conceptual models are informal externalizations of the mental models, which are communicated to others. Semi-formal conceptual models are final working models or operational models. Elicitation and analysis procedures are involved in the production of intermediate knowledge bases. Elicitation follows introspection of mental models and conceptual models. Analysis procedures draw upon communication processes with conceptual models and the semi-formal conceptual models. Analysis procedures are also required for the production of computer knowledge bases, in conjunction with implementation procedures that use formalisations of semi-formal conceptual models. The development of intermediate knowledge bases and computer knowledge bases inform each other by means of the analysis procedures. Shaw and Woodward view the processes and procedures as bi-directional; the development of the knowledge bases and the various levels of models mutually aid each others' development. The image of acquisition presented has multiple layers of knowledge, which are closely interconnected by cognitive processes and acquisition procedures.

Now, for the considerations of diagrammatic KA (DKA) it is a matter of identifying diagrammatic versions for each of the knowledge and procedural components of Shaw and Woodward's framework. What are the diagrammatic forms of mental models, conceptual models and semi-formal conceptual models? How can knowledge elicitation, analysis and implementation procedures be conducted with diagrams? Are diagrammatic representations suitable formalisms for building, or incorporating into, intermediate knowledge bases and computer knowledge bases? The focus of this paper will be on elicitation and analysis procedures from conceptual models and semi-formal conceptual models.

---

[1]Shaw and Woodward's term is *models of the conceptual models,* but *semi-formal conceptual models* is used as it is less cumbersome and somewhat more descriptive.

In the paper research on diagrammatic representations and reasoning that is relevant to DKA is first considered. The main body of the paper will consider the potential of two forms of diagrammatic representations for KA, as a means to being to identify some of the issues for DKA. Conventional Cartesian graphs and a special class of diagrams, called Law Encoding Diagrams (Cheng, 1994, 1995a, in press), will be considered. They are both well suited to expressing qualitative and quantitative relations among multiple variables. A discussion of the issues raised by the examples then follows, with brief consideration of how to develop methodologies and tools for DKA.

2 Diagrammatic Knowledge Representations and Reasoning

There has been substantial interest in reasoning and problem solving with diagrammatic representations in Artificial Intelligence, cognitive science and cognitive psychology. There have been various attempts to produce generative taxonomies of visual representations (e.g., Lohse *et al.*, 1994; Bertin, 1983), but these are too general to be useful for examining DKA. Work that can address components of Shaw and Woodward's (1990) framework will be briefly reviewed to provide some insights about the benefits of diagrams for KA and to flag some potential difficulties.

To begin, consider the nature of expert mental models. Although there has been much work on expertise (e.g., Chi *et al.*, 1988) and diagrammatic reasoning (e.g., Narayanan 1992), only a few studies of expert reasoning with diagrams have been conducted. Most notable is Koedinger and Anderson's (1990) work on *diagrammatic configuration schemas* (DCSs). DCSs are diagrammatic perceptual chunks. By comparing novice and expert geometry problem solvers, they found that structural constraints in the form of diagrammatic whole-part relations were used by experts as an efficient knowledge representations. Experts performed better, because they have schemas that combine diagrams with information relevant to common problem states (configurations). They solve problems by searching for DCSs that are applicable to the problem situation, matching parts of the given situation with the diagrams in DCSs. The information in the slots of active DCSs becomes available for inferences. Some implications for DKA flow from the existence of DCSs. By assuming that knowledge in a domain is encoded in DCS-like representations, this can guide and productively constrain knowledge elicitation, analysis and implementation. When an expert draws a diagram during elicitation, the general form of DCSs may be taken as a template within which to try to organise the expert's knowledge. During analysis DCS-like templates may suggests how to maximize the completeness of the knowledge, by explicitly identifying empty slots and seeking information to fill them. Given representations in the form of DCSs, the implementation of a KBS should be largely based around the search of the space of DCSs for those that are applicable to the target problem. These are fairly strong recommendations, but it should be noted that the applicability of Koedinger & Anderson's theory beyond geometry problem solving is yet to be fully demonstrated.

Moving from mental models to conceptual models and semi-formal conceptual models, consider the seminal paper on diagrammatic representations by Larkin &

Simon (1987), entitled 'Why a diagram is (sometimes) worth 10,000 words'. By building and comparing computational models of problem solving with diagrammatic and sentential representations, they demonstrated that there are benefits in the processes of search and recognition in problem solving with diagrams. In diagrams information needed for particular inferences is often found at the same location. This locational indexing makes the search for pieces of relevant data easier and reduces the effort to recognise what rules (productions) are applicable, by limiting the amount of symbolic matching that is required. This work is important to DKA, because it implies that consideration must be give to the way information is indexed within diagrams. Locational indexing is important, but this may not be apparent from experts' own descriptions of their diagrams or from observations of diagrams in use. Thus, during elicitation in which diagrams are drawn, care must be taken to understand how and where the experts' focus of attention resides in the diagram, at different stages in problem solutions.

On the machine side of the KA process, there are various lines of related work. There has been much work on graphical interfaces for knowledge engineering (see, Jones, 1988, for a review). Eisenstadt and colleagues (Eisenstadt *et al.,* 1990) use the term *visual knowledge engineering* (VKE) to refer to the synthesis of visual programming tools, program visualization tools, a sound knowledge engineering methodology, and AI programming support tools. The difference between DKA and these approaches to visual knowledge engineering is that DKA is attempting to obtain knowledge from experts that would normally be expressed in diagrams, and that may necessarily require diagrams. VKE, on the other hand, aims to re-present information, which is already expressed in a conventional propositional notation, in a graphical or visual format, to aid KBS development. Thus tables, abstract labelled networks and flow charts are common representations in VKE, but (Cartesian) graphs and structural or configurational diagrams will be used in DKA.

Of interest to DKA are techniques for parsing diagrams. Individual techniques exist for particular classes of diagrams, mostly network or node-link diagrams (e.g., Lutz, 1986). The development of techniques for parsing graphs and configurational diagrams would enhance diagrammatic elicitation, analysis and implementation procedures. However, the prospect of effective engines that would translate diagrams into standard propositional representations is remote, because of the high information content of diagrams and the wide variety of forms of problem solving they support, especially those that exploit perceptual inferences. An alternative is to directly incorporate diagrams in intermediate or computer knowledge bases. For intermediate knowledge bases a partial solution is to store diagrams alongside related knowledge from the target domain (perhaps as bit maps).

For computer KBSs there is work that suggests that systems may in the future use diagrammatic representations. For example, Koedinger & Anderson (1990) have built a simulation model that uses diagrammatic configuration schemas for geometry problem solving, to demonstrate the sufficiency of DCS. In addition to processes to search its space of schemas, the model also possesses the capability to parse a limited set of geometrical objects. Furnas (1992) has built a rule based system, with an architecture similar to a standard production system, that reasons with bitmaps. Rule conditions identify small bitmap patterns and rule actions specify changes to those patterns. Other problem solving systems that possess diagrammatic representations are described by Funt (1977), Novak (1977) and Shrager (1990). Unlike Furnas's system, which reasons with diagrams only, these other systems integrate propositional representations with the diagrams. This raises the important issue of multiple representations in expert reasoning, which was directly addressed by Tabachneck *et al.* (1994). They found

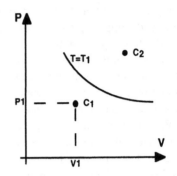

Fig. 1. A simple Cartesian Graph

that an expert uses the unique features of each representation for different purposes. Diagrams are used as place holders and to summarise information, whereas verbal expression are used to give semantic meaning and for making causal explanations.

Diagrammatic representations and reasoning has been studied in some detail, but the problem here is to understand the possible uses of diagrams in the processes of KA. Some of the research has direct implications for DKA, but this section has been somewhat speculative. In the remainder of the paper, the focus will be on concrete examples of diagrammatic representations and how they may be used for KA.

3 Elicitation with Cartesian Graphs

Cartesian graphs are a common form of diagrammatic representation, which can be found in a wide variety of domains. In Shaw and Woodward's terms, graphs are often used as conceptual models but are also commonly found as semi-formal conceptual models. For example, an expert's pencil sketch graph on the back of an enveloped to explain a process to colleague would be a conceptual model, but a printed graph in an plant operating manual is a semi-formal conceptual model. We will consider how the knowledge in such graphs can be elicited for the development of intermediate knowledge bases.

Typical Cartesian graphs define at set of axes so that points in a co-ordinate space can be identified. Figure 1 shows a P-V co-ordinate space (say pressure and volume). The magnitudes of a point in the graph is obtained by reading values off the appropriate axes; for example, for case C_1 the values are (V_1, P_1), as shown by dashed lines in the Figure 1. Families of points can be identified by the curves in the space; for example, the curve in Figure 1 is a contour for a particular value of another variable T. Similarly, families of curves can be shown by multiple lines in the graph; in Figure 2, three curves for different values of U are shown.

Simple graphs may be used in various ways for KA. Because the axes define a co-ordinate space, it is possible to distinguish different states. For example, suppose an expert sketches Figure 1 during a knowledge elicitation session. It is apparent that the space can be divided into two regions either side of the central curve, and that cases C_1 and C_2 fall in different regions. By further questioning the expert, it may be possible to find distinguishing characteristics for the regions, for instance, that points above the curve represent "critical" cases but those below are "normal" cases. There is information in the graph which may help to refine the distinction between critical and normal cases, by considering the shape and location of the curve in the co-ordinate space. Thus, critical cases are likely when both V and P are large, but unlikely when both P and V are small. Further, when either V or P is large but the other is small, there is a moderate possibility that the cases will be critical.

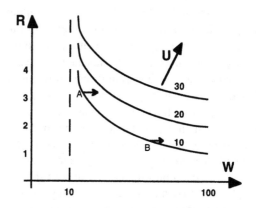

Fig. 2. A more complex graph

The purpose of a graph like Figure 1 may not be to distinguish different state spaces or regions, but could be to specify the relation between the variables P and V. If the graph is only a rough sketch, it is possible to infer that the P appears to be a monotonically decreasing function of V. If the graph is drawn more accurately, with scales to the axes, it may be possible use a curve fitting technique to find a equation describing the relation. Guidance about the appropriateness of different techniques can come by further questioning the expert. For example, a simple linear approximation may be sufficient when the curvature of the line is low and the expert is uncertain about its precise shape. Fitting polynomials to curves is a somewhat more sophisticated option for graphs that experts can draw more accurately. With further elicitation, it may be possible to select a suitable order for the polynomial, using the expert's knowledge of the number of characteristic operating modes of the target system, which might correspond to the number expected roots. If the expert says that the relation is periodic, then Fourier analysis may be used. The usefulness of the outputs of such analytical techniques for the eventual KBS will depend on the nature and tasks of the domain.

A greater variety of knowledge can be obtained from more complex graphs, like Figure 2, which an expert may have carefully drawn or that might be found in the documentation for a domain. In Figure 2 three curves for particular values of U are shown in a W-R co-ordinate space. The values on the axes permit quantitative facts to be inferred from the graph; for example, when $W=100$, it happens that R and U are linearly related. Although the graph's axes indicates that R and U continue to infinity, we may take the values on the axes as delimiting likely ranges of values that are of interest in the domain, unless otherwise specified. The graph not only gives the relations among variables but also the ranges over which the relations are known to hold. For example, the graph shows that there is a limiting minimum value of $W(=10)$, when R is large. It may be the case that there is a relation for R and W to the left of the asymptote, but this cannot be inferred from the graph.

Suppose that the line for $U=20$, in Figure 2, is a boundary between critical and normal cases, as in the previous graph. In this graph the contours for values of U provides useful information about the proximity of particular states to the boundary. For example, an expert may indicate that the area between curves for $U=10$ and $U=20$ should be treated as a warning zone. A rule may be formulated which states that if the R and W are such that the warning zone is entered, then corrective action should be taken to prevent the system moving nearer criticality. Further, given the shape of the warning zone it is possible to infer, when R is constant and $U=10$, that a small change in W is more dangerous at point A than it is at B, as shown by the arrows in Figure 2. For case B action must be taken promptly, even for small increases of W.

The examples illustrates some of the forms of knowledge that are encoded in graphs and that may be elicited using them. These include: qualitative relations among variables; rates of change of variables with respect to each other; algebraic approximations to relations; different systems states or cases of phenomena, plus boundary conditions for them; and, sensible ranges over which to consider the variables, for which the relations are valid. Although all these forms of information can be obtained by conventional propositional KA techniques, there are benefits in using a graph. In graphs, as with most diagrams, information that is often needed for particular inferences is often found at the same location in the diagram (Larkin and Simon, 1987). Typically information is neatly integrated within a diagram, so it is likely to be easier to obtain related information from a graph or diagram than from propositional knowledge structures. Experts can effectively use the conventions for constructing graphs as constraints to produce such compact and coherent packages of knowledge. Some properties of diagrams are perceptually obvious and require little effort to identify, such as the gradients at different points on a curve. Further, important information in diagrams often appears as emergent features (Koedinger, 1992), such as the set of curves tending towards an asymptote in Figure 2. This means acquisition of derived or inferred knowledge can be easier with diagrams than propositional representations, which may require more cognitive effort.

We now move from considerations of elicitation with single graphs to deal with knowledge analysis with multiple graphs.

4 Analysis with Cartesian Graphs

Cartesian graphs are a flexible yet formal form of knowledge representation, so they can also be used in knowledge analysis procedures. Such procedures are used for the refinement of intermediate knowledge bases and for the development of computer knowledge bases. An example is examined in which graphs are used for consistency and completeness checking.

Consider a simple hypothetical example of KA for the dynamic control of a fermentation process, in which the yield rate, Y, of the process is proportional to the product of three variables, say, temperature deviation from some optimum, dT, nutrient concentration, C, and oxygen concentration, G. Suppose the expert has during an initial elicitation phase identified Y, dT and C as pertinent variables, and has drawn different graphs to show the relations among the variables under various

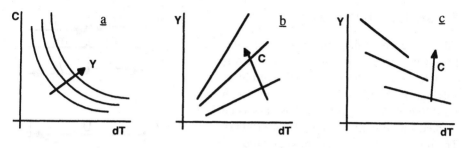

Fig. 3. Different perspectives in multiple graphs

conditions. During an analysis phase the consistency of the knowledge may be tested by examining the form of the graphs. If the expert had drawn Figure 3a and 3b for the process then there is no problem, because the graphs are consistent; both show that $Y \propto C \cdot dT$. However, if Figures 3a and 3c were drawn, then comparing these graphs reveals a difficulty, because Y and dT do not both increase together (with C constant). There are at least three possible reasons for the inconsistency. First, one of the graphs could be wrong. On telling the expert about the problem, the expert may simply recognise that one of the graphs is in error. Second, the model of the process may be incomplete, perhaps a hidden variable is influencing the process. For example, under Figure 1c the oxygen concentration, G, may be to high, so causing temperature dependent aerobic degeneration of the product to occur. Finally, the graphs may not apply over a consistent range of one of the variables, but by extending that range the incompatibility might be resolved. For example, all three graphs in Figure 3 would be consistent, if Figures 3b and 3c apply disjointly to low and high value ranges of dT, respectively. This would imply that Figure 3a is only showing the left hand side, low dT values, of a larger U-shaped curve. More direct inferences could be made about the ranges given information regarding the values on axes of the graphs.

Analysis in DKA is feasible with Cartesian graphs. The potential benefits are similar to the benefits noted for knowledge elicitation. Graphs allow powerful perceptual inferences to be made, such as visually joining Figure 3c to the right of Figure 3b and imagining that the sets of lines form inverted 'U' shaped curves. Equivalent inferences can be made with algebraic representations of the processes, but it is not simple to generate a formula that will have the correct form (shape) for the full range of all three variables. Similar, it is likely that inconsistencies will be more readily spotted in a set of graphs than in a set of abstract equations or other propositional representations. Graphs are a common form of representation, that most experts may find more natural to use than existing propositional representations in KA.

Graphs are not the only form of diagrams. The next two sections consider a class of diagrams that may provide other benefits to KA.

5 Law Encoding Diagrams

This is a class of diagrammatic representations with some interesting properties and is used for various forms of expert problem solving. Problem solving and learning with Law Encoding Diagrams (LEDs) has been studied empirically (Cheng 1994, 1995a). The role of LEDs in some important discoveries in the history of science has been investigated and computationally modelled (Cheng, in press; Cheng and Simon, 1995). Interactive computer based discovery learning environments have been built using LEDs for various domains (Cheng 1995a, 1995b). This section describes LEDs and considers some of the forms of problem solving that may be done with a particular LED. The next section considers how LEDs may be used for KA.

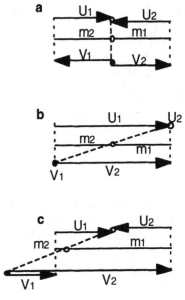

Fig. 4. 1DP Diagrams

A Law Encoding Diagram is a representation that encodes the underlying relations of a law, or a system of simultaneous laws, in the structure of a diagram by the means of geometric, topological and spatial constraints, such that each instantiation of a single diagram represents an instance of the phenomenon or one case of the law(s).

LEDs are effective for various forms of reasoning and problem solving, because they are representations at an intermediate level abstractions, which bridge the conceptual gulf between abstract general laws and descriptions of the behaviour of phenomena. LEDs are specialized computational devices for particular domains, that exploit the benefits of reasoning with diagrams, whilst ensuring that problem solving is grounded in the correct laws of a domain.

Figure 4 shows three examples of a LED, call the One-dimensional property diagram, 1DP diagram. Each 1DP diagram represents a single one-dimension head-on collision between two elastic bodies. In this domain there are six variables of interest, which are represented by diagrammatic elements in 1DP diagrams. The lines (vectors) u_1 and u_2 are the velocities of the two bodies before impact, and the lines v_1 and v_2 are the velocities afterwards. The subscripts indicate the two bodies, body-1 and body-2. The masses of the bodies are shown by the lines m_1 and m_2. Their relative sizes show the magnitudes of the variables. Each instantiation of a LED, a single diagram, represents one instance of the phenomenon; the 1DP diagrams in Figure 4 depict three collisions. For example, in Figure 4a the two bodies have the same mass and bounce off each other with the same speeds but in opposite directions.

The collisions domain is not one that we would attempt to learn about by doing KA, as it is already well understood in physics. However, it is a good domain to introduce LEDs, to show some of their properties and demonstrate the kinds of reasoning that can be done, and thus to see some of their potential for DKA. The underlying laws of the domain are momentum conservation and energy conservation. An impression of the complexity of relations that may encoded in LEDs can be seen by inspecting the algebraic forms of the laws;

$$m_1 u_1 + m_2 u_2 = m_1 v_1 + m_2 v_2 , \qquad \ldots 1$$

and

$$\tfrac{1}{2} m_1 u_1^2 + \tfrac{1}{2} m_2 u_2^2 = \tfrac{1}{2} m_1 v_1^2 + \tfrac{1}{2} m_2 v_2^2 , \qquad \ldots 2$$

respectively.

Laws are captured in LEDs by rules that constrain the geometric, spatial or topological structure of the diagrams. There are three such law-encoding constraints for the 1DP diagram. (i) The tails of the initial velocity arrows and the tips of the corresponding final velocity arrows must be in line vertically, so the total length of the u_1—u_2 line equals the total length of the v_1—v_2 line. (ii) The total length of the mass line, m_1—m_2, equals the length of the velocity lines. (iii) The small circles indicate the ends of the lines that are not fixed by the previous two constraints; the circles must lie in a straight vertical or diagonal line.

Cheng (1995a) describes the forms of reasoning and problem solving that are feasible with LEDs. These include: quantitative calculations; qualitative reasoning; configurational reasoning; debugging and trouble shooting; reasoning about extreme cases; analysis of complex interactions; extending LEDs to incorporate wider ranges of phenomena; and, high level conceptual explanations, which use notions of physical and temporal symmetry. Two examples of problem solving with 1DP diagrams are considered to give an impression of the capabilities of LEDs.

A common problem, especially in text books, is to find values of dependent variables (unknowns) given the values of independent variables (knowns). For example, what are the final velocities of two bodies in an impact, given that they approach from opposite directions with the same speed, but one is ten times heavier than the other (m_1/m_2=10)? Quantitative problems are relatively easy to solve with 1DP diagram, by drawing a diagram to scale, using the constraints given above, and measuring the required values. Figure 4c shows the diagram for the given problem, with the mass line divided in the ratio 10:1, showing the final velocities are v_1=0.6 and v_2=2.6. Given the simple geometric constraints that define 1DP diagrams, it is possible to compute precise answers using simple geometry. It is as easy to solve quantitative problems for other combinations of unknown variables, such as m_1 and m_2 given the 4 velocities.

For a representation to be generally useful in the present domain it should cope with collisions involving three or more bodies. For example, how can the behaviour of the balls in Newton's Cradle be explained (the executive toy with five suspended balls). What will happen when two balls hit three coming in the opposite direction? 1DP diagrams apply only to pairs of colliding bodies, so it initially seems that they cannot be used to explain complex interactions in Newton's cradle. However, the idea of pairs of impacts suggests that 1DP diagrams might be used in a (de)compositional manner, by treating the whole as a series of independent pair-wise collisions. This is possible because a single diagrammatic element may be shared in more than one 1DP

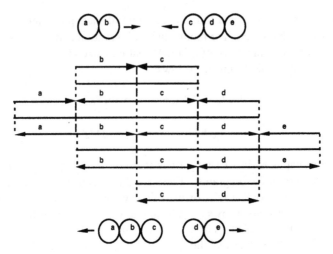

Fig. 5. Explaining Newton's Cradle

diagram. Figure 5 is a diagram for the given problem composed of six 1DP diagrams from Figure 4a. The first row shows ball b hitting ball c, and rebounding equally. The second row shows balls a and b colliding and similarly balls c and d. The collisions propagate until finally balls a, b and c go in the opposite direction to balls d and e. This is a good example of the compositionality of LEDs, a property that will be useful in DKA.

The two examples of problem solving with 1DP diagrams illustrate how LEDs can be the basis for some types of expert problem solving. A partial explanation of the effectiveness of LEDs, which is somewhat different to those mentioned above, is to view LEDs as perceptual chucks, similar but not identical to Koedinger & Anderson's diagrammatic configuration schemas. Although the DCS have only, so far, been found in geometry problem solving, it seems that much of Koedinger & Anderson's findings are applicable to LEDs, as they employ significant geometric constraints. Given the similarity between LEDs and DCSs, the observation in section 2, that it might be appropriate to use DCSs for DKA, may also be valid for LEDs. The next section considers DKA with LEDs.

6 LEDs for KA

The 1DP diagram is a highly specialised LED for a particular set of relations (Equations 1 and 2), so it is not suitable for general use in KA. There are other classes of LEDs that may be used, although one will be considered here — Algebra Triangle, AT, diagrams. (A specialised subset of AT diagrams have been used in a computer based tutoring system for electrical circuits, which allows the user to interactively manipulate the diagrams on screen, Cheng, 1995b.)

Figures 6a and 6b show the basic form of AT diagrams, using the fermentation example introduced in section 4 above. The height of the triangle is the value of dT and the length of the base is Y. The bold line beginning at the apex is a unit line and at its other end is a perpendicular line, *unit perpendicular*, whose length is C. These

AT diagrams encode the rela-
tion $Y=dT \cdot C$. Thus as C or dT
independently increase Y will
increase. Each diagram represents one set of values of the
variables; in Figure 6a dT is
greater than unity but in Figure
6b it is less than unity. Though
mathematically equivalent, it is

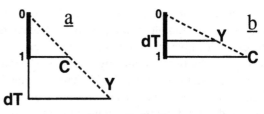

Fig. 6. AT diagrams

possible to conceptualize these AT triangles as encoding the relation $C=Y/dT$. Thus,
we would consider that C will increase as Y increases with dT held constant, but C
will decrease as dT increases with Y constant.

DKA with this class of LEDs could progress by the identification or
construction of AT diagrams, to find structures in which the changes to the variables
are consistent with the expert's expectations. It is assumed that the AT diagrams are
directly manipulable objects on a computer screen. For the fermentation process
example, an expert would initially identify the relevant variables and attempt to map
them into AT triangles. Knowing how AT triangles encode qualitative relations
among the variables, such as those mentioned in the previous paragraph, this would
suggest which variables should be mapped onto the height, base and the unit
perpendicular. The acceptability of the mapping can be checked by generating
different cases, particularly extreme ones, to see whether they match the expert's
predictions. Given an acceptable AT diagram, it is possible to infer a variety of rules
to be added to an intermediate or computer knowledge base. A rule could be quan-
titative/algebraic, if the expert is able to make a close numerical match between the
AT diagram and the process (e.g., If the process is fermentation and $dT=$<u> and
$C=$<v>, then $Y=$<u>*<v>). Alternatively, if the AT diagram is only an approximation
to the behaviour of the process, qualitative rules could be inferred (e.g., If the process
is fermentation and Y is increasing and dT is decreasing, then C is rapidly increasing).

Like the 1DP diagrams, AT diagrams can be used in a compositional fashion to
deal with complex interactions or relations. As the lines in the AT diagrams represent
variables, it is possible for a line to be shared by more than one AT triangle. Suppose
an expert introduces a new variable, G, to be incorporated into the model, Figure 7
shows three examples of composite AT diagrams that include G. Algebraically the

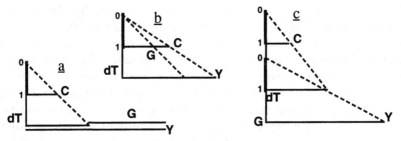

Fig. 7. Composite AT diagrams

relations that they encode are (a) $Y=dT \cdot C+G$; (b) $Y=dT(C+G)$; and, (c) $Y=dT \cdot C \cdot G$. This is a small sample of the possible AT diagram structures for four variables, but the examples give an impression of the expressive power of this class of LEDs for encoding relations. Again, by interactive manipulation of the diagrams, experts would be able to judge whether the changes among the variables are consistent with their knowledge of the target process. Quantitative or qualitative rules may be inferred directly from the structural form of the composite AT diagrams.

The examples demonstrate the feasibility of KA with LEDs, but the full potential for elicitation and analysis with AT diagrams, and LEDs in general, is yet to be investigated. However, it is possible to make some predications of how and why LEDs may be effective for KA based on the existing research with LEDs for problem solving and learning. The fundamental purpose of LEDs is to make the important relations of a domain readily accessible using the structure of diagrams. The potential uses and benefits of LEDs flow from this. LEDs may be effective for: (i) finding qualitative relations among variables; (ii) building algebraic models of systems; (iii) examining extreme and special cases; (iv) identifying general constraints among variables; (v) exploring rates of change among variables; and, (vi) if scales are provided for their elements, LED may be used for quantitative problem solving. As the relations among the variables are apparent from the structure of the diagram, it is likely that LEDs will be good for eliciting and analysing the forms of knowledge just listed. The cognitive effort required to generate and make inferences with LEDs is less than that of other representations, because they are diagrammatic and are at an intermediate level of abstraction. They are models that bridge the gap between abstract relations and concrete instances. The rules governing the structure of composite AT diagrams are simply defined and can be translated into algebraic formulas in a routine and straightforward manner. Particular instances can be examined by manipulating the shape of a LED within its diagrammatic constraints and unusual cases spotted as they appear as distinctive patterns.

7 Discussion: Research Issues for DKA

The possibility of DKA has been demonstrated using graphs and AT diagrams and some of the potential benefits have been discussed. Research on DKA is in its infancy, but the examples and the review of research on diagrammatic reasoning highlights various research issues for the field. This section deals with five of them.

The first issue concerns the need for tools to support DKA. KA can be greatly facilitated by computer based tools, which may improve the effectiveness of construction and revision of knowledge bases. In the case of DKA, tools will be particularly important, because diagrams are external representations that require a physical medium in which to be drawn. Tools will greatly reduce the effort needed for the drawing and re-drawing many different versions of graphs or composite AT diagrams. Direct on screen manipulation of LEDs will be essential to enable experts to simply examine and refine the diagrams. DKA tools are quite feasible with modern computers and can draw upon the same technology used in existing discovery environments that deploy interactive LEDs for learning (Cheng, 1995a, 1995b). For example, in a graph based DKA tool, should the users be (i) allowed to sketch curves on screen, or (ii) should they select curves from an on-line library? The first option gives the user greater flexibility, but requires computational machinery to interpret and encode the shape of the curves. In the second option, pre-coded descriptions of the curves could circumvent some of the problems of on line parsing of the graphs. However, this option relies on the library containing all the conceivable forms that a user might require.

Following DKA tools is the issue of devising effective ways to use the tools. Sketches of possible procedures were given in the above examples, but theoretically and empirically founded methodologies are needed. A systematic approach to the analysis of graphs is required and could be loosely based on the guidelines for structured interviews (mentioned by Shadbolt & Burton, 1989). These guidelines or protocols might consist of series of queries to the expert, to ensure the correctness and completeness of the information needed to interpret graphs. The protocols will need to consider the nature of the axes, the form of the curves, the role of other features in the co-ordinate space (e.g., asymptotes), and typical cases of reasoning with the graph. For example, take the axes, it is necessary to know whether the expert has assumed that they are linear or logarithmic, whether the origin coincides with zero values of the variables, and whether positive changes map onto upward and rightward movements along the axes.

A general protocol for DKA would be useful, but the diversity of diagrammatic representations makes this a remote possibility. An alternative is to decompose diagrams into separate problem solving functions and develop protocols associated with each function. A set of such functional roles of diagrams has been devised by Cheng (1996b). Previous work on reasoning with diagrammatic representations, see section 2, will also help to guide the development of methodologies. For example, perceptual schemas may be used as templates to encode knowledge associated with emergent features at particularly in locations in a diagram.

The third issue is the need for procedures to generate propositional rules from diagrammatic representations for use in existing KBSs. The translations will need to maintain the accuracy, completeness and consistency of the expressions generated, with respect to the original diagram. Some of the kinds of information that are available from graphs was considered in sections 3 and 4 above, but there are others, including: areas "under" the curve to the abscissa or ordinate (integration); interpolation to points between curves; possible extrapolation beyond the given ranges; and, the existence of symmetries which are often useful in reasoning. Achieving an appropriate balance the breadth of information and economy of knowledge in the translation is hard problem. Methods to match particular kinds of information in diagrams to specific forms of problem solving will have to be considered.

The fourth issue concerns the use of special representations for DKA, such as AT diagrams. The cost of learning to conceptualizing relations in terms of unfamiliar representations, implemented as contrived (rather than natural) elicitation techniques, may outweigh the potential benefits of having DKA tools in the first place. However, the diversity of kinds of diagrams suggests the possibility of marrying particular diagrams to different forms of knowledge or problem domains, or even to cope with the preferences of different experts. For example, a knowledge engineer might use AT diagrams with experts who are familiar with geometric reasoning, but adopt a graph based DKA tool for those who are not.

The final issue is mentioned to acknowledge its importance in the long term, but it is not considered in detail. This is the role of role of multiple representations in expertise. In particular, the integration of diagrams and propositional knowledge will be necessary for complete diagrammatic KBSs. Investigating DKA in relative isolation is the first step towards the more complex issue of integrating representations.

8 Conclusion

Diagrammatic knowledge acquisition has been somewhat neglected in KA. Here the feasibility of DKA has been shown, with some support from previous work on diagrammatic representations and reasoning. The identification and discussion of issues for study provides a context for future research. The development of graph and LED based KA tools, to investigate the issues discussed in the paper, has just been awarded funding. The construction of graph and LED based tools will involve the modifications to existing mechanisms used in interactive graphical learning environments. The work will be mainly focused on procedures for knowledge elicitation and knowledge analysis (to use Shaw and Woodward's conceptualization for the last time).

References

Bertin, J. (1983). *Seminology of Graphics: Diagrams, Networks, Maps*. Wisconsin: University of Wisconsin Press.

Cheng, P. C.-H. (1994). An empirical investigation of law encoding diagrams for instruction. In *Proceedings of the 16th Annual Conference of the Cognitive Science Society*. (pp. 171-176). Hillsdale, NJ: Lawrence Erlbaum Associates.

Cheng, P. C.-H. (1995a). Law encoding diagrams for instructional systems. *Journal of Artificial Intelligence in Education*, **6**(4).

Cheng, P. C.-H. (1995b). *AVOW tutor version 1.0: Instruction manual* (Technical Report No. 31). ESRC Centre for Research in Development, Instruction and Training, University of Nottingham.

Cheng, P. C.-H. (in press). Scientific discovery with law encoding diagrams. *Creativity Research Journal*.

Cheng, P. C.-H. (1996a). Problem solving and learning with diagrammatic representations. In D. Peterson (Eds.), *Forms of Representation* Intellect Books.

Cheng, P. C.-H. (1996b). Cognitive analysis of the functional roles of diagrams. Submitted to the *18th Annual Conference of the Cognitive Science Society*.

Cheng, P. C.-H., & Simon, H. A. (1995). Scientific Discovery and Creative Reasoning with Diagrams. In S. Smith, T. Ward, & R. Finke (Eds.), *The Creative Cognition Approach* (pp. 205-228). Cambridge, MA: MIT Press.

Chi, M. T. H., Glaser, R., & Farr, M. J. (Eds.). (1988). *The Nature of Expertise*. Hillsdale, NJ: L. Erlbaum Associates.

Eisenstadt, M., Domingue, J., Rajan, T., & Motta, E. (1990). Visual knowledge engineering. *IEEE Transactions on Software Engineering*, **116**(10), 1164-1177.

Funt, B. V. (1977). Whisper: A problem-solving system utilizing diagrams and a parallel processing retina. In *Fifth International Joint Conference on artificial Intelligence*, (pp. 286-291). San Mateo, CA: Morgan Kaufmann.

Furnas, G. W. (1992). Reasoning with diagrams only. In H. Narayanan (Eds.), *AAAI Technical Report on Reasoning with Diagrammatic Representations (Report No. SS-92-02)* (pp. 118-123). Menlo Park, CA: AAAI.

Jones, S. (1988). Graphical interfaces for knowledge engineering: an overview of relevant literature. *Knowledge Engineering Review*, **3**(3), 221-248.

Koedinger, K. R. (1992). Emergent properties and structural constraints: Advantages of diagrammatic representations for reasoning and learning. In N. H. Narayanan (Eds.), *AAAI Technical Report on Reasoning with Diagrammatic Representations (SS-92-02)* Menlo Park, CA: AAAI.

Koedinger, K. R., & Anderson, J. R. (1990). Abstract planning and perceptual chunks: Elements of expertise in geometry. *Cognitive Science*, **14**, 511-550.

Kulpa, Z. (1994). Diagrammatic representations and reasoning. *Machine Graphics and Vision*, **3**(1/2), 77-103.

Larkin, J. H., & Simon, H. A. (1987). Why a diagram is (sometimes) worth ten thousand words. *Cognitive Science*, **11**, 65-99.

Lohse, G., Biolsi, K., Walker, N., & Rueter, H. (1994). A classification of visual representations. *Communications of the ACM*, **37**(12), 36-49.

Lutz, R. (1986). *Diagram parsing - A new technique for artificial intelligence* (Research Paper No. CSRP.054). School of Cognitive and Computing Sciences, University of Sussex.

Narayanan, H. (Ed.). (1992). *AAAI Technical Report Reasoning with Diagrammatic Representations (SS-92-02)*. Menlo Park,CA:AAAI.

Novak, G. S. (1977). Representations of knowledge in a program for solving physics problems. In *Proceedings of the 5th International Joint Conference on Artificial Intelligence*, (pp. 286-291).

Shadbolt, N., & Burton, M. (1989). Knowledge elicitation: a systematic approach. In J. R. Wilson & N. E. Corlett (Eds.), *Evaluation of Human Work* London: Taylor & Francis.

Shaw, M. L. G., & Woodward, J. B. (1990). Modeling expert knowledge. *Knowledge Acquisition*, **2**(3), 179-206.

Shrager, J. (1990). Common-sense perception and the psychology of theory formation. In J. Shrager & P. Langley (Eds.), *Computational Models of Scientific Discovery and Theory Formation* (pp. 437-470). San Mateo, CA: Morgan Kaufmann.

Tabachneck, H. J. M., Leonardo, A. M., & Simon, H. A. (1994). How does an expert use a graph? A model of visual and verbal inferencing in economics. In A. Ram & K. Eiselt (Eds.), *Proceedings of the 16th Annual Conference of the Cognitive Science Society*. (pp. 842-847). Hillsdale, NJ: Lawrence Erlbaum Associates.

An Approach to Measuring Theory Quality

Edgar Sommer

GMD (German National Research Center for Information Technology)
AI Division (I3.KI)
Schloss Birlinghoven, 53757 Sankt Augustin, Germany
Fax +49(2241)14-2072, email eddi@gmd.de

Abstract. The quality of theories produced with the help of machine learning algorithms is usually measured in terms of accuracy and coverage. This paper reopens the issue of understandability of induced theories, which, while prominent in the early days of ML, seems to have fallen from favor in the sequel. This issue is especially relevant in the broader context of using ML as an aide in design and maintenance of knowledge bases for knowledge based systems. The guiding question is: beyond accuracy, what constitutes a good theory? An attempt at surveying relevant work in the fields of linguistics and cognitive psychology is made. The sympathetic reader will find this somewhat motivates the author's personal intuitions about the quality of a theory, hinging on understandability. These intuitions, in turn, point toward some simple criteria that may help in measuring quality. By way of consolation for those who do not share the author's intuitions, the criteria proposed here are objective in the sense that the measurements they provide may be evaluated from a number of contrary perspectives. Some empirical results are given in the context of theory restructuring: redundancy elimination and introduction of new intermediate concepts.

1 Symbolic and Subsymbolic Representations

One of the basic arguments for symbolic, and against subsymbolic AI (neural networks, genetic algorithms, etc.) [Smolensky 87] has to do with inspectability: the result of a successfully trained neural network, for example, is essentially a black box; either it solves the problem at hand, or it does not. If it does, we — as observers of the system — do not know *why*; we have not learned anything about the problem. If it does not, we do not know why either; we have no possibility of correcting this or that sub-procedure in a goal-directed, insightful manner; or of changing the input format in a specific way because we have recognized a certain bit of information is missing; or of adding x hidden units because they were obviously missing.

In symbolic AI, we are dealing with "knowledge": our representation consists of symbols meant to be interpreted by humans. Consequently, the result of a successfully run learning algorithm is a set of rules we can inspect, interpret, evaluate — understand. If the result shows satisfactory performance in the problem at hand, we may even have learned something about the domain. If it does not, we can hope to inspect it, and discover why, and make specific changes, either to the representation, or the learning algorithm, or just to the rules themselves. This, at least, is the promise symbolic systems must live up to. Quinlan points out in his foreword to [Piatetsky-Shapiro/Frawley 91], regarding what qualifies as "knowledge":

Michie [Michie 86] identifies concept expressions as those correct and effectively computable descriptions that can also be assimilated and used by a human being.

In Machine Learning, early work[1] was accompanied by the call for a bias toward comprehensibility [Michalski 83, Sec. 4.3.1], but there was the problem of deciding what constitutes a comprehensible result. [Carbonell 89] makes the distinction between discriminant and characteristic concept definitions, proposing that while most work in ML has focussed on producing the former, the latter are "far easier to communicate to users and often prove to be more usable when they must be interpreted by some other part of the performance system." Next to being more understandable, characteristic definitions are more robust in sense that they are more likely to remain valid when the knowledge base is scaled up or its scope is expanded. More recently, [Emde 94] has taken up and formalized this conviction in the COLA system, which makes use of information on unclassified examples in constructing characteristic definitions: definitions containing more information than strictly necessary to discriminate positive from negative examples.

Kodratoff [Kodratoff 94] notes many user/application accounts show that low understandability is often the main reason for the low acceptance of knowledge based systems: the functioning of ill-structured systems cannot be duplicated by the domain experts, in the sense that they understand the inferences involved, so that for critical applications, the users have no confidence in the systems' answers. Consequently, one measure for the quality of a theory is its understandability. But how to measure understandability?

2 Quality & Understandability

Beyond AI, this problem has been addressed in various subfields of linguistics, psychology and philosophy of science. Since the early work of Karl Popper on a theory of simplicity [Popper 33], and Occam's razor before that, there has been a vague consensus on the notion that utility, understandability and simplicity of theories are interconnected. There is, however, no consensus on how to measure simplicity: our intuitive concept of simplicity is vague and not directly transferable to the task of comparing two empirically equivalent theories. Furthermore, it is pragmatic and subjective: in the final analysis, we are less interested in whether theories fulfill some objective criterion of simplicity, than in whether they *seem* understandable to *us* [Kutschera 72, p. 309ff.]. It is, nevertheless, the task of such diverse fields as linguistics, psychology and philosophy of science to formulate such criteria. [Kutschera 72, Chapter 4.2], for instance, (carefully) postulates that a theory is simpler

- the less rules it contains,
- the shorter and easier to survey (*übersichtlich*) these are, and
- the more parsimonious the vocabulary of the theory is.

Even such basic criteria of structural simplicity are hard to formalize and test in the concrete case. Moreover, they may be contradictory: depending on what the beholder

---

[1] "Early" work as far as the artificial intelligence approach to ML is concerned.

considers to be *übersichtlich*, fulfilling this criterion may necessitate violating the last, i.e. the structure of a theory may be improved by extending its vocabulary (I return to this in the following). Kutschera notes that a propositional theory consisting of three axioms given in [Kutschera 67, Section 1.3] is simpler in terms of *length and overview*, than the equivalent consisting of eleven axioms [Kutschera 67, Section 2.4.2.4], but the latter is simpler in terms of *constructing proofs*[2].

Furthermore, these postulations, as intuitive as they may be, are not (and, perhaps, may not be) empirically validated. The field of (psycho-) linguistics experienced a phase during which attempts were made at producing such validation[3]:

1. In a study of text comprehension, [Kintsch/Keenan 73] find that the time needed to read a text grows as the number of propositions increases, even when the number of words or syllables remains constant.
2. Mandler [Mandler 67] finds a marked improvement in recall of isolated verbal material if the subject is offered in advance clue words that enable him to categorize the material: the category designations function as nuclei around which structures are built up, and structuring is known to facilitate the storing of material.
3. Lesgold [Lesgold 72] records superior recall for sentences with pronouns than for sentences with two separate propositions.
4. On a more philosophical note[4], [Hörmann 81, Chapter 14] concludes that "the organization of the material of the sentence in predicative units constitutes a basic property of the process of understanding."

With some effort, we can reinterpret these findings to fit into the context of assessing the understandability of logical theories. The basis for such reinterpretation is the supposition that there is common ground between text or sentence understanding on the one hand, and the understandability of a logical theory on the other, and that results in the former have some bearing on the latter. Without wanting to take the metaphor too far, the syntactic form of a logical theory could be cautiously likened to a text; the ground clauses (facts) could be compared to individual (single proposition) sentences within the text. Relations are then potential statements; where they occur in non-ground clauses (rules, relations between relations), they are separate propositions of a compound sentence.

This supposition cannot be "proved". We can only make it more plausible by noting that a given logical theory could easily be transformed into an intelligible though inelegant natural language text, and (less easily) back again. To do this, we need only define a sentence template for each relation in the theory; using such templates, any fact or rule, and even derivation in the theory can be "explained" in natural, if somewhat formulaic, language form. Moreover, any natural language sentence that adheres to the template syntax can be parsed back into the corresponding logical construct.

This parallel is also substantiated in Kintsch's theory of texts as hierarchies of propositions [Kintsch 74]. There, a proposition is a predicator followed by one or more arguments, which matches well with the instance of a relation in a logical theory.

---

[2] There is a cross-reference here to explanation based learning and the "utility problem".

[3] A phase of optimism which seems to have fallen from favor in the sequel, as far as I can tell. See, for instance, [Biere 89, Chapter 2.1].

[4] Hörmann's work is at least as much cognitive psychology as linguistics.

After issuing this caveat, the first finding above (1) could perhaps be mapped onto the length of individual clauses in a theory: a theory consisting of few long clauses is harder to follow, duplicate mentally, understand, than one of with shorter clauses, even if it is of the same absolute size. Most certainly this applies doubly if the size is reduced. Clauses have to be understood as a whole, so the shorter they are, the more the theory as a whole will make sense to the human observer.

(2) could be mapped onto the terminology used in the theory: while excess concepts will detract, meaningful, heavily used concepts will improve a theory by functioning as mental markers, "nuclei around which structures are built up". On a very detailed level, a single literal in a clause will be easier to handle mentally than an equivalent conjunction of literals — even before its meaning is understood: it gives an "advance clue". Once it has been understood, i.e. the concept's definition has been inspected and found plausible, the "marker" will be much easier to interpret and *locate* in a collection of clauses.

(3) falls into the same context: intermediate concepts that implement a short notation for more complex, recurring partial premises, allows both superior recall and better structuring of the mental model, which seem to be basic building blocks for understanding. In a sense, the use of new intermediate concepts adds an anaphoric structure to the theory-as-text, by substituting a simple referent for the more complex partial premise. Anaphora have been shown to improve the comprehensibility of texts by aiding the detection of structure (or conversely, the building of structure; see [Gernsbacher 90]).

In reading a text, the atomic units for an habitual reader are not the letters of the alphabet, but rather words and even phrases. The units of understanding are composites of these atoms, i.e. propositions and sentences. In "reading" (the syntactic form of) a theory, the atomic units are the symbols that represent the concepts and their arguments. The units of understanding are the clauses. Hence, the smaller (shorter) these are, the easier the theory as whole is to digest mentally.

At this point, we should note that there is a significant difference between assessing the understandability of single sentences/clauses and of texts/theories (see e.g. [Sanford/Garrod 81, Chapter 1], [Kutschera 72, p. 311ff.]). Arguably, the introduction of new concepts into the theory might increase the difficulty of understanding *individual* clauses, as the reader must now refer to additional clauses that define these new concepts (assuming the reader is familiar with the basic input concepts of the theory). The introduction of new concepts will increase the understandability of the theory *as a whole*; it adds structure to the theory, which is known to facilitate the storing of material in memory (see, for instance, [Bock 78]), and by extension, improve understandability.

More generally, Hörmann's conclusion (4) can be understood as an argument for more structure in a theory. Intermediate concepts provide such structure. If they are well-chosen, they organize a theory into sensible sub-theories, which can be inspected and understood in turn. What constitutes a well-chosen concept? In an investigation of concept formation in humans[5], [Wygotski 64] notes that concepts arise when there is specific need for them within a purposeful activity directed towards the solution of a specific goal. Similarly, [Barsalou 83] describes *ad-hoc categories* that are created for the solution of a specific task, but may become fully accessible concepts if they are

---

[5] See [Wrobel 94, Chapter 2] for a detailed discussion.

used frequently. In Section 5, the evaluation criteria developed in the following will be applied to different versions of a theory produced by a restructuring strategy inspired, in part, by these findings: recurring partial premises are used define new intermediate concepts, which in turn are used to reformulate the original rules. [6]

3 Some intuitions about the quality of a theory

On the whole, the sympathetic reader may follow me in seeing these results as support for some basic — and essentially unprovable — intuitions about the quality of a theory, with emphasis on understandability. Backward references to appropriate findings above are given in brackets; note though that some, notably Hörmann's more general cognitive postulate 4, are reflected in almost all of the intuitions in some way, and Kutschera's postulates as representatives of findings from the philosophy of science (see the beginning of the previous section), map easily, so that no explicit reference is made to them.

1. Intermediate concepts, sparingly introduced, are a Good Thing. [(2), (3)]
   - They introduce new terminology *where it is needed or used*.
   - They add structure to the inferences performed by the system, by relocating frequent "partial inferences" — satisfiability tests of common partial premises in the flat version of the theory — to clearly marked sub-theories: the sets of rules where the concepts are defined (see next).
2. Similarly, a deep inferential structure is more understandable and easier to maintain and modify, than a flat one, because it is more modular. [(2), (4)]
   - First, a "deep" theory provides strata of concepts, reflecting a problem solving strategy in the domain (input vs. intermediate vs. goal concepts, see e.g. [Fu/Buchanan 85]). Each level can be inspected on its own, while the problem solving strategy in a flat theory consists of a single, complex inference from input to goal.
   - Second, each intermediate concept in itself defines a sub-theory that can be inspected on its own.
   - Such sub-theories naturally provide a modularization of the theory, increasing the probability that problems can be pinpointed and fixed in a local manner, rather than having to regard the theory as a whole whenever a problem arises.
3. The more rules define a concepts, the harder it is to grasp. [(1)]
4. Long rules are harder to understand than short rules. [(1)]
5. It is probably not a Good Thing if the encoding of a theory costs more (in some information-theoretic sense) than the encoding of the instances it covers/derives/explains. Likewise, a theory requiring less cost is probably preferable to an equivalent one requiring more. [(1)]
6. The more variables made reference to in a rule, the harder it is to understand.

---

[6] Jan Zytkow <zytkow@cs.twsu.edu> tells the anecdote of a system of rewards and penalties instituted at the Polish Academy of Science: a researcher must pay the research community $1000 for each new *concept* she introduces in a publication, and receives $300 each time it is used. Cast into our setting, this enforced parsimony would mean the value of a new intermediate concept must be measured by determining how often it is *used* in the resulting theory (although here I would prefer a relative rather than absolute count).

7. The more *non-head* variables[7] in a rule, the harder it is to understand.
8. The more constants appear in a rule, the less general value it has. This is, of course, a question of how the representation language is designed, but different induction algorithms show differing behavior in this respect, and constants can be eliminated by introducing appropriate concepts (see Section 5).
9. Non-generative rules — in which some arguments of the conclusion are not described in the premise — are not a Good Thing. Besides being less descriptive since they give no clue as to the nature of these arguments, they can be used only for backward-chaining from instantiated queries, and there only with caution: the non-generated arguments are unconstrained, thus allowing nonsensical instantiations.
10. The less instances a rule covers/derives/explains, the less inclined we will be to accept it (and invest effort in understanding it). Note that simply reiterating the presented examples is a result that fits in the inductive logic framework as it is usually stated, e.g. [Muggleton/deRaedt 94]. Thus the specificness of the rules in a theory must play a role in evaluating its quality.
11. The more instances are multiply covered/derived/explained, the less inclined we will be to accept the theory (and invest effort in understanding it).

This last point should not be confused with the issue of logical redundancy, even if it is closely related. In general, a logically reduced theory is preferable to a redundant one, and this is covered by findings (1) and (4), since a logically redundant theory is perforce longer and less "well organized" than its reduced counterpart. In contrast, no form of logical redundancy need be present when instances are multiply covered[8].

The discerning reader will notice a lack of backward references in the latter half of the list. While this may also be due to my inability to find appropriate results in the psycholinguistics literature, consider that intuitions 6, 7, 8 and 9 are concerned with the arguments of clause literals (rule premises). This topic is not easily mapped onto text understanding issues, so experimental results are scarce. Similarly, 10 and 11 are concerned with concept instances, which would not seem to fit well into the text understanding analogy either. All of these intuitions do fit well, however, into the more general postulates made by Kutschera (see the beginning of the previous section), although as noted, these have received no empirical validation.

4 Criteria for Measuring Theory Quality

These intuitions immediately point out criteria that can be measured in a given (form of a) theory, regardless of whether one agrees with the intuitions. The criteria fall into two basic categories: those that can be computed without knowledge of the extensions of concepts, and those based (in part) on such knowledge. These can be called semantic (extensional) and syntactic (intensional) criteria. In the following, the individual criteria are described briefly, and some indication of the scope and meaning of their values is given. Backward references to appropriate intuitions in Section 3 are given in brackets;

---

[7] Variables used in the body of a rule that do not appear as arguments of the goal concept.

[8] Logical (intensional) vs. extensional redundancy is discussed in Section 5.2. Note that some forms of redundancy may actually increase understandability, as well as reliability ([Bruynooghe 82] and intuition 9 above).

note though that some, notably 1 and 2, are reflected in almost all of the criteria in some way.

4.1 Semantic Criteria

Semantic criteria measure a theory's quality relative to the number and nature of the known instances of the goal concept, not in any deeper cognitive sense.

Instances/rules ratio: $Ratio$ This an indication of how many rules are necessary to achieve the current coverage. $Ratio = \frac{|Pos_{goal}|}{|R_{goal}|}$, where Pos_{goal} is the set of positive instances of the goal concept, and R_{goal} is the set of rules having the goal concept as conclusion. [Intuition 3, 10]

Average coverage: $AvCov$ MOBAL's inference engine IM2 [Emde 89] maintains derivation information for each statement (fact) in the theory. This gives access to the set of instances covered/derived by a given rule. The cardinality of these sets are added up for each rule covering the goal concept, and divided by the number of rules, yielding an average coverage per rule. $AvCov = \frac{\sum_{i=1}^{n} |cov(r_i)|}{|R_{goal}|}$, where $cov(r_i)$ is the set of instances covered by rule r_i. [Intuition 10]

Redundancy index: Red $Red = 1 - \frac{Ratio}{AvCov}$, i.e. a normalized ratio between the two previous criteria. The closer this value is to 1, the more "redundant" the theory is, in the following sense: ideally, each instance should be covered by only one rule in the theory; if this is the case, then $Ratio = AvCov$ and consequently $Red = 0$. The more instances are multiply covered, the larger $AvCov$'s value, while $Ratio$'s remains constant, so that $Red \rightarrow 1$. [Intuition 3, 10, 11]

Compression index: $Comp$ The size of (the syntactic form of) Pos_{goal}, and any subset of the theory, is computed in a way similar to that proposed in [Muggleton/Buntine 88]: each symbol (constant, variable, predicate symbol) has size 1; a syntactic object, such as a fact or premise literal in a rule, has the size $\sum symbols$.

For example, the `may-operate` concept that plays a role in all of the figures has three arguments (person, component and operation; see Section 5); each instance thus "costs" 4 symbols; there are 1215 known positive instances in the testbed KB, so the extension size is 4*1215=4860 symbols.

Using the same method, the size of the rule set is computed, and the compression index $Comp = \frac{Size(R_{goal})}{Size(Pos_{goal})}$. This value indicates compression in the following sense: the closer it is to 0, the more has been gained by using rules to derive instances, as opposed to simply remembering the extension of the goal concept. The value $Comp = 1$ indicates nothing is gained — ruleset and extension size are equal. $Comp > 1$ indicates that it is more costly to remember the theory than the instances. [Intuition 3,11,5]

4.2 Syntactic Criteria

Syntactic criteria measure a theory's quality intrinsically, without making reference to the known extensions of the involved concepts. To pay homage to the difference between flat and deep theories, the values of the following criteria are computed separately for the **top-level** ruleset (R_{goal}) and the **required** ruleset (Req_{goal}), i.e. the union of R_{goal}

and the set of those rules defining intermediate concepts used in the premises of R_{goal}. In a flat theory, the two are identical; in a deep theory, the required ruleset is a superset of the goal concept ruleset. In the following, R denotes such a set of rules, either the top-level or the required theory.

Theory depth: $Depth$ This value reflects the maximum number of inferences required to answer a goal query. $Depth = 1$ for flat theories. Recursive definitions are ignored (cut off at level one); this means such theories are not adequately captured by this criterion, but the alternative would be to allow a value "infinite", which would not be very informative either. [Intuition 1,2]

Average rule length: AvL $AvL = \frac{\sum_{r \in R} |prems(r)|}{|R|}$, i.e. the average number of premise literals in the rules of R. [Intuition 4]

Average number of variables: $AvVars$ $AvVars = \frac{\sum_{r \in R} |vars(r)|}{|R|}$, i.e. the average number of variables appearing in the rules of R. [Intuition 6]

Average number of non-head vars: $AvNHead$
$AvNHead = \frac{\sum_{r \in R} |\{vars(r) - vars(concl(r))\}|}{|R|}$, i.e. the average number of non-head variables appearing in the rules of R. [Intuition 7]

Average number of constants: AvC $AvC = \frac{\sum_{r \in R} |consts(r)|}{|R|}$, i.e. the average number of constants appearing in the rules of R. [Intuition 8]

Ruleset size: $Size$ The size is computed as described above. In comparing a flat (Γ_{flat}) and a deep (Γ_{deep}) version of a theory, we must compare the sizes of top-level and required rulesets. Following the arguments in Sections 2 and 3, it is valid to compare the sizes of R_{goal} in both versions, as a decrease in the size of the top-level ruleset would seem to increase understandability, even if such comparison does not take into account that the flat version requires no additional rules — the latter is taken into account by comparing $Size(R_{goal_{\Gamma_{flat}}})$ with $Size(Req_{goal_{\Gamma_{deep}}})$. Similarly, compression is given for both top-level and required rulesets in deep theories. [Intuition 5,3,11]

5 Some Empirical Results

The criteria described above are implemented in the MOBAL system [Morik et al. 93, Sommer et al. 96] as part of the analysis & restructuring tool RRT [Sommer 94b, Sommer et al. 96, Sommer 95c]. Restructuring refers to any change in a theory (knowledge base) that improves its structure in some way, while retaining the set of computed answers, notably

- the elimination of redundant rules, and of redundant premise literals in the body of a rule,
- the elimination of intermediate concepts through unfolding, and
- the introduction of intermediate concepts through folding.

5.1 Evaluating the introduction of intermediate concepts

I concentrate on the last two here — redundancy is discussed in Section 5.2, where the criteria are used to compare the results of different approaches to eliminating redundancy. In [Sommer 94c, Sommer 95b] the notion of "stratifying" a given theory (knowledge base) was introduced, essentially separating the inductive properties of inverse resolution (IR) [Muggleton/Buntine 88] from its (re-) structuring properties. Following a specific strategy, FENDER performs a number of inter- and intraconstruction steps on a given ruleset, restructuring by introducing new intermediate concepts, *retaining* the set of computed answers of the theory. In other words, FENDER performs inverse resolution on given clauses, without generalizing them. The result is a new inferential structure that is deeper and more modular, and possibly easier to understand and maintain. The new intermediate concepts are intensionally defined and put to immediate use; they make implied relationships explicit by exploiting similarities and differences between original clauses of the theory.

Figure 3 shows the criteria values computed by RRT for two versions of the SPEED application [Sommer et al. 94], a knowledge base governing the security policy of distributed telecom switching stations. It describes a network of routing switches with the associated management operations, such as read, create or delete a log, add or remove a subscriber, read or change a switch table. The goal concept, may-operate(<user>, <component>, <operation>), specifies which employees of which company may perform which operations on which components in the network. Relevant information in this context concerns various attributes of the employees, companies, switches and operations involved, and relationships between them.

The original inferential structure, 30 rules induced by RDT [Kietz/Wrobel 91] from 1215 examples and background knowledge, is "flat", going in a single step from input concepts to goal (see also Figure 1). Note that this will usually be the case when rules are produced by machine learning algorithms from ground data. One example of the 30 original non-redundant goal-concept rules:

```
owner(X, Y) & has-dept(Y, Z) & manages(Z, X) & works-in(U, Z)
& operator(U) & optype(V, threshold-read)
→ may-operate(U, X, V).
```

It is to be understood as follows: "If an employee works in the department that manages a switch, and that department belongs to the company that owns the switch, and the employee has operator status, then the employee may perform operations of type Threshold-Read on that switch".

For comparison, the right column of Figure 3 shows the numbers on the theory restructured by FENDER (see also Figure 2). We see that coverage is unchanged but the number of top-level rules has been reduced to two, significantly reducing the instances/rules ratio and average coverage. FENDER achieves this by introducing four new concepts into the theory. In the following, constructed predicates have been renamed for clarity. Note also that if they are deemed relevant and their definitions have been understood by the user, these new concepts and their user-supplied names make explicit valid relationships between objects of the problem domain; they add structure to the theory on the "knowledge level" as well as on the implementational level (recall the discussion in Section 2, especially finding (2)).

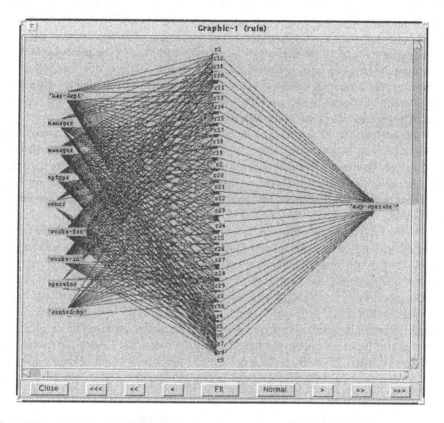

Fig. 1. Inferential structure of (flat) rulebase before stratification (left to right: input concepts used in rule premises → top-level rule layer → goal concept)

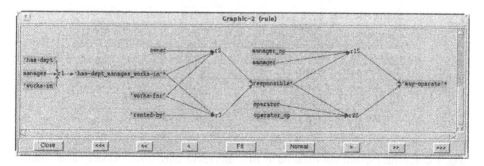

Fig. 2. Inferential structure after stratification with FENDER (inference depth 3, left to right: input concepts → intermediate-level 1 rules → intermediate concepts 1 → intermediate-level rules 2 → intermediate concepts 2 → top-level rules → goal)

Concepts invented by FENDER   The first concept found by FENDER makes a relationship between components, departments and users explicit that is implicit in all of the original rules:

has-dept(C,D) & works-in(U,D) & manages(D,S)→**cu_manages(S,C,U)**

Rewriting the original rules by using this new concept (folding) does not reduce the number of rules, but makes them simpler, both by shortening them and by eliminating any reference to departments, i.e. eliminating a non-head variable from the top-level rules. The second makes use of the first, and is disjunctively defined:

rented-by(S,C) & works-for(U,C) & cu_manages(S,C,U)→ **responsible(S,U)**

owner(S,C) & works-for(U,C) & cu_manages(S,C,U) → **responsible(S,U)**

Folding this into the rules reduces their number, since any occurrence of either the one or the other definition body is replaced, so that several pairs of rules may "melt" into one. Note also that the top-level rules are again shortened and any reference to companies is eliminated.

The third and fourth concepts introduced by FENDER, manager_op(OP) and operator-_op(OP), group the constants found in the original rules according to the context they appear in. This eliminates constants from the top-level rules and further reduces their number, so that finally, the 30 are subsumed by these two:

responsible(S,U) & manager_op(OP) & manager(U)→ may-operate(U,S,OP).

responsible(S,U) & operator_op(OP) & operator(U)→ may-operate(U,S,OP).

This definition of the goal concept is arguably easier to understand than the original one, as it contains less clauses than the original, and the individual clauses are shorter and use fewer variables. This difference is reflected in the criteria values in Figure 3 below.

Evaluation Criteria	Original	FENDER
$|R_{goal}|$	30	↝ 2 (20)
$Ratio = \frac{|Pos_{goal}|}{|R_{goal}|}$	40.5	↝ 607.5
$Av.Coverage = \frac{\sum_{i=1}^{n} |cov(r_i)|}{|R_{goal}|}$	40.5	↝ 607.5
$RedundancyIndex = 1 - \frac{Ratio}{Av.Coverage}$	0.0	↝ 0.0
$Syntactic\ Size\ of\ R_{goal} :\ Size(R_{goal})$	750	↝ 22 (151)
$Compression = \frac{Size(R_{goal})}{Size(Pos_{goal})}$	0.154	↝ 0.004 (0.031)
$Inference\ Depth$	1	↝ 3
$Av.\ Length\ of\ clauses$	7.0	↝ 3 (1.50)
$Av.\ \#Vars\ per\ clause$	5.0	↝ 3 (1.55)
$Av.\ \#NonHead\ Vars\ per\ clause$	2.0	↝ 0 (0.15)
$Av.\ \#Constants\ per\ clause$	1.0	↝ 0 (0.75)

Fig. 3. Comparison of original (induced by RDT) and restructured (FENDER) versions of SPEED with 1215 example instances of may-operate. Values for the required theory are given in parantheses; see Section 4.2.

5.2 Evaluating theory reductions

The criteria may also be used to evaluate the results of reduction operators, i.e. methods that identify parts of a theory that may be deleted without changing the set of computed answers. In [Sommer 96], we have discerned between two approaches to detecting redundancy in theories:

- **intensional**, or logical redundancy, exemplified by generalized subsumption [Buntine 88], which relies on the definitions of concepts (their *intensions*) to detect parts of a theory that logically follow from the rest and are therefor unnecessary, and
- **extensional** redundancy, which relies on representative facts (concepts' *extensions*) to detect parts of a theory that, when removed, do not alter rules' performance; this is often used by machine learning algorithms in a post-processing step to reduce the learned rules.

Both approaches must grapple with two forms of redundancy in theories: **clause** redundancy, which is indicated when entire rules are found to be unnecessary, and **literal** redundancy, which is indicated when some part of a rule's premise is found to be unnecessary.

Forms of both approaches to detecting redundancy have been incorporated in RRT along with FENDER and the evaluation methods described in this paper. The following paragraphs briefly illustrate the differences between the two approaches and the two forms of redundancy, using the the criteria to compare results; a more complete and technical discussion would require more space than we have here and is given in [Sommer 96]. We note here, however, that there is a fundamental trade-off between the two approaches, so that they complement each other and are both valuable tools in the broader restructuring context: intensional analysis relies on a completeness assumption that all valid deductive relationships between concepts are explicitly noted in the form of rules. Obviously, this assumption cannot be made in general, particularly when rules are being induced from facts — in this event, there will be no deductive relationships between any of the concepts of the theory (other than the concept to be learned). Extensional analysis is not subject to this condition, since it relies only on representative facts, i.e. a least Herbrand model of the theory. On the other hand, any change in this model — more or other facts — may invalidate the results of extensional analysis; even monotonic growth of the theory — some facts are added — may have this effect. In this light, intensional analysis is deductively justified, while extensional analysis is inductively justified and so subject to the same caveats as induction in general.

Literal redundancy: Reducing individual rules Our testbed is a version of the SPEED domain used in the previous section, with 1215 positive instances of the the goal concept may-operate(<user>,<component>,<operation>), and the 30 rules induced by RDT [Kietz/Wrobel 91]. These rules are not clause redundant, in fact no instance is covered by more than one rule (even though RDT does not guarantee such results per se). As the rules have been induced from facts, no background theory relating concepts to one another is available, so that Θ-subsumption [Plotkin 70] is the only applicable form of intensional analysis. No rule is subset of another, so intensional analysis offers no form of reducing the ruleset.

	Original	Reduce	Allow Generalizations
#Rules	30	$\rightsquigarrow$ 30	$\rightsquigarrow$ 15
$Inst/RulesRatio$	40.5	$\rightsquigarrow$ 40.5	$\rightsquigarrow$ 81
$TheorySize$	750	$\rightsquigarrow$ 615	$\rightsquigarrow$ 240
$Compression$	0.154	$\rightsquigarrow$ 0.126	$\rightsquigarrow$ 0.049
$Av.Length$	7	$\rightsquigarrow$ 5.5	$\rightsquigarrow$ 4
$Av.Vars$	5	$\rightsquigarrow$ 5	$\rightsquigarrow$ 4
$Av.NonHead$	2	$\rightsquigarrow$ 2	$\rightsquigarrow$ 1
$Req.InputConcepts$	9	$\rightsquigarrow$ 8	$\rightsquigarrow$ 5

Fig. 4. Reducing individual rules (Literal redundancy)

Extensional analysis, on the other hand, finds one or more premise literals in each rule that can be dropped without changing the rule's coverage, so that the average number of premise literals is reduced from seven to 5.5, and the size of the theory is reduced from 750 to 615 symbols. Moreover, one concept has been eliminated entirely from the list of required minimum inputs[9].

Allowing generalizations — accepting reduced versions of the rule that cover more examples than the original, as long as this remains within the confines of the overall set of known examples — has an even more marked effect: the average number of premise literals is reduced from seven to four, and the size of the theory is reduced from 750 to 240 symbols. The list of required minimum inputs is reduced from nine to five. Most significantly, the number of rules has been halved, from 30 to fifteen, because the deletion of literals has rendered pairs of rules identical (i.e. they differed only in the literals dropped). These results are summarized in Table 4.

Clause redundancy: Reducing a set of rules Here the testbed is a version of SPEED containing a large number of rules from a variety of sources (RDT, GOLEM [Muggleton/Feng 90], FOIL [Quinlan 90], LINK [Sommer 94a], FENDER, user input and a procedure that produces random permutations of rules). This represents the situation encountered when machine learning and restructuring are used in concert to design and maintain a complex knowledge base. The rules are both literal-redundant and, since several algorithms have been applied independently, clause redundant.

Intensional reduction here is able to spot the rules that are random permutations of others, but not, for instance, rules that make use of synonymous concepts, such as those produced by repeated calls to FENDER. Extensional reduction is able to weed out all rules up to the two constructed by FENDER (Section 5.1), thus attaining the best possible result. These results are summarized in Table 5.

---

[9] RRT computes a list of concepts that must be present to compute a given goal; if all reference to a concept is dropped in the course of rule reduction, then this concept is no longer required to compute the goal and hence drops from the list.

	Original	Intensional	Extensional
#Rules	260	⤳ 109	⤳ 2
$Inst/Rules Ratio$	4.67	⤳ 11.14	⤳ 607.5
$Av.Coverage$	60.75	⤳ 86.2	⤳ 607.5
$Redundancy Index$	0.92	⤳ 0.87	⤳ 0.0
$Theory Size$	5605	⤳ 1844	⤳ 22
$Compression$	1.153	⤳ 0.379	⤳ 0.004
$Av.Length$	5.76	⤳ 4.1	⤳ 3
$Av.Vars$	4.67	⤳ 4.23	⤳ 3
$Av.NonHead$	1.67	⤳ 1.23	⤳ 0
$Av.Constants$	0.98	⤳ 0.96	⤳ 0
$Req.Input Concepts$	9	⤳ 9	⤳ 5

Fig. 5. Intensional and extensional reduction (Clause redundancy)

6 Conclusion

Understandability has not been in the focus of more recent work in Machine Learning, but as we move from the laboratory to applications that are to be used by non-scientists, it gains importance, to the point where a faulty program that is understood is preferred over a better one that is essentially a black box. Dissenting voices are often heard when this topic comes up (for example the podium discussion on comprehensibility at ECML'94 and the workshop on comprehensibility & ML at IJCAI'95 [Nedellec 95]), but there is a sizable number of applications "out there" where the ability of suppliers to explain the inner workings of their product to potential customers is at least as important as the products' performance [Kodratoff 94].

The SPEED application is a case in point: a system governing the security policy of distributed telecom switching stations is well and good, but if the inherent policy is not *visible* — inspectable, understandable, perhaps even modifiable — then potential customers (telecommunication service providers) will turn away. They will stick to their unwieldy extensional databases or even plain lists of explicit permissions and prohibitions, rather than use a compact and elegant theory they do not understand.

This paper has attempted to point towards measures of quality beyond accuracy and coverage of induced rules. These measures hinge on the idea of understandability, which surely cannot be formalized, but with the help of findings from beyond ML, may be approached in a quantitative way. Whether the progression of values from left to right column in Figure 5.1, 4 and 5 constitutes an increase or a decrease in quality may be left to personal taste, or decided by one or more simple evaluation functions reflecting these tastes.

What is missing in these pages is empirical evidence for the hightened understandability of the deep version of a theory. This would require extensive tests with separate groups of subjects, one for flat and one for deep versions of a theory — and since there are many alternative ways of adding intermediate concepts, several groups subjected to different deep versions. The investigations of (psycho-) linguistic and psychological literature has not been altogether enlightening in this respect: accounts of empirical tests to determine or measure understandability are sparse, and there does not seem to be a consensus on how to measure it. The findings from philosophy of science — that the concept of understandability is vague, pragmatic and subjective, and that objective criteria to measure it have limited practical value, since we are less interested in theories that fulfill them than in theories that *seem* understandable to *us* — are comforting, but not constructive.

The criteria developed in this paper are useful in *characterizing*, at least, the differences between empirically equivalent theories. Whether the progression of values in Figures 5.1, 4 and 5 constitutes an increase in quality *must*, perhaps, be left to personal taste of the beholder, but the criteria are valuable tools for making this decision. They also allow the formulation of goals and requirements in complex modeling or learning tasks, such as "apply all available learning algorithms until $AvCov > Ratio$", "discard theories whose $AvL > 6$ or $Comp \geq 0.5$", or "restructure until $AvNHead \leq \frac{AvVars}{2}$".

Flexible, concurrent maintenance of multiple theories would be an exciting application and continuation of the work of Werner Emde on representation of multiple worlds [Emde 91]. Donato Malerba of University of Bari[10] points out that the criteria developed in here could be used as a means of communication between agents cooperating on a complex multi-predicate learning task, and is currently conducting research along these lines.

In a similar vein, restructuring operators taken together with the evaluation criteria, could form the basis of a system that autonomously performs experiments in producing, evaluating and categorizing empirically equivalent versions of given theories.

Acknowledgments This work was funded in part by ESPRIT Project ILP (P6020). I thank Katharina Morik and Jörg-Uwe Kietz at the University of Dortmund and my colleagues Werner Emde and Stefan Wrobel here in the ML group at GMD for many interesting discussions. An earlier version of this paper appears as [Sommer 95a]; my thanks to the organizer, Claire Nedellec, and the reviewers and participants of that workshop for constructive comments and discussion.

The restructuring tool RRT, including FENDER, intensional & extensional reduction operators, unfolding and the evaluation methods described here, is available as a part of MOBAL via WWW at `http://nathan.gmd.de/projects/ml/mobal.html` or FTP at `ftp://ftp.gmd.de/gmd/mlt/Mobal/`

References

[Barsalou 83] L. W. Barsalou. Ad hoc categories. *Memory & Cognition*, 11(3):211 – 227, 1983.

[Biere 89] Bernd Ulrich Biere. *Verständlich-Machen*. Max Niemeyer Verlag, Tübingen, 1989.

[Bock 78] M. Bock. *Wort-, Satz-, Textverarbeitung*. Kohlhammer, Stuttgart, 1978.

[Bruynooghe 82] Maurice Bruynooghe. Adding redundancy to obtain more reliable and readable Prolog programs. In Michel Van Caneghem (ed.), *Proceedings of the First International Logic Programming Conference*, pp. 129–133, Marseille, France, 1982. ADDP-GIA.

[Buntine 88] W. Buntine. Generalized Subsumption and its Applications to Induction and Redundancy. *Artificial Intelligence*, 36:149–176, 1988.

[Carbonell 89] Jaime G. Carbonell. Paradigms for Machine Learning. *Artificial Intelligence*, 40:1–9, 1989.

---

[10] Personal communication; `malerba@lacam.uniba.it`

[Emde 89] Werner Emde. An Inference Engine for Representing Multiple Theories. In K. Morik (ed.), *Knowledge Representation and Organization in Machine Learning*, pp. 148–176. Springer, New York, Berlin, Tokyo, 1989. Also: KIT-Report Nr. 64, TU Berlin, 1988.

[Emde 91] Werner Emde. *Modellbildung, Wissensrevision und Wissensrepräsentation im Maschinellen Lernen*. Informatik-Fachberichte 281. Springer Verlag, Berlin, New York, 1991. PhD thesis.

[Emde 94] Werner Emde. Inductive Learning from very few Classified Examples. In *Proc. 7th European Conference on Machine Learning (ECML-94)*, 1994. also available as GMD Tech. Report.

[Fu/Buchanan 85] Li-Min Fu and Bruce Buchanan. Learning Intermediate Concepts in Constructing a Hierarchical Knowledge Base. In *Proc. 9th International Joint Conference on Artificial Intelligence*, pp. 659–666, San Mateo, CA, 1985. Morgan Kaufman.

[Gernsbacher 90] M. A. Gernsbacher. *Language Comprehension as Structure Building*. Lawrence Erlbaum, Hillsdale NJ, 1990.

[Hörmann 81] Hans Hörmann. *To Mean — To Understand: Problems of Psychological Semantics*. Springer-Verlag, 1981.

[Kietz/Wrobel 91] Jörg-Uwe Kietz and Stefan Wrobel. Controlling the Complexity of Learning in Logic through Syntactic and Task-Oriented Models. In Stephen Muggleton (ed.), *Proc. 1st Int. Workshop on ILP*, pp. 107 – 126, Viana de Castelo, Portugal, 1991. Also in S.Muggleton (ed.), Inductive Logic Programming, Academic Press, 1992.

[Kintsch 74] W. Kintsch. *The Representation of Meaning in Memory*. Erlbaum, Potomac, MD, 1974.

[Kintsch/Keenan 73] W. Kintsch and J Keenan. Reading rate and retention as a function of the number of propositions in the base structure of sentences. *Cognitive Psychology*, 5:257 – 274, 1973.

[Kodratoff 94] Yves Kodratoff. Guest Editor's Introduction (The Comprehensibility Manifesto). *AI Communications*, 7(2):83 – 85, 1994.

[Kutschera 67] Franz von Kutschera. *Elementare Logik*. Wien, 1967.

[Kutschera 72] Franz von Kutschera. *Wissenschaftstheorie*, volume II. Wilhelm Fink Verlag, München, 1972.

[Lesgold 72] A. M. Lesgold. Pronominalization: a Device for Unifying Sentences in Memory. *Journal of Verbal Learning and Verbal Behavior*, 11:316–323, 1972.

[Mandler 67] G. Mandler. Organisation and Memory. In K. W. Spence and J. T. Spence (eds.), *The Psychology of Learning and Motivation*, volume 2, pp. 189 – 196. Academic Press, New York, 1967.

[Michalski 83] Ryszard S. Michalski. A Theory and Methodology of Inductive Learning. In *Machine Learning — An Artificial Intelligence Approach*, volume I, pp. 83–134. Morgan Kaufman, San Mateo, CA, 1983.

[Michie 86] Donald Michie. The superarticulacy phenomenon in the context of software manufacture. *Proceedings of the Royal Society of London*, A 405:185–212, 1986.

[Morik et al. 93] K. Morik, S. Wrobel, Jörg-Uwe Kietz, and W. Emde. *Knowledge Acquisition and Machine Learning*. Academic Press, London, 1993.

[Muggleton 87] Stephen Muggleton. Structuring Knowledge by Asking Questions. In Ivan Bratko and Nada Lavrač (eds.), *Progress in Machine Learning — Proc. Second European Working Session on Learning (EWSL)*, Wilmslow, UK, 1987. Sigma Press.

[Muggleton/Buntine 88] Stephen Muggleton and Wray Buntine. Machine Invention of First-Order Predicates by Inverting Resolution. In *Proc. Fifth Intern. Conf. on Machine Learning*, San Mateo, CA, 1988. Morgan Kaufman.

[Muggleton/deRaedt 94] Stephen Muggleton and Luc deRaedt. Inductive Logic Programming: Theory and Methods. *Journal of Logic Programming*, 19/20:629 – 680, 1994.

[Muggleton/Feng 90] Stephen Muggleton and Cao Feng. Efficient Induction of Logic Programs. In *Proc. First Conf. on Algorithmic Learning Theory*, Tokyo, 1990. Ohmsha Publishers.

[Nedellec 95] Claire Nedellec (ed.). *Proc. IJCAI Workshop on Machine Learning and Comprehensibility*, Claire.Nedellec@lri.fr, 1995.

[Piatetsky-Shapiro/Frawley 91] G. Piatetsky-Shapiro and W. Frawley. *Knowledge discovery in databases*. The MIT press, 1991. (editors).

[Plotkin 70] Gordon D. Plotkin. A note on inductive generalization. In B. Meltzer and D. Michie (eds.), *Machine Intelligence*, volume 5, chapter 8, pp. 153–163. American Elsevier, 1970.

[Popper 33] Karl Popper. *Die beiden Grundprobleme der Erkenntnistheorie : aufgrund von Ms. aus d. Jahren 1930 - 1933*, volume 18 of *Die Einheit der Gesellschaftswissenschaften*. Mohr, Tübingen, 1933. edited by Troels Eggers Hansen, appeared 1979.

[Quinlan 90] J. Ross Quinlan. Learning Logical Definitions from Relations. *Machine Learning*, 5(3):239 – 266, 1990.

[Sanford/Garrod 81] A. J. Sanford and S. C. Garrod. *Understanding Written Language*. Wiley and Sons, Chichester, 1981.

[Smolensky 87] P. Smolensky. Connectionist AI, Symbolic AI, and the Brain. *Artificial Intelligence Review*, 1:95 – 109, 1987.

[Sommer et al. 94] E. Sommer, K. Morik, J.M. Andre, and M. Uszynski. What On-line Learning Can Do for Knowledge Acquisition. *Knowledge Acquisition*, 6:435–460, 1994.

[Sommer et al. 96] E. Sommer, Werner Emde, Jörg-Uwe Kietz, and Stefan Wrobel. Mobal 42 User Guide ((always) Draft). Arbeitspapiere der gmd, GMD, 1996. Available via WWW http://nathan.gmd.de/projects/ml/lit/mlpublist.html.

[Sommer 94a] E. Sommer. Learning Relations without Closing the World. In *Proc. of the European Conference on Machine Learning (ECML-94)*, Berlin, 1994. Springer-Verlag.

[Sommer 94b] E. Sommer. Restructuring in Horn clause knowledge bases. Technical report, ESPRIT Project ILP (6020), 1994. ILP Deliverable GMD 2.1.

[Sommer 94c] E. Sommer. Rulebase Stratification: an Approach to theory restructuring. In *Proc. 4th Intl. Workshop on Inductive Logic Programming (ILP-94)*, 1994. Available via WWW http://nathan.gmd.de/projects/ml/lit/mlpublist.html.

[Sommer 95a] E. Sommer. An Approach to Quantifying the Quality of Induced Theories. In Claire Nedellec (ed.), *Proc. IJCAI Workshop on Machine Learning and Comprehensibility*, 1995. Available via WWW http://nathan.gmd.de/projects/ml/lit/-mlpublist.html.

[Sommer 95b] E. Sommer. Fender: An approach to theory restructuring. In Stefan Wrobel and Nada Lavrac (eds.), *Proc. of the European Conference on Machine Learning (ECML-95)*, volume 912 of *Lecture Notes in Artificial Intelligence*, Berlin, 1995. Springer-Verlag.

[Sommer 95c] E. Sommer. Mobal's theory restructuring tool RRT. Technical report, ESPRIT Project ILP (6020), 1995. ILP Deliverable GMD 2.2.

[Sommer 96] E. Sommer. *Theory Restructuring*. NN, 1996. (submitted).

[Wrobel 94] Stefan Wrobel. *Concept Formation and Knowledge Revision*. Kluwer Academic Publishers, Dordrecht, Netherlands, 1994.

[Wygotski 64] L. S. Wygotski. *Denken und Sprechen*. Conditio humana. S. Fischer, 1964. (First published in Russian 1934, english translation "Thought and language" 1962 by MIT Press).

Some Late-Breaking News from the Data Mines and a Preview of the KOALA System: A Prospector's Report

Franz Schmalhofer and Christoph Kozieja

German Research Center for Artificial Intelligence (DFKI)
Erwin-Schrödinger-Strasse, Postfach 2080
D-67608 Kaiserslautern, Germany

Abstract

It has been widely advertised that the numerous large databases which exist in the various industries, administrative offices and in the public domain (e.g. the world-wide-web) would indeed be very valuable data mines from which important and previously unknown knowledge could be harvested when machine learning procedures would be applied as mining tools. The present research evaluates the prospects of discovering such knowledge from industrial databases. Three different databases are considered and three different machine learning tools (conceptual clustering, neural net, and inductive logic programming) are applied in an experimental fashion. From these experiences it could be concluded that the tool box philosophy has severe limitations in highly structured industrial application areas. It was thus suggested that higher order conceptualizations of machine learning should be developed which are easier to apply and understand by the user. A preview of the KOALA system which is currently under development is then presented. By applying constraint satisfaction over hierarchically structured domains, the KOALA system allows the user to have his own machine learning application being configured according to the domain ontologies and the specific needs of a given field of application.

1 Introduction

It has been widely advertised that the numerous large databases which exist in the various industries, administrative offices and in the public domain (e.g. the world-wide-web) would indeed be very valuable data mines from which important and previously unknown knowledge could be harvested (Frawley et al., 1992) when machine learning procedures would be applied as mining tools (Moulet & Kodratoff, 1995). Thereby the implicit but nevertheless very useful knowledge could be extracted from the data mines. In other words, it has been proposed that very valuable and important information or knowledge is often not explicitly represented in the databases but only implicitly encompassed and that machine learning and other data mining tools would be well suited for explicating such implicit knowledge from a single database or a combination of several different databases.

The present research evaluates the prospects of discovering such knowledge from databases in different fields of application. Three different databases were considered and three different machine learning tools (conceptual clustering, neural net, and inductive logic programming) were applied in an experimental fashion. On the basis of this experimental demonstration, some quite general conclusions will be drawn about the currently popular data mining scenario as well as about the presently available machine learning tools.

In order to overcome the identified limitations, a more flexible and a more user-driven application of machine learning techniques is proposed and the scenario of cooperative knowledge evolution (cf. Schmalhofer & Tschaitschian, 1995) is further developed. The practical implications of this scenario which stresses the importance of the comprehensibility of machine learning are then demonstrated by a new architecture for machine learning. This architecture is called KOALA which stands for the configuration and automatization of learning applications. In the KOALA architecture, a user-driven configuration of data filter, machine learning and visualization modules is achieved by utilizing the constraint satisfaction techniques that have been developed in the ConPlan project (cf. Meyer auf'm Hofe & Tschaitschian, 1995) in combination with a knowledge base that formally describes the different machine learning components in an abstract and user comprehensible manner (Schmalhofer & Auerswald, 1995; Schmalhofer & Aitken, 1995). The flexibility of combining and configuring different machine learning components in a user comprehensible manner is thereby accomplished by constraint satisfaction techniques which allow a user to specify hard and soft as well as hierarchically ordered constraints. In the next section of this paper we will describe three data mines from different industries which we are considering as potential sources for harvesting invaluable knowledge. Section 3 will then describe the experimental application of the mining tools and furthermore discuss the application results in terms of more general applications. Section 4 will present the KOALA system and section 5 will conclude the paper by a general discussion.

2 The Data Mines

We will describe three different collections of data. The first database is from the area of medicine and health and describes the so called adverse events which were observed when some specific drug was administered to patients. By a more comprehensive and knowledge based (as opposed to statistical) utilization of this information, additional valuable knowledge about the side effects and the interaction of various drugs can be discovered.

The second database comes from the engineering sciences where the results from systematic experiments with new production materials (e.g. new kinds of glass mat reinforced thermoplastics) or from experiments with new manufacturing techniques (e.g. welding by ultrasonic waves) are kept in various databases. From such databases valuable knowledge can be obtained about what would be the optimal parameters in some industrial production process that employs such new materials or manufacturing techniques (cf. Hinkelmann et al., 1994).

The third data mine which will be considered is of a quite different kind. It consists of all the visual images which are collected by some image processing device that is used for rapidly classifying manufactured products according to whether or not they contain faults. The collection of all visual images can be very valuable for finding the best classification procedure in combination with the most diagnostic attributes for detecting faulty products.

2.1 Adverse Events in Clinical Trials

Before a new medical drug can be released on the market, large scale clinical studies must be performed in several hospitals where the new drug is administered to those patients who are most likely to benefit from the drug. Such clinical studies (so called phase III studies) are required by law. These studies aim to evaluate drug efficacy as well as drug safety with respect to potential side effects and interactions with other substances. In the course of such a study, a variety of adverse events may occur which must be classified and explained to determine whether they are caused by the drug under investigation. This decision is made by clinical project managers and drug safety managers using information and knowledge from numerous heterogeneous sources. The results of these studies are kept in large statistical databases. The statistical analyses are usually performed only with respect to the experimental drug that is under evaluation. Since the patients also consume other drugs in these studies (so called concomitent drugs), a conjoint analyses of all the available data could reveal quite important knowledge of the negative (and also positive) interaction of different substances. Since there is also general medical knowledge available, knowledge-based machine learning procedures which utilize this medical knowledge may be more successful in discovering new knowledge than purely statistical procedures. The prospects of discovering valuable knowledge by the application of machine learning procedures are thus quite good.

2.2 Parameter Specification in Product and Production Planning

In the material sciences, there is much research that evaluates the properties and the behavior of the various materials after some (potential) production procedure has been applied. In such scientific experiments, one may thus determine the maximum tension that can be applied to some material or its module of elasticity after it has been heated and pressed. Different parameters can thereby be systematically manipulated. Another example for such experimental research is the determination of the thickness of some compound material at the different locations of a press.

Table 1 shows some data and a segment of a database with such experimental results. More specifically, the upper section of Table 1 shows the thickness of some compound material after it has been heated and subsequently pressed by 18217 Joule and 24835 Joule. For the different locations which are identified by x- and y-coordinates, the thickness of the material is shown in mm. This particular experiment is referred to as charge 3. There are two more experiments which were conducted in the same manner but employed different parameter values (different temperatures, different pressures). These two experiments are referred to as charge 1 and charge 2. The lower section of Table 1 shows some segment of the database, where each experimental data point is simply represented by the thickness and its location in terms of x- and y-coordinates. Obviously, a complete database as well as the complete experiments are indeed much more complex (for more detail see: Kempf et al., 1995).

It can be shown that such experimental results from the material sciences could be extremely valuable for the product engineers who work as practitioners and have to

Distribution of Thickness					
X | Y	0 mm	200 mm	400 mm	600 mm	800 mm
0 mm	5,6	6,2	6,1	5,8	6,0
200 mm	6,0	7,0	6,7	6,6	6,2
400 mm	6,0	6,5	7,0	7,0	6,4
600 mm	5,6	6,6	6,8	6,8	6,4
800 mm	5,8	6,4	6,2	6,2	6,0

Database

Charge 1:

thickness(7.4, 400, 600)

thickness(7.4, 600, 400)

thickness(6.5, 0, 200)

...

Charge 3:

thickness(7.4, 200, 200)

thickness(7.4, 400, 400)

thickness(7.4, 600, 400)...

Table 1: Empirical results from an experiment in the material sciences which shows the thickness of some pressed material as a function of its location in the press. The lower section shows a segment from a respective database.

determine the optimal parameter values when designing and manufacturing their products. For example a product engineer may have to determine how long somecompound material should be heated before it is pressed. Since the available databases are very detailed and also quite heterogeneous, it is indeed difficult for a product engineer to extract the knowledge that is relevant for his task (cf. Hinkelmann et al., 1994; Kempf et al., 1995). Indeed, this knowledge is not explicitly represented but must be inferred or discovered. The application of datamining tools could thus provide the possibility of disclosing the knowledge which is relevant for the product engineer.

2.3 Two Dimensional Images

Data mines do not need to exist explicitly. In some application areas, data can be collected so rapidly that the stream of collected data may be considered as a data mine even when they are only selectively stored in a database. The processing of two dimensional color or black and white images can be considered as a data mine. Consider the previously mentioned quality control system where the images of different products must be collected and analyzed in real time so that faulty products can be immediately detected. In this application, the stream of collected images may be viewed as a data mine where machine learning procedures may be applied to continuously monitor and improve the performance of the quality control system.

3 Application of Mining Tools

In the previous section, three quite different data mines were identified from which valuable knowledge may be extracted by machine learning tools. In the VEGA project, an environment has been developed which allows to explore and validate declarative knowledge (Abecker et al., 1995). This environment uses a visual programming environment and follows the toolbox approach to machine learning. In principle, there are several similarities to the Clementine system (Khabaza & Shearer, 1995) and the machine learning toolbox (Sleeman, 1994). The knowledge evolution system of the VEGA project thus allows the interactive exploration of knowledge bases by inductive components. Since it is an open architecture, it also provides the possibility to link foreign tools so that three different tools which are available from the machine learning archive could be applied to the described data mines. These three tools were AutoClassC (Stutz & Cheeseman, 1994) as a conceptual clustering system, Atree (Armstrong et al., 1990) as a neural network and Clint (DeRaedt, 1992) as an inductive logic programming procedure.

3.1 The Mining Tools

AutoClassC

AutoClassC is a Bayesian classification system that induces classes from a database. It uses Bayesian statistics to determine the most probable number of classes, their probabilistic descriptions, and the probability of every object being a member of each class. It searches for a classification with the highest a-posteriori probability. The program starts with a specific number of classes that is to be determined by the user and then searches for a constellation of classes that maximizes a likelihood criterion. Finally, it generates three reports which show the various probabilities of an object being a member of the different classes. AutoClassC is thus one of several different algorithms which perform conceptual clustering.

Atree

Atree is a program which simulates adaptive logical nets. An adaptive logical net is a kind of neural net. A training set and a test set are used as input data. Atree uses the training set to determine the different links in the neural net and to determine the best fitting function between the input and the output nodes of the net. The test set is then used to determine the correctness of the learned function with respect to the desired input and output values.

Clint

Clint is an interactive inductive logical program (ILP) that can learn new predicates on the basis of given examples. It thereby attempts to define the new predicates in terms of already defined predicates. It applies anti-unification to find the most specific generalization from the presented examples.

3.2 Results of the Application

In our initial attempts of discovering new knowledge from three described data mines, we pursued the specific discovery questions which were most interesting with respect to the specific application domain: How can one detect yet unknown interactions of drug substances from the databases of adverse events? How can one determine the optimal production parameters (e.g. the required heat in the tunnel oven, the energy in Joules that should be applied for pressing the desired product, like a car seat) from the experimental results in the material sciences? How can one discover the most diagnostic attributes and attribute values for detecting faulty products by harvesting the appropriate knowledge from the datamines of two dimensional images. By pursuing these questions, we encountered a large host of quite different problems and it became quite difficult to sort things out. Was the problem that the discovery task was too ill specified? Was the problem that the domain expert did not sufficiently understand the available machine learning tools? Was the problem that the machine learning tools were not sufficiently suited for processing highly structured inputs? Or was the problem that knowledge acquisition in the form of a model building activity was needed for exploiting these datamines? These are only some of the questions which were raised.

In order to obtain more concrete indications of potential difficulties, our efforts were restricted to one of the three datamines, namely the databases from material sciences and this database was furthermore quite severely simplified. We thus obtained the representation of the different data points that are shown in Table 1 as our experimental data mine. In order to obtain valuable information about the optimal parameters in a production process, the thickness of a given material had to be determined as a function of the physical location in the press (i.e. its x- and y-coordinates). Since the measured data points were sparse, intermediate points needed to be interpolated. Since measurements were available in different databases, these results should be integrated to obtain better estimates. The lower right panel of Figure 1 shows a graphical representation of the desired result. The estimated areas of an equal thickness are thereby indicated by identical shades.

A potential user was then selected to apply the three mining tools in the best possible way to the databases from the material sciences. This user had some general but no detailed knowledge about statistics and the particular machine learning techniques. He studied to some degree the technical descriptions which were available over the Internet. Since we did not want him to become an expert of the specific machine learning tools the time of studying was, however, restricted not to exceed a couple of days.

The user decided to apply AutoClassC for determining the different classes of physical locations where the material would show an equal thickness. In other words, the x- and y-values were used as attributes for determining class membership and an identical thickness or y-value served as the criterion for belonging to the same class. It was quite difficult to determine the appropriate probabilistic model which AutoclassC should apply: single-normal, single_multinomial or ...? All together, the user performed five consecutive runs of AutoClassC. The upper left section of Figure 1 shows a typical segment of the output. Also, the 5th attempt caught some of the classification which is shown as the desired result in Figure 1. Since the numbers indicating class membership are rather randomly assigned by AutoClassC, they needed to be postprocessed and rearranged so that they would become comprehensible.

AutoClass	Atree

AutoClass

CROSS REFERENCE:
CASE NUMBER => MOST PROBABLE CLASS

    AutoClass CLASSIFICATION for the 25 cases
    with log-A<X/H>
    (approximate marginal likelihood) = -166.511
    and using models   charge.model - index = 0

Case#	Class	Prob	Case#	Class	Prob	Case#	Class	Prob
1	2	0.98	10	1	0.98	19	0	0.99
...			...			...		
2	2	0.99	11	1	0.99	20	0	0.99
9	0	0.97	18	0	0.99			

Atree

7.40 11	7.40 11	1.0 1	1.0 1
7.30 10	7.0 8	0.0 0	0.0 0
6.30 3	6.0 1	0.0 0	0.0 0
6.20 3	6.20 2	1.0 1	1.0 1
...			
6.0 1	5.90 0	0.0 0	1.0 1
5.90 1	5.90 0	1.0 1	1.0 1
5.80 0	6.30 3	0.0 0	0.0 0
6.20 3	6.20 2	1.0 1	1.0 1
5.80 0	7.0 8	0.0 0	1.0 1
6.20 3	6.20 2	1.0 1	1.0 1

ERROR HISTOGRAM
Out by 0 levels 26
Out by 1 levels 4
Out by 3+ levels   0

Clint

New positive example
is_connected(7.4, 400, 600, 7.4, 600, 400)
Lowerbound does not cover a negative example:

```
* is_connected(_X, _Y, _Z, _U, _V, _W) if
    elevation(_U, _W, _V)  and elevation(_U, _V, _W) and
    elevation(_U, _W, _Z)  and elevation(_U, _Z, _W) and
    elevation(_U, _V, _Y)  and elevation(_U, _Y, _V) and
    elevation(_U, _Z, _Y)  and elevation(_U, _Y, _Z) and
    elevation(_X, _W, _V)  and elevation(_X, _V, _W) and
    elevation(_X, _W, _Z)  and elevation(_X, _Z, _W) and
    ...
    equal(_U, _U)   and equal(_U, _X)   and
    equal(_X, _U)   and equal(_X, _X)   and
    height(_U)   and height(_X) .
Attempt to generalize ...
```

Desired result

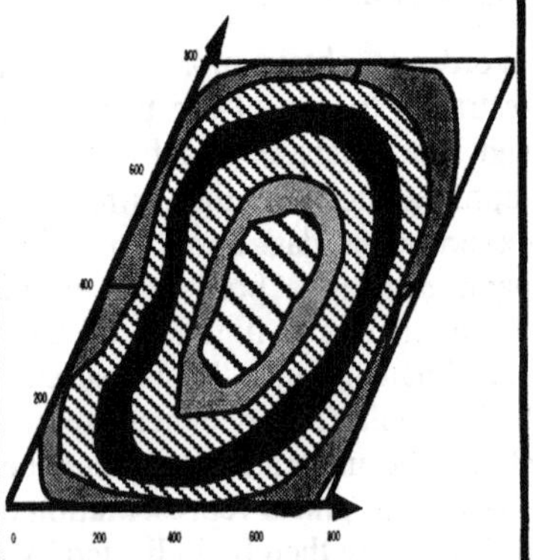

Figure 1: Some results from the applications of AutoClassC, Atree, Clint together with a graphical representation of the desired result.

Atree was applied for learning that two different points (expressed in terms of their x- and y- values) should be connected and thereby determine a line of equal thickness, when they have the same thickness (or z-value). Some of the cases were used as training set and the other cases as test set. Altogether, five runs of Atree were performed. The upper right panel of Figure 1 shows some of the output produced by Atree. The last run of Atree showed that the function „is_connected" was learned relatively well, but again comprehending the results in terms of the specific application needs was quite difficult. At best Atree provided only a partial contribution to the solution of the (reduced) application problem.

Clint was presented with examples of the form „is_connected(6.3, 200, 800, 6.3, 600, 0)", where the six numbers represent the thickness of the material (e.g. 6.3) and the x- and y- coordinates of two locations which showed the same thickness. Clint was then supposed to learn that two points are connected whenever their thickness is identical. It turned out that a few auxiliary predicates (elevation, eaqual, height) needed to be defined before Clint would at least come close to induce the desired predicate and produce the output which is partially shown in the lower left panel of Figure 1.

3.3 Conclusions

The purpose of applying the different machine learning tools to realistic databases and real life problems in three application domains was not so much to determine which of the different tools would perform best. There are already plenty of experimental comparisons among different machine learning tools and the proceedings of the machine learning conferences are full of such comparisons. The purpose of our experimental evaluation was more to identify the quite common problems which arise when machine learning is applied for discovering new knowledge in some application domain, where this application domain has in no way been considered when the specific learning tool was developed. Neither the developers of AutoClass, or Atree, or Clint had even thought of applying their tools to any of the three data mines which we have described.

Why should these tools then be useful in a specific application domain? According to the popular toolbox philosophy they would be applicable because machine learning procedures are viewed as generic tools and such generic tools are useful in many domains. Similar to a hammer which can be useful for driving a nail into the wall as well as for trashing a porcelain vase, machine learning would be useful for discovering the most relevant concepts in medicine as well as the most diagnostic attributes in the material sciences.

The results from our little exercise can be expressed in quite general terms: When a machine learning tool does not have an appreciation of the ontological and structural properties of an application domain, it will at best produce some partial results which require expensive postprocessing before the desired learning result is achieved. Such an appreciation of the ontological and structural properties requires that the machine learning tool provides appropriate representation constructs. Alternatively, a learning tool could be quite selectively applied to the values of some selected attributes. In such a situation it must be clarified how the learning result relates to the other conceptual structures of the domain. In other words, a successful application of learning tools to databases and domains which have their own ontologies requires the solution of the knowledge acquisition problem where the generic structures of the machine learning tool must be matched to the domain structures of the application field. Obviously, there is no guarantee that an easy match can be found.

When machine learning is to be applied to some realistic application domain, the toolbox approach (for references see Sleeman, 1994) puts all the burden on the user. This assessment is also true, when there is some advisory system as part of machine learning toolbox. In a way, it was the fault of our user that he was not more knowledgeable about the specific algorithms and not more creative in adjusting them to the specific problems. With enough time and effort spent, they surely could have been successfully used. But such an assessment simply is not fair to the user. Such an accusation of the user is similar to refuting the complaints of a user in the 60s, who complained that assembly languages are so difficult to use. What is needed instead is a higher order conceptualization of machine learning which is easier to apply and understand by the user. Instead of the toolbox approach we are thus proposing a user centered configuration of machine learning components in combination with filter and visualization components that are partially automatically configured according to user requirements. They can be thus more easily applied to different application domains and the learning procedures as well as the learning results are more comprehensible. This configuration approach to machine learning is currently pursued in the KOALA project. We will thus give a preview of the KOALA system which is currently under development. The configuration system is thereby based on constraint satisfaction procedures over hierarchically structured domains, which have been developed in the ConPlan project (Meyer, 1994; Meyer auf'm Hofe & Tschaitschian, 1995).

4. The KOALA System

The KOALA system attempts to enhance the applicability and comprehensibility of machine learning tools by cooperative knowledge evolution, where understanding and meaning emerges through user interactions. In a way, each user is developing (i.e. configuring) his own machine learning system, by applying techniques of end-user programming.

4.1 System Architecture

Figure 2 shows the architecture of the KOALA system. There is a knowledge base which formally describes the different machine learning, filter, visualization and other post processing procedures at different levels of abstractions. The descriptions are expressed in terms of behavior descriptions, a kind of knowledge level specification which is easily comprehensible to users (Schmalhofer & Aitken, 1995). The corresponding machine learning and related components are stored in respective libraries (LIB-ML and LIB-FILT). The user may enter his requirements in terms of input/output specifications as well as by nonfunctional requirements (speed, costs, etc.). The CONSTRUCTOR component will then attempt to configure an appropriate procedure. The CONSTRUCTOR presents intermediate results to the user and the user can interactively refine or revise his previously stated requirements and component specifications.

This configuration system has been developed so that it can handle incremental specifications of a problem, that the user can interactively guide the inference and constraint satisfaction processes and that it can operate with an FILT/ML-KB which contains only incomplete knowledge. A partial or complete specification of a procedure may be tested with a number of examples and such test results can furthermore be used for modifying or completing a specification. After some iterations, a user may be satisfied with the achieved configuration. The ML-COMPILER will then select, combine and appropriately instantiate the respective modules from the libraries and the specified machine learning procedure can be exported and applied to the specific problem at hand.

Since at the most general level, the specifications of requirements and components are expressed in the terminology of the user and since the user is himself active in configuring and testing the different modules, the configured machine learning procedure as well as the learning results which are achieved by applying this procedure are more comprehensible to the user. In other words, the user is not simply confronted with the achieved learning results but new knowledge evolves in a cooperative manner (cf. Schmalhofer & Tschaitschian, 1995)

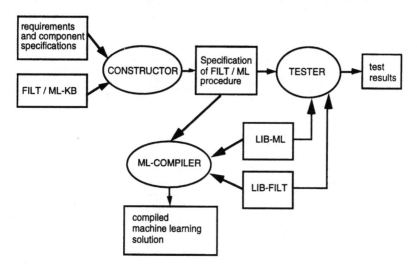

Figure 2: Architecture of the KOALA-System for achieving a cooperative knowledge evolution between user and system

4.2 User Interface

Figure 3 shows the user interface of the KOALA system. A list of previously used requirements and components are shown in the *requirements and components* window. Each component is thereby described by its name and several parameter values (for a more detailed description see section 4.3). ID3 is for example described as a learning procedure that generates rules from classified examples, that is not incremental (one shot) and uses a hypothesis space as *knowledge* and search procedures as learning *skills*. Results from the actual test runs of a component would be shown in the column labelled *performance*. The user may select one or several items from this list of *requirements and components* and drag them to the *current list of requirements*. All entrances in the *current list of requirements* can be edited and new requirements can also be entered by typing them. After some requirements and/or components have been entered and priorities have been assigned to them, the user may activate the CONSTRUCTOR. The CONSTRUCTOR will now begin to (partially) configure a solution for the specific requirements and will present intermediate results in the window labelled *current solution infos*. Based upon this feedback, the user may decide to revise his requirements and the CONSTRUCTOR will then process the updated requirements. In cases where the user feels that he would like to proceed without the assistance of the CONSTRUCTOR, he can himself specify a configuration by entering it into the window labelled *user supplied solution*. The currently active solution of the configuration problem will always be visualized in the window labelled *visualization of procedure*.

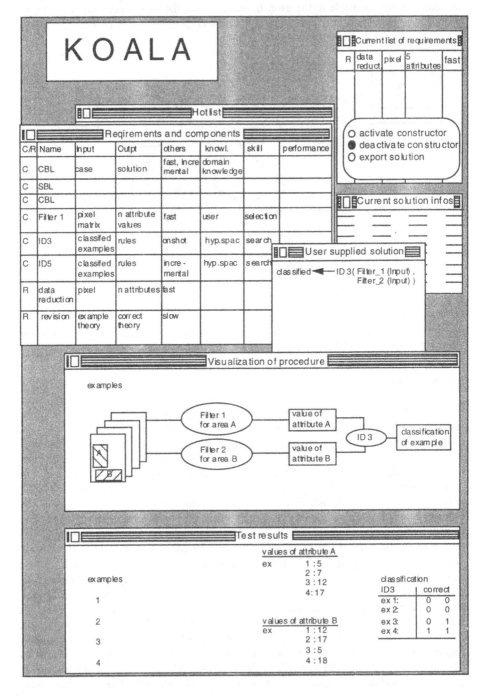

Figure 3: User Interface of the KOALA System

The user can now select some or all of the components and data sets for performing test runs. The results of such test runs will be displayed in the window labelled *test results*.

After the user is satisfied with some given configuration he can request that the configured solution is exported and the ML-COMPILER will then link and instantiate the corresponding modules from the respective libraries.

4.3 Description of the Machine Learning Components in the Filt/ML-KB

The machine learning components are described in terms of behavior descriptions (Schmalhofer & Aitken, 1995) which are a kind of knowledge level specification. The behavior description B of each component consists of four parameters together with the various relations R among them: $B=(g,k,s,p, R_{gk}, R_{gs}, R_{gp}, R_{ks}, R_{kp}, R_{gks},....R_{gksp})$. The g-parameter describes the purpose of a component in terms of the required inputs and the to be achieved outputs. The k-parameter describes the knowledge which is used and must be supplied to the learning procedure. The s-parameter describes the skills which are used by the learning method. Finally, the p-parameter describes the performance of the component in terms of actual test examples. The following list shows the different parameter values which resulted from describing several learning components in general terms that can be easily understood by the different users.

$G =$ {({cases},{problem_solutions}),({examples},{rules}),
({examples classification},{rules}), ({examples selection},{rules}),
({examples selection},{schema}), ({examples theory},{revised theory}))}

$K =$ {{domain_knowledge}, {heuristics}, {hypothesis_space,
information_measure}, {domain_knowledge heuristics }}

$S =$ {{analogy}, {search}, {explanatory coherence}}

$P =$ {{medicine}, {material science}, {quality control}}.

With this terminology, a conceptual clustering procedure is for example described as generating rules from examples, $g=$({examples},{rules}), by using search as a learning skill, $s=${search}, and a hypothesis space with an information measure as knowledge, $k=${hypothesis_space, information_measure}. And this procedure may have been tested in the area of medicine, $p=${medicine}.

Such a global description of a machine learning component is certainly not sufficient for configuring a concatenation of several filter-, learning- and visualization components so that they would accomplish a certain input-output performance. In addition, each component is therefore also described at a micro level and these micro level descriptions are associated with their respective macro level descriptions. Since CONSTRUCT accepts specifications which are expressed in predicate calculus, the micro level descriptions are expressed in predicate logic. A complete description of a machine learning component would require too much space for being presented here. We will therefore only present typical segments of a learning procedure which we have recently developed.

We will present a description of a generic learning procedure, namely a procedure for learning abstractions from plans and cases by translating some concrete plan into a more coarse grained representation language. This learning procedure is particularly important for obtaining the more general descriptions of the interactions of different pharmaceutical substances from the databases of adverse events (see section 2.1) This machine learning tool has been termed PABS for plan or program abstraction (Schmalhofer et al., 1993; Schmalhofer et al., 1995). It is performed by determining appropriate state- and sequence abstraction mappings. The g-parameter thus specifies that an abstract plan will be generated from the concrete plan, so that the induced state- and sequence abstraction mappings are appropriately related to one another.

G: Given some concrete plan P_c and an initial state description S_0

construct an abstract plan P_a with

$(\exists \ f_{St})$ (IsStateAbstractionMapping $(f_{St}, L_c, L_a) \wedge$

$(\exists \ f_{Seq})$ $(\exists \ Sq_c)$ $(\exists \ Sq_a)$ (IsInducedStateDescriptionSequence $(P_c, S_0, Sq_c, L_c) \wedge$

IsInducedStateDescriptionSequence $(P_a,$ ApplyFunction $(f_{St}, S_0), Sq_a, L_a) \wedge$

IsSequenceAbstractionMapping $(f_{Seq}, Sq_c, Sq_a) \wedge$

$(\forall \ x)$ $(x \in$ Domain $(f_{Seq}) \rightarrow$

IncludesPair $(f_{St},$ ApplyFunction $(Sq_c,$ ApplyFunction $(f_{Seq}, x))$,

ApplyFunction $(Sq_a, x)))))$

Furthermore:

- IsStateAbstractionMapping (f, L_1, L_2) is an abbreviation of:

    IsFunction $(f) \wedge (\forall \ x) (\forall \ y)$ (IncludesPair $(f, x, y) \rightarrow$

    IsStateDescription $(x, L_1) \wedge$ IsStateDescription $(y, L_2) \wedge (\forall \ S)$ (IsState $(S) \rightarrow$

    (valid $(x, S) \rightarrow$ valid $(y, S))))$

This means that f is a function which maps the state descriptions from the concrete description L_1 to the abstract description language L_2.

- IsSequenceAbstractionMapping (f, Sq_1, Sq_2) is an abbreviation of:

    $(\forall \ x)$ $((x \in$ Domain $(f) \leftrightarrow (x \in$ Domain $(Sq_2)) \wedge$

    $(x \in$ Image $(f) \rightarrow (x \in$ Domain $(Sq_1))) \wedge$

ApplyFunction (f, min (Domain (Sq2))) = min (Domain (Sq1)) $\wedge$

ApplyFunction (f, max (Domain (Sq2))) = max (Domain (Sq1)) $\wedge$

$(\forall\ x_1)\ (\forall\ x_2)\ (x_1 \in$ Domain (f) $\wedge$ $x_2 \in$ Domain (f) $\wedge$ $x_1 < x_2$

$\rightarrow$ ApplyFunction (f, x_1) < ApplyFunction (f, x_2))

It means that f would be a sequence abstraction mapping for the state sequences Sq_1 and Sq_2 where Sq_2 has a more coarse grained granularity (For more details see Schmalhofer et. al. 1993; p.214).

- IsPlan (P, L) is an abbreviation of:

    IsFunction (P) $\wedge$ $(\forall\ o)\ (o \in$ Image (P) $\rightarrow$ IsDescribedOperator (o, L)) $\wedge$

    Domain (P) $\subseteq$ N $\wedge$ $(\exists\ n)\ (n \in$ N $\wedge$ $(\forall\ y)\ (y \in$ Domain (P) $\leftrightarrow$ $0 < y \leq n))$

This description describes the linear plan consisting of the operators $(o_1, o_2, ... , o_n)$.

The k-parameter specifies that concrete and abstract description languages and sets of operators are used as knowledge in learning.

K: concrete and abstract description languages: L_c, L_a

Sets of operators O_c und O_a, that are described in L_c and L_a , respectively.

The s-parameters describe the skills of calculating the various mappings.

S: Skill I

Input: P : Plan specified in L_c; S_0 : initial state described in L_c

Output: Sq : Sequence of state descriptions described in L_c

Functionality: IsPlan (P, L_c) $\wedge$ IsStateDescription (S_0, L_c) $\rightarrow$ IsInducedStateDescriptionSequence (P, S_0, Sq, L_c)

This partial example may be sufficient for demonstrating how behavior descriptions are utilized in the KOALA-system: The macroscopic behavior descriptions provide a terminology which is easy to comprehend for the different users. A user can thus much better determine which machine learning components are most promising for achieving the desired result. The microscopic descriptions are a more refined specification which allows the CONSTRUCTOR of the KOALA-system to configure a learning procedure that would achieve this result.

Discussion

With this research we have attempted to evaluate the prospects of harvesting important knowledge from industrial databases. Some initial experimental evaluation of applying some machine learning tools to different data mines revealed some severe limitations of the tool box philosophy. Since realistic databases and application domains carry with them quite well structured domain ontologies which cannot be ignored when some machine learning tool is applied, general tools and some application adviser are not sufficient for making data mining a success. It was therefore suggested to develop a general configuration system for concatenating various filter-, learning-, and postprocessing components by applying constraint satisfaction techniques over hierarchically structured domains. A preview of the KOALA system which achieves these objectives was then presented. The development of a configuration environment for a configurable learning system has also been proposed by Rouveirol & Albert (1994). The present proposal differs from the suggestions of Rouveirol & Albert in that it focuses on the conceptions of the users in the application domains, while Rouveirol & Albert have described learning tools in terms of language, search, and confirmation biases as the important aspects for controlling the application of the learning primitives.

Acknowledgements

This research was supported by grant 413-5839-ITW9304/3 from the BMFT. We would like to thank Harald Meyer auf'm Hofe and Jürgen Kempf for their contributions to this work.

References

Abecker, A., Boley, H., Hinkelmann, K., Wache, H. & Schmalhofer, F. (November 1995) An environment for exploring and validating declarative knowledge. Tech. Memo TM-95-03. Deutsches Forschungszentrum für Künstliche Intelligenz GmbH, Kaiserslautern. Also in: Proc. Workshop on Logic Programming Environments at ILP'S '95, Portland, Oregon, Dec. 1995.

Armstrong, W.W., Liang, J., Lin, D., Reynolds, S. (September 1990) Experiments using Parsimonious Adaptive Logic, Tech. Report TR 90-30, Department of Computing Science, University of Alberta.

DeRaedt, L. (1992) Interactive Theory Revision: An Inductive Logic Programming Approach. London: Academic Press.

Frawley, Piatetsky-Shapiro & Matheus (Fall 1992) Knowledge discovery in databases. AI Magazine.

Hinkelmann, K., Meyer, M. & Schmalhofer, F. (1994) Knowledge-base evolution for product and production planning. AI Communications: The European Journal on Artificial Intelligence, 7, 98-113.

Khabaza & Shearer (February 1995) Data mining with Clementine. In Colloquium on Knowledge Discovery in Databases. The Institution of Electrical Engineers.

Kempf, J., Andel, S., Schmalhofer, F. & Boley, H. (1995) Transformation einer fertigungstechnischen Anwendungsdatenbasis in eine deklarative Repräsentation. VEGA Report, August 1995, DFKI Kaiserslautern.

Meyer, M. (1994). Finite domain constraints: Declarativity meets efficiency, theory meets application. Doctoral dissertation, Computer Science Department, University of Kaiserslautern.

Meyer auf'm Hofe, H. & Tschaitschian, B. (1995) PCSPs with hierarchical constraint orderings in real world scheduling applications, in: Jampel, M., Freuder, E. and Maher M. (eds.) Notes on the CP'95 Workshop on Over-Constrained Systems.

Moulet M., & Kodratoff, Y. (1995) From machine learning towards knowledge discovery in databases. In Kodratoff, Nakhaeizadeh & Taylor (eds.) Statistics, machine learning and knowledge discovery in databases: Proceedings of the MLnet Sponsored Familiarization Workshop, Heraklion, Crete, Greece, 7-12.

Rouveirol & Albert (1994) Knowledge level model for a configurable learning system. In L. Steels, G. Schreiber & W. Van de Velde (eds.) A Future for Knowledge Acquisition, EKAW '94 Proceedings, Berlin: Springer-Verlag, 374-393.

Schmalhofer F., & Aitken, S. (1995) Beyond the knowledge level: Behavior descriptions of machine learning systems. In D. Fensel (ed.) Knowledge Level Modelling and Machine Learning: Proceedings of the MLnet Sponsored Familiarization Workshop, Heraklion, Crete, Greece, S. III.1.1 - III.1.15.

Schmalhofer, F., & Auerswald, M. (1995) Verhaltensbeschreibungen zur Charakterisierung von Lernsystemen auf der Wissensebene. In C. Globig & K.-D. Althoff (eds.) Beiträge zum 7. Fachgruppentreffen Maschinelles Lernen, Kaiserslautern, August 1994, Kaiserslautern: Zentrum für Lernende Systeme und Anwendungen, Fachbereich Informatik. Universität Kaiserslautern, 28-36.

Schmalhofer, F., Bergmann, R., Boschert, S. & Thoben, J. (1993) Learning program abstractions: Formal model and empirical validation. In G. Strube & K. F. Wender (eds.) The Cognitive Psychology of Knowledge, Amsterdam, Elsevier: North Holland, 203-232, 1993.

Schmalhofer, F., Reinartz, Th., & Tschaitschian, B. (1995) A unified approach to learning in complex real world domains, Applied Artificial Intelligence, An International Journal, vol 9., No 2, 127-156.

Schmalhofer, F.& Tschaitschian, B. (1995) Cooperative knowledge evolution for complex domains. In G. Tecuci & Y. Kodratoff (eds.) Machine Learning and Knowledge Acquisition: Integrated Approaches, London: Academic Press, 145-166.

Sleeman, D. (1994) Towards a technology and a science of machine learning. Artificial Intelligence Communications, 7, 29-38.

Stutz, J. and Cheeseman, P. (1994) AutoClass - a Bayesian Approach to Classification. In Maximum Entropy and Bayesian Methods, Cambridge, 1994, J. Skilling and S. Sibisi (eds.) Dordrecht, The Netherlands: Kluwer Academic Publishers.

A Knowledge Acquisition Tool for Multi-Perspective Concept Formation

João José Furtado Vasco, Colette Faucher, Eugène Chouraqui

DIAM-IUSPIM - Université d'Aix Marseille III Av. Escadrille Normandie-Niemen
F-13397 Marseille Cedex 20 France
Diam_ef@vmesa11.u-3mrs.fr

Abstract. In this paper, we describe an architecture for helping in the construction of concept hierarchies. This architecture is based on machine learning and on cognitive psychology studies in concept formation. Our basic assumption is that concept formation should be considered as a goal-driven, context-dependent process and, therefore, that the hierarchical organization of concepts should be represented in different perspectives. The core of our architecture is a learning system that generates multi-perspective hierarchies. The evaluation of the architecture is realized from a perspective of both the comprehensibility and the prediction power of the generated knowledge.

1 Introduction

Knowledge acquisition (KA) for knowledge-based systems concerns the development of knowledge models for problem solving in specific domains. Machine learning systems are an alternative to automate the KA process, optimizing expert participation. In particular, incremental concept formation systems [Fisher 87] construct hierarchical abstract representations from *observations* (non-classified description of specific entities, events or situations), by recognizing regularities among them. These systems are especially interesting for the initial modeling phases in which the domain concepts and the relationships between them are identified.

From a KA perspective two factors are essential to be examined in machine learning systems: How understandable the knowledge they generate is and how flexible the system is to provide and receive feedback to and from the user (the interaction factor). Concept formation systems need in particular concentration on understanding considerations, since their objective is to construct abstract representations to better comprehend the world and to make predictions about it. Thus it is essential that these abstract representations (concepts) be easily interpretable by an expert, allowing him to do associations with the real-world entities which he manipulates. As for the interaction between the learning system and the user, its necessity has become evident for supporting revisions in the generated knowledge. In addition, feedback to the user can improve the presentation of new examples.

In order to create a KA tool for helping an expert to express and to elaborate concepts of his domain, we have defined a concept formation architecture called CONFORT. This architecture is based on cognitive psychological studies which suppose that concept formation is a goal-driven process [Barsalou 83],[Seifert 88]. This assumption leads us to consider that concept hierarchies should be viewed from different perspectives, which can have different hierarchical organizations according to the usage determined by the expert's categorization goals. The core of CONFORT is FORMVIEW, a learning algorithm of incremental concept formation that uses observations to generate multi-perspective concept hierarchies.

CONFORT addresses the understanding and the interaction factors mentioned above. In spite of the subjectivity involved with the former notion, our claim is that concept hierarchies generated from both a goal and a context familiar to the expert can be more easily interpreted by him. Regarding the interaction factor, the user receives an assistance of the system as regards the properties' relevance he should present. Another feedback given by the system concerns the identification of relationships between perspectives. In addition, CONFORT generates concept hierarchies that have good power to infer properties as a byproduct of the classification of unseen observations.

In this paper, we describe the main ideas of both CONFORT and FORMVIEW showing their characteristics for helping in KA, namely the multi-perspective representation, the incremental concept formation process, and the heuristics used to give feedback to the expert. Furthermore we analyze the hierarchies generated from FORMVIEW from the prediction accuracy and the understanding angles.

This article has the following organization. In Section 2, we highlight considerations on concept formation from a machine learning perspective. In Section 3, we describe the CONFORT architecture. Section 4 describes the concept formation algorithm FORMVIEW. In Section 5 we evaluate FORMVIEW and show how the representation it generates can be exploited. Section 6 describes related works, and finally in Section 7, our conclusions are stated and future researches are indicated.

2 Background

2.1 Basic definitions

In order to design a software architecture for helping KA, our researches are focused on the human's concept formation process. Therefore, our work is fundamentally based on psychological findings about concepts and categories.

We consider a concept refers to an idea or notion by which people can understand some aspects of the world[Hampton 93]. A category is a set of entities (objects, events, actions, states, etc.) which are grouped together on the basis of some criterion of categorization. Thus, a concept provides a way to categorize the world into those entities that instantiate the concept, and those that do not. Below, we define more formally some of these notions as well as others that will be important to the comprehension of this article. Given

E   set of entities to categorize E=$\{e_1, e_2, ..., e_n \mid n \in N \}$

$\mathcal{P}$(E)   set of parts of E, called *categories*

A   set of *attributes* describing the entities of E. Ex: A=$\{$Age, Sex, Tail$\}$

$\upsilon(a)$ set of possible values of the attribute a of A, υ(Age)=$\{$Young, Adult$\}$

V   set of values of all the attributes $\in$ A; V=$\{\upsilon(k) \mid k \in A\}$

O   an *observation* describing an entity e;O=$\{p_i=(a,v) \mid a \in A, v \in \upsilon(a)\} \in \mathcal{P}(A \times V)$
       we call p_i a *property* of O $(1 \leq i \leq n)$; n $\leq$ card(A).

H   a strict hierarchy (disjoint categories) to establish on E :
       H is an oriented acyclic graph H=$(\mathcal{P}(E)$, π, R) where R is the maximal element following the partial order relation π (specialization relation).

PV   set of perspectives reflecting the categorization goals. PV=$\{pv_1, pv_2,..., pv_n\}$

H↑pv is a hierarchy H established on E reflecting a perspective pv ($\in$ PV)

2.2 Concept Formation from a Machine Learning Perspective

Machine learning systems build concepts in *intension* from exemplars of their *extension*. In this context, we concentrate on learning from observation systems or conceptual clustering [Michalski 86],[Fisher 87]. These systems recognize regularities among a set of non-preclassified entities or events and induce a concept hierarchy that organizes these observations. Generally, concept formation systems can be defined by means of a quadruplet(H, I, C, µ) [Thaise 91] , where :

- H is the possible space of concept hierarchies;
- I is the set of observation about entities to be categorized;
- C is a partitioning of all these entities into conceptual categories C_i which are structured hierarchically($C \in$ H) and optimizing a defined quality criterion;
- µ is the set of operators of construction or organization of categories which we can apply to the members of H to generate C.

A concept formation algorithm is reduced to a hill-climbing search, in H, for a hierarchy of conceptual categories C that covers all the entities described in I and that optimizes the evaluation function $f(C, I)$ measuring the quality criterion. The fundamental point of this research concerns the application of the µ's operator that produces an optimal value for $f(C, I)$. On incremental concept formation, entities are treated one after another as soon as they are observed. The classification of new entities is made by their adequacy for the existing conceptual categories.

A typical incremental concept formation system is COBWEB [Fisher 87]. It is a pioneer system influenced by research in cognitive psychology on *basic level, probabilistic concepts* and *typicality effects* [Rosch 76][Fisher 93]. It has given rise to many successors(BRIDGER[Reich 92] and CLASSIT[Gennari 89] are examples).

3 CONFORT Main Characteristics

CONFORT presupposes that goals of categorization exist (supplied by one or more experts) prior to initiation of the process. Categorization uses a scheme to weigh an observation's properties based on prior expectations of the relevance of particular properties within the task domain. Both the properties' relevance and the relationships between these properties are represented in a GDN (Goal Dependency Network) [Michalski 86] according to the categorization goals. Property relationships are implications between initial observed properties(typically surface properties) and those dependent on the expert domain(usually functional properties). Thus, an observation is represented by the observer's defined properties and eventually by the GDN's inferred ones. Alternatively, different experts can supply the system with different observations describing the same entity. In other words, the moment that an expert observes and describes the entity, he can already determine the properties which are particular to his viewpoint.

A goal-driven concept formation process leads us naturally to a multi-perspective representation, since goals have influence on the perception of the properties as well as on the determination of relevance for context-specific features. Consequently, this situation favours the generation of different hierarchical organizations. For instance, to achieve the goal of buying a pet for a child, one would consider beauty and low price as relevant properties. As a result, animal hierarchical organization which reflects this particular situation would probably differs from the perspective of a veterinary surgeon for whom other properties (e.g. physiological) would be relevant.

The use of a multi-perspective concept representation has opened up various alternatives for helping in knowledge acquisition. The most obvious advantage is to allow an expert to isolate a specific perspective where the hierarchy is organized according to his point of view and where he treats only the relevant attributes. We can thus suppose that these hierarchies are more understandable.

The second particularity of the multi-perspective representation is the existence of a communication channel among hierarchies representing different perspectives. This communication channel, called *bridge*, allows FORMVIEW to produce inference rules associating categories in different perspectives. These rules are eventually presented to the expert, encouraging him to provide the system with feedback. The rule discovery procedure helps in KA, because unknown relations are identified and because the expert can teach the system representative observations. Bridges will be presented precisely in Section 4.

The core of our architecture is FORMVIEW, a concept formation algorithm that generates multiple hierarchies and uses a category quality measure that can take into account the relevance of an observation's properties and the generated categories in other perspectives. Figure 1 illustrates the main ideas of CONFORT. Observe the possibiliy of feedback, thus the expert can act in a supervised manner, informing observations with their associated categories. Conversely, FORMVIEW provides feedback to the expert, suggesting which properties should be defined as relevant as well as determining their values in order to obtain hierarchies with good prediction power.

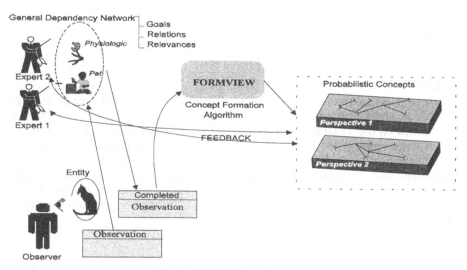

Fig. 1. CONFORT architecture

4 FORMVIEW: Constructing Multi-Perspective Concept Hierarchies

4.1 Knowledge Representation in FORMVIEW

An important feature of CONFORT and particularly of FORMVIEW is that they were developed in an Object Oriented Representation (OOR) context. We have integrated them into the frame-based language Objlog+[Faucher 91] permitting an automatic construction of frame hierarchies. The details and advantages of this integration are beyond the scope of this paper, and can be obtained in [Vasco 95a].

Description of Inputs

The main FORMVIEW's input is one or several (following different perspectives) observations describing an entity that belongs to E. FORMVIEW uses as additional data a goal dependency network (GDN)[Michalski 86]. For this paper, it suffices to say that in a GDN, for each categorization goal, the expert can define a degree of relevance (in the interval [0,1]) for each property that he considers important to that goal. In addition, the existence of a property can lead to the occurrence of another one so that implication is also represented in the GDN.

Description of Concepts

FORMVIEW constructs *probabilistic concepts* [Smith 81]. These concepts have the probability that an observation is classified into the category represented by the concept C,P(C), all possible values for their attributes and each such value having its associated *predictability* and *predictiveness* [Fisher 87]. The predictability is the conditional probability that an observation x has value v for an attribute a, given that x is a member of a category C, or $P(a=v|C)$. The predictiveness is the conditional probability that x is member of C given that x has value v for a or $P(C|a=v)$. Formally, given a set of entities E, and a hierarchy $H\uparrow pv$ built on E which representes a perspective pv. In FORMVIEW, all category of entities C of $H\uparrow pv$ define the probabilistic concept CP below:

$CP = \{(a, \upsilon(a), PD, PP)| a \in A\}$

Where PD=the set of the predictabilities for each $v \in \upsilon(a)$

PP =the set of the predictiveness for each $v \in \upsilon(a)$ (1)

We name the pair (a, v), $v \in \upsilon(a)$, a property of CP

FORMVIEW constructs multiple probabilistic concept trees which represent different points of view corresponding to different choices of categorization goals (GDN's goals). In our work, the basic ideas on a multi-perspective representation were based on the TROPES model[Marino 90]. The main feature of this model is the existence of oriented links, called *bridges*, between hierarchies that represent different perspectives. Two types of bridges are possible: unidirectional and bi-directional. Bi-directional bridges represent set equality relation while unidirectional ones represent set inclusion relation. Precisely, a bridge between a category C of a perspective pv ($C \in H\uparrow pv$) and another category C' in another perspective pv'($C' \in H'\uparrow pv'$), noted as bridge(C,C'), is defined as:

$$bridge(C,C') = \begin{cases} 1 \Leftrightarrow C = C'(bi-directional) \\ 0 \Leftrightarrow C \subset C'(unidirectional) \\ -1 \Leftrightarrow C \not\subset C'(no-bridge) \end{cases}$$ (2)

When observations which are covered by a node (a concept representing a category) C are included into the set of observations which are covered by a node C' in another perspective, a bridge from C (source node) to C' (target node) is established. If the extension of C' is also included in C, a bi-directional bridge is created. Notice that both set inclusion and set equality relations accept the application of the transitivity property (horizontally, among perspectives), which is similar to the vertical transitivity authorized by the specialization relation in a hierarchy. In addition, the specialization relation in one hierarchy allows FORMVIEW to establish *hidden bridges* between the children of a bridge's source node and a bridge's target node. Figure 2 illustrates two hierarchies following two perspectives and the bridges between them.

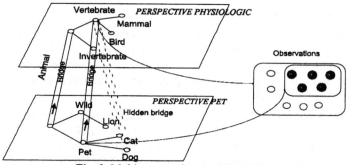

Fig. 2. Multi-perspectives in CONFORT

4.2 The Utility Measure

FORMVIEW constructs hierarchies while privileging their prediction power. Its evaluation function is, like many of its predecessors, based on the Gluck and Corter's work on cognitive psychology[Gluck 85], who have defined a function to discover, within a hierarchical classification tree, the basic level category. Category quality, called *category utility*, is defined as the increase in the expected number of properties that can be correctly predicted given knowledge of a category over the expected number of correct predictions without such knowledge. Category utility in FORMVIEW, called *semantic utility*, takes into account the relevance of properties defined by the expert in the GDN. In fact, we consider that the increase in the expected number of properties to be predicted depends on the relevance of the considered properties. Thus, let be $P_{cp}=\{p_1, p_2,...,p_p\}$ the set of properties of a probabilistic concept *CP*. The semantic utility *UCs*, of a category C, which CP represents is :

$$UCs(C) = \left(\sum_{i=1}^{p} \Delta(pi) P(pi|C) P(C|pi) - P(C) P(pi)^2 \right)$$

(3)

Where $\Delta(p_i) = $ (GDN's relevance of p_i + $P(p_i)$))

FORMVIEW computes the utility of a partition of categories, as the mean of semantic utilities of each partition category. However, it can use, during concept hierarchy construction from a particular perspective, additional information from other hierarchies which represent other perspectives. This is possible because of bridges. In this case, FORMVIEW's additional strategy is to determine a *complete* partition (P^{com}) with categories of other hierarchies: Those are target of bridges established from sources that are categories from the initial partition. Since several irrelevant bridges can be established, FORMVIEW considers only those confirmed by the expert (the *valid* bridges).

It is important to point out that the target categories, which will make part of the complete partition, contribute to the category utility calculation only with properties that are not present in the concept that represents the source category. In addition, if there are several target categories with the same property, FORMVIEW selects those having the highest predictability. We call these properties as *useful* ones.

The rational behind these two latter strategies is that a *complete* partition and its *useful* properties define a complete concept, independent from a particular perspective. Thus, the prediction power is improved because a greater quantity of properties can be induced as a result of the classification of a new entity.

4.3 The Concept Formation Process

At first, from an observation O, FORMVIEW searches the relationship between properties of such an observation and other properties in the GDN. This can provoke modifications in the initial observation structure since a complete observation OC^t for a perspective t ($\in$ PV) possesses the properties of the initial observation O plus those inferred from the GDN.

From complete observations, FORMVIEW generates several hierarchies reflecting different perspectives or points of view according to GDN's categorization goals. Each GDN categorization goal determines a perspective to consider, then a specific hierarchy. The concept formation procedure of FORMVIEW is a hill climbing search for the best partition that can be generated from the application of the operators for hierarchy construction. More precisely, to categorize a new observation OC^t among the sub-concepts of a given concept (partition P_0), FORMVIEW can :

- modify the partition P_0 incorporating OC^t in one of the P_0's categories and giving rise to the partition $P_a = \{C_1,..., C_i,...,C_r,...,C_k\}$; With C_i, C_r having the two best utilities to categorize OC^t that is to say $UCs(C_i) > UCs(C_r) > UCs_z(C_z)$ ($0 < z < k$, $z \neq i, r$).
- modify P_0 creating a new concept C_c for receiving OC^t, giving rise to the partition P_c ($P_c = P_0 \cup \{C_c\}$)
- modify P_0 merging the two concepts C_i et C_r in one C_{ir}, giving rise to the partition P_f ($P_f = P_0 - \{C_i, C_r\} \cup \{C_{ir}\}$)
- modify P_0 splitting C_i in its sub-concepts C_{il} $\{C_{il} | 1 \leq l \leq ql$, giving rise to the partition P_s ($P_s = P_0 - \{C_i\} \cup \{C_{i1}, C_{i2}, ..., C_{iq}\}$.

The choice of the partition into which to integrate OC^t will be that which optimizes the category utility UCs. Notice that the partition used in the UCs computing is the *complete* partition for each operation; that is to say, FORMVIEW takes into consideration the *valid* bridges between perspectives. Thus, we have the complete partitions P^{com}_0, P^{com}_a, P^{com}_c, P^{com}_f, P^{com}_s. Notice also that in this computing FORMVIEW considers only the *useful* properties of each complete partition.

Another FORMVIEW feature is the management of bridges between perspectives. This procedure is carried out when an observation is incorporated into a node of a hierarchy that represents a certain perspective. At this moment, FORMVIEW descends other hierarchies which have already treated the current observation in order to compare the set of entities which are covered by the chosen node with those covered by nodes of hierarchies developed from other perspective. Thus, it can build bridges between perspectives or even undoes unidirectional bridges from the chosen node to nodes in other taxonomies that did not treat the current observation.

The basic FORMVIEW's control structure is summarized in Table 1. There we can see the functions *FORMVIEW* and *PrincipalLoop*.

FORMVIEW
1. From the first observation O_0, to find out the complete observations for each goal t (OC_0^t)
2. Create the roots R^t for each perspective based on the complete observations $(R^t = OC_0^t)$
3. For each perspective t
   3.1 For the next k observations O_k
      3.1.1 Compute the complete observation for the perspective t (OC_k^t)
      3.1.2 PrincipalLoop (R^t, OC_k^t)
PrincipalLoop (C, O)
1. Incorporate (C, O)
2. Compute the partitions P^{com}_a, P^{com}_c, P^{com}_f, P^{com}_s, from the partition P_0 of C's sub-concepts
3. Choose the best partition PB; PB=max(UCs(P^{com}_a), UCs(P^{com}_c), UCs(P^{com}_f), UCs(P^{com}_s))
4. Choose the best category CB from PB; CB=max(UCs(C_k)) $(1 \le k \le card(PB))$
5. If PB$\ne P^{com}_c$ then replace C by CB and return to 1

Table 1 . FORMVIEW's control structure

4.4 An Example of Multi-hierarchies Generation

We will now consider an example of categorization in FORMVIEW. We have defined two perspectives. In order to facilitate comparisons, in perspective 1, we do not define anything in the GDN. Perspective 2 possesses a statement defining the relevance of the property *FoodType=Packaged* and its implication to *Character=Smart*. The tiny GDN and the observations used in this example[Martin 94] are described in Table 2.

GDN Perspective2 (Foodtype=Packaged(rel=1) ==> Character=Smart)							
NAME	FOUND	FOODTYPE	MOBILITY	COVERING	REPROD.	LEGS	APPEARS
FINCH	INSIDE	PACKAGED	FLIES	FEATHERS	PRODEGGS	2	PLAIN
ANGELFISH	OUTSIDE	FRESH	SWIMS	SCALES	PRODEGGS	0	PRETTY
MACAW	INSIDE	PACKAGED	FLIES	FEATHERS	FERTILIZES	2	PLAIN
HAMSTER	INSIDE	PACKAGED	WALKS	HAIR	FERTILIZES	4	PLAIN
LEOPARD	OUTSIDE	FRESH	WALKS	HAIR	PRODEGGS	4	PRETTY
PIGEON	OUTSIDE	FRESH	FLIES	FEATHERS	FERTILIZES	2	PLAIN
GOLDFISH	INSIDE	PACKAGED	SWIMS	SCALES	PRODEGGS	0	PRETTY
GUPPY	INSIDE	PACKAGED	SWIMS	SCALES	FERTILIZES	0	PLAIN

Table 2 Animal observations and a tiny GDN

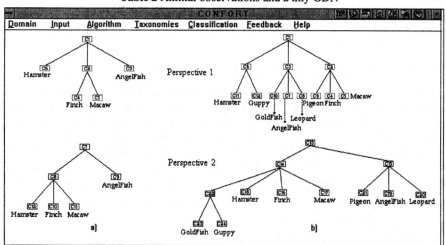

Fig. 3. Extensional view of hierarchies generated from the observations from Table 3

After 3 observations the generated hierarchies are the same ones. However, the fourth observation(*Hamster*) leads to a different hierarchy organization since from the perspective 2, FORMVIEW generates a hierarchy that cluster *Hamster*, *Finch* and *Macaw* because they share the *FoodType=packaged* and *Character=Smart* properties (Figure 3a). These properties, defined in the GDN with high relevance, accentuate the relation between observations in which they occur. Figure 3b shows the hierarchies generated from all observations of Table 2. There, we can realize the two different clusters that reflect the importance of the GDN's specified properties.

4.5 Interacting with the Expert: The Feedback Module

We have argued the importance of providing feedback to the expert. Having explained the FORMVIEW concept formation process, we can describe the strategies used in CONFORT to implement feedback.

The feedback module consists of two heuristics. The first one is to show the expert inference rules generated from bridges. These inference rules represent relationships between categories in different perspectives. Consider the example depicted in Figure 2: a possible inference rule is *If PET then VERTEBRATE*. Hidden bridges also give rise to inference rules like *If DOG then VERTEBRATE*. To provide inference rules favors presentation of selected observations, since if the expert disagrees with an inference rule, he can inform the system about an observation that invalidates such rule.

The second heuristics is to suggest to the expert which properties and their relevance values should be defined in the GDN so as to improve prediction power for a whole hierarchy. The basic idea is to do emerge from data the properties that could be considered relevant. This strategy relies on attribute dependence(or attribute correlation) in the way that was defined by Fisher[Fisher 87]. He has pointed out the relationship between attribute correlation and the ability to correctly infer an attribute's value using a probabilistic concept hierarchy. In order to account this relationship, he has defined a measure of attribute correlation derived from category utility. Formally, The dependence of an attribute A_m on other n attributes A_i can be defined as:

$$M dep(A_m, A_i) = \frac{\left(\sum_i^n \sum_{j_i} P(A_i = V_{ij_i}) \sum_{j_m} \left[P(A_m = V_{mj}|A_i = V_{ij_i})^2 - P(A_m = V_{mj_m})^2 \right] \right)'}{n} \quad (4)$$

Where V_{ij_i} signifies the j_ith value of attribute A_i and $A_i \neq A_m$.

In fact, this function measures the average increase in the ability to guess a value of A_m given the value of a second attribute A_i. We can thus determine those attributes that depend on others and, as a consequence, those that influence the prediction of others. We mean by *influent attributes* those that, if we know theirs values, allow good prediction about the value of others. Our claim is that defining relevant attributes from *influent* ones improves the prediction power of probabilistic concepts. We have defined the total influence *Tinfl* of an attribute A_k on others A_m as:

$$Tinfl(A_k) = \frac{\sum_m M dep(A_m, A_k)}{m} \quad (5)$$

Where $A_k \in A$, $A_m \in A$, $A_k \neq A_m$

Our claim is that attribute correlation gives a measure to ponder attribute influence and, consequently, attribute relevance in a GDN. Actually attribute relevance in this context means how much an attribute correlates with others.

5 Evaluation of FORMVIEW

We have used three criteria to evaluate FORMVIEW. The first criterion consists in determining the accuracy of prediction of individual properties from the classification of "unseen" observations. The second criterion concerns prediction power of an entire group of properties also from the classification of "unseen" observations. Finally, we have analyzed FORMVIEW according to the facility of interpretation of the generated concept hierarchies.

5.1 The Experimentation Methods

To classify unseen observations is a very common procedure for assessing the performance of machine learning systems. Fisher has proposed to use it for measuring prediction capacity of concept formation systems. In this kind of procedure, the observation set is divided into 2 subsets: one is used for training and the remaining subset is used for testing. During the testing procedure, one property of the observation is saved and masked as « unknown ». The idea is to classify this observation into the hierarchy constructed from the training subset and to infer the unknown property from the host in which the observation has been integrated. If the inferred property is equal to the saved value before the masking then the hierarchy has made a good prediction. In order to collect statistically the prediction power of a hierarchy, the test is rerun for each property of the observation and, later, with the training and testing subsets having different quantity of observations.

A variation of the first test is to measure the capacity of concept formation systems to reproduce a complete group of properties by only observing another group. This kind of test was used in particular in design domains[Reich 92], since these domains are characterized by the existence of a group of properties called *specification properties* and another group called *design properties*. The idea is to compute the ability of the algorithm for matching the observation's specification properties with those of the host as well as to measure the « quality » of the inferred design properties.

The third criterion by which we have evaluated FORMVIEW concerns the understanding of the knowledge it generates. Considerations about comprehensibility involve much subjectivity. However, since we have developed a goal-driven, context-dependent process, we believe the hierarchies provided by FORMVIEW can be more easily understood and interpreted if compared with others generated without context-dependency. In fact, the use of a multi-perspective representation allows the generation and visualization of more compact hierarchies because only the relevant properties to a particular perspective are considered.

At first, we will describe the tests which measures the prediction of a simple unknown property, afterwards we will describe the tests for prediction of a group of properties. The first experimentation was realized using a *zoo* domain since it better illustrates the notion of multiple perspectives. As for the second test, we have chosen a design domain: the *Pittsburgh* bridge domain. Considerations about comprehensibility, according to the criteria we have defined, will be made during the analyses of both tests. We use COBWEB as the basic parameter of comparison.

5.2 The Domains

The *zoo* domain was taken from the UCI machine-learning dataset consisting of 53 observations with 18 attributes describing animals. We have divided this dataset into two sets of observations which are described by 10 and 11 properties each one. In fact we have adapted this domain through the insertion of some special attributes for reflecting two perspectives: the *pet* and the *physiologic* perspectives. The *pet* perspective has the following attributes : *name, found, foodtype, predator, venomous, appears, origin, owner, age, intelligence and price.* The *physiologic* one has : *name, found, foodtype, mobility, covering, reproduction, legs, predator, breathes, venomous, tail* and *type.*

The other domain used in our work was the Pittsburgh bridge domain also taken from the UCI dataset. This domain was explored by [Reich 92], where he shows the suitability of concept formation systems like COBWEB to design domains. Our project has as its final goal to use FORMVIEW in this kind of domain therefore we have considered essential to test it for such a domain. Briefly, design domains are characterized by having a set of specifications properties which define the user needs and a set of design properties which describes the artifact's characteristics. The bridge domain contains descriptions of 108 bridges built in Pittsburgh since 1818. Each observation is described by 12 properties of which 7 are specification properties and 5 are design properties.

We have also tested FORMVIEW with the soybean domain but we won't describe precisely the results here. Basically these results are the same as those obtained with the zoo domain.

5.3 Results and Discussion

Prediction of a Single Property in the Zoo Domain

The first step of our tests consists in generating two hierarchies reflecting two different perspectives and in comparing their average prediction power with the prediction power of a unique hierarchy generated from COBWEB. The hierarchy generated from COBWEB is obtained from observations with 19 attribute-value pairs whereas FORMVIEW generates two hierarchies from two sets of observations. The first one with 11 properties and the other with 12 (there are 5 properties which are common to the two perspectives).

Our objective with this test is to know if only the fact of separating the observations into two sets representing two perspectives could provide a better prediction power. We have used the *unseen observation test* to compare the prediction power between FORMVIEW's hierarchies and COBWEB's one. The results of this comparison are depicted in Figure 4. The y axis shows the average of prediction for each property of the unseen observations.

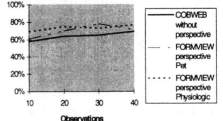

Fig. 4. Comparison between FORMVIEW and COBWEB

Defining Attribute Relevance in the GDN:

In these later tests, we do not have defined any information in the GDN. The second phase of our experiments consists in analyzing the effects provoked on the generated hierarchies after having informed the properties' relevance in the GDN. This new situation requires a more careful analysis because it can influence the prediction power as well as the understanding of the generated hierarchies. The use of the properties's relevance by FORMVIEW produces hierarchies where the relevant properties are best discriminated at the first levels. That occurs because the integration of an observation will be privileged into category hosts which equal the weighted(relevant) properties, since in this situation the category utility measure tends to maximize.

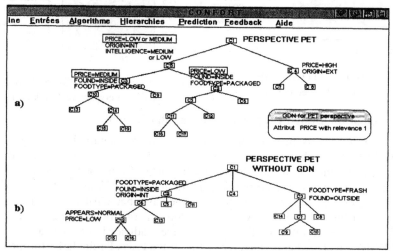

Fig. 5. Hierarchies generated by FORMVIEW with and without GDN

Observe, for example, the *pet* hierarchy of Figure 5a (only *normative* properties, high predictability and predicteveness, [Fisher 87] are described). The *PRICE* attribute is crucial to the interpretation of the generated categories and this corresponds to the expert intuition (represented in the GDN). Our claim is that this situation allows an expert to use a *divide-to-conquer* strategy since if he interprets the first level of a hierarchy, he can focus on the comprehension of the remaining, and so on. It is important to point out that if we did not define any property relevance, the hierarchy in Figure 5a would have been very different. The *pet* hierarchy without GDN, for example, is depicted in Figure 5b.

However the use of property relevance in the GDN does not assure that the generated hierarchies will increase their prediction power because the expert's subjective opinion about the relevance of a property might not be represented in the data. Therefore, it is important to analyze the effects that the definition of property relevance in a GDN can cause on the prediction power of the hierarchies generated from such a GDN.

The results of the comparison between the prediction power of COBWEB's hierarchy and a hierarchy generated from FORMVIEW using a GDN can be seen in Figures 6 and 7. The values of the GDN were obtained from the application of the attribute dependence measure defined in Section 4.5. The attribute dependence for each attribute was mapped in the range [0,1]. These results as well as others obtained from different domains ratify our claim that giving a strong relevance to *influent* properties is a good heuristic for improving prediction power of probabilistic concepts.

Remember that the expert is responsible to define property's relevance. However, CONFORT's philosophy is to suggest which properties are important (in the sense *influence* of a attribute) rather than to let the expert define them without any guidance. In this way, the expert can search a compromise between his knowledge and the data.

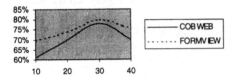

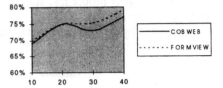

Fig. 6. COBWEB and FORMVIEW using a GDN - Perspective *Pet*

Fig. 7. COBWEB and FORMVIEW using a GDN - Perspective *Physiologic*

Prediction of the Design Properties in the Bridge Domain

The next test consists in evaluating the power of the hierarchies generated from FORMVIEW to predict a group of properties. We have again defined attribute relevance as a function of the attribute dependence. In this test, we use the bridge domain since it represents a design domain. In this kind of domain, the specification properties guide the hierarchy construction, we have then attributed a high value of relevance for these properties. As a result, global hierarchy coverage is better than COBWEB. The results of these tests have indicated us the adequacy of FORMVIEW in constructing hierarchies for design tasks. Particularly, for the bridge domain we could verify another feature of FORMVIEW: the possibility of highlighting a specific property. Actually, Reich[Reich 92] has pointed out the importance of the PERIOD property in the bridge domain. FORMVIEW can naturally represent this importance obtaining, as a result, hierarchies with good prediction power. Figure 8 shows the predictive accuracy of FORMVIEW, using a GDN with all the specification properties having relevance equal to 1(called GDN2 in Figure 8). Also in Figure 8, we can see the predictive accuracy of FORMVIEW, using a GDN with only the property *PERIOD* as relevant(called GDN1 in Figure 8).

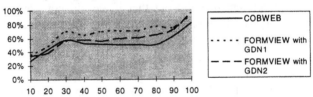

Fig. 8. Results obtained from FORMVIEW with GDN

The effects on the understanding of the hierarchies generated in this domain are analogous to the test in Section 5.3.

5.4 Using Bridges for Classification

Until now we have evaluated the performance of FORMVIEW with some traditional methods used in concept formation. These analysis allowed a comparison with COBWEB, situating FORMVIEW with regard to other works of the same type. However an important characteristic of CONFORT is the existence of the bridges between perspectives, which allows us to define different mechanisms of classification.

Below we analyze briefly an alternative way of classification of unseen observations by using bridges. Bridges are a useful heuristic in the classification process because they allow the horizontal navigation between perspectives like a multi-expert cooperation. The search of unknown values is performed from a principal perspective and, via bridges, properties not existing in this perspective can be induced from the secondary perspectives. For instance, suppose the hierarchies presented in Figure 2. In order to classify an incomplete observation describing an animal into these hierarchies, if FORMVIEW adopts the *PHYSIOLOGIC* perspective as the principal one and the animal can be classified as MAMMALS, it can infer the unknown values for the properties of this perspective such as *walk for mobility* and *fertilizes for reproduction*. Furthermore, through the bridge between the categories *PET* and *MAMMALS* it can infer, from the perspective *PET,* that the observed animal should *have good appears, be smart* and *have price low or medium.*

6 Related Work

Much of this research is based on machine learning systems of concept formation specially on Fisher's COBWEB[Fisher 87]. The different representation used by FORMVIEW is responsible for the major differences between them. COBWEB organizes its conceptual knowledge into a unique hierarchy whereas FORMVIEW can generate several ones from the expert's goals. For example, where COBWEB would eventually learn the concepts *pet-bird, wild-bird, pet-mammal* and *wild-mammal,* FORMVIEW learns *pet* and *wild,* and *bird* and *mammal,* in two different hierarchies representing different perspectives. In addition, CONFORT as KA architecture aims to facilitate active collaboration with the expert.

Actually the difference between CONFORT and the other concept formation systems is due to the KA philosophy of the former. This philosophy is inspired in the *sloppy modeling* approach proposed by Morik[Morik 89]. Systems that follow this approach support KA by providing a tool for the user to enter knowledge as well as by providing, via machine learning, additional feedback to the user about the structure of such an informed knowledge.

Another system that has similarities to our approach is AQUINAS[Boose 88]. In this system, the process of expertise elicitation is based on the psychological theory PCT (Personal Construct Theory), which argues that knowledge can be acquired in a constructive manner via dichotomies between properties. These dichotomies give rise to repertory grids which can be represented from different experts' perspectives. From the repertory grids, AQUINAS can construct multiple hierarchies via a clustering analysis method. Instead of an alternative method to hierarchical concept formation, we view this method as complementary approach to that used in CONFORT. In fact, the definition of the relevance and relationships of properties in the GDN, as well as the definition of properties which will compose an observation, can be improved by interview methods like those based on PCT.

7 Conclusion and Future Research

We have defined a software architecture for assisting in the incremental construction of concept hierarchies. This architecture has a learning algorithm which generates multiple probabilistic concept hierarchies representing different perspectives. We have evaluated the FORMVIEW algorithm as regards its prediction power and comprehensibility. The first results obtained with the use of property relevance are encouraging. However, additional tests are necessary, mainly with regard to evaluate the performance of FORMVIEW with a larger quantity of perspectives. In fact, a real application with an expert evaluation will help to identify the points to be improved.

The architecture described in this paper is a tool for helping only in the early phases of the KA process. Improvements with the use of a most complex representation (like composite observations) and with the use of other tools for later phases will be necessary for more realistic results. The insertion of CONFORT in a complete workbench like MOBAL[Morik 94] can be an alternative. We envisage to implement an explanation module that will allow the expert to better understand the integrationof an observation in a hierarchy.

Another line of research by which our approach can be expanded is the learning of the categorization goals. Recently, some researchers have argued that the identification of the user's learning goals is an important aspect of the learning problems [Ram 95], [Michalski 94]. This process should be characterized as an active and dynamic, as one in which the system has the capacity to generate its own goals.

Finally, we point out that CONFORT will be used as a tool for the construction of frame hierarchies. The probabilistic information generated by FORMVIEW is used for creating frame's facets which define default values, and sufficient and necessary properties[see Vasco[95a] for details].

Acknowledgments

The first author's work was supported by the Brazilian Research Council(CNPQ) grant 200522/93-0, SEPROCE and UNIFOR. We thank Doug Fisher for his kindness to find a time to discuss this paper.

References

[Barsalou 83] Barsalou, L.W.: *Ad Hoc Categories*. Memory and Cognition,11(3),1983.

[Boose 88] Boose, J., Schema, D., Bradshaw, J.: *Recent Progress in AQUINAS: A Knowledge Acquisition Workbench*. EKAW, 1988.

[Faucher 91] Faucher, C.: *Elaboration d'un langage extensible fondé sur les schemas le langage objlog+*. Thèse de doctorat, Université de Droit, d'Economie et des Sciences d'Aix-Marseille, 1991.

[Fisher 87] Fisher, D.H.: *Knowledge Acquisition via Incremental Conceptual Learning*. Machine Learning, vol 2, numero 2, 1987.

[Fisher 93] Fisher, D., Yoo, J.: *Categorization, Concept Learning, and Problem-Solving: A Unifying View*. The Psychology of Learning and Motivation. Vol 29. 1993.

[Gennari 89] Gennari, J.H, Langley, P., Fisher, D.: *Models of Incremental Concept Formation*. Artificial Intelligence, 40, 1989.

[Gluck 85] Gluck, M. A., Corter, J.E.: *Information, uncertainty, and the utility of categories*. Proc. of the 7th Annual Conference of the Cognitive Science Society. Irvine, CA, Lawrence Erlbaum , 1985.

[Hampton 93] Hampton, J. Dubois, D.: *Psychological Models of Concepts: Introduction*. In Categories and Concepts: Theoretical Views and Inductive Data Analysis. Academic Press, 1993.

[Marino 90] Marino, O., Rechenmann, F., Uvietta, P.: *Multiple Perspectives and Classification Mechanism in Object-Oriented Representation*. Cognitiva 90, 1990.

[Martin 94] Martin, J., Bilman, D.: *Acquiring and Combining Overlapping Concepts*. Machine Learning, 16, 121-155, 1994.

[Michalski 86] Michalski, R., Carbonnel, J., Mitchell, T.: *Machine Learning, An Intelligence Approach*. Vol II. Morgan Kaufmann, CA. 1986.

[Michalski 94] Michalski, R.: *Inferential Theory of Learning: Developing Foundations for Multistrategy Learning*. In Machine Learning: A Multistrategy Approach. Michalkski(Ed).Vol.IV. M.Kaufmann, 1994.

[Morik 89] Morik, K.: *Sloppy Modeling*. In Knowledge Representation and Organization in Machine Learning,Morik (Ed). Spring-Verlag, 1989.

[Morik 94] Morik, K.: *Balanced Cooperative Modeling*. Michalski and Tecuci(Eds), Machine Learning: A Multistrategy Approach. Vol. IV. Morgan Kauffmann, 1994.

[Ram 95] Ram, A., Leake, D.: *Goal-driven Learning*. MIT Press, 1995.

[Reich 92] Reich, Y., Fenves, S.: *Inductive Learning of Synthesis Knowledge*. International Journal of Expert Systems. Vol 5, Num. 4, 1992.

[Rosch 75] Rosch, E., Mervis, C.: *Family Resemblances: studies in the internal structure of categories*. Cognitivie Psychology 7, 1975.

[Seifert 89] Seifert, C.: *A Retrieval Model Using Feature Selection*. Proc. of the 6th Int. Workshop on Machine Learning. Morgan Kaufmann. 1989.

[Smith 81] Smith, E.E, Medin, D.L.: *Categories and Concepts*. Library of Congress Cataloging in Publication Data. Cognitive Science, 1981.

[Thaise 91] Thaise: *L'approche logique de l'intelligence artificiel*. Tome 4: De l'apprentissage artificiel aux frontières de l'IA. Chapitre 1, 1991.

[Vasco 95a] Vasco, J.J.F, Faucher, C., Chouraqui, E.: *Frame Hierarchies Construction using Machine Learning*. 6th ASIS Conference. SIG/CR Classification Research Workshop. Chicago, 1995.

[Vasco 95b] Vasco, J.J.F., Faucher, C., Chouraqui, E.: *Knowledge Acquisition Based on Concept Formation Using a Multi-Perspective Representation*. Florida Artificial Intelligence Research Symposium FLAIRS/95. 1995.

Knowledge Discovery in Databases: Exploiting Knowledge-Level Redescription

James Cupit* and Nigel Shadbolt

Artificial Intelligence Group, Department of Psychology, Nottingham University,
email [jc,nrs]@psyc.nott.ac.uk

Abstract. Within this paper, we analyse the nature of knowledge discovery in database. We conclude that it is similar to that of knowledge acquisition, yet unique in that it employs pre-existing data collected for reasons other than analysis. The post-hoc nature of KDD means that the database is often unfit for analysis using traditional machine-learning techniques. We present a methodology for KDD that attempts to overcome this problem. Knowledge elicitation techniques are employed to define the structure of an appropriate learning dataset and to relate this structure to the raw database. The raw database is then redescribed in terms of the new structure before machine learning tools are applied. We also present CASTLE, a software workbench designed to support this methodology, and illustrate it's usage upon a worked example drawn from the Sisyphus-I room allocation problem.

1 The nature of knowledge discovery in databases

Advances in computer science, such as cheaper memory, faster processing and remote access via the Internet, has meant increasingly large databases can be compiled, processed and stored. The increased growth in the amount of stored data has, however, lead to what Frawley et al (1991) claim is "..a growing gap between data generation and data understanding".

A wide range of data analytic techniques derived from statistics and machine learning are available to aid in the understanding of data. Whilst such data-mining techniques offer insight over databases, it appears that, at a deeper level, one must consider a variety of factors influencing reasoning, learning and the communication of knowledge to ensure the sensible usage of such techniques. Such consideration represents a methodology for knowledge discovery in databases (KDD) that ensures the results of analysis are both comprehendable and useful.

We would like to guarantee that KDD results in knowledge that both satisfies the desired problem-solving needs and is easily understood by existing experts within the domain. The goals of KDD are thus essentially similar to that of traditional knowledge acquisition for expert systems construction.

---

* This work was supported by award of a Phd studentship from the Department of Psychology, Nottingham University.

We believe that the application areas of KDD are of sufficient complexity to warrant the construction of an explicit model of expertise as in knowledge acquisition. For example, we may be asked to analyse a database of fault reports for the purpose of improving diagnostic accuracy or identifying design flaws. Diagnosis and design represent complex acts of problem-solving that may warrant the usage of intermediate semantics to describe the domain and particular inferential methods to realise the problem-solving goals. Knowledge acquisition methodologies have been specifically developed to overcome the issues of complexity found within such problems. It makes sense to employ insights from the field of KA to facilitate KDD.

This perspective appears at odds with other opinions concerning KDD. These typically view the process as the identification of informative patterns within a database, such as the induction of relations between database fields or the identification of salient clusters. The induction of relations between fields and the identification of clusters may play an important role within an efficient KDD process but does not constitute the process itself. The overall process, as in KA, should involve developing and extending a conceptual model of expertise. In the following section we briefly detail current KA methodology and relate it to the process of KDD.

1.1 Knowledge discovery as model construction

It is now accepted that knowledge acquisition is best conceived as the interpretive process of constructing models of expertise within a domain. The results of knowledge acquisition activity, such as using a machine learning tool with a database or an elicitation technique with an existing expert, are not directly transferred into the model. It is rather the case that the composition of a model is determined through the negotiated interpretation of such results between knowledge engineers, domain experts and others involved in the life-cycle of an expert system. The implications of such an approach for KDD are clear. One should not treat the output of analytic techniques as knowledge per se but as suggestive cues that require evaluation within the context of existing knowledge before becoming part of any conceptual model.

The knowledge within such a model can be categorized as residing at one of three distinct layers, the domain-layer, inference-layer and task-layer. Within this paper we will concentrate on the acquisition of domain knowledge. Such knowledge can be specified as a set of terms used to describe the domain together with a coherent set of relationships between such terms. As such knowledge is acquired in relation to a particular task, it should be noted that domain models may therefore embody certain assumptions that are specific for the use that is made of it (Wielinga et al, 1992). This view follows from the philosophical position that problem-solving purpose underpins the semantic content of terms (Wittgenstein 1958, Austin 1955). Within our worked example of room assignment, the domain model will consist of a set of terms used to describe individuals and offices and a set of relations that together afford the ability to assign individuals to offices.

Current knowledge acquisition methodology (eg, Breuker et al, 1987, Terpstra et al, 1993, Chandrasekaran 1988) stresses the importance of acquiring domain knowledge in the context of a model of expert inference. This specifies, in an abstract, domain-independent fashion, the problem-solving roles that domain descriptions must fulfill and the inference steps that must be performed upon these descriptions. Inference steps and problem solving roles are organized into a flow diagram highlighting the dependencies between them.

Within our worked example of room allocation, an applicable inference-model may be that of "transform and propose" (see figure 1). This model is an example of synthetic design, constructed from a library of model components currently under development (O'Hara, 1993). A solution is proposed rather than being selected from a pre-enumerated set; the initial input is first transformed into a specification for the solution before it is proposed. Within a complete model of expertise, this would be augmented with a task-layer model of how such inferences are sequenced and controlled during problem-solving.

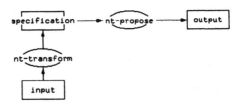

Fig. 1. Transform and propose inference model

Inference models within KDD may appear non-essential. Within expert systems construction an inferential model is essential to specify the functionality and design of the resultant expert system (Cupit et al, 1994). However an important feature of modeling methodology is also to employ inference models to structure the acquisition of domain knowledge (Shadbolt and Wielinga, 1990). At the very least this could be of importance within the KDD process. The a priori possession of an inference model allows domain knowledge acquisition to become focussed upon acquiring the domain terms and relationships that serve the problem solving roles and inference steps specified at the inference layer. Inference models may serve to organise and partition discovered knowledge. Thus within our worked example, we are seeking terms describing rooms and individuals which will act as both input to the problem solving process and as an intermediate specification of the resultant design. We are also seeking to acquire relationships that will serve to transform the initial input and, similarly, those that serve to propose a solution.

More importantly, a strong interaction between domain- and inference-level models may exist. Certain domain ontologies may only be applicable to certain modes of inference. If discovered domain knowledge cannot be related to the inference model being employed by the user, then it may prove difficult to employ. For example, an existing user may perform diagnosis through the method of cover and differentiate. This method relies on knowledge that rules out certain suspected causes, for example

```
IF   flat battery is suspected
AND the car lights work
THEN flat battery is not the cause
```

Discovered knowledge supplied in a form that fits this general template can be considered more useful as it directly fits the users preferred pattern of inference. We thus believe that in KDD, inference models may play an important part in structuring activity and ensuring the utility of results.

1.2   KDD as a qualitatively distinct task

So far we have attempted to characterise KDD as similar to traditional KA in terms of it's goals and process. We do, however, believe that the nature of KDD is such that it constitutes a qualitatively different task to that of KA.

It might be claimed that KA relies upon the presence of human expertise whilst KDD assumes its absence. Within KA, it is often assumed that the goal is to capture existing expertise within a domain model. The term knowledge discovery, however, implies some sense of advancement; new knowledge must be acquired during the analytic process. This distinction places an emphasis upon the usage of automated analytic techniques to discover new relationships.

This emphasis is, however, misleading. It is not uncommon for expert systems to be commissioned in domains where existing expertise is incomplete or distributed between a number of experts. Under such circumstances it is necessary to collect knowledge from a variety of sources, human expert and machine analysis, to produce a model whose content surpasses any that has previously existed. KA methodology is thus used to operating in domains characterised by partial expertise.

Moreover, it is not that case that knowledge elicitation techniques simply extract that which is already explicitly known and that new knowledge is always discovered through automated machine analysis. Numerous knowledge elicitation techniques operate by allowing an expert to behave then interpreting his behaviour; such techniques can be viewed as turning implicit skill into explicit knowledge. In cases where skilled behaviour is evident but explicit knowledge is absent, KDD could, theoretically, be achieved through elicitation tools alone. For example, important clusters or high-level factors could be identified by asking an expert to perform a card sort over cases.

An over-emphasis on automated analytic techniques within KDD has led the discipline to be compared to machine learning (ML) and statistics, as opposed to KA (Mannila, 1995). This undermines the role existing expertise may play during the knowledge discovery process. Knowledge acquired through elicitation with existing experts can be usefully exploited before, during and after automated analytic techniques are invoked. Usage of existing knowledge to bias learning has become an increasingly large area of research within AI. For example, Schlimmer et al (1991) present a learning tool that can employ structural knowledge acquired from other sources to bias the learning search. Similarly, Thomas et al (1993) present a system which exploits "inference-level" bias; learning is performed in the context of a particular model of inference. It is a moot point how successful KDD can be without some ability to involve an experts opinion on putatively interesting patterns discovered during the process. Our approach requires the input of an expert informant for this purpose.

It has also been claimed that KA and KDD differ in the specificity of their goals. Whilst KA attempts to construct a knowledge base satisfying pre-determined problem-solving goals, KDD is more exploratory, aiming simply to discover interesting regularities (Manilla, 1995, Frawley et al, 1991). Research in KDD has thus concentrated on developing pattern detection techniques; for example, Piatesky-Shapiro (1991) presents a learning tool capable of extracting every exact, or near exact rule, that may be found within a database. We doubt, however, that KDD is always an exploratory process. Whilst the undirected analysis of data may supply results that can be considered of interest, a large proportion of clients commissioning KDD work will have well-defined analytic goals. We thus consider exploratory analysis to be important but it should not be the sole preoccupation of KDD.

A seemingly obvious difference between KDD and KA is that KDD relies heavily upon an existing database as a primary analytic resource. It is implicit when commissioning an KDD application that a database exists that might, when analysed by machine or human expert, result in the extension of domain knowledge. This does not, however, alone justify KDD as qualitatively distinct; KA can involve the usage of machine learning and statistical analysis as a source of knowledge. There is however a difference between as regards the type of data analysed.

It has been noted that the size of the database being analysed, in terms of the number of cases and fields it contains, is much larger within KDD (Mannila, 1995). Research has thus concentrated upon improving the efficiency of basic algorithms (Piatesky-Shapiro 1991) and the imposition of bias to control the learning search (Russel and Grosof, 1990, Ganascia et al, 1993). We do not deny the importance of such research in improving the performance and usability of learning algorithms to acquire relations between database terms. The above problems, however, appear surface manifestations of a deeper distinction between KDD and KA data analysis. We believe the essential difference between KDD and KA is the post-hoc nature of the database being analysed.

Whilst databases specifically collected for usage as an analytic data-set may be formulated in accordance to the problem-solving purpose, pre-existing organizational databases may be structured to satisfy different requirements (Cupit and Shadbolt, 1994). The databases available to KDD are likely to contain numerous attributes and cases that are irrelevant to the purpose of analysis. Significant domain terms may be absent from the database. It is not guarranteed that an appropriate number of cases will exist. We believe that the post-hoc analysis of any database of even very small datasets can constitute KDD. In such cases, existing expertise must be employed to carefully distinguish between signal and noise within the analytic results.

The problems of post-hoc analysis amount to more than ensuring that tools can operate over databases, determining which fields and cases are relevant to the analytic task and carefully evaluating results.

More serious problems may be encountered when one considers distinctions between domain representations employed for data storage in contrast to those employed during problem solving. We consider it unlikely that an organizational database will contain attributes that directly represent the intermediate domain descriptions employed during problem-solving. In fact, we believe it will often be the case that expert domain representations act to summarize and explain domain data. Semantics are invoked to reference significant patterns within the data and to postulate unobservable causes and effects to explain these patterns. For example, our domain database within the room allocation task consists simply of an individuals name, his role within the organization, his research project and his room number. Room allocation expertise is likely to describe individuals and rooms in terms of higher-level attributes relevant to the problem that explains why certain individuals are allocated certain rooms with particular people.

Experts may thus often employ semantics at a higher level of abstraction than that found in the initial database. It appears likely that different individuals within different problem-solving contexts will employ different abstraction rules. That is, they may have made different ontological commitments in the way semantics are related to extensional patterns of data. Contemporary epistemology stresses that the semantic content of terms may be formulated with respect to problem-solving utility. Different goals or inferential methods may result in different reifications being made to describe the domain. Experts have also been noted as being capable of re-ontologising their knowledge from different ontological perspectives according to the problem-solving context. In essence, the way in which we represent data and describe the patterns of association within in it are dependent upon the overall problem-solving goal, a range of secondary strategic demands (for example, available time, desired accuracy, the avoidance of certain types of error) and the inferential method employed (for example, systematic diagnosis or heuristic classification).

Such findings have a direct impact upon the process of KDD. Frawley et al (1991) states "discovered knowledge is represented in a high-level language. It need not be directly used by humans, but it's expression should be understandable by human users". Understandability, from our perspective, relies not simply upon natural language vocabulary but upon an ontological commitment that is ultimately shaped by the overall context of analysis. Given the post-hoc nature of KDD, it is unlikely that the problem-solving context surrounding data collection and subsequent analyses remains constant. Whilst the learning tool may induce relationships of known accuracy, the terms employed may be difficult to interpret as they are not directly drawn from an appropriate ontology employed by experts. Comprehending the relationships induced by a learning tool applied to database during KDD may thus prove difficult.

In domains where expertise is absent or partial, the simple application of learning tools to the raw, static database is also unlikely to support the process of developing expertise within a domain. It is noted that novices and expertise differ in terms of their internal representation of domains. Developing expertise thus involves internal representational change. Such change amounts to more than the development of new relations between a fixed set of semantic primitives. New intermediate terms are invented and their definition revised to facilitate comprehension of the domain (Chi et al, 1988). Whilst the results of analysis over raw data may prove insightful, we seek a methodology for KDD that supports the acquisition of terms as well as relations between terms.

2 Representational redescription within KDD

The mismatch between semantics within the database and those employed by domain experts raises a number of issues that cannot be tackled by the enhancement of analytic tools. Any analytic tool is constrained to operate over a pre-supplied set of semantics. Numerous techniques such as cluster analysis, factor analysis, inductive logic programming and neural network analysis can suggest stable extensional patterns within the data that may warrant the creation of semantics. Given the importance of problem-solving context, they cannot, however, always guarantee that such patterns are optimal, or indeed appropriate. They can not provide such patterns with natural language terms. Human expertise will always be required to shape and name new semantic terms according to their needs. Within this section we detail a methodological framework for KDD and outline the structure of a software workbench, CASTLE, that naturally supports this process.

We perceive KDD to be an iterative cycle of activity, as shown in figure 2. This involves the key stages of exploratory analysis, knowledge elicitation, representational redescription and machine learning. Significant domain terms will be elicited from a user using exploratory techniques to provide suggestive cues. These terms are then related by the user to terms within the raw database through the definition of logical rules. Representational redescription will be employed to flexibly revise and extend the original database so that learning operates over a dataset that represents the domain using the experts terms, as opposed to those in the initial database. The results of learning will be fed back to the user and the domain terms will, if necessary be revised and learning repeated.

To illustrate our approach we shall employ a worked example drawn from the Sisyphus-1 problem definition (see related papers within Int. J. Human-Computer Studies, 1994, 40). We assume the presence of a pre-existing database of 15 cases supplied within the problem definition. Each case within the database

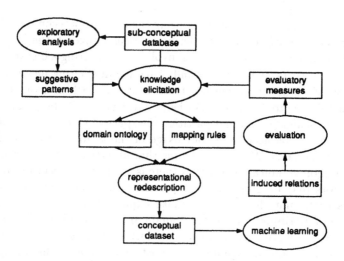

Fig. 2. The iterative cycle of KDD activity

represents an individual and records his role within the organization, the project he works on and his room number. We aim to construct a conceptual model of the expertise involved in allocating an individual to an office. For the purposes of this example we shall assume that the task is currently performed by an individual possessing little expertise. They have derived a solution that is acceptable through trial and error over several years but have little explicit knowledge as to how this was derived.

We realise this is an extremely small dataset. Moreover it is taken from a rather traditional KBS application. Nevertheless, it demonstrates how knowledge redescription may be useful even in apparently simplistic problems; we show how a new property of the data is constructed and put to application in problem-solving. This example also has the merit of being familiar to the KA community for expository purposes.

2.1 Knowledge elicitation and exploratory analysis

The first stage of modeling involves eliciting an inference structure and putative domain ontology from the expert. An appropriate inference structure is acquired within the GDM construction tool developed during the VITAL project (Shadbolt et al, 1993). We shall assume that inference-level elicitation revealed that the allocator does not simply allocate a room directly but transforms the initial input into a design specification which is then used to propose a suitable solution. A suitable model is thus that of "transform and propose" (see figure 1). Specified within this domain, a description of an individual requiring office space will be transformed into a specification of his required room; an appropriate location can then be proposed.

At the domain level we are thus looking for an appropriate set of semantics to describe the domain. This is achieved using the elicitation technique of laddering (Corbridge et al, 1994) using a laddering tool customized towards representing the structure of a database. Laddering involves constructing a hierarchical tree of important constructs; it is thus not only effective in eliciting new domain terms but also the structural relationships between them. Each node in the hierarchy of terms within the tool represents either a database attribute, possible values of these attributes and factors that partition the space of attributes in a meaningful fashion. It should be noted that our usage of the term "factor" is much wider than that in statistics. We do not assume that all attributes comprising a factor possess common variance; merely that there is a conceptual relationship between them. Factors may be employed to represent either inference-layer or domain-layer constructs and thus serve to make explicit background theories of the significance of attributes within the domain and the problem-solving roles they may fulfill. Such theories can be documented within CASTLE though a hypertext system that maintains a page for each construct within the hierarchy. Figure 3 show the initial case structure defined within CASTLE. The attributes contained within the initial database are define beneath the factor "raw-data". Factors have been defined to represent the problem-solving roles within the model. The attribute room number has been associated with the problem-solving role of output. No other teleologically significant attributes have so far been associated with these roles; unfortunately, the expert cannot explicitly state what these are.

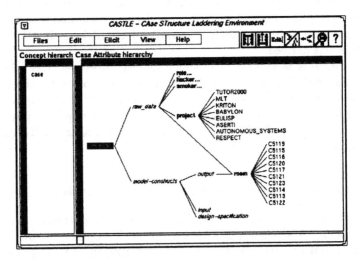

Fig. 3. The initial case structure

At this point a range of knowledge elicitation techniques, such as card sorting and repertory grid analysis (Shadbolt and Burton, 1989) may be of use. We shall assume that this approach fails; our expert feels he cannot sensibly perform the tasks required by each technique.

Exploratory analytic techniques may also aid in this process. The usage of a rule induction tool at this stage is not, however, possible. Such a tool can only discover relationships between the input description (the description of the person being allocated an office) and specific room numbers. Such rules are uninformative and do not fit our inferential model; we wish to discover relationships between input descriptions and a abstract design specification of an appropriate room.

A range of other exploratory techniques are more applicable. Cluster analysis, for example, might be employed to suggest a hierarchical organisation of rooms. A hierarchical structure does not, however, directly serve any problem-solving role within our inference model; it would, however, be applicable within a model involving hierarchical refinement, such as heuristic classification. Within our "transform and propose" model we wish to acquire domain terms that represent rooms in terms of their abstract design properties.

Principle component analysis (PCA) might thus be a suitable choice. The result of PCA is a set of components that summarizes the variance of numeric measures. Components are extracted in sequence; the 1st component accounts for the maximum amount of variance whilst the last accounts for lowest. Analysis of the amount of variance accounted for by each allows one to determine which components represent signal as opposed to noise. As fields within the database are categorical, it is necessary to translate such fields into binary measures. Analysis of the loadings of each room number onto components accounting for a large proportion of the variance, might be suggestive of an underlying dimension. For example, if room C5125 and C5123 load positively onto the 1st component, whilst C5119 and C5114 load negatively, the expert might be able to name the dimension that makes each room within a pair similar yet each pair different. Using PCA in such a fashion is thus similar to triadic elicitation within repertory grid analysis; in this case, however, the choice of which elements to identify similarities and differences between is non-random but based upon shared correlation between existing database fields.

A problem with PCA, however, is that it is an unsupervised process that is not directed towards isolating dimensions that are teleologically significant within respect to our problem solving goal. PCA attempts to summarize all of the variance of all fields within the database. In this case, we are only concerned with the variance in room numbers. We could indirectly bias the process by supplying the technique only with attributes we perceived as teleologically significant and hope that a dimension was extracted that indicated a shared variance between room numbers and these attributes. Our expert is, however, unsure as to what these are. A more appropriate choice is thus back-propagation in a three layer neural network (Rummelhart and McClelland, 1986). Back propagation can be thought of in terms of a heuristic "supervised PCA". The result of learning is a set of dimensions (hidden units) that maximally account for the variance of target outputs. Each weight between a hidden and target unit can be thought of as a component loading.

Figure 4 shows the weights within a trained neural network connecting the first two hidden units to target room numbers This is suggestive to our expert; the pattern of weights of the first unit indicates a teleologically significant difference between room C5119 and C5120. Our expert names this as room centrality. Similarly, the pattern of weights for the second unit suggest the dimension of room size. The database structure is thus extended to include attributes representing these dimensions.

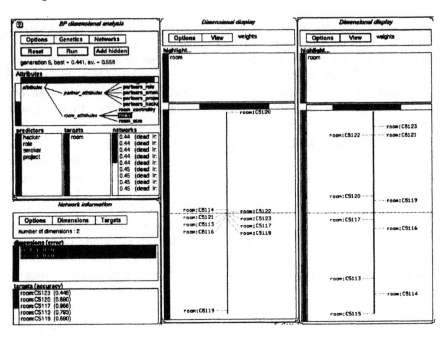

Fig. 4. Back-propagation used for investigative analysis

2.2 Representational redescription

As mentioned earlier, employing a induction tool over the raw database to induce rules entailing room number would not prove useful. It would, however, prove useful to induce rules entailing room size and room centrality. Whilst we have extended our database structure to include the fields room centrality and size, we do not, however, have any values for these fields. There is, however, enough information within the database to infer the field values. The expert thus defines a set of logical rules to map these new attributes to the existing detail. An example rule is shown in figure 5.

These rules are actively employed by CASTLE to infer new attribute values. In cases where user-entered data violates these mapping rules, the user's value is still displayed within the editor, though it is marked to denote a logical inconsistency. This feature may be used to maintain consistency within a case when entering new detail as any entries violating a logical rule will be brought to the users attention. Similarly when more than one value is inferred, the user is informed of a contradiction arising from conflicting rules. The provision of a truth maintenance system is essential in aiding definition of appropriate mapping rules. If rules entailing the values of a particular attribute are poorly formulated then either a large proportion of values remain unknown or a large number of conflicts occur. An appropriate mapping rule results in few unknown values and few contradictions. Whilst the rules defined within this example are instances of simple attribute value abstraction, the rules definable within CASTLE may be of any logical complexity and may also make usage of standard numerical operators when referencing numerical/ordinal attributes. This allows the introduction and inference of arbitrarily defined attributes within a case structure.

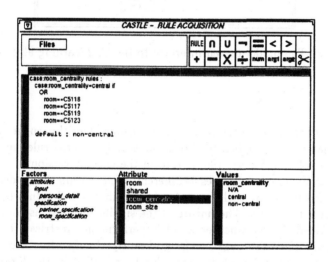

Fig. 5. The logical rule defining room centrality=central

2.3   Machine learning

It is now possible to employ a learning tool to induce rules that transform the input description of an individual into a design specification of an appropriate room. We shall concentrate upon the acquisition of rules that entail one aspect of this specification, room centrality. CASTLE contains a version of the Cn algorithm reformulated at the knowledge level; the model-based interface to the tool is shown in figure 6. The Cn algorithm (Clark and Niblett, 1979) operates by searching the space of rules in a top-down beam-first search fashion. An initial rule is extended by adding every possible extra condition; the set of extended rules are then evaluated and a specified number of these are extended in the next iteration.

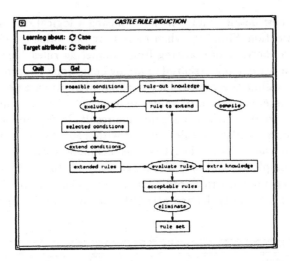

Fig. 6. The model-driven interface to the Cn2 learning algorithm

The knowledge-level reformulation of a learning algorithm suggests a number of biases that can be applied to direct the search towards rules in a desirable form (Rouveirol and Albert, 1994). Within the current version of the tool it is possible to apply a range of biases at different points within the model. Rules can be constrained to always include particular attributes and values by modifying the initial rule to extend. The nature of the significance test used in evaluation can be modified to test whether a rule's performance metrics (true and false positives, true and false negatives) significantly change after a condition has been added. Rule-out knowledge can also be supplied in the form of control rules that, when satisfied, remove possible extensions to a rule. For example, if it is known that all secretaries do not smoke, or that all smokers are researchers, then the algorithm can be explicitly directed to avoid rules containing such values as conditions. This knowledge may be explicitly provided by the user or may be discovered by the algorithm during the course of learning itself. When evaluating an extended rule, it may be found that it no longer covers any cases or, alternatively, that its coverage is unaffected. Such findings are used to produce extra domain knowledge which are, in turn, automatically compiled into control rules excluding certain rule extensions.

Learning resulted in the set of rules which were then fed back to the expert for evaluation. It was felt that a number of rules resulted from accidental and contingent patterns within a relatively small dataset and did not constitute valid knowledge of how to propose a specification. For example, no valid justification could be found for placing people working on a particular project in non-central rooms. A number of rules did, however, appear to suggest that the role of an individual might determine the specification of room centrality.

2.4 Repeating the process

Having performed some investigative analysis, defined a putative domain ontology in the form of new fields and field values, employed a learning tool over data redescribed in these terms and evaluated the results we can now repeat the cycle of KDD activity. After examination of the rules induced above, it was postulated that the degree of social contact associated with certain roles may be a significant feature. The background theory of the domain suggests that people whose role requires a high degree of interaction with other staff members should be placed in central offices as they can easily be accessed. It was decided to encode the construct of social interaction as a new attribute within the database. It's values (namely high and low) were then mapped to existing detail. The value of high was inferred if the persons role was either a manager, secretary or group head was the value of low as inherited by default.

Learning was then re-applied and the results appear to validate our hypothesis, see figure 7. We believe the discovery of social contact as a teleologically significant term within the domain ontology may not have been made if the synergetic usage of exploratory techniques, elicitation techniques and learning within an iterative cycle of KDD had not been followed. It is certainly not present in any of the reported approaches to the original Sisyphus-1 experiment.

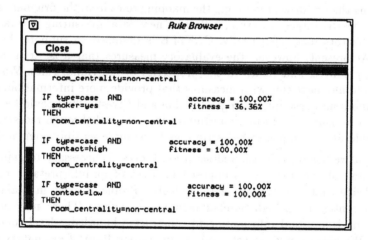

Fig. 7. The results of learning after the introduction of social contact

3 Conclusions and further research

We hope that the simple worked example presented above illustrates the power of synergetically employing elicitation and learning to acquire, evaluate and revise the structure of domain descriptions and inferential relations. This stands in opposition to the practice of employing a single acquisition technique to realize a modeling goal. It also illustrates the ease with which database redescription can be achieved within the CASTLE workbench to extend, revise and reformulate databases to introduce knowledge-level semantics and to intelligently pre-process training data.

We believe it also serves to illustrate the importance of background theories in composing the content of training sets and interpreting the results of machine learning. Some initial learning results were dismissed since no background theory could be invoked to explain them. The results of learning, when evaluated in the context of a background theory, was, however, suggestive of higher-order semantics that did constitute an appropriate characterization of the domain in the context of the problem solving goal and the inference method employed to realize it.

From our perspective, the role of machine learning as an experimental technique to test and evaluate a background theory is as important as a tool that directly acquires problem solving knowledge. The CASTLE workbench should be thought of as an environment supportive of such experimentation as opposed to an interface to a learning algorithm. The failure of learning tools to induce useful and meaningful relationships often indicates that the conceptual framework for comprehending the domain requires revision. This may sometimes involve re-factorising the database, modifying the mapping rules from the original database structure to the target structure, collecting new data, measuring new factors or existing factors more specifically. CASTLE is designed to support these processes. At present, however, the evaluatory measures that arise from machine learning are weak and relate to the properties of individual rules. Work is in progress to augment this with measures that provide more information. For example, minimum description length (Quilan and Rivest, 1994) could be used to provide a measure of information compression achieved through redescriptions. This would allow competing redescriptions to be more sensibly compared.

Whilst we believe that the redescription process is necessary to gain an understanding of the domain, as opposed to a set of un-interpretable rules, we acknowledge that it is fraught with difficulty. Problems exist in dealing with datasets containing a high number of unknown values. There may not exist enough sub-conceptual information to construct a knowledge-level conceptualization. We also do not, as yet, possess any strong form of evaluatory criteria to determine where a model requires modification. A failure to learn is a very weak form of evaluation. We are currently examining how this feedback can be strengthened to suggest weaknesses within the model and, if possible, to provide techniques that support the process of constructing domain conceptualizations where little expertise exists and to automatically suggest modifications for the user to implement and evaluate. Identifying appropriate knowledge-level redescriptions of the original data in this simple worked example was relatively unproblematic; all were instances of simple attribute value abstraction. In more complex domains, however, appropriate redescriptions may be harder to identify and define. An increased range of techniques is necessary to advise and critique the development of such knowledge-level primitives.

A second important source of guidance concerning the formulation of appropriate domain descriptions may arise from a more explicit use of inference-level models of expertise. We believe that fully comprehending how a particular domain term is inferred within a database may warrant the usage of more complex problem models found within traditional knowledge acquisition methodologies (eg, Terpstra et al, 1993 O'Hara, 1993). Different problem solving models may require different representations (for example, semantic networks, conceptual hierarchies or production rules) to afford efficient visualization and inference. Different models may also operate differentially over different domain ontologies. We ultimately aim to employ the structure of such problem solving models to increase our ability to determine target representations, representational structures and effective KDD techniques at the onset of domain model construction. Even within a relatively simple database the issues of appropriate epistemological redescription still apply. It isn't a matter of how large the attribute space or putative set of domain terms, it is an issue of their utility within the overall problem-solving context. Nor is it a matter of the size of the dataset. As we have seen significant insights can derive from small as well as large databases as long as KA supplements the pattern detection process.

Whilst our approach requires validation in more complex domains, we believe the CASTLE workbench represents a template for future tools supporting this process.

References

Austin, J.L. (1955) How to do things with words. Oxford University Press, New York.

Breuker, J., Wielinga, B., Van Someren, M., De Hoog, R., Schreiber, G., De Greef, P., Bredeweg, B., Wielemaker, L., Billault, J-P., Davoodi, M. and Hayward, S. (1987) Model Driven Knowledge Acquisition: interpretation models. ESPRIT Project P1098 Deliverable D1. University of Amsterdam and STL Ltd.

Chandrasekaran, B. (1988) Generic tasks as building blocks for knowledge-based systems: the diagnosis and routine design examples. The Knowledge Engineering Review, 3(3), 183-210.

Chi, M.T.H., Glasser, R. and Farr, M.J. (1988) The nature of expertise. Hillsdale, NJ: Lawrence Erlbaum.

Clark, P. and Niblett, T. (1979) The CN2 induction algorithm. Machine Learning 3, 263-283.

Corbridge, C., Rugg, G., Major, N., Shadbolt, N. and Burton, M. (1994) Laddering : technique and tool use in knowledge acquisition. Knowledge Acquisition (1994), 6, 315-341.

Cupit, J., Major, N. and Shadbolt, N. (1994) REKAP : A methodology for the automated construction of real-time and distributed knowledge-based systems. Proceedings of AI'94.

Cupit, J. and Shadbolt, N. (1994) Representational redescription within knowledge intensive data-mining. Proceedings of JKAW 1994.

Frawley, W. Piatetsky-Shapiro, G. and Matheus, C.J. (1991) Knowledge Discovery in Databases: An overview. In Piatetsky-Shapiro and Frawley (eds). Knowledge discovery in databases (1991). AAAI Press.

Ganascia, J., Thomas, J. and Laublet, P. (1993) Integrating models of knowledge and machine learning. Proceedings of ECML, 1993. pp 396-401. Springer-Verlag.

Mannila, H.(1995) Aspects of data mining. In Kodratoff, Nakhaeizadeh and Taylor (eds) Statistics, Machine Learning and Knowledge Discovery in Databases. MLnet workshop notes, ECML-95.

O'Hara, K. (1993) A Representation of KADS-I Interpretation Models Using A Decompositional Approach. In Löckenhoff, C. Fensel, D. and Studer, R. (Eds.) Proceedings of the 3rd KADS Meeting. pp 147-169. Siemens AG, Munich.

Piatetsky-Shapiro, G. and Frawley, W. (eds). (1991) Knowledge discovery in databases. AAAI Press.

Quinlan, J.R. and Rivest, R.L. (1994) Inferring decisions trees using the minimum description length principle. Information and computation. 80. pp 227-248.

Rouveirol, C. and Albert, P. (1994) Knowledge level model of a configuable learning system. Proceedings of EKAW 1994. pp. 374-393. Springer-Verlag.

Rummelhart, D.E and McClelland, J.L. (eds). (1990) Parallel Distributed Cognition: Explorations in the Microstructure of Cognition: vol 1, Foundations (pp. 318-62), Cambridge, MA: MIT Press.

Russel, S.J., and Grosof, B.N. (1990) Declarative bias: an overview. In Change of representation and inductive bias. ed. by P Benjamin.

Terpstra, P., Van Heijst, G., Shadbolt, N. and Wielinga, B. (1993) Knowledge Acquisition Process Support Through Generalized Directive Models. In David, J-M., Krivine, J-P. and Simmons, R. (eds.) **Second Generation Expert Systems**, pp 428-454. Springer-Verlag.

Thomas, J. Ganascia, J and Laublet, P. (1993) Model-based knowledge acquisition and knowledge-biased machine learning: an example of a principled association. In Procdeedings of IJCAI workshop 16, Chambery.

Shadbolt, N. and Burton, M. (1989) The empirical study of knowledge elicitation techniques. SIGART Newsletter, 108, April 1989.

Shadbolt, N., Motta, E. and Rouge, A. (1993) Constructing knowledge-based systems. IEEE software, November, 34 -39.

Shadbolt, N. and Wielinga, B. (1990) Knowledge based knowledge acquisition: the next generation of support tools. In B.J. Wielinga, B. Gaines, G. Scheiber and M. Van Sommeren (eds) Current Trends in Knowledge Acquisition, 313-338, Amsterdam. IOS Press.

Schlimmer, J. Mitchell, J and McDermott, J. (1991) Justification-based refinement of expert knowledge. In Piatetsky-Shapiro and Frawley (eds). Knowledge discovery in databases (1991). AAAI Press.

Wielinga, B.J., vad de Velde, W., Schreiber, G. and Akkermans, H. (1992). The Common KADS Framework for knowledge modelling. Proceedings of the 7th KA workshop, Banff, Alberta, Canada.

Wittgenstein, L. (1958) Philosphical Investigations. Blackwell, Oxford.

Towards Painless Knowledge Acquisition

Derek Sleeman &
Fraser Mitchell

Department of Computing Science
King's College
The University
Aberdeen AB9 2UE
Scotland UK
email: <sleeman,mitchell>@csd.abdn.ac.uk

Abstract

This paper argues that there is a discernible trend in Knowledge Acquisition towards systems which are easier for the domain expert to use; such systems ask more focused questions and questions at a higher conceptual level. Two systems, REFINER+ and TIGON which illustrate this trend are described in some detail; these have been applied in the domains of patient management and diagnosis of turbine errors respectively. Other trends noted include:

- *Co-operative* systems for Knowledge Acquisition/Problem Solving[1].
- The re-use of existing knowledge(bases)

Additionally, the relationship of the TIGON system to Data Mining is discussed; as is the inference of diagnostic rules for dynamic systems from the systems performance data.

Acknowledgements: EPSRC CASE studentship for Fraser Mitchell; many helpful discussions with Dr. Rob Milne of Intelligent Applications (the Industrial sponsors). Similarly the activities of REFINER and REFINER+ (Sunil Sharma and Mark Winter) were supported by SERC and EPSRC studentships.

1. Introduction

Given this audience, it is clearly not appropriate to give a detailed history of how Knowledge Acquisition/Knowledge Elicitation techniques have evolved, but simply to note some trends:

- many of the "newer" techniques like sorting & laddering (Diaper, 1989) are more "specialised" or perhaps one should say more limited than the "original" techniques of Protocol Analysis (Ericsson & Simon, 1984) and Interviewing. That is, a narrower range of knowledge is acquired by these techniques.

---

[1] Because we believe it is *essential* that Inferred/Acquired Knowledge is *used* to solve relevant problems in order to demonstrate its efficacy, we associate Problem Solving with Knowledge Acquisition. Indeed we would further argue that Knowledge Acquisition, Knowledge Refinement and Problem Solving are all intimately interrelated activities.

- many techniques are now computer-based e.g., the Repertory Grid (Boose, 1990) and Sorting methods (Diaper 1989) are part of the ProtoKew system (Reichgelt & Shadbolt 1992)

- KA tools, which acquire information for a *particular* PSM (Problem Solving Method), appear to be easier for the domain expert to use as they ask more focused questions. Examples of such systems include MORE (Kahn, 1988), MOLE (Eshelman, 1988), SALT (Marcus, 1988), S-SALT (Leo et al., 1994) and OPAL (Musen, 1990).

Although, the PSM-based systems are a considerable improvement over earlier approaches, we believe, in some circumstances, it is possible to use information which already exists on-line, and only to seek the occasional guidance from the domain expert. In an earlier paper (Sleeman, 1994), we talked about there being a trend "towards painless Knowledge Acquisition". In the next sections we discuss, in some detail, the REFINER & TIGON systems, implemented in Aberdeen which illustrate this theme; in section 4, we attempt to relate this work to existing systems in KA & ML, and to discuss what we believe are additional emerging themes.

2. The REFINER & REFINER+ Systems

REFINER is a system which accepts a number of labelled examples, or cases, and infers a prototypical description for each of the classes; the labelling of the cases is done by the domain expert/oracle. A more succinct description is often produced if background knowledge is available, however REFINER is able to produce prototype descriptions even when it is not available. An inconsistency occurs when:

- an example matches a prototype other than its assigned class
- an example does not match the appropriate inferred prototype

The system then presents the domain expert with a variety of options which are able to remove the current inconsistency:

(1) specific case(s) be reclassified
(2) edit case(s) e.g., the values of particular attributes
(3) add new descriptions to all cases (so that it is possible to discriminate between 2 cases)
(4) modify the background domain knowledge
(5) shelve case(s)

These mechanisms are discussed in greater detail in Sharma & Sleeman (1988).

REFINER was implemented initially as an incremental algorithm, and deals with a single (inconsistent) task. A particular task, as seen above, could be accommodated in many ways and so the expert chooses one (sometimes arbitrarily). When a further inconsistent example is processed, it might well necessitate the system "undoing" an earlier decision. Thus a "batch" algorithm has been implemented in the REFINER+ system, which has been shown to be very much more efficient (Winter & Sleeman, 1995).

2.1 Summary of REFINER+

The problem of getting expert users to articulate their knowledge is well documented. We would like to argue that REFINER+ allows this information to be obtained in a fairly painless way. In fact, the actual cases used in the above examples are extracted from the records of patients receiving long term therapy for Hypertension, and were taken directly from the hospital's database and transformed by a suite of programs into a format suitable for REFINER+. The expert, however, was additionally asked to confirm classes to which each of the cases belonged.

REFINER+ does a great deal of processing of cases, and then presents the expert with a list of modifications which would be able to remove particular inconsistencies. Once confronted with highly focused information, humans are often good at suggesting ways of overcoming discrepancies. Thus, REFINER+ seems to have many of the desirable features of an aide, and nicely illustrates the theme of co-operative problem-solving.

2.2 Planned Extensions to REFINER+

- Encourage the expert to say which classes she/he sometimes becomes confused between (for which he finds a differential diagnosis difficult). For example, if he says that cases of classes A and D are hard to distinguish, then the descriptions of these classes should have considerable overlap in the REFINER+ representation. If they do *not*, REFINER+ might, for example, systematically check the features of the two "difficult" cases to determine whether some piece of background knowledge is missing. For example, the system, might check to see if the two drugs being used in the cases are related. Additionally, one might ask the expert why he thought the two cases were difficult to differentiate, and then use this information directly.

- Determine the effect of expanding ranges of values; use background knowledge to generalise inferred class descriptors, for example to test whether it is possible to replace *arm* by *limb*.

- Add a facility to ask the expert why she/he selected a particular option to remove an inconsistency; and the reasons chosen for *not* selecting the other options. (The plan is to extract information from these explanations which will enhance the system's background knowledge, thus making REFINER+ more effective when it processes subsequent example sets.)

3. The TIGON System[2]

There is a large source of knowledge that is often overlooked by the knowledge engineer; namely, information generated by the process that is being modelled. This is especially true in the industrial sector where processes are often monitored and the data archived for safety and accounting purposes. Unfortunately this data when in its raw form, is unusable by a standard knowledge acquisition tool; what is

---

[2] This section is based on a paper presented by F. Mitchell, D. Sleeman and R. Milne to the IEE Colloquium on Knowledge Discovery in Databases, 1st and 2nd February 1995.

needed is some way of extracting the useful information, the patterns, from the data. In other words some form of *data mining* needs to be performed. (See Piatetsky-Shapiro & Matheus (1992) for a general overview of the subfield.)

Data mining systems are useful for detecting trends in large quantities of data, but they function best when given some guidance. This is the role, we suggest, for the expert. In such "hybrid" systems, the system does most of the KA, but the expert determines what sort of knowledge should be acquired and from which sources.

The TIGON system is being developed to detect and diagnose faults in a gas turbine engine. It is based on the work of, and uses the same data as, the ESPRIT TIGER project[3], which has "manually" produced a series of KBs to undertake fault detection and diagnosis for two turbines. The aim of the TIGON project is to produce analogous rule bases for these turbines "automatically". An additional aim is to modify the TIGON-produced KBs so that they are applicable to further turbine systems. To this end we have developed a methodology that enables TIGON to mine the data that has been routinely collected by the on-line computer while the turbine is operating.

The TIGON system is made up of four co-operating subsystems - a Learning Module which learns the fault detection and diagnosis models; a Monitoring Module that monitors the turbine's behaviour and detects when it is behaving abnormally; a Diagnosis Module that tries to determine what is causing the abnormality; and a Transformation Module that transfers the knowledgebases to further turbines. In this paper we consider the Learning Module, which, like REFINER, generally produces more succinct descriptions when it is provided with appropriate background knowledge. The Monitoring and Diagnosis Modules are merely interpreters for the code generated by the Learning Module and are therefore of little interest; the Transition Module is still being developed and will be described subsequently.

3.1 The Domain

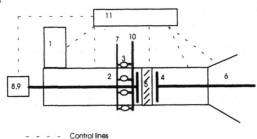

1) Air intake	5) Control nozzles	9) Helper turbine
2) Air compressor	6) Air exhaust	10) Steam injection
3) Combustion chambers	7) Fuel delivery system	11) Control unit
4) Turbine	8) Starter turbine	

Figure 1. Gas Turbine Engine

[3] ESPRIT Project No 6862, *Real-Time Situation Assessment of Dynamic, Hard to Measure Systems.* (See Milne (1993) for an overview of the project)

Gas turbine engines[4] are a type of internal combustion engine that are used throughout modern industry for the pumping of fluids and power generation, and in jet aircraft as their source of propulsion. They are expensive, and often occupy crucial roles in the plant in which they are sited. (For example, at the Exxon petrochemical plant in Scotland, where the majority of the training data for the TIGON project comes from, if the turbine breaks down, most of the plant shuts down at a cost of £100,000 per hour.) For this reason, it is important to know immediately when things start to go wrong so that the fault in the turbine can be corrected before the entire turbine has to be shut down. Less important, but desirable, is diagnostic information which helps the engineer detect the nature and the location of the fault.

3.2 The Data

There are essentially 3 sources of data:

- the information about the turbine's parameters which is recorded automatically by an "on-board" PC (see section 3.2.1)
- the data dependency diagram which indicates which parameters are affected when another parameter changes (see section 3.2.2)
- the labelling of the datasets which specifies the state which the domain expert (the turbine engineer) believes the turbine is in. This is discussed in section 3.2.3.

3.2.1 The Turbine's Parameters

As mentioned above the TIGON project uses data previously collected from the turbine at Exxon. This data comes from a PC connected to the turbine's controller which saves the values of prespecified variables at 1 second intervals. This data collection occurs at a specified period daily, *and* when some of the turbine's parameters are out of range. Figures 2-5 give examples of data collected.

Figure 2. Normal Running

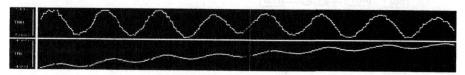

Figure 3. Normal Running with oscillations and load change.

---

[4] See Rolls Royce (1986) for technical information about gas turbines.

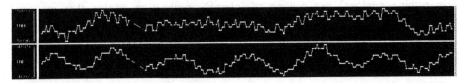

Figure 4. Fuel pressure transmitter problem.

Figure 5. Turbine tripped (i.e. shut-down)

All the above graphs show the values for the low pressure shaft speed (TNL) and the high pressure shaft speed (TNH), collected at one second intervals.

3.2.2 The Data Dependency Diagram

In most turbines there are around 160 variables to be considered. Obviously to search for possible relationships between all combinations of variables would take a prohibitively long time. It would also be largely pointless, as often only a *small* subset of the variables are interdependent. So TIGON requires the expert to enter a data dependency diagram to indicate which variables effect other variables. An example of such a data dependency diagram is given in

Figure 6. (Note, the dependency diagram is literally drawn by the expert, using a TIGON subsystem, and is very easily changed to allow the expert to ask *what-if* questions or to examine the behaviour of a specific set of links.)

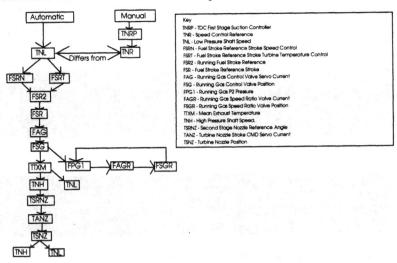

Figure 6. Data dependency diagram (names in boxes represent sensor variables)

3.2.3 Labelling the Datasets

As part of standard procedures, the engineer in charge of the turbine monitors its performance and regularly annotates the data collected. Labels used so far in this domain include

- Normal operation with constant (low, medium and high) load
- Normal operation with increasing/decreasing load
- Normal operation with the steam helper turbine becoming engaged
- One of several known faults (e.g. a particular nozzle sticking)
- Unusual, but otherwise normal states, e.g. start-up
- Controlled shutdown.

and, of course, combinations of the above.

3.3 The Methodology of the TIGON System Learning Module

The Learning Module can be summarised as:

1. Expert provides a data dependency diagram for the system to be modelled (see section 3.2.2)

2. Data labelled by the expert and split up into training and testing data sets by the knowledge engineer

3. Data filtered (i.e. separate out "start up" states from "normal-steady" states operations)

4. Use data dependency diagram and *normal* data to infer ranges and relationships which together form a model of the turbine's *normal* behaviour

5. System repeats stages 3-4 for *abnormal* data

6. System compares a particular *abnormal* model both with the *normal* model and all the other *abnormal* models to see if this particular *abnormal* state can be uniquely detected.

7. The discrepancies are used along with the label to produce a series of diagnostic rules that uniquely identify (as far as is possible) a particular *abnormal* state; this is repeated for each abnormal state

8. The diagnostic rules produced in 7 are generalised

9. Code is generated for the detection and diagnosis rulebases

10. The rules produced in 9 are used with the test datasets (both *normal* and *abnormal*)

11. Expert critiques results and points out where detection failed or diagnosis was wrong.

12. If the expert is not satisfied with the results he/she has a series of options including

- refining the labelling of the dataset
- modifying the turbine's data dependency diagram (a fairly drastic measure)
- removing datasets
- adding further datasets

·If the expert is satisfied with the results, the process stops, otherwise steps 3-12 above are repeated.

As can be seen, the expert is only involved in stages 1, 2, 11 and 12.

3.3.1 Segmenting the Data (stages 2 & 3)

In order for TIGON to learn a concept, it must have example data in which that behaviour is manifested, and the associated concept name. In the case of the TIGON project, this is provided by the expert taking data from the turbine's controller, segmenting the data in such a way that in each segment the turbine is in the same state (i.e. in segment 1 the turbine is running normally, in segment 2 there is a load change, etc.), and then labelling that data segment accordingly.

In the case of the TIGON project, much of the data collection, segmentation and labelling had been done by the expert as part of the TIGER project. Some of the labelling used has been listed in section 3.2.3.

This initial segmentation is often not enough to provide a suitable search space for the system to do data mining and will lead to excessively complex and incomplete results, as well as taking longer than we might like. To overcome this, the system does a further segmentation of the data using data filters. These data filters are used to describe discrete turbine states, such as constant load, steam injection on, steam injection at 80%, etc., all of which can be described in terms of signals from the turbine controller, certain ranges of sensor values or Boolean combinations of these values. Most of these filters are pre-defined although the user can define his or her own.

All these data segments are then split in two in an arbitrary manner by the knowledge engineer who designates some as *test* data and some as *training* data.

3.3.2 The Data Mining (stages 4 & 5)

After the last phase of data segmentation has been carried out, data mining can begin. TIGON is first given the normal training data and from it, generates a model for the normal behaviour. The model is made up of three components. Firstly, the range of values noted for each variable when the turbine is behaving normally.

Secondly there is the qualitative component which describes the links in the dependency diagram as qualitative relationships showing the expected behaviour e.g.

$$FSR2_{tn}(increasing)->FSR_{t0}(increasing)$$
To be read as - If FSR2 at time tn is increasing then
FSR at time t0 should also be increasing.

So if FSR2 had increased and FSR was not increasing then that would suggest that something was not functioning correctly.

The third, and most important, component produces a set of semi-quantitative descriptions. Here a curve fitting function tries to infer a numerical relationship between the variables using the dependency diagram as a template. This relationship can be of two forms:

$$FSR_0 = 1.375E28 * FSR2_0^5 + 5.214E - 32 * FSR2_0^4 + 1723 * FSR2_0^3 + 45254 * FSR2_0^2 + 455 * FSR2_0^1$$
$$+ 3463$$

Or

$$FSR2_0 = \text{MINIMUM}\left(FSRN_0, FSRT_0\right)$$

The current function finder uses the standard linear regression technique of "method of least squares" to find a polynomial that best fits the data. The system then also scores some basic functions (minimum, maximum, equals and average) and the relationship that provides the best overall fit to the data is chosen. As can be seen there is a temporal aspect to the relationship. This is necessary because mechanical influences can often take time to propagate through the system. The temporal offset is calculated on a best fit basis, i.e. each variable on the right hand side is calculated for a range of temporal offsets[5] and the temporal offset that gives the best result is chosen.

These three descriptions together, form a model of the turbine's expected behaviour. Further, TIGON creates, for each of the labelled *abnormal* datasets, a knowledgebase using the same method.

3.3.3 Building the Diagnostic Knowledgebase (stages 6, 7 & 8)

Once all the knowledgebases for the labelled abnormal datasets have been created, TIGON then compares a particular non-standard knowledgebase with the normal knowledgebase and all the other abnormal KBs and notes where there are any difference(s) in either the variable ranges, or in the qualitative relationships[6]. These discrepancies are then stored with the name of the appropriate state. (The label of the abnormal dataset being a description of the abnormality, its location and the time which it occurred.) The next stage attempts to find a *unique* description for each of the abnormalities; this involves comparing the descriptions of the several abnormal KBs. The result of this stage is either unique descriptions of abnormal states or a list of abnormal states which cannot be completely discriminated.

These discrepancy and label pairs can then be used to produce a fault diagnosis KB. The fault detection KB contains a description of the abnormality (the discrepancy) and the type and location of the abnormality (the label). However, it is extremely unlikely that there will be datasets for all possible abnormalities, so TIGON needs the ability to reason about "unseen" abnormalities. This will be done by generalisation of existing abnormalities. Each of the discrepancy-label pairs will be examined to see if the same abnormality type occurs in more than one location. If an abnormality does exist in more than one location, then TIGON will attempt to

---

[5] Under normal circumstances the turbine should take no longer than 5 seconds to react to a change in condition, so TIGON searches in the range 0-5 seconds. Some faults cause the turbine to take longer to react, but they will be dealt with by the diagnostic rulebase.

[6] Due to the fact that many different polynomials can represent the same function, comparing the quantitative relationships is unlikely to yield much useful information and so will not be attempted.

generalise the discrepancies noted for that abnormality. This generalised discrepancy, along with a label giving the abnormality type (but not, obviously, the location of the abnormality), will also be added to the fault diagnosis KB. This generalisation facility will, we believe, be important when the KBs are transferred to further turbines.

3.3.4 Code Generation (stage 9)

As the system needs to diagnose a fault whilst still monitoring the turbine for other faults that may occur, the Diagnosis and Monitoring Modules need to run in real time. For this reason, the fault detection and fault diagnosis knowledgebases are currently converted to LISP and then compiled before the system is used for monitoring. (This should give sufficient speed, although it is acknowledged that the knowledgebase might have to be cross compiled to a faster language like C.)

3.3.5 System Testing and Subsequent Refinement (stages 10, 11 & 12)

After the knowledgebases have been created they are tested on a simulator, using the test data, to see how they perform. If TIGON detects a fault that has not happened or fails to correctly detect or diagnose a fault, then the knowledgebases are incomplete and need to be refined. In TIGON we are opting for co-operation specifically between the expert and the system at this stage.

An important facility of the TIGON system is that the results of the testing are displayed on the data dependency diagram - using a convention which distinguishes between the three aspects of the model (variable range, qualitative & quantitative). Correct predictions are shown in green and incorrect predictions are shown in red. This enables the expert to quickly see the areas of the data dependency diagram (and hence the data) which need his/her attention.

TIGON provides an extensive WHAT-IF facility which allows the expert to explore a variety of possible changes including, changing the labels on the data segments, deleting data segments, adding new data segments and changing the data dependency diagram.

3.4 The Monitoring Module and the Diagnosis Module

The Monitoring Module runs the fault detection KB as obtained by the Learning Module (section 3.3.2). It is also be responsible for keeping a history of the data. When it detects what it suspects is a fault, it will call the Diagnostic Module. The Diagnosis Module uses the fault diagnosis KB created by the Learning Module (section 3.3.3) to try to determine the fault. By having the Monitoring Module and Diagnosis Module separated in this way, it will enable the Monitoring Module to continue functioning and maybe detect further errors by activating the Diagnosis Module again, while the first instantiation of the Diagnosis Module is still determining the initial fault.

3.5 Results & Discussion

At the moment only the fault detection part of TIGON has been implemented. The code to generate the fault diagnosis rulebase has not yet been fully implemented. However we have still been able to produce some promising results from the system.

When TIGON is trained on the particular "normal" dataset[7] used by the TIGER project, it is able to learn satisfactorily all but two of the relationships and ranges in the data dependency diagram[8]. When trained on this "standard" dataset or any known normal dataset, TIGON can, with a high degree of accuracy, distinguish between normal datasets and abnormal datasets, for any dataset taken in the 24hrs after the training dataset was taken.

By expanding the amount of training data we can increase the time for which the predictions are accurate up to 1 month, after which time the fault detection KB has to be relearned. TIGON seems to learn best if approximately 5 datasets are used to learn the relationships and about 10-15 to learn the variable ranges. Using less datasets than this seems to result in poorer predictive capabilities, using more datasets than this lengthens the time taken to learn without noticeably improving the results.

TIGON has also been tested on another turbine (or more accurately part of a turbine) and although the results have yet to be fully analysed, it appears that TIGON can also learn a fault detection KB for this turbine.

The diagnostics in TIGON can at present detect broad classes of fault. These classes correspond roughly, not to a fault, but how the turbine responds to a particular *type* of fault. More work is currently being done to separate the fault manifestation from the turbine's attempts at fault recovery, so as to more accurately pinpoint faults that arise.

As the TIGON system is still under development, it has not yet been tried on other domains. However it seems likely that TIGON's methodology and its approach to representing fault determination and diagnostic information should make it suitable for other domains, especially those involving dynamic processes, such as furnace control, management of water purification plants, other types of turbine (e.g. hydro-electric turbines), and perhaps parts of human physiology.

3.6 TIGON Summary

In essence, TIGON takes 3 kinds of information which are readily available, namely: the performance data, the data dependency diagram, and the labelling of data-sets, and infers diagnostic rules for the several abnormal states. We argue that the information which is acquired on the turbine's performance is "free" as it is already being collected automatically. We further argue that 2 other kinds of

---

[7] This dataset was considered by the expert to be the best "standard" dataset from all the data collected for the TIGER project, and was their baseline dataset.

[8] After subsequent discussion with the people on the TIGER project, it was realised that the two relationships in question were of such a complex nature, that it was extremely unlikely that our system would have been able to infer the necessary rules.

information are very easy for the turbine engineer to provide; indeed, the data-dependency diagram should be available from existing design documents, and the labelling of performance data segments is something which the turbine engineers do as part of their standard monitoring procedures.

Another significant feature of the TIGON system is it's WHAT-IF facility. More generally, we argue that TIGON is a good example of a co-operative system which does a great deal of data analysis, and then presents summaries in a form which enables the domain specialist to make high-level decisions in order to remove inconsistencies detected in the data analysis phase.

4. Related Work and Discussion

We wish to argue that the systems reported in the last 2 sections can be usefully considered under the following headings:

- Knowledge Acquisition which requires minimal input from the domain expert.
- Co-operative Knowledge Acquisition and Refinement systems.
- Re-use of existing knowledge, an important theme identified by Neches et. al. (1991)

Sections 4.1, 4.2 & 4.3 will consider the contributions which systems, including REFINER+ and TIGON have made to these themes. Additionally, we wish to point out that TIGON also contributes to two further themes, namely data mining and the inference of diagnostic rules from the systems performance data; these themes are discussed in sections 4.4 and 4.5

4.1 Knowledge Acquisition Which Requires Minimal Input From the Expert.

Many systems have contributed to this theme, including inference systems such as ID3 (Quinlan, 1986), CN2 (Clark & Boswell, 1991) and C4.5 (Quinlan, 1993) which have created decision trees and rules from example sets. In a sense, one could argue that case base reasoning systems also contribute to this theme. For example, HYPO (Ashley, 1990) produces legal decisions on the basis of a current case and a databank of previous cases. The Ripple-down rules algorithm (Compton & Jansen, 1990) should also be mentioned here.

However we would like to argue that TIGON produces diagnostics for a much more demanding situation - namely for a dynamic process and on the basis of information produced by the system itself. Also we would like to stress that TIGON is not attempting to simplify an existing theory or rule-set as does EBL and Reinforcement Learning (Mitchell et al., 1986), but rather to create a rule base from low level empirical data and a high level causal graph.

4.2 Co-operative Knowledge Acquisition and Refinement Systems.

Many KA systems have acquired knowledge interactively - for example AQUINAS (Boose, 1990). However by using the term *co-operative* we wish to imply that the expert is given a more significant role in the process than simply the inputting of data. In the MOLE system (Eshelman, 1988), the user is asked to decide whether there are causal links between pairs of nodes; in DISCIPLE (Kodratoff & Tecuci, 1987) the expert is asked to decide whether a system-generated example is a member of the concept under discussion. Similarly in REFINER and REFINER+, the user is asked to choose between a number of options to remove an inconsistency in a set of cases. In TIGON, the user is asked to suggest changes to the set of cases, the causal graph or the descriptors used to help remove inconsistencies reported by the system in the current dataset.

4.3 Re-use of Existing Knowledge

This is one of the important themes in Knowledge Systems development which has been highlighted in Neches et. al. (1991). In Milne and Gausch's (1994) system they extract diagnostic rules from the code of the controller. King, Stewart and Tait (1995) extract from existing CADCAM diagrams, constraints to be applied to the variables; this information is then used as components of rules for both an Expert System and an Intelligent Tutoring System. Additionally TIGON has been able to re-use design information; in this system it becomes the data dependency diagram.

4.4 TIGON and Data Mining

TIGON is a very basic data mining system; it is not a "conventional" KDD system as strictly there is no database and very little searching for information is done. In fact it could be argued that TIGON is more akin to some of the earlier scientific discovery systems such as BACON (Langely et al. 87) or the early KDD work such as FORTY-NINER (Zytkow & Baker 91) in that they use expert specified dependent variables to guide the search. Also, the reduced search time allows the expert to use the system more interactively, and to try out new theories and relationships, using the philosophy proposed in the KDW system (Piatetsky-Shapiro & Matheus 1992).

4.5 Inferring Diagnostic Rules for Dynamic Systems From the Systems Performance Data

So far most of the work in this area has mainly concentrated around the use of ANNs (Artificial Neural Networks) (Fu, 1994; Penman & Yin, 1994), in particular MLP's (Multi Layer Perceptrons) using the backpropagation algorithm for training. These systems have the advantage that they are relatively easy to set up and train. Unfortunately, the standard MLP is non-incremental, slow to learn, cannot use background knowledge and what it does learn is not readily understandable by humans. Recently systems (in particular KB-ANN (Towell & Shavlik, 1994)) have tried to overcome these problems. KB-ANN inputs a tree of symbolic rules containing an incomplete domain theory and uses that tree to form the basis of a NN which is then trained using examples from the domain, and after training is complete, the resultant network is converted back into a tree. TIGON uses a somewhat similar idea, in that TIGON uses the data dependency diagram to form the basis of a network, and then uses domain data to "revise" the parameters in the links. What makes TIGON different is that it is not limited to purely quantitative values of the weights, as an ANN is, but rather it can also learn the qualitative relationships between nodes in the network. Further, because of the nature of the domain, TIGON can learn suitable ranges of values for the variables in the network. One feature that KB-ANN does have that TIGON does not is the ability to add or remove links in the network. In TIGON we have chosen not to do this as it would create a *much* larger search space.

5. Final Comment

We have argued above why it was necessary to implement REFINER and TIGON as co-operative systems. We now wish to argue that it is appropriate/necessary to build co-operative Knowledge Acquisition/Problem Solving systems when the following conditions hold:

- there is a very large amount of data which thus makes it impossible for the domain expert to "eyeball" the complete data-set and hence data mining/ML techniques need to be used.

- the domain is complex, and so it is *not* feasible for a domain expert to articulate in advance, a complete domain theory. However, it is often feasible for the domain expert to select, from a set of options produced by the system, one(s) which will resolve *particular* inconsistencies.

Thus we envisage many situations where symbiotic interactions between man and machine can be used to great advantage.

6. References

K D Ashley (1990) Modelling legal argument: Reasoning with cases and hypotheticals. Cambridge MA: MIT Press, Bradford Books

P Clark & R Boswell (1991) Rule Induction with CN2: Some recent improvements. In *Proceedings of EWSL-91*, Y Kodratoff (ed.) Springer-Verlag pp463-481

P Compton & R Jansen (1990) A Philosophical basis for knowledge acquisition. *Knowledge Acquisition, 2*, pp241-257

D Diaper (1989) Knowledge Elicition: Principles, techniques and applications. Sussex: Ellis Horwood

K A Ericsson & H A Simon (1984) Protocol Analysis. Cambridge, Mass: MIT Press.

L Eshelman (1988). MOLE: a knowledge-acquisition tool for cover-and-differentiate systems". In S. Marcus (Ed.), *Automating Knowledge Acquisition for Expert Systems*. Norwood, Mass: Kluwer Academic, pp 37-80.

L Fu (1994) Neural Networks in computer Intelligence. McGraw-Hill Inc.

G Kahn (1988). MORE: From Observing Knowledge Engineers to Automating Knowledge Acquisition. In S. Marcus (Ed.) *Automating Knowledge acquisition for Expert Systems*. Norwell, Mass: Kluwer Academic, pp 7-35.

B King, A P Steward & J I Tait (1995). Towards Automated Knowledge Acquisition for Process Plant Diagnosis. *IEE Colloquium on KDD, Digest No 1995/021 (B)*, February 1995.

Y Kodratoff & G Tecuci (1987) What is an example in DISCIPLE? In *Proceedings of the 4th International ML workshop*, Uni. Of California, Irvine. Publ: Morgan-Kaufmann pp 160-166

P Langley, H A Simon, G Bradshaw & J M Zytkow (1987) *Scientific Discovery: An account of the creative Process*. Cambridge, Mass. MIT Press

P Leo, D Sleeman & A Tsinakos (1994). S-SALT: A problem solver plus knowledge acquisition tool which additionally can refine its knowledge base. In *Proceeding EKAW-94*.

S Marcus (1988). A knowledge acquisition tool for propose-and-revise systems. In S Marcus (Ed), *Automating Knowledge Acquisition for Expert Systems*. Boston: Kluwer Academic, pp 81-123.

R Milne (1993). ESPRIT TIGER project, Knowledge Acquisition Summary - FEP.

R Milne T Gausch (1994) Automatic Diagnostic Development on a programmable logic controller. *In Applications & Innovations in Expert Systems 11*. (R Milne & A Montgomery eds.) Oxford: Information Press, p99-110.

F Mitchell, D Sleeman & R Milne, (1995) KA the KDD way or How to do Knowledge Acquisition without completely annoying your expert. *IEE Colloquium on KDD, Digest No 1995/021 (B)*, February 1995.

T M Mitchell R M Keller & S T Kedar-Cabelli (1986) Explanation-based generalisation: A unifying view. *Machine Learning I, I*, pp 47-80

M A Musen (1990) An editor for the conceptual models of interactive knowledge-acquisition tools. In *The Foundations of Knowledge Acquisition*, J Boose & B G Gaines (eds) London: Academic Press, pp135-160

R Neches, R Fikes, T Finin, T Gruber, T Senator & W Swartout, (1991) Enabling technology for knowledge sharing. *AI Magazine*, 12, pp 36-56

J Penman & C M Yin (1994) Feasibility of using unsupervised learning, artificial neural networks for the condition monitoring of electrical machines. In *IEE Proceedings of Electr. Power Appl., Vol 141 No 6.*

G Piatetsky-Shapiro & W J Frawley (eds.) (1991) Knowledge Discovery in Databases. AAAI Press

G Piatetsky-Shapiro & C J Matheus (1992) *Knowledge Discovery Workbench for Exploring Business Databases.* International Journal of Intelligent Systems, Vol. 7, No. 7, September 1992.

J R Quinlan (1986) Induction of decision trees. *Machine Intelligence, I* pp81-106

J R Quinlan (1993) C4.5 Programs for Machine Learning. Publ: San Mateo, CA:Morgan Kaufmann

H Reichgelt & N Shadbolt (1992). PROTOKEW: A knowledge based system for knowledge acquisition. In: *Artificial Intelligence Research Directions in Cognitive Science,* D Sleeman & N O Berson, (eds.) Publ Hove: LEA, pp 171-202.

Rolls-Royce plc, (1986) The Jet engine, Rolls-Royce plc.

S Sharma & D Sleeman (1988) Refiner: A Case-based Differential Diagnosis Aide for Knowledge Acquisition and Knowledge Refinement. *In Proceedings of EWSL-88,* D Sleeman (eds.) Pitman: London, pp201-210.

D Sleeman (1994) Some Recent Advances in KB Systems Building. *Research and Development in Expert Systems XI, Proceedings of Expert Systems 94,* Oxford: Information Press, p3-16

G G Towell & J W Shavlik (1994) Refining symbolic knowledge using neural networks. *Machine Learning IV,* R Michalski & G Tecuci (eds) pp405-429

M Winter & D Sleeman (1995). REFINER+: An Efficient System for Detecting and Removing Inconsistencies in Example Sets. In *Research & Development in Expert Systems XII* M A Bramer J L Nealon & R Milne (eds). Oxford: Information Press, pp 115-132.

J M Zytkow & J Baker (1991) *Interactive Mining of Regularities in Database* In Knowledge Discovery in Databases, G Piatetsky-Shapiro & W J Frawley (eds.) AAAI Press.

The Acquisition of a Shared Task Model

Frances Brazier, Jan Treur and Niek Wijngaards

Artificial Intelligence Group,
Department of Mathematics and Computer Science
Vrije Universiteit Amsterdam
De Boelelaan 1081, 1081 HV Amsterdam, The Netherlands
E-mail: {frances, treur, niek}@cs.vu.nl

Keywords: shared task model, strategic interaction, cooperative agents, design support.

Abstract The process of the acquisition of an agreed, shared task model as a means to structure interaction between expert users and knowledge engineers is described. The role existing (generic) task models play in this process is illustrated for two domains of application, both domains requiring diagnostic reasoning. In both domains different levels of interaction between an expert user and a diagnostic reasoning system are distinguished.

1 Introduction

Decision support systems are most often designed to provide expert users with the information they need to solve a problem. More extensive support, however, is provided by knowledge-based systems that not only are capable of performing complex computation but that also are equipped with explicit knowledge of the decision process. The acquisition of such knowledge is not as trivial as it may seem. Although experts differ in their approaches to problems, in almost all situations different alternatives are thought through and compared. Decision support systems ideally support experts in this process. Not only the opportunity to influence the approach taken by systems (for example the sequence of tasks) is of importance, but also the opportunity to influence the more local levels of strategic reasoning involved in decision making processes.

User centered task analysis is essential to the design of such systems (Barnard, 1993; Brazier & Treur, 1994). The tasks users perform in specific decision making situations must be identified, in addition to relations between tasks. The designer of a system (in general a knowledge engineer) and one or more experts must reach a common understanding of the tasks involved in a specific decision making process. The types of decisions an expert user would prefer to make him/herself and the ways in which an expert user would like to be able to influence a system's reasoning, must be identified.

In this paper the role a shared task model can play as a means to acquire a common understanding of a task in interaction with expert users, is described. During an acquisition process different types of interaction between expert users and a system designed to support such users, can be identified. Three levels of interaction are introduced below in Section 2. In Section 3 existing (generic) task models used to structure the knowledge acquisition process are introduced. In Sections 4 and 5 the process of acquisition is described for two domains for which shared task models have been devised in practice, on the basis of which system architectures have been developed.

2 Knowledge Acquisition

To structure the exchange of knowledge between a knowledge engineer and an expert user often mediating representations are used (e.g., Ford, Bradshaw, Adams-Webber & Agnew, 1993). From our perspective, one of the results of knowledge acquisition (and task analysis) is a shared task model: a model which both the knowledge engineer and one or more expert user(s) agree to be an acceptable representation of the task structure for which support is to be provided.

2.1 Explicit Interaction

Within a shared model different types of tasks are distinguished: some of which may require interaction between the user and the system, and others which may not. Different types of information may be exchanged, depending on the subtask. These different types of information are used to define different levels of interaction.

Object level interaction is the interaction required to acquire specific facts about a current situation. This type of interaction in often modelled during the development and design of knowledge-based systems.

In addition, however, experts often reason about the approaches they take, comparing strategies and results. Systems designed to support expert users should therefore support such types of explicit meta-reasoning. Expert users should be able to influence the strategies employed by a system influencing factors such as specific goals, heuristics, preferences, assumptions, etc. Interaction at this level, is called *interaction at the level of strategic preferences* or *strategic interaction*.

Although a shared task model is the result of negotiation with one or more experts, it is not necessarily "the" correct model of a task for all problems in all domains. Expert users may wish to influence, for example, the sequencing or choice of subtasks in a particular situation. Interaction at this level, the level of *task model modification*, allows for individual expert users to adapt the task model to their own needs.

To model the knowledge required at these three levels of interaction within the task model, a task based framework for the design and development of compositional systems is required.

2.2 Declarative Compositional Approach

DESIRE (Langevelde, Philipsen & Treur, 1992; Brazier, Treur, Wijngaards & Willems, 1994, 1995) is a framework for the design and development of compositional systems. The framework provides support for the specification and implementation of compositional task models. These models include knowledge of the following types (comparable types of knowledge are distinguished in task analysis approaches such as KAT/KTS (Johnson & Johnson, 1991, 1993)):

1 knowledge of the task structure: task (de)composition,
2 knowledge of sequencing of tasks and goals: control (de)composition,
3 knowledge of knowledge structures,
4 knowledge of information exchange,
5 knowledge of task delegation.

Within the DESIRE framework different levels of abstraction are distinguished for each of these five types of knowledge. Tasks are defined at different levels of abstraction, resulting in a task (de)composition. Different levels of abstraction are also found within knowledge structures such as taxonomies, to which tasks refer. Sequencing of tasks and goals, and information exchange are defined not only at the level of primitive tasks, but also between composed tasks (and between composed tasks and primitive tasks), again providing a levelled structure of abstraction. Task delegation, the last of the five types of knowledge, can also be defined at all levels within a task model. More abstract tasks may be delegated to more than one party, whereas more specific tasks are often delegated to one particular party.

Within the DESIRE framework a distinction is made between the task dimension and the knowledge dimension. Together the knowledge structures define the knowledge dimension, related to the task dimension, but separately defined.

2.3 Task Models

A shared task model, as a mediating representation, is the result of negotiation between a knowledge engineer and one or more experts. The purpose of the negotiation is to acquire a common understanding of the task. An expert has extensive (often implicit) knowledge of a domain and of his/her task and strategies. A knowledge engineer has knowledge of existing models of related tasks which may or may not be applicable, and of ways to modify and combine such models for the domain at hand. Abstract task models are often used to structure the knowledge acquisition process.

Within the DESIRE framework (Langevelde *et al.*, 1992; Brazier *et al.*, 1995), a number of such abstract task models, generic task models, exist which are used for this purpose. These models have been defined on the basis of experience and logical analysis. The concept of a generic task, introduced by Chandrasekaran (1986, 1990) and Brown and Chandrasekaran (1989), is comparable to the notion of *generic task model* in that they are both generic with respect to domains. Generic task models within the DESIRE framework, however, are generic with respect to both tasks and domain: generic task models can be refined with respect to the task by *specialisation* (e.g., further decomposition of a subtask) and refined with respect to the domain by *instantiation* (e.g., addition of domain-specific knowledge). Moreover, the way a generic task model is specified in DESIRE is more declarative (with semantics based on temporal logic) than the way generic tasks are described in Chandrasekaran (1986, 1990) and Brown and Chandrasekaran (1989). The integral approach to levels of abstraction within the DESIRE framework supports the use of generic task models during knowledge acquisition. Different levels of abstraction and composition play a role during the negotiation phase.

2.4 The Common KADS Approach

The Common KADS model set (see de Hoog, Martil, Wielinga, Taylor, Bright and van de Velde, 1994) includes: an organisation model, a task model, an agent model, an expertise model, a communication model and a design model. An *organisation model* analyses the impact of a system in and on an organisation. A *task model* describes the tasks related to the realisation of a function in an organisation independent of the agent responsible for the performance of the tasks. A task model, however, when complete, relates each task to an agent. Agents are described in an *agent model*. The capabilities of an agent are described in an *expertise model*. Strategic knowledge is defined by inference and task aspects of the problem solving knowledge included in an expertise model. Communication tasks, defined in a *communication model*, are specified in terms of user models (defined in an agent model) and transfer tasks (defined in an expertise model). Important decisions made during the design of an application together form the *decision model*.

Not all of the three levels of interaction distinguished above in section 2.1 are easily distinguished within the Common KADS framework. Object level interaction is defined by transfer tasks. How interaction at the level of strategic preferences or task model modification can be modelled is less clear. One option is to use the task layer of the expertise model, another is to use the REFLECT principle (see van Harmelen, Wielinga, Bredeweg, Schreiber, Karbach, Reinders, Voß, Akkermans, Bartsch-Spörl & Vinkhuyzen, 1992). Using the task layer to model these levels of interaction may not be appropriate, as domain specific (strategic) knowledge is involved, which then would not be specified at the domain layer and inference layer of the expertise model. This is, therefore, not a very elegant solution. The REFLECT approach models an entire expertise-model in the domain layer of another expertise model. Explicit strategic reasoning can be modelled within this approach, but entails the (recursive) combination of two expertise models for this purpose.

Reasoning about states of different reasoning processes is quite common in, for example, multi-agent situations. The Common KADS framework does not include constructs or models which can be used for this purpose. The semantics of DESIRE, however, based on temporal logic (states and transitions between states) has been designed to model interaction between components (which may be tasks) by explicit specification of transitions between states.

From the above it follows that the way in which the three levels of interaction are incorporated into one knowledge based system is not as transparent in Common KADS as in DESIRE. In DESIRE the levels of abstraction and temporal semantics facilitate the modelling of these levels of interaction.

3 Generic Task Models for Diagnostic Reasoning

In most situations in which diagnosis is required not all relevant facts are known in advance. In practice, in fact, diagnosis is not often based on complete information. The acquisition of additional (test) information is an essential part of most diagnostic processes. In general, diagnosis includes a number of subprocesses such as: the determination of hypotheses, the choice of applicable tests, the performance of tests, and the interpretation of test results. Strategic considerations such as the suitability of a test, the likeliness of a hypothesis being true, and the cost and effect of a test, play an important role in these processes. A number of existing (generic) task models for diagnostic reasoning in which strategic knowledge is explicitly modelled are described in this section. These models are used in interaction with experts to structure acquisition of shared task models of diagnostic reasoning for specific domains of application. The process of knowledge acquisition is illustrated for two such domains in Sections 4 and 5.

In Section 3.1 a generic model for diagnostic reasoning is described. Two specialisations of this model are presented in Sections 3.2 and 3.3. The relation between the models and the different levels of interaction distinguished in Section 2.1 is discussed in Section 3.4.

3.1 The SIX Architecture for Diagnostic Reasoning

As described above shared task models are acquired in interaction with experts, using existing (generic) task models to structure the process of knowledge acquisition. A generic task model of diagnostic reasoning designed for this purpose (Treur, 1993; Brazier & Treur, 1994) is shown in Figure 1.

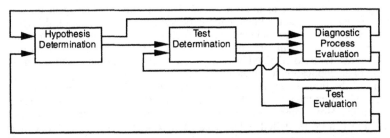

Fig. 1. SIX: a generic task model of diagnostic reasoning.

In this model four tasks are distinguished: *hypothesis determination, test determination, test evaluation* and *diagnostic process evaluation*. Hypothesis determination reasons about the appropriateness of possible hypotheses within a given state of the diagnostic process and determines which hypotheses are to be further investigated. Test determination analyses the current state of the diagnostic process with respect to test performance and determines which tests are most appropriate. Test evaluation performs the tests, and determines the relation between the test results and the current hypotheses. Diagnostic process evaluation analyses the implications of the test results for the hypotheses and determines which hypotheses are rejected and which are confirmed. On the basis of an analysis of the current overall state of the diagnostic process, the decision to conclude the diagnostic process may be made. If, however, the diagnostic process is continued, the required subsequent processes (for example, determination of hypotheses or tests) are identified.

Diagnostic reasoning processes can be based on *causal* or on *anti-causal* domain knowledge. In the first case derivations about the domain follow the direction of causality: the predicted observable consequences are derived from hypotheses (possible causes), after which (some of) the predicted observations are verified. For this type of reasoning causal knowledge is required that specifies how the causal consequences of hypotheses can be derived (e.g., represented by a causal network).

In the second case the domain knowledge is used to derive hypotheses from information on observables (symptoms). Here the direction of derivation is against the direction of causality: it proceeds from observable findings (in particular, those that actually were observed) to the causes. For this type of reasoning, knowledge is required that specifies how hypotheses can be derived from observable findings: this type of knowledge is called anti-causal knowledge.

In both cases strategic reasoning is required to determine the appropriate hypotheses on which to focus and the appropriate tests to be performed, as modelled by the generic task model for diagnostic reasoning SIX described above. This generic task model can be refined by specialisation to two slightly different models for diagnostic reasoning based on causal domain knowledge and anti-causal domain knowledge, respectively. These specialisations are described in Sections 3.2 and 3.3.

3.2 A Specialisation of the Generic Task Model for Anti-causal Diagnostic Reasoning

The specialisation for diagnostic reasoning based on anti-causal domain knowledge is obtained by decomposing the test evaluation task into two subtasks: *test performance* and *results interpretation*, as shown in Figure 2.

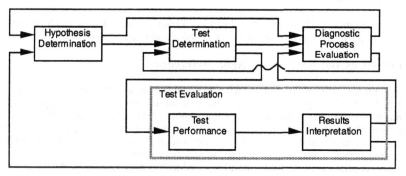

Fig. 2. A task model for diagnostic reasoning based on anti-causal knowledge.

Test performance is responsible for the "execution" of the tests selected by test determination. The results of the test may be acquired directly by object level interaction with an expert user, or may be acquired automatically from other systems. No further reasoning about the domain is performed in this task. The acquired test information is used by results interpretation to draw conclusions about the hypotheses, by means of the available anti-causal domain knowledge.

3.3 A specialisation of the Generic Task Model for Causal Diagnostic Reasoning

The specialisation for diagnostic reasoning based on causal domain knowledge is obtained by decomposing the test determination task into two subtasks: *test generation* and *test selection*, as shown in Figure 3.

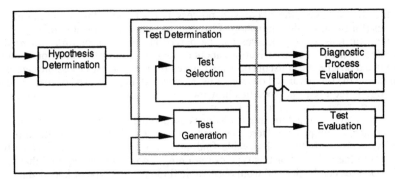

Fig. 3. A task model for diagnostic reasoning based on causal knowledge.

Test generation takes the hypothesis on which it is focussed as its input and using causal domain knowledge observable causal consequences are derived. These observable causal consequences are predictions of the findings that should be observed if the hypothesis hold. The predicted findings, influenced by the assumed hypothesis, are suitable candidates for tests to be selected. Test selection analyses the candidates and selects one or more tests on the basis of this analysis.

3.4 Interaction Levels in the Generic Task Models

In Section 2.1 three levels of interaction were distinguished. In this section the levels in the SIX model for diagnostic reasoning are discussed.

Object level interaction

The test evaluation subtask employs object level interaction with a user. The execution of tests may require users to provide (additional) information to the system.

Interaction at the level of strategic preferences

Strategic preferences are related to each subtask at the meta-level. Strategic preferences in the hypothesis determination subtask may influence the choice of hypotheses (e.g. frequency of occurrence, likelihood given a situation, preference of the user, ...). Strategic preferences in the test determination subtask may influence the choice of tests (e.g. based on cost of the tests, duration, predictive power, order of execution, preference of the user, ...). Strategic preferences in the diagnostic process evaluation subtask influence whether the system continues it search for (more) rejected and/or confirmed hypotheses or not.

Interaction at the level of task model modification

The user of the system influences which subtask is activated when. Knowledge of the sequence in which subtasks are activated may be overridden by users. For example, a user may look at the results of several settings for the strategic preferences for the test determination subtask before proceeding to the test evaluation subtask.

4 A Shared Task Model for Soil Sanitation

One domain in which a shared task model was developed in interaction with experts is the domain of soil sanitation (Boelens, 1991). During the acquisition process the generic task model of diagnostic reasoning (SIX) presented above played an important role. This model was used to structure interaction with the experts. In this section the domain of soil sanitation is introduced, an indication of the required functionality of a support system is given and finally the acquisition of the shared task model is described.

4.1 Soil Sanitation

Soil sanitation is a relatively young but fast-growing area of expertise. Polluted soil is found in many locations (in the Netherlands at least several thousand) and depending on the severity of the pollution the soil may need to be sanitized. At the level of provincial and local authorities the problem of soil sanitation usually is encountered during urban renewal. Pragmatic solutions are often chosen. Such solutions are based on two major decisions: how the site is to be sanitized and how the soil can be disposed.

Several procedures have been formulated concerning soil sanitation. Inventory research provides an indication of the different types of contaminations. Initial investigations aim to provide a global insight in the nature and concentrations of the contaminants. Further investigation concentrates on the nature, extent and concentrations of the contaminations as well as the spreading-probabilities. The goal of these investigations is to provide enough information for the sanitation procedure. The sanitation procedure consists of a comparison of the possible sanitation alternatives on environmental, technical and financial aspects. Sanitation is planned and executed.

The domain of sanitation consists of types of contaminations found (heavy metals, cyanide, aliphatic or hydrocarbons, aromatic compounds, and volatile helogenic hydrocarbons) and types of soil (sandy, loamy, loamy and clayey, peaty, and mixed). These types are only top-levels of taxonomies. Possible (general) sanitation techniques are: removing the contamination, prevent spreading of the contamination (isolation), or change of the function of the site. When removing the contamination either the soil is not removed (in situ techniques) or the soil is dug up. A soil sanitation alternative is a plan: one or more pollution remedial techniques are applied to the polluted site.

4.2 Acquisition of a Shared Task Model for Soil Sanitation

Experts working in the domain of soil sanitation were aware of the need for more support in choosing the best soil sanitation alternative. Although large bodies of knowledge are available the experts lacked support for flexible use of that knowledge. Ideally, the experts should be able to influence the use of the knowledge, when knowledge is used and what sanitation alternatives or tests may be investigated.

The following knowledge was readily available in pre-defined procedures and/or algorithms:

- How to choose remedial techniques based on their technological features and the situation at the polluted site.
- How to combine pollution remedial techniques into sanitation alternatives.
- How to predict the results of sanitation alternatives, based on the situation at the polluted site.
- How to compare sanitation alternatives to environmental standards or constraints.
- How to weight between various (groups of) evaluation criteria for sanitation alternatives.
- How to perform sensitivity analysis to determine which type of additional investigations is most effective with regard to selecting the best alternative.

Initial analysis of the experts' reasoning process to find the best alternative for a specific situation given the option to collect additional information about the situation, is, in fact, a form of diagnosis. Experts agreed that this generic task model (the generic task model for diagnostic reasoning, described in section 3.1) provided a basis for subsequent discussion. The mapping of the terminology in the domain to the terminology in which the generic task model is presented, was relatively straightforward: sanitation alternatives in this domain are hypotheses, performance of "additional investigation" is the performance of tests, and acquired information corresponds to test results. The resulting task decomposition is shown in Figure 4.

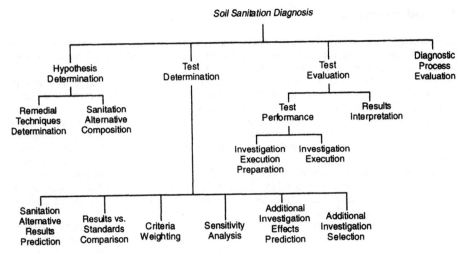

Fig. 4. Task decomposition of Soil Sanitation Diagnosis.

Hypothesis determination

During knowledge acquisition it became clear that the determination of the most appropriate sanitation alternatives, should be seen as two separate tasks. The first is the determination of the most appropriate technique for the reduction of one or more pollutants at a polluted site (*remedial techniques determination*). The second is the formulation of alternatives (i.e. hypotheses) on the basis of the available remedial techniques (*sanitation alternative composition*).

Test determination

The most extensive refinement of the generic task model was made with respect to test determination. Different subtasks were identified using different types of knowledge (including the knowledge mentioned above) to determine the most appropriate test.

Predictions about the (expected) reductions of pollutants at a particular site, are made using the available knowledge mentioned above (*sanitation alternative results prediction* task). Available knowledge is also used to determine the goodness of reductions, measured against directives on soil sanitation and construction materials (*results vs. standards comparison* task). Separate knowledge is available to decide how important different criteria are in the evaluation of sanitation alternatives (*criteria weighting* task).

Experts employ sensitivity analysis to determine which tests are most interesting in view of existing uncertainties (*sensitivity analysis* task). The knowledge experts have of models to predict the effect of tests on the criteria was also identified as a separate task (*additional investigation effects prediction* task). On the basis of the knowledge obtained by the performance of the above mentioned subtasks, a decision is made as to which additional investigations should be performed taking cost and duration (*additional investigation selection* task).

Test performance

Before actually performing tests experts reason about the information they expect to acquire and the way in which additional investigations should be performed (*investigation execution preparation*). This task is distinguished from the actual performance of the additional investigations (*investigation execution* task).

Results interpretation

Further decomposition of results interpretation was not necessary: the results of the tests are interpreted.

Diagnostic process evaluation

Experts recognized the appropriateness of a task for evaluation of the status of the process. On the basis of this analysis experts decide whether to pursue further analysis of a situation, or not.

Levels of interaction

Within the final version of the shared task model all three levels of interaction were modelled. Object level interaction is of importance in the test evaluation subtask, interaction at the level of strategic preferences in hypothesis determination and test determination subtasks, interaction at the level of task model modification in the task control process (using information provided by the diagnostic decision subtask).

5 Acquisition of Shared Task Models in Diagnosis of Chemical Processes

In a completely different domain, namely the domain of nylon production, the same SIX model was used during knowledge acquisition to structure discussions with an expert in this field. The expert involved identified the need for a system to support him in the diagnostic process, hopefully reducing the need for frequent on-site diagnosis. The nylon production process was described in detail and a few examples of types of problems with which the expert is confronted were discussed. As it was unclear how, in general, the expert structured his process of diagnosis, the two specialisations of the SIX task model described in Section 3: the causal and the anti-causal SIX task models, were introduced.

Initially, the process of nylon production in principle is based on causal knowledge in the domains of physics and chemistry, the knowledge engineers involved expected the diagnostic process to be based on causal reasoning. The SIX task model for causal diagnostic reasoning was introduced. Further discussion and analysis of cases of diagnostic processes, however, showed that during the diagnostic process in this domain hypotheses themselves could be confirmed or rejected on the basis of direct observation, i.e., no causal or anti-causal knowledge at all was required. In addition cases were identified in which hypotheses which could not be confirmed or rejected on the basis of direct observation, played an important role. In these cases the expert used anti-causal knowledge to derive hypotheses from observed findings. At this point the SIX task model for anti-causal diagnostic reasoning was introduced. The two models were compared, and the expert concluded that, in general, the anti-causal model was most applicable even though he realised that in some, more exceptional (and complicated) situations, the causal model would be more applicable (in which observable findings are derived from hypotheses). Hypothesis determination was further refined: a (limited) number of possible hypotheses are first identified, one of which is chosen for further examination. The first task is delegated to the system, the second to the expert user. By modelling the task in this way, the expert user explicitly and directly influences the reasoning process. The need for such strategic interaction was identified during the knowledge acquisition process.

The shared task model designed for diagnostic Nylon-6 production process is a specialisation of the generic task model for diagnostic reasoning based on anti-causal knowledge, presented in Section 3.3. The first version of a system for diagnosis of Nylon-6 production processes based on this model, has been implemented and is currently being evaluated. In other domains in the same chemical plant, the causal model has shown to be more applicable.

6   Discussion

To model a task in which an expert user and an intelligent decision support system collaborate, appropriate intermediate representations of the task at hand must be designed. The acquisition of a shared task model as an intermediate representation of the task (within which different levels of specificity are modelled), has been addressed in this paper.

The knowledge involved in a collaborative task, to the extent modelled in an agreed shared task model, includes the knowledge of different types of interaction involved within: (1) knowledge of the task structure, (2) knowledge of sequencing of (sub)tasks and goals, (3) knowledge of the knowledge structures, (4) knowledge of information exchange, and (5) knowledge of task delegation. These five types of knowledge are explicitly modelled in the declarative compositional framework for the design of complex reasoning tasks, DESIRE. Within the DESIRE framework existing abstract models of generic tasks, provide a means to structure initial interaction with the expert user during the acquisition of a shared task model. A number of agreed, shared task models have been used to develop applications (decision support systems) in different domains.

In this paper the principles behind the DESIRE approach to user-centered system design are presented and illustrated on the basis of the development of two applications of diagnostic decision support systems. In the first application, decision support in the domain of soil sanitation, one of the existing generic task models for diagnostic reasoning based on anti-causal knowledge provided a means to structure knowledge acquisition. The shared task model developed for this domain was, in the end, a specialisation of this existing generic task model.

In the second domain discussed in the paper, diagnosis of chemical processes, two existing generic task models for diagnostic reasoning were introduced: the first one based on causal knowledge, and later in the acquisition process the model based on anti-causal knowledge. In contrast to the knowledge engineers' expectations, the model based on causal knowledge was not in line with the expert's diagnostic approach. The anti-causal model, however, was useful: the acquisition process resulted in a shared task model for diagnostic reasoning of Nylon-6 production as a specialisation of this model.

The declarative nature of knowledge specification in DESIRE (for both examples), was of particular importance to modelling strategic preference interaction between the user and the decision support system. Explicit, declarative representation of strategic knowledge (for which modelling primitives exist within DESIRE) allows strategic knowledge itself to be subject of interaction, both from the user to the system (which preferences hold, which relations between preferences exist, etc. influencing the system's reasoning strategy), and from the system to the user (which preferences have been fulfilled, to which extent, etc.).

Not only the knowledge acquisition process (and task analysis) is structured on the basis of this shared model, but also the design of the interaction between the user and system. Three different levels of interaction between an expert user and an intelligent design/decision support system are distinguished in this paper: object level interaction, strategic preference interaction and interaction required for task model modification, each requiring specific modelling techniques. The role an agreed shared task model can play as the basis for modelling the necessary functionality of interaction between an expert user and the system, and thus as the basis for the design of an interface, is discussed in (Brazier & Ruttkay, 1993; Brazier, Treur & Wijngaards, 1996).

The role of shared task models in situations in which more than two parties (agents) are involved, is a current focus of research. A shared task model is an agreed model: in some situations agreement may be reached between more than two parties (resulting in a situation comparable to the situation described above for two parties), but in other situations different models of a task may exist between parties, thus requiring "attunement" between parties. Such collaborative tasks are currently being analysed, providing insight in the extensions required to the DESIRE framework.

Acknowledgements

This research has been (partially) supported by the Dutch Foundation for Knowledge-based Systems (SKBS), within the A3 project "An environment for modular knowledge-based systems (based on meta-knowledge) for design tasks" and NWO-SION within project 612-322-316, "Evolutionary design in knowledge-based systems".

References

P.J. Barnard (1993). Modelling users, systems and design spaces. In *Proceedings of HCI International '93*, Elsevier, Amsterdam, 1993, pp. 331-336.

J. Boelens (1991). *Soil sanitation and strategic interaction.* Masters thesis, Department of Mathematics and Computer Science, Vrije Universiteit Amsterdam, 1991.

F.M.T. Brazier and Zs. Ruttkay (1993). A Compositional, Knowledge-Based Architecture for Intelligent Query User Interfaces. In: S. Ashlund, K. Mullet, A. Henderson, E. Hollnagel and T. White (eds.), *Adjunct Proceedings of the INTERCHI '93* (INTERACT '93 + CHI '93), 1993, pp. 145-146.

F.M.T. Brazier and J. Treur (1994). User centered knowledge-based system design: a formal modelling approach. In: L. Steels, G. Schreiber and W. Van de Velde (eds.), "A future for knowledge acquisition," *Proceedings of the 8th European Knowledge Acquisition Workshop, EKAW '94.* Springer-Verlag, Lecture Notes in Artificial Intelligence 867, 1994, pp. 283-300.

F.M.T. Brazier, J. Treur and N.J.E. Wijngaards (1996). Modelling Interaction with Experts: The Role of a Shared Task Model. In: W. Wahlster, ed. *Proceedings of the 12th European Conference on Artificial Intelligence, ECAI'96.* John Wiley & Sons, Ltd, 1996. To appear.

F.M.T. Brazier, J. Treur, N.J.E. Wijngaards and M. Willems (1994). A formalisation of hierarchical task decomposition. In: D. Fensel (ed.), *Proceedings of the ECAI '94 Workshop on Formal Specification Methods for Knowledge-Based Systems*, 1994, pp. 97-112.

F.M.T. Brazier, J. Treur, N.J.E. Wijngaards and M. Willems (1995). Formal specification of hierachically (de)composed tasks. In B.R. Gaines and M.A. Musen, eds. *Proceedings of the 9th Banff Knowledge Acquisition for Knowledge-Based Systems Workshop KAW '95*, Calgary: SRDG Publications, Department of Computer Science, University of Calgary, 1995, Volume 2, pp. 25/1-25/20.

D.C. Brown and B. Chandrasekaran (1989). *Design Problem Solving; Knowledge Structures and Control Strategies.* Research Notes in Artificial Intelligence, London: Pitman, 1989.

B. Chandrasekaran (1986). Generic tasks in knowledge-based reasoning: high-level building blocks for expert system design. *IEEE Expert*, 1986, Vol. 1, pp. 23–30.

B. Chandrasekaran (1990). Design Problem Solving: a Task Analysis. *AI Magazine*, 11 (4), Winter 1990, pp. 59-71.

K.M. Ford, J.M. Bradshaw, J.R. Adams-Webber, and N.M. Agnew (1993). Knowledge Acquisition as a Constructive Modeling Activity. In: K.M. Ford and J.M. Bradshaw (eds.), *Knowledge Acquisition as Modeling, International Journal of Intelligent Systems*, Wiley and Sons, 1993, Vol. 8, Nr. 1, pp. 9-32.

F. van Harmelen, B. Wielinga, B. Bredeweg, G. Schreiber, W. Karbach, M. Reinders, A. Voß, H. Akkermans, B. Bartsch-Spörl, and E. Vinkhuyzen (1992). Knowledge-Level Reflection. In: B. Le Pape, and L. Steels (eds), *Enhancing the Knowledge Engineering Process -- Contributions from ESPRIT*, Elsevier Science, Amsterdam, The Netherlands, 1992, pp. 175-204.

R. de Hoog, R. Martil, B. Wielinga, R. Taylor, C. Bright and W. van de Velde (1994). *The Common KADS model set.* Deliverable DM1.1c of ESPRIT Project P5248 "KADS-II", 1994.

H. Johnson and J. Johnson (1991). Task Knowledge Structures: Psychological basis and integration into system design. *Acta Psychologica*, 1991, Vol. 78, pp. 3-26.

H. Johnson and P. Johnson (1993). Explanation facilities and interactive systems. In Gray, W., Hefley, W. & Murray, D. (eds.), *Proceedings of the 1993 International Workshop on Intelligent User Interfaces*, New York, ACM, 1993.

I.A. van Langevelde, A.W. Philipsen and J. Treur (1992). Formal Specification of Compositional Architectures. In: B. Neumann (ed.), *Proceedings of 10th European Conference on Artificial Intelligence, ECAI'92*, Wiley and Sons, 1992, pp. 272-276.

J. Treur (1993). Heuristic reasoning and relative incompleteness. *Journal of approximate reasoning*, Vol. 8, 1993, pp. 51-87.

The Group Elicitation Method: An Introduction

Guy Boy

European Institute of Cognitive Sciences and Engineering (EURISCO)
4, avenue Edouard Belin, 31400 Toulouse, France
Tel. (33) 62 17 38 38; FAX (33) 62 17 38 39
Email: boy@onecert.fr

Abstract. This paper presents the Group Elicitation Method (GEM), a brainwriting technique augmented by a decision support system for constructing a shared memory. GEM has been successfully used in four industrial projects to elicit knowledge from experts. In particular, in three of them it was used to elicit end-users' knowledge for the design of new knowledge-based user interfaces. An example is developed in the aeronautical domain. This paper discusses the properties of such a method and the lessons learned. Finally, we discuss the leverage effect of GEM as a decision support tool and a computer-supported meeting environment.

Keywords. Knowledge elicitation, decision support systems, collaborative work, participatory design, design techniques, evaluation, methodology.

1 Rationale

"The most successful designs result from a team approach where people with differing backgrounds and strengths are equally empowered to affect the final design." (Tognazzini, 1992 page 57).

For many years, theories and practices of knowledge acquisition for knowledge-based systems (expert systems) tended to focus on how to elicit and represent knowledge from a single expert. This reflected a position which was dominant both in cognitive psychology and artificial intelligence (AI) in the 1970s and 1980s, where cognition was seen as a product of isolated *information processors* (Newell & Simon, 1972).

Real-world multi-expert situations are very significant. Knowledge is usually elicited from combined individual knowledge elicitation results or group meetings. The latter is more appealing since it adds a necessary cross-feedback and consensus-seeking from the experts. There are five classical types of meeting activities that need to be further emphasized: idea generation, issue discussion, negotiation, conflict resolution and team building. It is, however, recognized that meetings are time-consuming, inefficient, and unadapted to reaching consensus. In addition, they provide poor or incomplete consideration of alternatives, unequal participation (domination of a few members), a lack of meeting memory and a lack of satisfaction with the meeting process (Neal & Mantei, 1993). For instance, several experts may work together to investigate appropriate solutions to a design or evaluation issue. A crucial problem is to derive an acceptable consensus from a group of experts who share neither the same background nor the same objectives. It is not uncommon that experts do not understand each other.

The *brainwriting* technique was introduced more than two decades ago to facilitate the generation of ideas or viewpoints by a group of people (Warfield, 1971). This method can be used to stimulate a group of experts with the goal of silently expressing their expertise on a precise issue (Boy, 1991). It enables a group of experts to construct a writen shared memory. Each person takes a sheet of paper and reads the issue to be investigated. He/she then adds several viewpoints and put it back on the table, where the set of papers constitutes a shared memory of the meeting. The process of choosing a piece of paper, reading, writing viewpoints and replacing the paper on the table, is continued until each person has seen and filled in all the papers. Thus each person is continually confronted with the viewpoints of the others and can react by offering a critique or new viewpoints. Generally, a considerable number of viewpoints can be amassed with this procedure.

This paper introduces an integrated method that combines Warfield's original technique, and a decision-support system that enhances the analysis of brainwriting results: *Group Elicitation Method* (GEM). It has been tested in four industrial projects, in carrying out 24 full experiments that have involved more than 170 people. In particular, in three of them it was used to elicit end-users' knowledge for the design of new user interfaces. In order to illustrate the use of GEM, we develop an example of one of the experiments about user interface design that were run. More specifically, we have used GEM to derive user interface artifacts from an elicited graph of problems that experts think are illustrative of air traffic management functions. The properties of such a method and the lessons learned are discussed. Finally, we discuss the leverage effect of GEM as a decision support tool and a computer-supported meeting environment.

2 Description of GEM

A typical GEM session takes a full day, and consists of six phases conducted by a knowledge elicitation facilitator:

- issue statement formulation and choice of the participants;
- viewpoints generation;
- reformulation of these viewpoints into more elaborate concepts;
- generation of relations between these concepts;
- derivation of a consensus;
- critical analysis of the results.

2.1 Issue statement and participants

The first crucial and difficult phase is to state the issue to be investigated by a group of participants. It often takes a few application domain experts to state this issue. We found that the type of checklist proposed by Nielsen *et al.* (1986) for semi-structured interviews was a good starting point for the formulation of issue statements. GEM is currently implemented using the following checklist as a guideline:

- What is the goal of the engineered system that we plan to design or evaluate?
- How is the system or its equivalent being used? (current practice, observed human errors)
- How would you use this system? (users' requirements)

- What do you expect will happen if the corresponding design is implemented? (e.g., productivity, aesthetics, and safety issues)
- How about doing the work this way! (naive and/or provocative suggestions)
- What constraints do you foresee? (pragmatic investigation of the work environment)

Six to ten domain experts are chosen to participate in the GEM experiment. Experience suggests that the optimal number of participants for an interesting session in a reasonable time frame is about seven. In the experiments that we have carried out, most participants were end-users mixed with a few designers.

2.2 Viewpoints generation

The issue statement is then given to the participants, and they are asked to provide their opinions or *viewpoints* on the formulated issue. In the running example, the issue is:

- Could you write problems that you think are illustrative of air traffic management functions from the perspective of the design of new datalink pilot interfaces?

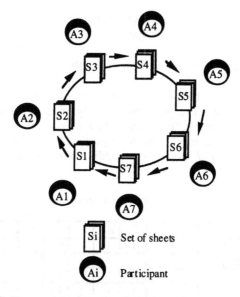

Fig. 1. There are n participants and n sets of sheets (n=7 in this figure). The viewpoint generation starts when each participant Ai writes on a set of sheets Si ($1 \leq i \leq n$). Then, Ai passes on Si to Ai+1 (note that An+1=A1), until Ai sees his/her orginal set of sheets Si again.

For the first ten minutes, each participant writes a list of viewpoints on his/her sheet. Then each participant passes his/her sheet to the person next to him/her. At this stage, each participant faces a list of viewpoints generated by someone else (Figure 1). There are three possibilities of action: agreement, disagreement or new viewpoint. In the first case, the participant mentions his/her agreement and may add more comments reinforcing the original viewpoint. In the second case, each participant mentions his/her disagreement and explains why he/she does not agree with the original viewpoint. In the third case, he/she just adds a new viewpoint to the list. This process continues until all participants have seen all sheets. One of the main advantages of this method is that participants are not influenced by outspoken people as is often the case in conventional meetings.

2.3 Reformulation into more elaborated concepts

These viewpoints are then analyzed, and reformulated into a list of *concepts*. The knowledge elicitation facilitator is free to create the concepts that he/she feels are the most appropriate. They can be refined as the reformulation process goes on. The creation/reformulation process is typically performed in front of the participants, so they can react and propose changes. This phase may take between one and two hours. It involves four types of operations that correspond to the concept clustering mechanisms that were described and used in the COBWEB system (Fisher, 1987):

- classifying the viewpoint with respect to an existing concept (a class of viewpoints);
- creating a new concept;
- combining two concepts into a single concept; and
- dividing a concept into several concepts.

2.4 Generation of relations between these concepts

Each participant is then asked to provide his opinion on the *relative priorities* of these concepts. He/she fills out a triangular matrix presenting the concepts in rows and columns. Basically, each matrix "box" is filled by a score. For example, he/she starts at line 1, second box, if concept 1 is *more / equally / less* important than concept 2, then he/she writes *+1 / 0 / -1* in the corresponding box, and so on. This phase takes about thirty minutes.

Table 1. Example of a priority matrix generated by a participant.

	2	3	4	5	6	7	8	9	10	11	12	13	14
1	-1	-1	-1	-1	0	-1	-1	-1	0	0	-1	0	0
2		-1	-1	-1	-1	-1	-1	-1	0	0	-1	-1	0
3			1	0	1	0	1	1	1	1	1	0	1
4				-1	1	-1	0	-1	1	0	-1	-1	0
5					1	0	1	0	1	1	0	0	1
6						-1	-1	-1	0	0	-1	-1	0
7							1	0	1	1	0	0	1
8								-1	1	1	-1	0	1
9									1	1	0	1	1
10										0	-1	-1	0
11											-1	-1	0
12												1	1
13													0

2.5 Derivation of a consensus

A *consensus* is derived using a computer program. We call *global score of a relation* the sum of all the scores of one relation among the participants. The global score matrix is the sum of all the matrices generated by all participants. To each global score is attached a standard deviation measuring the inter-participant consistency of the global score of the relation. This phase leads to the expression of a consensus among the participants (at the time they were consulted). This consensus is expressed using four types of typical parameters (normalized with respect to the number of participants and the number of generated concepts).

The *mean priority* (MP) of a concept corresponds to the mean of the scores assigned to a concept with respect to the other concepts for all the participants. The value range of the mean priority is the interval [-100, +100]. This enables the distinction of the "positive" concepts from the "negative" concepts. For instance, if all the participants provide the score +1 for a concept compared to all the other concepts, then the mean priority of this concept is +100.

The *inter-participant consistency* (C) of a concept corresponds to the mean of the standard deviations of all global scores. It is related to a consensus on the choice of subjective criteria. It conveys a degree of confidence in the mean priority with respect to the set of participants.

The *mean priority deviation* or *stability of a concept* (D) corresponds to the standard deviation of the mean priority with respect to the global scores of a concept. This parameter is useful to better characterize the priority concepts. The smaller D is, the more stable the group judgment is.

The *global consensus* (GC) expresses a global score of the group consensus on the investigated issue. This parameter is useful for comparing several groups.

2.6 Critical analysis of the results

GEM is a semi-formal method that the participants tend to accept and even rely on to enhance cooperation. We have observed that a critical analysis of the generated concept network is very constructive and reinforces the consensus. Experience shows that this phase may take between thirty minutes and one hour. A report is finally prepared by the knowledge elicitation facilitator.

Using GEM as a conceptual design tool makes it possible to gather together designers, management and end-users. It has been observed to be extremely useful in several cases, e.g., design of a computer interface for hostesses onboard airplanes; design of a maintenance instructor workstation; design of a classroom; design of a user interface for a new aviation communication system. An essential common factor into these cases was that the implementation of GEM helped bridge the gap between designers and end-users.

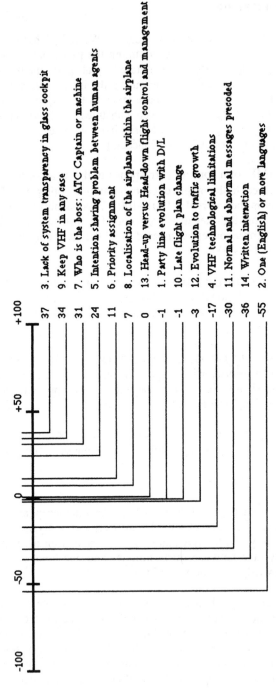

Fig. 2. Visualization of relative priorities.

3 Illustrating GEM using an example

3.1 Synthetic results from a typical GEM experiment

The expert group included nine experts in air traffic management (ATM). These participants generated 160 raw viewpoints on conceptual issues related to the design of new datalink pilot interfaces. This type of user interface is knowledge-based in the sense that designers need to know the essential viewpoints of pilots on the way air-ground communication would be influenced by the introduction of new communication media. After the viewpoint generation, each participant read his set of sheets, and a synthesis was carried out. Fourteen concepts were constructed by the group (Figure 2). The relative priorities of the 14 concepts have been generated by the participants by filling out matrices 14x14. Table 2 gives the resulting priority order of the concepts with respect to the mean priority (MP). The inter-participant consistency (C) and the mean priority deviation or stability (D) of each concept are also given. Each concept is described by a list of viewpoints (see Appendix for more details).

Table 2. Mean priority ordering.

Rank	MP	C	D	Concept
1	37	30	74	3. Lack of system transparency in glass cockpits
2	34	66	74	9. Keep VHF in any case
3	31	58	71	7. Who is the boss: ATC, Captain or machine
4	24	46	68	5. Intention-sharing problem between human agents
5	11	49	74	6. Priority assigment
6	7	58	65	8. Localization of the airplane within the airplane
7	0	90	63	13. Head-up vs. head-down flight control and managt
8	-1	19	76	1. Party line evolution with datalink
9	-1	70	70	10. Late flight change
10	-3	82	69	12. Evolution of traffic growth
11	-17	36	75	4. VHF technological limitations
12	-30	79	82	11. Normal and abnormal messages precoded
13	-36	94	73	14. Written interaction
14	-55	45	69	2. One (English) or more languages

3.2 Example of a GEM analysis

In order to better understand the way such an analysis is performed, it is developed for the first four concepts. Note that the following analysis example is extracted from a real-world experiment. Thus, we have tried to simplify it as much as possible to reach a larger audience even if some terms are kept as used by experts.

- Concept 3, Lack of system transparency in glass cockpit, 9, Keep VHF in any case, and 7, Who is the boss: ATC Captain or machine, are the best scored by the participants. This means that a traditionalist approach to cockpit changes is recommended. They lead to the elicitation of four generic requirements: system transparency; oral communication; sensory feedback; redundancy; confidence in technology; urgency handling. These requirements are motivated by two crucial observations: the complexity of ATM planning and replanning; the need for situation awareness and context continuity. The participants were concerned with potential confusion due to written language, the overload of the visual channels, degraded modes, and they are not sure that datalink would provide a picture of the whole. In conclusion, the participants ask for a natural interaction that ensures easy to acquire feedback, confidence and transparency.

- Concept 5, *Intention sharing problems between human agents*, is also a priority. A synthetic voice generator and a message acknowledgment aid have been advocated. Obviously, they would be additional systems to manage. The main value of this concept is to advocate a datalink system that would enhance the cross-check between pilots. In conclusion, a good datalink system on board would increase intention sharing between human agents.

Experience is necessary for comparing parameters in Table 2. It is more the relative values that are important than the values themselves. The more we perform GEM experiments, the more this analogical processing improves and becomes easier. Figure 1 provides a visual appreciation of the relative priority of the concepts constructed by the group. It was found to be very useful.

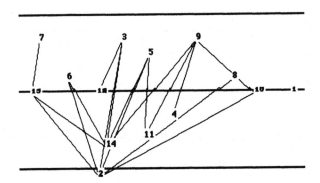

Fig. 3. Consensus graph. The middle horizontal line represents the zero mean priority level. The top (bottom) line represents the 50% (-50%) mean priority level.

The consensus graph (Figure 3) provides information on the strength of the relations between the concepts. It shows which concepts are responsible for the priority of another one. High priority concepts are at the top of the graph, and low priority concepts are at the bottom of the graph. A link between two concepts (presented using their number) shows that the participants have arrived at a consensus on the comparison between these two concepts. For instance, the group reached a consensus to say that concept 2 is of much less priority than concepts 3, 5, 6, 8, 10 and 13. Conversely, there is no consensus to say that concept 4 is of higher priority than concept 2. There is no real consensus for concept 1.

4 GEM properties and lessons learned

In this section, the validity of GEM is discussed on the basis of 24 experiments involving an average of seven participants per experiment. These experiments were conducted with experts from a wide range of aeronautics-related domains. For the last six experiments, the participants have filled in a questionnaire including the following questions:

- Q1: What did GEM bring to you?
- Q2: Could you compare GEM to other knowledge elicitation methods (inteviews, questionnaires, field studies, classical engineering analysis)?
- Q3: What are the positive attributes of GEM (e.g., rapidity, creativity, efficiency, productivity, formal aspect, cooperative aspect)?
- Q4: What are the negative attributes of GEM (e.g., brainwriting procedure, influence of the knowledge elicitation facilitator, non transparency of consensus calculations, shallow knowledge elicited)?
- Q5: What do you find useful and unique about GEM?
- Q6: In which kind of task would you recommend the use of GEM (e.g., requirement gathering, design, development, training, maintenance, marketing)?
- Q7: Which phase of GEM would you improve first?
- Q8: What should the knowledge elicitation facilitator know (e.g., domain, task, problem, GEM)?
- Q9: If this method was chosen by your organization, would you recommend training a knowledge elicitation facilitator to use it?
- Q10: Would you reuse GEM by yourself as a knowledge elicitation facilitator?
- Q11: Would you advertize this method to your colleagues?
- Q12: Do you think that an extended computer-supported GEM would improve the current paper-supported GEM? Why?

The main advantages and flaws of GEM are discussed using the answers to the above questions along four dimensions:

- design as collaborative writing;
- analytical and learning process;
- GEM as a semi-formal mediating decision support;
- the social construction of knowledge (Barrett, 1992).

4.1 Design as collaborative writing

Writing has several advantages as well as drawbacks. Participants involved in a GEM experiment, casually write short statements that usually include stronger viewpoints than if they were giving the same information orally. Generated viewpoints are more or less specific episodes that can be subsequently endorsed or contradicted.

Sometimes there are problems due to the fact that people cannot understand other participant's handwriting. This flaw supports the decision to develop an extended computer-supported GEM (see section 5). They may interpret other participant's arguments incorrectly. This flaw is eventually corrected during the reformulation phase. By trying to understand each other's terminology and conceptual analyses, participants incrementally construct and agree on an ontology of the domain. As the GEM progresses in time, participants start to write for the others instead of writing for themselves by adapting their own language to what they have just read. This is called *empathy* [7], i.e., participants need to understand the needs and abilities of others if they want to communicate. The difference between talking and writing lies in the fact that they have more time and opportunity to express their viewpoints in an undisturbed atmosphere. The properties described in this section are strongly supported by the answers of the particpants to questions Q1, Q4 and Q7.

4.2 Analytical and learning process

During the viewpoint generation phase, by reading each others' statements, each participant allows his/her attention to be focused on the precise details of the argumentation. This *read and write* dialogue also involves both event-driven reactive behavior and reflective/deliberative behavior. In any case, the fact that people need to read involves cognitive processes of interpretation, understanding and reformulation. These are typical analytical processes. Positive reinforcement contributes to the validity of the viewpoint. A negative statement or refutation provides an alternative view. This alternative view is usually due to either a different background (the interpretation is different because the participant does not have the same knowledge as the originator of the initial viewpoint), or a different perspective (even if the current participant has the same knowledge as the viewpiont generator, he/she does not have the same data/information). This is endorsed by the answers to questions Q2 and Q3. In particular, 76% of the answers to Q3 support the cooperative aspect of GEM.

In this context, it is possible to talk about a logic of *discovery*. The indeterminate nature of the result of interactions between the participants as rational agents (*ratification* effect) creates a situation of investigation and confrontation of knowledge. By reading each others' statements and, in the later phases of GEM, by visualizing conceptual structures that the group generates, participants re-examine their own knowledge. The resulting effect is a crucial added value of GEM: participants learn, and subsequently are more motivated to accept the result. This was observed in each GEM experiment that we carried out and confirmed by the answers to Q5. In the beginning, most participants were very skeptical about the use of GEM since they thought that they could not come to an agreement with each other. GEM not only provided a consensus derived according to normative parameters such as MP, C, D, and GC, but also an indisputable written agreement. All groups were very motivated and enthusiastic after each GEM experiment (answers to questions Q10 and Q11). Team building is a meeting activity that we found important in multi-expert knowledge acquisition to further guarantee the social recognition of elicited knowledge (this is supported by answers to Q1).

4.3 GEM as a group knowledge design process

Visual feedback enables participants to explicitly perceive the course of the *knowledge design process*. Participants see the viewpoint generation as a sequential process, i.e., they generate their own viewpoints and react to each other's viewpoints using the sequentiality of writing. It is also a parallel process since all participants generate viewpoints at the same time (reducing elicitation time). The difference between a regular meeting and this phase is that the participants discuss viewpoints that are already explicitly expressed. The ontology of the domain that is explored has been cognitively constructed by reading and writing. This is extremely different from verbal expression of the same viewpoints; verbal expression is usually ephemeral.

GEM is based on social interactions mediated by an incrementally-constructed shared memory (from answers to Q5 and Q12). During the generation phase, participants are collaboratively involved in a creative activity using the sheets that are progressively filled in. During the reformulation phase, they cluster the viewpoints into concepts that are compared during the relation generation phase. The GEM can be seen as a decision making process among generated concepts. Generated concepts are *good enough* solutions that are accepted by the participants. Consensus ratings are computed and used as mediating relative trends to guide designers and evaluators in their final decision-making process.

> "It is obviously impossible for the individual to know 'all' his/her alternatives or 'all' their consequences, and this impossibility is a very important departure of actual behavior from the model of objective rationality." (Simon, 1976— cited in Winograd & Flores, 1986, page 21).

During the generation of relationships between concepts, participants may introduce inconsistencies such as concept 1 more important than concept 2, concept 2 more important than concept 3, and concept 1 less important than concept 3 (as expressed in answers to Q4). This is usually due to the fact that participants do not have the same priority attributes in mind when they compare two concepts and then two others. Experience shows that the number of generated inconsistencies is usually small, and that GEM experiments tend to converge towards satisfactory results, i.e., globally accepted by the participants during phase 6 of GEM. *Inconsistency checking* can be extremely useful to measure the validity of the results. This is actually achieved using the mean priority deviation D.

4.4 The social construction of knowledge

As Winograd and Flores (1986) stated, the rationalistic view of cognition is individual-centered. Using GEM, several viewpoints on a given issue can be generated, cross-referenced, and refined. They are incrementally reformulated and structured into concepts. These concepts are socially constructed as written objects seen from different viewpoints. They can be used either as a basis for argument or taken for granted.

GEM differs from personal construct theory methods (Kelly, 1955) that resulted in the incorporation of repertory grids as a major elicitation technique (Shaw & Gaines, 1993; Boose, 1984). Although GEM recognizes Kelly's dichotomy corollary that, "A person's construction system is composed of a finite number of dichotomous constructs" (in Shaw & Gaines, 1993), and tries to represent the hierarchical structure of Kelly's organization corollary that, "Each person characteristically evolves, for his convenience of anticipating events, a construction system embracing ordinal relationships between constructs". Unlike repertory grid methods, GEM does not attempt to characterize the ordinal relationship types (internal attributes). Instead, each priority matrix (see Table 1) represents a set of personal relationships (external attributes that need to be further determined by eliciting relevant attributes of each participant). In other words, instead of asking one participant to elicit explicit distinctions between concepts (internal attributes as semantic descriptors), GEM attempts to elicit individual ordinal relationships. These relationships may be typed by an examination of participants' profiles (external attributes as viewpoints or pragmatic context). This examination is usually done during the critical analysis of the results (phase 6).

We elicited several criteria that were used for such a construction of knowledge (during the reformulation phase):

- *Simplicity*. For reasons of comprehensibility, if the expression of a concept is too complex, it must be split into several simpler concepts. The simplicity of a concept is usually a function of the number of viewpoints that generated it.
- *Interest*. The interest of the participants in a concept is provided by the number of positive reinforcements of its various viewpoints. It may be considered also to be inversely proportional to the number of its strongly contradicted viewpoints.
- *Robustness*. The robustness of a concept is a measure of how much the participants support it. This, in turn, depends on the robustness of the initial viewpoints and backgrounds of the participants.
- *Corroboration*. By corroboration, we mean validation by exterior knowledge which is provided during reformulation discussions. We here consider that a concept is corroborated if other concepts reinforce its constituting viewpoints.

GEM is both creative and normative (supported by answers to Q1). It is creative in that it enables the participants to generate new ideas that would not be possible to capture using a questionnaire. It is normative due to the consensus process generated. In particular, the normative aspect of GEM comes from the integration of a voting mechanism (generation of relationships between concepts), a concept clustering technique for reformulating viewpoints as concepts, a consensus formula based on priority matrices, and priority parameters that provide guidance in the elicitation/decision-making process. Following the answers to Q8, Q9 and Q10, and our own experience, a good knowledge elicitation facilitator must have implemented GEM a few times in order to get a reasonable grasp of the tool.

5 On-Going Research

5.1 Extended computer-supported GEM

GEM has been upgraded using communication types similar to Flores et al' (1987) types used in the *Coordinator*. The *Coordinator* (Flores et al., 1988) was a computer-mediated communication system that supported dialogue in the form of explicit speech acts (Winograd & Flores, 1986). By providing explicit communication types, the *Coordinator* overcame weaknesses in communication by making people aware of the nature of their transactions. Even if the *Coordinator* provided a framework too strict for dialogue, explicit types such as endorse, contradict (background), contradict (perspective), new viewpoint, enable a first raw categorization of viewpoints generated during the second phase (brainwriting) of GEM. Other categories can be added of course. The current prototype is implemented using Hypercard stacks. Each participant faces a stack of GEM sheets (cards) where he/she can enter his/her viewpoints. Each card is equiped with a menu of default communication types that may or may not be used and/or modified.

5.2 Enhanced hypertextual elicited knowedge

Viewpoints generated in phase 2 of GEM are hypertext nodes related to each other by typed links described in section 5.3. We have adapted the CID system (Boy, 1991) to describe each viewpoint using descriptors. New links can be derived between viewpoints using these descriptors as semantic relationships. We have shown in previous work that CID is a good tool to semantically correlate hypertext nodes (Boy, 1992). Using this technique, the elicitation of concepts is much improved (phase 3 of GEM). We have recently used it to correlate GEM results from five groups (50 partcipants all together). This exercise has shown the feasibility of such an approach. Once each concept has been derived, it is described by its various viewpoints. A new hypertext structure is then developed from the results of phase 4 of GEM where the nodes are concepts, and links are consensual relationships between concepts. The degree of consensus of a relationship depends on the degree of reinforcement provided by the group. The more a relationship is consensual, the more it can be considered as an attribute of the related concepts. Phase 6 of GEM usually enables the participants to elicit this attribute. If a concept is not linked to any other concepts (see Figure 3), one can consider that the criteria of importance is not explicit enough to characterize the relationship. It follows that such a concept needs to be analyzed in more detail.

The extended computer-supported GEM (ECS-GEM) is comparable to systems such as VisionQuest developed by Collaborative Technologies, the Capture Lab developed by EDS or the Facilitator developed by Qsoft (Neal & Mantei, 1993). In addition to these existing systems, GEM properties elicited in section 4 have guided the design of ECS-GEM.

6 Conclusion

This paper presents the *Group Elicitation Method* (GEM) that has been extensively used for user interface design or evaluation taking into account various viewpoints of a group of potential users. GEM facilitates the gathering of people with very different backgrounds. Compared to other methods such as structured or prompted interviews, card sorting or twenty questions (Tognazzini, 1992), GEM integrates group meeting properties, analytical benefits of writing and computer-supported decision-making guidance (Neal & Mantei, 1993). A GEM session takes a full day. This is a great advantage since results can be assessed directly, and expert end-users are extremely difficult to gather together for design or evaluation purposes.

As a decision support tool, GEM can be used for design as well as for evaluation. Even if we have used GEM for the design of new systems, we have observed that it would be useful for evaluating existing systems and suggesting alternatives.

We have observed that GEM is a method that relies on the skills and the expertise of a knowledge elicitation facilitator during the reformulation phase. In other words, one must learn to use it before applying it to complex cases. A checklist is proposed to state the issue to be investigated. Four types of operations are provided to guide the reformulation of viewpoints into concepts. GEM currently uses a minimal set of computer programs that help the knowledge elicitation facilitator to suggest directions in the knowledge design process. Derived concepts charts and tables using typical parameters such as mean priority, inter-participant consistency, stability of a concept, and global consensus, provide relative trends and a basis for problem solving and decision making.

A question that arises from these experiments concerns the *full* computerization of the method. The extended computer-supported GEM qualifies for being a full *group support system* (GSS). McLeod (1992) defines a GSS as an "interactive computer-based system that combines communication, computer and decision technologies to support problem formulation and solutions in group meetings." GEM uses decision technology to support problem formulation and solutions in a brainwriting meeting environment. We have already developed a system that meets all these requirements. Industry people still prefer to write on paper using a pen, and to have the knowledge elicitation facilitator write on a white board and interact with them directly. The aim of our current research is to investigate new computer tools that will integrate these requirements, in particular the impression of the physical presence of the other participants and the facilitator.

Acknowledgements

Many people contributed to the current state of the GEM. Among them, I owe thanks to Catherine Logé who helped me develop the first version of the GEM assistance programs, Rosel Schmengler who strongly encouraged the use of GEM at Air France for an innovative experiment, Jean-Pierre Daniel who helped me organize several GEM experiments at Aerospatiale on the assessment of the use of electronic mail and the development of a corporate memory, Jean-François Schmidt of Airbus Training who provided us with a very interesting application on the redesign of an instructor workstation, the FANSTIC group that participated in the work that is illustrated here, and all the participants of various GEM experiments that were and will be carried out for the improvement the method. Alfred Attipoe, Markus Durstewitz, Martin Hollender, Rachel Israel, Laurent Karsenty, Helen Wilson and anonymous reviewers provided astute advice towards improving the quality of this paper.

References

Barrett, E. (1992). Sociomedia—*The Social Creation of Knowledge.* MIT Press Book.

Boose, J.H. (1984). Personal construct theory and the transfer of human expertise. *AAAI-84 Proceedings.* pp. 27-33. California: American Association for Artificial Intelligence.

Boy, G.A. (1991). *Intelligent Assistant System.* Textbook. Published by Academic Press, London.

Boy, G.A. (1991). Indexing Hypertext Documents in Context. Proceedings *of the Hypertext'91 Conference*, San Antonio, Texas, December.

Boy, G.A. (1992). Semantic correlation in context: Application in document comparison and group knowledge design. *Proceedings AAAI Spring Symposium on Cognitive Aspects of Knowledge Acquisition.* J.H. Boose, W. Clancey, B. Gaines & A. Rappaport (Eds.). Stanford University, CA, USA.

Fisher, D.H. (1987). Knowledge Acquisition via Incremental Conceptual Clustering. *Machine Learning*, 2, pp. 139-172.

Flores, F., Graves, M., Hartfield, B. & Winograd, T. (1988). Computer systems and the design of organizational interaction. *ACM Transactions on Office Information Systems*, 6 (2), pp. 153-172.

Kelly, G.A. (1955). *The Psychology of Personal Constructs*. New York: Norton.

McLeod, P.L. (1992). An assessment of experimental literature on electronic support of group work: Results of a meta-analysis. *Human-Computer Interaction*, 7, pp. 257-280.

Neal, L. & Mantei, M. (1993). Computer-Supported Meeting Environments. Tutorial Notes. *Conference on Human Factors in Computing Systems, INTERCHI'93*. Amsterdam, The Netherlands.

Newell, A. & Simon, H.A. (1972). *Human Problem Solving*, Englewood Cliffs, N.J., Prentice Hall.

Nielsen, J., Mack, R.B., Bergendorff, K.H. & Grischlowsky, N.L. (1986). Integrated software usage in the professional work environment: evidence from questionnaires and interviews. In *Human Factors in Computing Systems, CHI'86 Conference Proceedings*, Mantei M. and Oberton P. (Eds.), pp. 162-167. New York: ACM Press.

Norman, D.A. (1992). *Turn signals are facial expressions of automobiles*. Addison-Wesley Publishing Company, Reading, MA.

Shaw, L.G. & Gaines, B.R. (19993). Personal construct psychology foundations for knowledge acquisition and representation. *Knowledge Aquisition for Knowledge-Base Systems. EKAW'93 Proceedings.* N. Aussenac, G. Boy et al. (Eds.). pp. 256-276. Berlin: Springer-Verlag.

Tognazzini, B. (1992). *Tog on interface*. Addison-Wesley Publishing Company, Inc. Reading, MA.

Warfield, J.N. (1971). *Societal Systems: Planning, Policy and Complexity*. Wiley, New York.

Welbank, M. (1990). An overview of knowledge acquisition methods. *Interacting with Computers*, 2 (1), pp. 83-91.

Winograd, T. & Flores, F. (1986). *Understanding computers and cognition-A new foundation for design*. Addison-Wesley Pub. Comp., Inc. Reading, MA.

Appendix - Example of a list of concepts and viewpoints on air traffic management (ATM) functions elicited from a group of nine experts in the Aeronautical domain

Concept 1. *Party-line evolution with datalink (D/L)*
- Party line (i.e., pilots can hear radio messages from other pilots and controllers) is an advantage in current ATM. How to keep party line with D/L?
- Acknowledgments. Intelligent message filter

Concept 2. *One (English) or more languages*
- Language concerns: some pilots only speak English (do not write or read)
- But D/L could help here; people often understand writing better than speech
- D/L can provide multi-language data bases
- Standardization, adherence to standard terminology checked by a computer

Concept 3. *Lack of system transparency in glass cockpit*
- Overload of visual perception channels with new technologies in high-workload situations (time pressure)
- New technology tends to load/overload visual perception channels

- Lack of sensory feedback in glass cockpit
- Get the picture of the whole

Concept 4. *VHF technological limitations*
- Misunderstanding in current very high frequency (VHF) communications
- Unload the burden of removing the noise from messages
- Limited bandwidth
- Necessity of waiting for availability of the channel (safety limitation)

Concept 5. *Intention sharing problem between human agents*
- Synthetic voice generator
- Message acknowledgment aid. In all cases, pilots and copilo ts need to cross-check all the time (cockpit resource management).Yet again another system!

Concept 6. *Priority assignment*
- D/L provides parallelism in information transfer
- New procedures in crew communications
- Synchronous versus asynchronous message transmission
- Situations needing quick responses? Intelligent message filter

Concept 7. *Who is the boss: air traffic control (ATC), captain or machine ?*
- Complexity of ATM planning, replanning
- Confidence in technology

Concept 8. *Localization of the airplane within the airplane*
- Easier with automatic down-link system
- Know the identity of neighboring aircraft
- Proximity warning system versus advice from ATC
- Current datalink systems (e.g., TCAS) may give conflicting commands

Concept 9. *Keep VHF in any case*
- Oral communication must be kept
- Voice creates situation awareness? (contested)
- Degraded mode, urgency
- When context is essential
- Increase the redundancy

Concept 10. *Late flight plan change*
- Voice communication remains the last

Concept 11. Normal and abnormal messages precoded
- Very few procedures available for abnormal situations (need to be learned)

Concept 12. *Evolution of traffic growth*
- Difficulty of adaptation of traffic growth
- D/L systems: from current limited capacity to higher capacity
- Adaptation to the congestion of the area

Concept 13. *Head-up versus head-down flight control and management*
- Risk of head down piloting with D/L

Concept 14. *Written interaction*
- Written language can introduce confusions such as misreading, typos...
- Confusing if pilots and controllers communicate in different languages
- Add very good acknowledgment messages

Formalising the Repair of Schedules Through Knowledge Acquisition

Janet Efstathiou

Department of Engineering Science, University of Oxford, Oxford OX1 3PJ, UK

Abstract. The generation and repair of schedules in the dynamic environment of a major UK automobile manufacturer provided challenging a testbed for real-time tools to support the schedulers. A tool was developed, described in the paper, featuring a distinction between schedule assessment and amendment, together with heuristic methods for dynamic iterative schedule repair. Some lessons were learnt on acquiring and structuring heuristic knowledge in these circumstances, with a view to selecting dynamically between the schedule repair heuristics. The paper concludes with a call for dynamic tools to assist the operators in a continued search for better understanding of their manufacturing processes and the impact of schedule changes.

1 Introduction

Manufacturing industry does not obey the tidy world assumptions usually explained at the outset of academic papers on schedule optimisation. In fact, real scheduling means having to cope with faulty materials, machines that break down, customers who change their minds and staff who go absent. These problems always occur at least some of the time, and so human schedulers need to have ways of repairing their schedules when things go wrong.

Human experts are already well skilled in repairing schedules to meet a number of goals simultaneously. If some of their methods could be captured and formalised into computer programs, then more effective and controlled time-dependent responses could be provided for schedule repair problems.

This paper describes some work done in collaboration with Rover Body and Pressings to uncover the methods employed by human schedulers to repair and amend schedules and to develop software which would support them in this task. This revealed a preference ordering over the schedule repair heuristics, which could be exploited to develop a simple deliberation algorithm.

The remainder of this paper is organised as follows. Section 2 describes some of the approaches to scheduling emerging in the literature, with reference to knowledge-based approahces. Section 3 describes the industrial collaborator, Rover Body and Pressings, with whom this project was carried out. Sections 4 and 5 describe the tools which were constructed to help understand the domain of schedule repair and the knowledge acquisition methods. Section 6 shows how the heuristics may be formalised and section 7 outlines a simple deliberation algorithm which may be used to support the automatic repair of schedules. Sections 8 and 9 discuss further how the generation and repair of schedules may be represented as the combination of user and computer, and how the tools should be flexible enough to capture the constantly evolving complexity of the factory and its environment. Section 10 concludes with a summary and ideas for further work.

2 Background

The traditional OR (Operations Research) approach to scheduling is being challenged by new approaches to managing schedules dynamically, arising principally from within the Artificial Intelligence community. Beck [1] listed several options for schedule repair and, earlier, Bona et al [2] listed schedule repair operations specifically for a press shop. Zweben [15] uses a method of iterative repair, where a complete but flawed schedule is improved with the help of a simulated annealing algorithm. Major work on schedule generation and maintenance has been carried out at Carnegie-Mellon, principally with the OPIS scheduler [13], the Cortes project [14] and the Coral project [12] for resource allocation. DAS (Distributed Asynchronous Scheduling) is an implementation of a generic scheduling methodology developed by Burke, Prosser and others at the University of Strathclyde (See [3, 4, 11]).

Within the literature on optimisation and comparison of heuristics, an alternative literature is beginning to emerge with a different focus – on the people who generate and maintain schedules. For example, the human-centred aspects of scheduling are considered in [8] who approach scheduling as a decision support problem, placing the operators at the centre of the scheduling task. They identify problem-solving tactics similar to those incorporated in the heuristics which will be described below. Through their work on case studies of actual scheduling practice, Little and Hemmings [9] emphasise the need for flexibility in scheduling and work management, either through high levels of control or intelligence in the workstations. Interrante and Rochowiak [6] focus on group scheduling in a dynamic workplace where communication between individuals and scheduling agents is important. McKay, Safayeni and Buzacott [10] emphasise the complex nature of the factory and the many social and organisational factors which contribute to the schedulers' tasks.

The combination of the entry of knowledge-based techniques into scheduling, together with the growing awareness of schedule generation and maintenance as a complex, social task, has brought the needs of the scheduler to the forefront. Knowledge should be acquired, not only for representation in the computer support provided to the operator, but also to enable the operator to learn more about the domain. This is consistent with the now established management philosophies of Total Quality and Just in Time jit, which lay emphasis on empowering and granting responsibility to the workers for the continual improvement of their own performance and that of their team.

3   Description of Domain

It would be possible to generate a complete new schedule each time a problem occurs, but that would mean that neither work force nor customers would know exactly what would be supposed to happen any time ahead, since a reschedule could occur at any time. Paying attention to the jobs already promised and under way means that rather than re-schedule, schedule repair could adjust the resources and tasks to accommodate as best as possible the required changes.

Another important requirement of scheduling in manufacturing is that schedule repairs must be carried out in a predictable amount of time. The time constraint is very important, since the cost to the factory of delivering late to a customer, in terms of damage to reputation as well as financial penalties particularly in a Just In Time domain, is much higher than the cost of holding some stock that an optimal program would declare to be unnecessary. Under Just in Time customer-supplier agreements, penalty clauses in contracts specify the fine that a manufacturer must pay their customers if they fail to deliver the specified goods at the specified time. These clauses can make people very anxious about not wasting time on overly fussy schedule repair. Satisficing is the main thing, rather than optimising.

This project was performed in collaboration with the Tri-Axis facility of Rover Body and Pressings in Swindon, UK. This facility is a large press capable of loading four pairs of dies simultaneously. Sheets of metal, cut to the required shape and size, are fed in at one end and fully formed metal panels emerge from the other. Set up time for the press is short, about 5 minutes. This is achieved by loading the next set of dies on tracks and preparing them for the press. When the current job is completed, the current dies are wheeled out and the new set of dies is wheeled into the press and prepared for running.

During the period of this project, the two Tri-Axis presses would be expected to manufacture up to about 80 different panels, in lot sizes from about 50 up to 2000. The panels were large car body parts, such as monosides (a car side panel from front to rear bumpers), door skins, door inners, bonnets, roofs and boots. Because many of these parts formed the outer skin of the car, the quality standards which were expected of the parts was very high. Deviations of a few microns in the surface appearance of the panels would cause them to be rejected by the customer. Some defects could be repaired by rework, but others had to be scrapped, an expensive business for large body panels.

The press could form car body panels at a rate of between 10 and 15 per minute. Some panels, such as doors, were formed in pairs so two finished panels were formed from a single blank sheet of metal. Finished panels were stored carefully in specially constructed pallets. This rate of production of large items meant that storage space would be filled very quickly. Deliveries of finished goods left several times a day to the customers' factories, so there was a rapid turnover of finished goods, which was necessary since the available storage space would have been quickly filled otherwise.

Raw materials were delivered to the facility as coils of steel, weighing from 10 to 20 tonnes each, on the day before a job was scheduled to be blanked, or cut into sheets of the required size. Steel was ordered from the supplier for a particular part, since the chemical content, thickness, surface finish and other properties were specified for each part. A coil of steel would be cut into blanks for the designated part on the day following delivery from the steel supplier and the job would expect to run on the day after. Finished goods would not remain on site for more than two days after forming.

The operation was fairly smooth running in theory, but the spare time between blanking, forming and despatch allowed leeway should anything go wrong. In fact, things did go wrong from time to time, and it was down to the human scheduler to cope as problems arose.

The human scheduler uses a semi-automated spreadsheet to collate the predicted stock levels for the end of the week with the shipping requirements for the two weeks ahead. Job lots are inserted into the schedules as stock levels are predicted to fall below the safety stock level designated for each part. Lot sizes are fixed for each part. The human scheduler must check that enough capacity is available each day for the required jobs to be completed on time. He must also order raw materials and receive requests from customers for changes to the parts or changes to delivery times. If any dies or the press fail or require urgent maintenance, he must adjust the existing schedule to cope with these demands as far as possible. As jobs are completed, the actual lot size must be updated in the spreadsheet and checks made to see whether the next planned job for that part must be adjusted. If a job takes longer than scheduled to complete the run, the times must be checked to see how seriously any other urgent jobs have been delayed. Furthermore, at any time a sizeable proportion of the parts were on try out, i.e. they were new dies that were being tested to see whether they conformed to the specifications on shape of the finished panel and whether the dies were operating well enough to participate in volume production.

A considerable amount of schedule disruption occurs. Data was gathered at the end of each week on the adherence of actual jobs to the jobs that had been planned at the start of the week. This data covered only the actual lot sizes and the days on which they were run, rather than the actual times. The data was analysed to calculate a lower bound for the number of change operations which were performed each week. A change operation is defined as a job cancellation, or a new job inserted to the schedule, a job moved early or late, or when the actual lot size deviates from the planned lot size by more than plus or minus 10%. Since the data were recorded at the end of the week and compared with the schedule prepared at the start of the week, any intermediate changes were obscured, so the lower bound to the number of schedule change operations only could be obtained. This showed that the human scheduler would be required to adapt the schedule about once each hour. This was confirmed through observation and interview, where schedule monitoring was described as a constant task.

Much time was spent with the human scheduler, observing how schedules were generated and repaired. The scheduler followed some quite subtle strategies for schedule repair. An example from part of a schedule is shown in Table 1 below. The job for part A on Tuesday was too large and was split in two, with 1600 running early on Monday and 2200 on Wednesday. This part runs regularly, once every two or three days, with a preference for a lot size of 2000 or more. Hence, it was desirable to run two jobs with the total production exceeding the original job. To make room for the new job on Monday, the planned job for part C was moved one day later to Tuesday and increased in size to fill partly the available capacity. To accommodate the new job on Wednesday, the original job for part B was moved one day later to Thursday.

This example occurred during early days in the life of the Tri-Axis press. Although this example covers only three parts from a schedule with many other parts as well, it does illustrate that there was spare capacity available and that jobs were not scheduled very close to the stock out date. This allows jobs to be moved safely one day later if pressure arises from other jobs, as happened with part B. The example does illustrate how schedule repair can become complex, involving more than one job to complete a repair. It ought to be stressed, however, that this was unusually complex for the time. The amount of capacity available meant that most of the repairs involved changes to one or two jobs only.

The complexity of the schedule amendment operations can be quite high, as shown by this example. This kind of operation would have only been possible under conditions when there was capacity available in the system and deadlines were not very tight. As the workload on the system increased, and the frequency of schedule repair became higher, so the schedule amendment operations tended to become more short term. The predictability of the system decreased because of the high probability of change occurring, either due to customer requests or internal problems. Because of the short horizon, it was not worth amending the schedule well in advance, since it was likely other changes would occur or be made. Hence, under greater workload, the schedule amendment operations tended to be simpler and more short term.

Table 1. Table 1. Example of how a schedule may be amended, (a) original schedule and (b) after amendment.

(a) Original schedule

Parts	Mon	Tue	Wed	Thurs
A		2500		
B			2200	
C	650			

(b) Amended schedule

Parts	Mon	Tue	Wed	Thurs
A	1600		2200	
B				2200
C	1000			

4 Description of Tools and Tethods

In order to study closely the schedule repair heuristics, a suite of software was designed and built, based upon the Excel 5 spreadsheet package which was in use at Rover. Two menus were added to the tool bar, one covering change operations and the other identifying useful data items which were frequently used in deciding whether and how to amend the schedule.

One menu, Amend Schedule, contained the change operations mentioned briefly in the previous section. These were elaborated as:

1. insert a job,
2. cancel a job,
3. move a job early,
4. move a job late,
5. increase lot size and
6. decrease lot size.

The Amend Schedule menu was equipped with macros to perform these tasks when a user moved the cursor to a job and selected one of the items from the menu.

In addition to performing the requested schedule adjustment, the software also recorded the task which was performed and its effects on certain crucial items of data on the schedule. Enough data was recorded to enable the amendment to be undone if the user should change his/her mind. The time at the start and the end of the change operation was recorded too. This enabled an estimate of the processing time involved in making the change and the thinking time prior to the change. A sample from the results table is shown in Figure 1. This also indicates that the column recording the type of change made was colour coded. This was very useful and provided an easy visual identification of the pattern of changes made, useful later in comparing the performance of the heuristic methods.

One of the crucial points about the scheduling support was the dynamic assessment of the schedule. The operators had already developed some assessment of their schedules, but this was extended to give a number of data items relating to performance of the press each day and for each part, as well as some global measures of schedule quality. The schedule assessment could be easily performed and displayed using a spreadsheet, but as the number of interesting data items grew, so it became more difficult to access them. Remember too that the number of parts to be scheduled increased and the scheduling horizon was extended, which also added to the difficulty of moving around the spreadsheet to find the required data item.

This problem was solved by adding the second menu which could call up some of the most important data items on the schedule. These are listed in Table 2 for the current version of the software. It can be seen from the table that the data items are grouped as global (i.e. referring to the whole schedule), by part (i.e. covering all the jobs and stock for the selected part), and by day (covering all the jobs for the selected day).

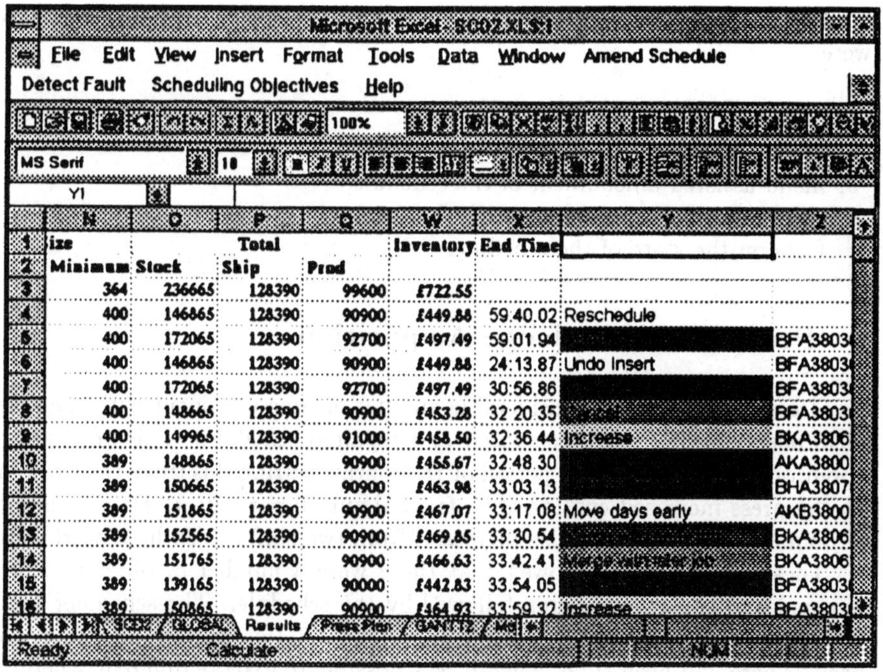

	N	O	P	Q	W	X	Y	Z
1	ize		Total		Inventory	End Time		
2	Minimum	Stock	Ship	Prod				
3	364	236665	128390	99600	£722.55			
4	400	146865	128390	90900	£449.86	59.40.02	Reschedule	
5	400	172065	128390	92700	£497.49	59:01.94		BFA3803
6	400	146865	128390	90900	£449.86	24:13.87	Undo Insert	BFA3803
7	400	172065	128390	92700	£497.49	30:56.86		BFA3803
8	400	148665	128390	90900	£453.28	32:20.35	Cancel	BFA3803
9	400	149965	128390	91000	£458.50	32:36.44	Increase	BKA3806
10	389	148865	128390	90900	£455.67	32:48.30		AKA3800
11	389	150665	128390	90900	£463.96	33:03.13		BHA3807
12	389	151865	128390	90900	£467.07	33:17.08	Move days early	AKB3800
13	389	152565	128390	90900	£469.85	33.30.54		BKA3806
14	389	151765	128390	90900	£466.63	33.42.41	Merge with later job	BKA3806
15	389	139165	128390	90000	£442.83	33.54.05		BFA3803
16	389	150865	128390	90900	£464.93	33:59.32	Increase	BFA3803

Fig. 1. Part of the Results file, showing some of the columns of data recorded together with the job changes.

Table 2. Data items available under Detect Fault menu.

Stockouts
Capacity
Maximum Imbalance
Minimum Imbalance
Largest Lot Size
Smallest Lot Size
Maximum Stock to Ship
Max Stock to Av Ship
Maximum Part Stock
Today's most urgent job
Next most urgent job
Today's least urgent job
Today's most postponable job
Today's most reducible job
Next earlier job
Next later job
Stockout time

The tools which were available, therefore, to assist knowledge acquisition were:

1. dynamic assessment of the schedule,
2. menu assistance for schedule assessment,
3. menu-assisted amendment of the schedule,
4. recording of all menu-driven schedule amendment operations, with their effects on the state of the schedule.

5 Process of Knowledge Acquisition

As already mentioned, a considerable amount of time was spent with the schedulers observing how they generated and repaired schedules. This amounted to about one day a week over a period of 18 months. During this time, the work load on the press increased considerably, from about 20 parts up to 80. The number of hours worked per week also increased from two shifts to 24 hour working.

These investigations showed that there were a number of objectives being pursued and constraints being followed by the scheduler. The scheduler's work pressure varied considerably during the course of this project and on a daily basis. There had been times when it was possible to explore different scheduling strategies in a fairly thoughtful manner, but when the work load on the press was higher, and capacity became a tight constraint, so there was less opportunity for exploring the schedule and a much greater emphasis on coping with the problems as they occurred.

Some software was written to model the schedule generation methods used at Tri-Axis, but it quickly became apparent that schedule repair played an important part in the working routine. A schedule would be generated on Saturday, but that could be amended approximately hourly during the working week. A trade-off became obvious between the complexity of the schedule generation algorithm and the flexibility of schedule amendment and repair. This point will be discussed again in sections 8 and 9.

It was not possible to record the operators in extended schedule repair sessions, so instead the repair process was investigated by the author performing extended schedule repair sessions on buggy schedules. Clearly, this will distort the conclusions, but some useful insights may still be obtained.

Buggy schedules were created and repaired manually in extended sessions, to explore the change in objectives and constraints which occur when a very poor schedule is repaired to one which achieves one or more objectives. A schedule would be created where new jobs could not be inserted until the existing stock for each part had dropped below that required for one day. This would typically lead to a schedule with many parts running out of stock, since there would not be enough capacity available to run all the required jobs each day to their usual lot size. This schedule could be repaired first by removing stockouts as far as possible. Once that had been achieved, it might be desirable to remove very large lots for parts with a relatively low demand for the duration of the schedule.

This might create a few stockouts, but these can be repaired by exploiting the capacity made available when the larger lots were reduced.

As well as tracking by software the schedule repair, written notes were made on the reasoning processes involved in choosing which objective to pursue and which amendment to perform. The operators at Rover were too busy and distracted to be able to sit down and carry out extended schedule repair tasks, so the data had to be gathered by the author from her own efforts to repair typical manufacturing schedules back at the University.

6   Formalising Heuristics

Once some observations had been obtained, it was possible to attempt to model the schedule repair process by writing and executing schedule repair heuristics. A number of objectives were selected and for each at least two anytime heuristics were prepared. A third menu, Scheduling Objectives, was added to the spreadsheet listing the selected objectives. These were:

1. Remove Stockouts
2. Reduce Maximum Imbalance
3. Improve Minimum Imbalance
4. Reduce Stock Holdings
5. Reduce Job Count
6. Reduce Average Lot Size

A number of heuristics were written for each of the objectives listed above. Some patterns emerged in the structure of heuristics which suggested some general principles of designing and writing heuristics.

First of all, the anytime design constraint meant that the heuristics had to repair the earliest fault in the schedule first. This could cause the schedule to be less than optimal, but the time penalties associated with slower but optimal results are too high to make the search for an optimal solution acceptable. Furthermore, work which is done to repair faults a long time from the present is likely to be undone again when the next repair is required, given the frequency of schedule repair, which was measured to occur about once per hour. But most importantly, the urgency of the work is sufficient that the most imminent jobs should be repaired first. Circumstances will change again in the future, causing repairs at points later in the schedule to be undone.

Another important reason for this pattern was that the heuristics had to be interruptible, with a partial solution available no matter when the heuristic was interrupted. Hence, the solution algorithm had to be incremental in nature, with a partial solution available at any time.

Another design choice in the heuristics was whether to keep to the preferred lot sizing policy as far as possible or to ignore it and insert small jobs where this would alleviate a problem. Another option is to amend repeatedly the standard lot sizes by a small amount until the objective is achieved or failure apparent.

This dilemma was resolved by making a preference for using standard lot sizes whenever possible. This gave rise to a more general principle of avoiding disruption to the existing schedule and schedule generation policy.

There is always a temptation to cover all possible cases and to make the calculation as accurate as possible. However, in real-time problems, this might lead to overly slow algorithms with a minor improvement in accuracy achieved. For the highly dynamic situations in the factory, the chosen policy was to write simpler heuristics, since this would be more likely to improve the time performance of the algorithms. Clearly, this decision could be subject to closer scrutiny with the help of simulations.

Related to the point in the previous paragraph, the complexity of the heuristics can be limited by choosing carefully how many objectives or constraints each heuristic should meet. Indeed, the heuristics may be differentiated according to the number of constraints or objectives they obey. This leads to a family of heuristics being possible for each objective.

Given that a number of heuristics may be written for a given objective, a partial ordering may be constructed over the heuristics according to the constraints and objectives they meet. It is postulated that this ordering is closely related to the preference ordering over the objectives and constraints. The mechanism is as follows. Since many constraints may be obeyed, it would be possible to construct a hierarchy of heuristics, with several heuristics violating one constraint, several more violating two constraints and so forth. However, the fact that a partial ordering of the heuristics, rather than a hierarchy, can be constructed implies that a preference order exists over the constraints.

During the experiments on debugging the schedules, it was clear that the objective of the schedule repair would shift as the repair progressed. For example, removing stockouts would be the over-riding objective at the commencement of repair, but as this objective was almost achieved, other objectives were considered, such as removing high levels of stock. This made sense, since these subsidiary objectives could be achieved better before all the stockout removals had been achieved. This shifting of objectives is difficult to capture algorithmically, using a weighted linear combination of criteria, for example. Such a linear weighted model assumes constant trade-off between the objectives or criteria, which would not account for the changing of desired objective as a function of their level of achievement. Another method of moving through the family of heuristics associated with each objective is required, therefore. This will be discussed briefly in the next section.

7   A Simple Deliberation Algorithm

It is desired to construct a deliberation algorithm which can choose dynamically between the heuristics according to some preference ordering over the heuristics while obeying the anytime constraints of being interruptible and providing a better solution the more time is available. An algorithm was constructed which fulfils these objectives, shown in Figure 2.

The algorithm works by iterating through a sequence of heuristics until the rate of progress towards the objective has declined so much that the least constrained heuristic must be applied to achieve any further progress towards the goal. This is achieved in the algorithm of figure 2 by applying the heuristics according to a preference order until the rate of progress towards to objective is less than SOI.rate.threshold, i.e. a threshold value here at whcih the Single Objective Inserts heuristic will be invoked.

The rate of progress toward the goal is computed per change operation rather than per unit time. This has a number of advantageous effects, most importantly removing the need to assess whether the rate of progress is greater or less than would be expected for the size of job, state of the schedule and power of the computer.

Fig. 2. Simple deliberation algorithm for selecting between three remove stockout heuristics.

```
improvement.rate.threshold := 1
SOI.rate.threshold := 0.3
decrementing.factor:= 0.9

while stockouts remain and improvement.rate.threshold > SOI.rate.threshold
      while rate.of.curing.stockouts > improvement.rate.threshold
           apply Inserts heuristic
      end.while

      while rate.of.curing.stockouts > improvement.rate.threshold
           apply Looking Early heuristic
      end.while

      improvement.rate.threshold := improvement.rate.threshold * decrementing.factor
end.while

while stockouts remain
      apply Single Objective Inserts heuristic
end.while
```

8 Comparison with Expert System Approach

It is instructive to compare this approach to schedule repair with that which would be adopted under the earlier kinds of expert system approach. To summarise the main features of this approach, recall that schedule assessment is available completely separately from schedule amendment. A few basic schedule amendment operations were identified from which a suite of schedule amendment operations could be built. The separation of amendment and assessment led to the construction of families of heuristics directed towards some objective, with preference orderings existing over the families of heuristics according the obedience to constraints and other objectives. The deliberation algorithm outlined in section 7 considers the rate of achieving the objective as the means of moving to the next heuristic in the preference order.

An expert system approach would seek to formalise the scheduler's expertise as an expert system, traditionally expected to be a set of rules. In a schedule repair expert system, one might expect the antecedents of the rules to consider the state of the schedule in order to select which repair heuristic to apply. Were the antecedents to consider only the rate of repair and direct the solution method to the next heuristic in the list, this would seem contrary to the usual practice in expert systems, where the next step in the reasoning process is driven by data from the state of the world, rather than from preferences and rate of achievement.

Another difference between this approach and the expert system approach is the amount of control and support which is permitted to the user. The expert system approach often seeks to represent the complexity of the domain within the expert system, encouraging the user to produce more elaborate models of their decision-making process, which may then be represented as rules. Within the highly dynamic of the factory, the configuration of the factory is always subject to modification, which would require the computer support to be updated. Furthermore, the managerial and marketing environment within which the facotry operates is also subject to constant revision. These changes, subtle and not so subtle, have to be detected and incorporated by the human scheduler. As already mentioned, many of these circumstances are short-lived and informal and may be poorly understood. Hence, it would be difficult to represent and maintain them in an expert system.

9   Locating Complexity

The approach to schedule generation and repair which was adopted in this work was to recognise that the highly dynamic nature of the factory environment could not be modelled in a computer program, but that the entire model of the plant resided in the combination of the computer program and the human scheduler's mental model. Hence, given the changeable nature of the plant, it was better to give the operator simple, basic tools with which to understand and control the plant, but which can also be adapted to build a more complex set of tools.

The highly dynamic nature of the factory derives from the short-lived nature of the constraints which arise from day to day. Furthermore, the objectives which drive schedule generation and repair can change on both short and longer terms. In the short term, objectives can change during the course of a repair, since an objective can become less important as its target is approached, allowing another objective to be pursued. On the longer term, changes to management and planning policies can mean that the constraints and objectives can alter fundamentally. The tools for representing these changes must be flexible and easy to use.

When a model of the factory is being constructed in a software package, the design of the software package dictates what may be represented and how easy it is to change. It is debatable whether all the changes to the factory could be anticipated at the outset for including in the model. Furthermore, even if they were to be included, the model would be more difficult to construct and one could imagine that the regular verification of the model would impose a burden on the users. This would lead to errors in the model, since it would likely occur that constraints and objectives might remain in the model after their useful lifetime had ended, since it would be too difficult and complex to check them on a regular basis. It often happens that the reason for a particular decision can be so long forgotten that no-one dares to change it, even though that constraint or objective is no longer valid.

Once the highly dynamic, complex nature of the factory has been recognised [5], the factory manager has two options. Either the factory must be simplified so that a simple computer model may be constructed, or the computer model must be simplified so that it supports the mental model and understanding of the human operator.

Some complexity is desirable in the factory, since this permits flexibility and responsiveness, but it also leads to unpredictability and unreliability. Complexity in the factory may be reduced in a number of ways. For example, the number of possible routes through the factory could be severely curtailed so that parts are made only on designated "home line" and on no others. Such a decision would reduce the shceduler's flexibility in coping with problems, but the rigourous enforcement of such a rule would require the scheduler and his/her manager to address the issues which give rise to the need to move jobs away from their home line. This would increase the predictability of the factory while making it simpler and less flexible.

In the complex, evolving environment of the modern factory, where the objective is to increase quality and delight the customer in a highly competitive global marketplace, the knowledge and understanding of the environment must increase and improve continuously so that the factory can remain in business and survive. Rather than construct monolithic models of the factory, we should be creating simple, flexible, short-lived models which help the schedulers to understand more about the plant and its processes. Such an approach admits that the complexity and knowledge cannot be captured on computer but must reside at least partly in the mind of the schedulers.

In order for this knowledge to grow and improve, the organisation, be it factory, school or whatever, must provide the social, technical and training support to enable knowledge and models to be shared between members of the organisation. This will help each person's model to be challenged, criticised and extended by the knowledge and experience of others. Hence, the model will reside in the minds of many members of the organisation, as well as the computer support.

10   Discussion and Further Work

This work has shown that it is possible to use a simple structure distinguishing schedule assessment and schedule repair to assist the user in generating and repairing schedules. This structure may then be enhanced with a number of objectives, which combine the schedule amendment and assessment functions. Investigations of the schedule repair process showed that the objectives of the repair process shifted according to the level of achievement of the objectives. This suggested the need for a flexible deliberation algorithm which could obey the anytime constraint and apply iteratively the various relevant heuristics. A simple deliberation algorithm has been suggested and demonstrated. The emergence of a structure to the heuristics was exploited in the deliberation algorithm, but this suggests other exciting possibilities for generic heuristics, raising the possibility of more flexible and expressive schedule generation and repair methods.

One of the problems with scheduling is the dynamic nature of the objectives. New objectives frequently emerge which were not considered at the time of writing the package, so that there is no capability in the language to express the new objective. For example, a new requirement might be that certain jobs run only at certain times of day, or that jobs should run in a fixed sequence, or should alternate with other jobs. The structured heuristics which are have been used in this work suggest that there might be a possibility to construct generic heuristics, which could use any objective function and a generic structure, producing a family of related heuristics differing on the number of constraints which they obey. Hence, so long as an objective function could be created (as is often possible with the flexibility of the spreadsheet based interface) and constraints identified, there may be the possibility of constructing a family of generic heuristics.

The anytime problems which have been addressed in this paper permit heuristics which may be interrupted at any point and a deliberation algorithm which also has this property. A related problem is how to achieve a debugged schedule within a fixed time budget. Thus, given a fixed, known amount of time, how are the deliberation algorithm's parameters to be adjusted so that a debugged schedule can be guaranteed at the end of the time allowed? One method would be to let the least constrained objective run through the schedule, then allow other repairing heuristics to undo the violations which the least constrained heuristic caused. Another possibility would be to combine the current methods of computing rate of progress with projections of when the goal is likely to be achieved to estimate how long to spend on each heuristic. This problem would require some knowledge of the likely rate of repair of each heuristic under different circumstances, something we were at pains to avoid earlier. Also, being based on statistical estimates, it could not guarantee a solution. Hence, the use of a single objective heuristic followed by an anytime repair heuristic would have more desirable properties.

References

1. Beck, H.A.: Design considerations for reactive scheduling. Technical Report, Artificial Intelligence Applications Institute, University of Edinburgh, (1982)
2. Bona, B., Brandimente P. and Greco C.: Some experiences in the application of AI in manufacturing and control. 29–45, in *Applications of Artificial Intelligence in Engineering V*, Volume 2, Manufacturing and Planning, G. Rzevski (Ed.), Computational Mechanics Publications, 1982, Springer-Verlag.
3. Buchanan, I., Burke P., Costello J. and Prosse r P.: in Artificial Intelligence in Manufacturing, (ed.) G. Rzevski, Computational Mechanics Publications, Southampton, (1988) 107–114.
4. Burke, P., Prosser, P.: Distributed Asynchronous Scheduling. 503–522, in Applications of Artificial Intelligence in Engineering V , Volume 2, Manufacturing and Planning, G. Rzevski (Ed.), Computational Mechanics Publications (1990), Springer-Verlag.
5. Frizelle, G.D.M.: An Entropic Measurement of Complexity in Jackson Networks, Working Paper in Manufacturing, 1995 No 13, Cambridge University Engineering Department, Mill Lane Cambridge CB2 1RX.
6. Interrante, L.D., Rochowiak, D.M.: Active Rescheduling and Collaboration in Dynamic Manufacturing Systems. Concurrent Engineering: Research and Applications, **2** 97–105
7. Wild, R.: Production and Operations Management. Fourth Edition, Cassell, london, 1989.
8. Lane, R., Evans, S.: Solving problems in production scheduling. Computer Integrated Manufacturing Systems, **8** (1995) 117–124
9. Little, D., A. Hemmings.: Automated assembly scheduling: a review. Computer Integrated Manufacturing Systems **7** (1995) 51–61.
10. McKay, K.N., Safayeni, F.R., Buzacott, J.A.: Schedulers & Planners: What and how can we learn from them. Invited paper, Proceedings of Intelligent Scheduling Symposium, November, San Francisco (1992) 51–66.
11. Prosser, P., Conway, C., Muller, C.: A constraint maintenance system for the distributed resource allocation problem. Intelligent Systems Engineering **1** (1992) 76–83.
12. Sathi, N., Fox, M.S., Goyal, R., Kott, S.: Resource configuration and allocation. IEEE Expert **7** No. 2 (1992) 26–35.
13. Smith, S.F., Ow, P.S., Potvin, J-Y., Muscettola N., Matthys D.C.: An integrated framework for generating and revising factory schedules. International Journal of Operations Research **41** (1990) 539–552
14. Sycara, K.P., Roth, S.F., Sadeh, N., Fox, M.S.: Resource allocation in distributed factory scheduling. IEEE Expert, **6** (1991) 29-40.
15. Zweben, M.: Repair for scheduling and rescheduling. IEEE Systems Man and Cybernetics (1992)

Acknowledgements This work was performed with the support of EPSRC under research grant GR/H 86455 and EPSRC Advanced Fellowship B/90/AF/1287, which are gratefully acknowledged. The support and co-operation of the industrial collaborators is also warmly acknowledged. I am grateful too to the referees for their helpful comments which have greatly improved this paper.

Intelligent Tools for Planning Knowledge Base Development and Verification

Steve A. Chien*

Jet Propulsion Laboratory, California Institute of Technology
4800 Oak Grove Drive, M/S 525-3660, Pasadena, CA 91109-8099
steve.chien@jpl.nasa.gov

Abstract. A key obstacle hampering fielding of AI planning applications is the considerable expense of developing, verifying, updating, and maintaining the planning knowledge base (KB). Planning systems must be able to compare favorably in terms of software lifecycle costs to other means of automation such as scripts or rule-based expert systems. Consequently, in order to field real systems, planning practitioners must be able to provide: 1. tools to allow domain experts to create and debug their own planning knowledge bases; 2. tools for software verification, validation, and testing; and 3. tools to facilitate updates and maintenance of the planning knowledge base. This paper describes two types of tools for planning knowledge base development: static KB analysis techniques to detect certain classes of syntactic errors in a planning knowledge base; and completion analysis techniques, to interactively debug the planning knowledge base. We describe these knowledge development tools and describe empirical results documenting the usefulness of these tools.

1 Introduction

A key bottleneck in applying AI planning techniques to a real-world problem is the amount of effort required to construct, debug, verify, and update (maintain) the planning knowledge base. In particular, planning systems must be able to compare favorably in terms of software lifecycle costs to other means of automation such as scripts or rule-based expert systems. An important component to reducing such costs is to provide a good environment for developing planning knowledge bases. Despite this situation, relatively little effort has been devoted to developing an integrated set of tools to facilitate constructing, debugging, verifying, and updating specialized knowledge structures used by planning systems.

While considerable research has focused on knowledge acquisition systems for rule-based expert systems [5] , and object-oriented/inheritance knowledge bases with procedures and methods [8], little work has focused on knowledge acquisition for specialized planning representations. Notable exceptions to this statement are [6] which uses inductive learning capabilities and a simulator to refine planning operators and [18] which uses expert traces to learn and a simulator to refine planning operators. However, in many cases a simulation capability

* This work was performed by the Jet Propulsion Laboratory, California Institute of Technology, under contract with the National Aeronautics and Space Administration.

is not available. In these situations the user needs assistance in causally tracing errors and debugging from a single example. This assistance is sorely needed to enable domain experts to write and debug domain theories without relying on AI people. Furthermore, planning knowledge base maintenance is often overlooked. Such tools are also invaluable in tracking smaller bugs, verifying KB coverage [2], and updating the KB as the domain changes. While these tools can draw much from causal tracking techniques used in rule-based systems [5], there are several aspects of planning systems which differentiate them from rule-based systems - their specialized representations and their temporal reasoning capabilities. Two specialized representations for planning are prevalent - task reduction rules and planning operators. These representations as well as the most common constraints (ordering and codesignation constraints) have evolved so that specialized reasoning algorithms must be adapted to support debugging.

Many types of knowledge encoding errors can occur: incorrectly defined preconditions, incorrectly defined effects, and incorrect variable specifications. Invariably the end result is a mismatch between the planners model of the legality of a plan and the model dictated by the domain (or domain expert). Thus, the end symptoms of a knowledge base error can be broadly classified into two categories.

Incorrect Plan Generation: This occurs when the planner is presented a problem and generates a plan which does not achieve the goals in the current problem context. In our experience, the current problem and faulty solution can focus attention in debugging the flaw in the knowledge base. By using the faulty plan to direct the debugging process, the user can often focus on the incorrect link in the plan (faulty protection or achievement) - allowing for rapid debugging.

Failure to Generate a Plan: This occurs when the planner is presented with a solvable problem, but the planner is unable to find a solution. In our experience this type of failure is far more difficult to debug. This is because the user does not have a particular plan to use to focus the debugging process. Thus, often a user would manually write down a valid plan based on their mental model of the domain, and then trace through the steps of the plan to verify that the plan could be constructed. Because our experience has been that detecting and debugging failure-to-generate-a-plan cases has been more difficult, our work focuses on: 1. verifying that a domain theory can solve all solvable problems; and 2. facilitating debugging of cases where the domain theory does not allow solution of a problem deemed solvable by the domain expert.

This paper describes two types of tools developed to assist in developing planning knowledge bases - *static analysis tools* and *completion analysis tools*. Static analysis tools analyze the domain knowledge rules and operators to see if certain goals can or cannot be inferred. However, because of computational tractability issues, these checks must be limited. Static analysis tools are useful in detecting situations in which a faulty knowledge base causes a top-level goal

---

[2] For work in verifying rule-based systems - see [13]. For work on rule base refinement using training examples (the analogue of a simulator for planning KB refinement) see [9].

or operator precondition to be unachievable - frequently due to omission of an operator effect or a typographical error.

Completion analysis tools operate at planning time and allow the planner to complete plans which can achieve all but a few focused subgoals or top-level goals. Completion analysis tools are useful in cases where a faulty knowledge base does not allow a plan to be constructed for a problem that the domain expert believes is solvable. In the case where the completion analysis tool allows a plan to be formed by assuming goals true, the domain expert can then be focused on these goals as preventing the plan from being generated.

The static analysis and completion analysis tools have been developed in response to our experiences in developing and refining the knowledge base for the Multimission VICAR Planner (MVP) [1, 2] system, which automatically generates VICAR image processing scripts from specifications of image processing goals. The MVP system was initially used in December 1993, and has been in routine use since May 1994. The tools described in this paper were driven by our considerable efforts in knowledge base development, debugging, and updates to the modest sized knowledge base for MVP.

The remainder of this paper is organized as follows. Section 2 outlines the two planning representations we support: task reduction rules and operators. Section 2 also briefly describes how these representations are used in planning. Section 3 describes static analysis rules for assisting in planning KB verification and development. Section 4 describes completion analysis rules for assisting in planning KB development.

2   VICAR Image Processing

We describe the static and completion analysis tools within the context of the Multimission VICAR Planner system, a fielded AI planning system which automates certain types of image processing [3]. MVP uses both task reduction and operator-based methods in planning. However, the two paradigms are separate, in that MVP first performs task reduction (also called hierarchical task network or HTN planning) and then performs operator-based planning. All of the task reduction occurs at the higher conceptual level and the operator-based methods at the lower level[4]. Consequently, MVP uses two main types of knowledge to construct image processing plans (scripts):

- decomposition rules - to specify how problems are to be decomposed into lower level subproblems; and

---

[3] We only briefly describe the MVP application due to space constraints. For further information on this application area, MVP architecture, and knowledge representation see [1, 2].

[4] MVP first uses task reduction [11] planning techniques to perform high level strategic classification and decomposition of the problem then uses traditional operator-based [15] planning paradigms to plan at the lower level

- operators - to specify how VICAR programs can be used to achieve lower level image processing goals (produced by 1 above). These also specify how VICAR programs interact.

These two types of knowledge structures are described in further detail below.

A key aspect of MVP's integration of task reduction and operator-based planning is that first task reduction is performed, then operator-based planning. Because of the order in which these are performed, these two types of knowledge can be checked separately.[5]

2.1 Task Reduction Planning in MVP

MVP uses a task reduction approach to planning. In a task reduction approach, reduction rules dictate how in plan-space planning, one plan can be legally transformed into another plan. The planner then searches the plan space defined by these reductions. Syntactically, a task reduction rule is of the form:

LHS	RHS
GI = initial goal set/actions	GR= reduced goal set/actions
C0 = constraints	$\Rightarrow$ C1 = constraints
C2 = context	N = notes on decomposition

This rule states that a set of goals or actions GI can be reduced to a new set of goals or actions GR if the set of constraints C0 is satisfied in the current plan and the context C2 is satisfied in the current plan provided the additional constraints C1 are added to the plan. C0 and C1 are constraint forms which specify conjuncts of constraints, each of which may be a codesignation constraint on variables appearing in the plan, an ordering constraint on actions or goal achievements in the plan, a not-present constraint (which is satisfied only if the activity or goal specified does not appear in the plan and never appeared in the derivation of the plan), a present constraint (which is satisfied only if the activity or goal specified did appear in the plan or derivation of the plan), or a protection constraint (which specifies that a goal or set of goals cannot be invalidated during a specified temporal interval. Skeletal planning[10] is a technique in which a problem is identified as one of a general class of problem. This classification is then used to choose a particular solution method. Skeletal planning in MVP is implemented in by encoding decomposition rules which allow for classification and initial decomposition of a set of goals corresponding to a VICAR problem class. The LHS of a skeletal decomposition rule in MVP corresponds to a set of conditions specifying a problem class, and the RHS specifies an initial problem decomposition for that problem class.

MVP also uses decomposition rules to implement hierarchical planning. Hierarchical planning [17] is an approach to planning where abstract goals or procedures are incrementally refined into more and more specific goals or procedures

---

[5] A more recently developed planner [3, 4] completely integrates these two planning paradigms. While natural extensions of static and completion analysis to this integrated planning approach exist, we have not as of yet explored such possibilities.

as dictated by goal or procedure decompositions. MVP uses this approach of hierarchical decomposition to refine the initial skeletal plan into a more specific plan specialized based on the specific current goals and situation. This allows the overall problem decomposition to be influenced by factors such as the presence or absence of certain image calibration files or the type of instrument and spacecraft used to record the image. For example, geometric correction uses a model of the target object to correct for variable distance from the instrument to the target. For VOYAGER images, geometric correction is performed as part of the local correction process, as geometric distortion is significant enough to require immediate correction before other image processing steps can be performed. However, for GALILEO images, geometric correction is postponed until the registration step, where it can be performed more efficiently.

This decomposition-based approach to skeletal and hierarchical planning in MVP has several strengths. First, the decomposition rules very naturally represent the manner in which the analysts attack the procedure generation problem. Thus, it was a relatively straightforward process for the analysts to articulate and accept classification and decomposition rules for the subareas which we have implemented thus far. Second, the notes from the decomposition rules used to decompose the problem can be used to annotate the resulting plan to make the output plans more understandable to the analysts. Third, relatively few problem decomposition rules are easily able to cover a wide range of problems and decompose them into much smaller subproblems.

2.2 Operator-based Planning in MVP

MVP represents lower level procedural information in terms of classical planning operators. These are typical classical planning operators with preconditions, effects, conditional effects, universal and existential quantification allowed, and with codesignation constraints allowed to appear in operator preconditions and effect conditional preconditions. For reasons of space constraints the operator representation is only briefly described here. (for a good description of a classical planning operator representation similar to ours see [15]). Thus, an operator has a list of parameter variables, a conjunctive set of preconditions, and for each effect (which is a conjunct) there is a (possibly null) set of preconditions.

```
Operator
    Parameters:    variable*
    Preconditions: Prec = Prop*
    Effects:       [Effecti = Prop* when Cpreci = Prop*]*
```

The above operator has the semantics that it can only be executed in a state in which all of the preconditions Prec are true. And when executed, for each effect set, if all of the conditional preconditions Cpreci are true in the input state, the effect Effecti occurs and all of the effects are true in the output state.

A description of the GALSOS operator is shown below.

```
operator GALSOS
            :parameters ?infile ?ubwc ?calc
            :preconditions
                    the project of ?infile must be galileo
                    the data in ?infile must be raw data values
            :effects
                    reseaus are not intact for ?infile
                    the data in ?infile is not raw data values
                    missing lines are not filled in for ?infile
                    ?infile is radiometrically corrected
                    the image format for ?infile is halfword
                    ?infile has blemishes-removed
                    if (UBWC option selected) then ?infile is uneven bit wt. corrected
                    if (CALC option selected) then ?infile has entropy values calculated
```

2.3 Different Tool Types and Representations

In order to facilitate this key process of knowledge acquisition and refinement we have been developing a set of knowledge-base editing and analysis tools. These tools can be categorized into two general types: (1) static knowledge base analysis tools; and (2) completion analysis tools. Because MVP uses two types of knowledge: decomposition rules and operator definitions, each of these tools can be used with each of these representations. Thus there are four types of tools:

- static rule analysis tools;
- static operator analysis tools;
- completion rule analysis tools; and
- completion rule analysis tools.

For each type of tool, it is possible to perform the analysis using propositional or full predicate checking. In propositional analysis, all actions and goals are considered optimistically only for the predicate or goal name. For example, when considering whether an operator could achieve a specific fact, "(radiometrically-corrected ?file1)", optimistic treatment means that any effect or initial state fact with the predicate "radiometrically-corrected" can be used. When considering whether an effect , "(radiometrically-corrected ?file1)", deletes a protected fact "(radiometrically-corrected ?file2)", one presumes that the arguments to the predicate can be resolved such that the conflict does not occur. Therefore the effect is not considered to delete the fact. The propositional analysis is used as a fast checking component to catch simple errors when debugging a knowledge base. The full static analysis is useful but restricted to more batch-like analysis due to its computational expense.

2.4 Problem Spaces for Knowledge Analysis

In our knowledge base development and refinement framework, the knowledge base is divided into a set of problem spaces. A problem space consists of a set of allowable sets of inputs and groundings. In the case of task reduction, inputs are non-operational goals, groundings are operational goals, and the problem space corresponds to a class of non-operational goal sets which can be reduced into operational goals. In the case of operator-based planning, inputs are goals, groundings are initial state facts, and the problem space corresponds to a class of goal sets which can be achieved from a general class of initial states. In both the task reduction and operator-based cases, the inputs are specified in terms of logical constraints over goals and groundings are specified in terms of a list of predicates which can be presumed true/operational.

These problem spaces represent a set of contexts in which the decomposition planner or operator planner is attempting to solve a general class of problems. Decomposing the overall problem solving process into these problem spaces and analyzing each in isolation dramatically reduces the complexity of the analysis process. Of course, this introduces the possibility that the knowledge base analysis is flawed due to a poor problem decomposition. Unfortunately, we know of no other way around this problem.

3 Static Analysis Tools

3.1 Static Analysis Tools for Task Reduction Rules

Static analysis tools analyze the knowledge base to determine if pre-specified problem-classes are solvable. The static analysis techniques can be used in two ways: 1. fast run-time checking using propositional analysis (called propositional static rule analysis); and 2. off-line knowledge-base analysis to verify domain coverage (called full static rule analysis).

In the case of static rule analysis, the analysis process is to verify that all legal sets of input goals can be reduced into operational goals/facts/tasks. The set of allowable input goals is formally specified in terms of logical constraints on a set of goals produced by the interface. Figure 1 describes the static rule analysis algorithm. Below we show a simplified problem space description for the navigation problem space, and use this to illustrate static rule analysis. Input goals are all combinations of:

(attempt-to-FARENC ?files)   (automatch ?files)
(manmatch ?files)   (curve-verify ?files)
(display-automatch-residual-error ?files) (display-manmatch-residual-error ?files)
(update-archival-sedr ?files)

Subject to the constraint that:
¬((attempt-to-FARENC ?files ?files) and (automatch ?files))
¬(curve-verify ?files) or (attempt-to-FARENC ?files)
¬(display-automatch-residual-error ?files) or (automatch ?files)
¬(display-manmatch-residual-error ?files) or (manmatch ?files)

Generally, the allowable sets of input goals are of the form "all combinations of these 5 goals except that goal4 and goal3 are incompatible, and that every time goal 2 is selected goal 1 must have parameter X and so on.

The output legal set of goals/facts/tasks are defined in terms of a set of operational predicates. For example, in the relative navigation example used above has the operational predicates: construct-om-matrix, and display-om-error.

This means that any goal/activity/fact produced using one of these predicates is considered achieved. Static rule analysis runs the rules on these allowable combinations and verifies that the decomposition rules cover the combinations (this corresponds to exhaustive testing of the task reduction rules). As described in Section 2.1, there are several types of constraints used in the task reduction rules. Some of these constraints do not make sense for a propositional analysis; how constraints are handled in the propositional analysis is shown below.

Table 1. Propositional vs. Full Constraint Handling

Constraint type	Propositional Case	Full Case
codesignation	ignored	tracked
not-present	ignored	tracked
present	propositional	tracked
ordering	tracked	tracked
protection	ignored	tracked

```
StaticRuleAnalyze(input-goals, operational-goals, rules)
initialize Q = (goals=input-goals, constraints={})
select a plan P from Q
        for each plan P' produced by reducing a goal in P using a
        task reduction rule w. constraints as below
        IF P' contains only operational goals return SUCCESS
        ELSE add P' to Q and continue
```

Fig. 1. Static Rule Analysis Algorithm

The principal difference between the propositional and non-propositional cases is that when predicates are transformed to the propositional case, constraint resolution optimistically presumes variable assignments will remove conflicts. For example, consider the plan and reduction rules shown below.

Plan1: activities: (foo c216) (bar c216) constraints: .....
Plan2: activities: (foo c216) (bar c211) constraints: .....
Reduction Rule1: if present: (bar ?a) not-present: (foo ?b)
Reduction Rule2: if present: (bar ?a) (foo ?a)

In the propositional case, both rule1 and rule2 apply to both plan1 and plan2.

In the full case, rule 1 does not apply either plan1 or plan2. In the full case rule2 applies to plan1 but does not apply to plan2. Note that in the propositional case, in order to presume that variables resolve optimistically, the analysis procedure need not compute all possible bindings. Rather, the analysis procedure resolves present constraints by presuming matching if the predicate matches and by ignoring not- present constraints (and others as indicated above). To further illustrate, consider the following example from the MVP domain. The input goals, relevant decomposition rules, and operational predicates are shown below.

Input Goals: (automatch ?files) (manmatch ?files) (display-manmatch-error ?files)

Decomposition Rules:

Rule1 LHS (automatch ?f1) (manmatch ?f1)

RHS (construct-om-matrix ?f1 auto-man-refined)

Rule2 LHS (display-manmatch-error ?f2) present (automatch ?f2) (manmatch ?f2)

RHS (display-om-error ?f2 auto-man-refined)

Operational Predicates: construct-om-matrix, display-om- error

In both the propositional and full static rule analysis cases both rules would apply in the analysis. Thus, both analyses would indicate that the input goals can be reduced into operational facts/activities.

3.2   Static Analysis Tools for Operator-based Planning

The static analysis techniques can also be applied to the MVP's operator-based planner component. This is accomplished by generalizing the planning algorithm. Again, as with the static rule analysis, the static operator analysis is considering a general class of problems defined by a problem space. As with the static rule analysis, a problem space defines an allowable set of goals and a set of operational predicates which are assumed true in the initial state.

In the propositional static operator analysis case, in order to treat the domain theory optimistically, we must assume that all protection interactions can be resolved by variable assignments. Because of the absence of protection constraints, the propositional operator static analysis corresponds to the propositional rule-based static analysis. An operator with preconditions P and effects E maps onto a rule with LHS P and RHS E. Conditional effects extend analogously.

The non-propositional static analysis case is handled by modifying a standard operator-based planner. The planner is changed by adding an achievement operation corresponding to presuming any operational fact is true in the initial state. We are currently investigating using more sophisticated static analysis techniques to detect more subtle cases where goals are unachievable [7, 16]. The full (e.g. non-propositional) operator static analysis algorithm is shown below in Figure 2

Figure 3 shows the subgoal tree generated by performing full static analysis on the operator planner problem space defined by: Input Goals: (compute-om-matrix ?fl manmatch) (update-archival-sedr ?fl manmatch) and Operational Predicates: project, initial-predict-source.

StaticOperatorAnalyzeFull(input, operational, operators)
initialize plan queue Q to (goals=input, constraints={})
select a plan P from Q
    for each plan P' produced by achieving a goal G using the following methods:
        1. use an existing operator in the plan to achieve G
        2. add a new operator to the plan to achieve G
        3.* if the goal is operational assume it true in the initial state
    resolve conflicts in P' (protections)
    IF P' has no unresolved conflicts and no unachieved goals
    THEN return SUCCESS
    ELSE add P' to Q and continue

Fig. 2. Static Operator Analysis Algorithm

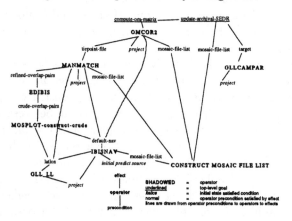

Fig. 3. Subgoal Graph Indicating Static Operator Analysis for Navigation Goals

4 Completion Analysis Tools

The second type of knowledge base development tool used in MVP is the completion analysis tool. In many cases, a knowledge engineer will construct a domain specification for a particular VICAR problem, test it out on known files and goal combinations. Two possible outcomes will occur. First, it is possible that the domain specification will produce an invalid solution. Second, it is possible that the planner will be unable to construct a solution for a problem that the expert believes is solvable.

In the case that the planner constructs an invalid solution, the knowledge engineer can use the inconsistent part of the solution to indicate the flawed portion of the domain theory. For example, suppose that the planner produces a plan consisting of steps ABCD, but the expert believes that the correct plan consists of steps ABCSD. In this case the knowledge engineer can focus on the underlying reason that S is necessary. S must have had some purpose in the plan. It may be needed to achieve a top-level goal G or a precondition P of A, B, or C.

Alternatively, if the ordering of operators or variable assignments is not valid in the produced plan, the knowledge engineer can focus on the protection or other constraint which should have been enforced.

The second possibility is that the domain specification fails to allow the desired solution. For example, the expert believes that the plan ABCD should achieve the goals, but the planner fails to find any plan to achieve the goals. In this case, detecting the flawed part of the knowledge base is more difficult, because it is difficult to determine which part of the domain specification caused the desired output plan to fail. In manually debugging these types of problems, the knowledge engineer would write out by hand the plan that should be constructed. The knowledge engineer would then construct a set of problems, each of which corresponded to a subpart of the failed complete problem. For example, if a failed problem consisted of achieving goals A, B, and C, the knowledge engineer might try the planner on A alone, B alone, and C alone, to attempt to isolate the bug to the portion of the knowledge base corresponding to A, B, or C, correspondingly.

Completion analysis tools partially automate this tedious process of isolating the bug by constructing subproblems. The completion analysis tools allow the decomposition or operator-based planner [6] to construct a proof with assumptions that a small number of goals or subgoals can be presumed achievable (typically only one or two)[7]. By seeing which goals, if assumable, make the problem solvable, the user gains valuable information about where the bug lies in the knowledge base. For example, if a problem consists of goals A, B, and C, and the problem becomes solvable if B is assumed achievable, the bug is likely to be in the portion of the knowledge base relating to the achievement of B. Alternatively, if the problem is solvable when either B or C is assumed achievable, then the bug likely lies in the interaction of the operators achieving B and C. The completion analysis tool is used by running the modified planner algorithm until either: 1. a resource bound of the number of plans expanded is reached; or 2. there are no more plans to expand. The completion analysis algorithm for the reduction planner is shown below in Figure 4 .

In the operator-based planner, completion analysis is permitted by adding another goal achievement method which corresponds to assuming that the goal is magically achieved. The completion analysis operator planner is then run until either 1. a resource bound of the number of plans expanded is reached; or 2. there are no more plans to expand. All solutions found are then reported back to the user to assist in focusing on possible areas of the domain theory for refinement.

---

[6] In the completion analysis for both the reduction planner and the operator-based planner there are choice points in the search in ordering plans in the search queue. In both cases, we use standard heuristics based on the number of outstanding goals and plan derivation steps so far. However, the static analysis techniques would work with any appropriate heuristic for this search choice.

[7] The number of goals assumable is kept small because allowing the planner to assume goals dramatically increases the search space for possible plans. It effectively adds 1 to the branching factor of every goal achievement node in the search space for the plan

```
CompletionReductionPlanner (input, operational, rules)
initialize Q = (goals=input, constraints=, assumptions=0)
IF resource bound return SOLUTIONS
ELSE select a plan P from Q
        for each plan P' produced by reducing P using a task reduction rule
            IF the constraints in P' are consistent
                IF P' contains only operation goals/activities
                    THEN add P' to SOLUTIONS
                    ELSE add P' to Q and continue
                ELSE discard P'
        for each plan P' produced by presuming the current goal achieved/operational
        IF P' contains only operation goals/activities
            THEN add P' to SOLUTIONS
            ELSE increment NumberOfAssumptions(P')
                IF NumberOfAssumptions(P') ≤ bound
                    THEN add P' to Q
```

Fig. 4. Completion Analysis for Reduction Rules

The basic completion analysis algorithm for the operator planner is shown below in Figure 5. The main drawback of the completion analysis tools is that they dramatically increase the size of the search space. Thus, with the completion analysis tools, we provide the user with the option of restricting the types of goals that can be presumed true. Currently the user can restrict this process in the following ways:

- allow only top-level (problem input) goals to be assumed;
- allow only goals appearing in a specific operators preconditions to be assumed;
- allow goals relating to an operator (appearing in its precondition or effects) to be assumed; and
- only allow certain predicates to be assumed.

Thus far, we have found these restriction methods to be fairly effective in focusing the search. Note that allowing certain goals to be presumed true corresponds to editing the problem definition (or domain theory) numerous times and re-running the planner. For example, allowing a single top-level goal to be assumed true for a problem with N goals corresponds to editing the problem definition n times, each time removing one of the top-level goals and re-running the planner each time. Allowing a precondition of an operator to be suspended corresponds to running the planner on the original problem multiple times, each time with a domain theory that has one of the operator preconditions removed. Manually performing this testing to isolate an error quickly grows tiresome. Furthermore, if multiple goals are allowed to be suspended, the number of edits and runs grows combinatorially. The completion analysis tools are designed to alleviate this tedious process and to allow the user to focus on repairing the domain theory.

CompletionOperatorPlanner(input, initial-state, operators)
initialize Q = (goals=input, constraints=, assumptions=0)
IF resource bound exceeded
    THEN return SOLUTIONS
    ELSE select a plan P from Q
           for each plan P' produced by achieving a goal using the following methods:
               1. use existing operator in the plan to achieve the goal
               2. add a new operator to the plan to achieve the goal
               3. use the initial state to achieve the goal
               4.* if the number of goals already assumed in P is less than the bound
                    assume the goal true using completion analysis;
                    the # of assumptions in the new plan is 1+ # in P;
                    resolve conflicts in P' (protections);
           IF P' has no unresolved conflicts and has no unachieved goals
               THEN add P' to SOLUTIONS
               ELSE add P' to Q and continue

Fig. 5. Completion Analysis for Operator Planner

As a side effect, running the planner only once is also computationally more efficient than running the planner multiple times. This is because the planner need explore portions of the search space unrelated to the suspended conditions fewer times.

Thus, the completion analysis techniques are generally used in the following manner. MVP automatically logs any problems unsolvable by the task reduction planner (unreducable) or operator-based planner (no plan found). The user then specifies that one of the top-level goals may be suspended (any one of the top-level goals is a valid candidate - the planner tries each in turn. The completion planner then finds a plan which solves all but one of the top-level goals - focusing the user on the top-level goal which is unachievable. The user then determines which operator O1 that should be achieving the goal, and specifies that the completion planner may consider suspending preconditions of O1. The completion analysis planner runs and determines which precondition P1 of O1 is preventing application of this operator. Next, the user determines which operator O2 should be achieving this precondition P1 of O1, and the process continues recursively until the flawed operator is found. For example, it may be that a protection cannot be enforced, thus preventing a precondition P1 from being achieved. In this case, suppose another operator O2 should be able to achieve P1. But suspending its preconditions does not allow the problem to be solved. This might hint to the knowledge engineer that the problem is in the protection of P1 from O2 to O1. Alternatively, it may be that no operator has an effect that can achieve P (perhaps the knowledge engineer forgot to define the effect or operator). Or that the effect has a different number of arguments, or arguments in a different order, or arguments of a different type. These types of bugs can be easily detected once the bug has been isolated to the particular operator. Another possibility is that a conditional effect that should be used has the wrong conditional preconditions. Again, once the bug has been traced to a particular operator, the debugging process is greatly simplified.

In order to further explain how the completion analysis tools are used, we now describe a detailed example of how the completion analysis tools are used. The graph below in Figure 6 illustrates this process from an actual debugging episode which occurred in the development of a portion of the planning knowledge base [8] relating to a problem called relative navigation [9]. Each of the following steps in the debugging process is labeled P if the planner performed the step; U if the user/knowledge engineer performs the step; or C if the completion analysis tool performs the step.

1. (P) The planner is unable to solve the original problem.

2. (U) The user initiates the debugging process by invoking the operator-based completion analysis tool specifying that one top-level goal may be suspended.

3. (C) The completion planner constructs a plan achieving all of the goals but the top-level goal of (compute-om- matrix ?om-matrix ?file-list ?file-list).

4. (U) The user then determines that the OMCOR2 operator should have been able to achieve the goal (compute-om-matrix ?om-matrix ?file-list ?file-list). The user then continues the debugging process by invoking the completion analysis tool specifying that a precondition of the OMCOR2 operator may be suspended.

5. (C) In response to the user request, the completion planner finds a plan achieving all goals except the OMCOR2 precondition (tiepoint-file ?tp ?file-list manmatch).

6. (U) The user then determines that the precondition (tiepoint-file ?tp ?file-list manmatch) should be achieved by the MANMATCH operator, and invokes the operator completion analysis tool allowing suspension of one of the preconditions of the MANMATCH operator.

7. (C) The completion planner then finds a plan achieving all goals but the precondition (refined-overlap-pairs ?rop- file ?file-list) of the operator MANMATCH.

8. (U) The user then determines that the precondition (refined-overlap-pairs ?rop-file ?file-list) should have been achieved by the EDIBIS operator and invokes the operator completion analysis tool allowing suspension of an EDIBIS precondition.

9. (C) The completion planner finds a plan achieving all goals but the precondition (crude-overlap-pair ?cop-file ?file-list) of EDIBIS.

10. (U) The user then determines that this precondition (crude-overlap-pair ?cop-file ?file-list) should have been achieved by the MOSPLOT-construct-crude-nav-file. This results in another invocation of the completion analysis tool allowing suspension of a precondition for MOSPLOT-construct-crude-nav-file.

11. (C) The completion analysis tool then finds a plan achieving all goals but the

---

[8] Note that this is the operator portion of the knowledge base relating directly to the task reduction rules shown in the example for static rule analysis.

[9] For the interested reader, navigation of the image is the process of determining the appropriate transformation matrix to map each pixel from the 2-dimensional (line, sample) of the image space to a 3-dimensional (x,y,z) of some coordinate object space (usually based on the planet center of the target being imaged). Relative navigation corresponds to the process when determining the absolute position of each point is difficult to compute so that the process focuses on determining the correct positions of each point relative to other points in related images.

precondition (latlon ?mf ?lat ?lon) for the operator MOSPLOT-construct-crude-nav-file.

12. (U) At this point, the user notices that the constructed plan for achieving the goals has assumed the instantiated goal (latlon &middle-file ?lat ?lon). This immediately indicates the error to the user because the user is expecting a file name as the second argument of the latlon predicate [10].

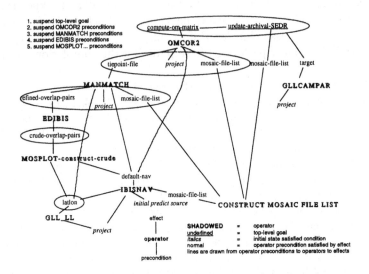

Fig. 6. Subgoal Graph for Completion Analysis Debugging

Unfortunately, we have as of yet not been able to determine any heuristics for controlling the use of these completion tools that allows for more global search or allows for less user interaction. However, in their current form, the completion analysis tools have proved quite useful in debugging the MVP radiometric correction and color triplet reconstruction knowledge base.

4.1 Impact of Debugging

In order to quantify the usefulness of the completion analysis tools, we collected data from a 1 week phase of domain theory development for the relative navigation portion of the domain theory. During this week, we identified 22 issues

---

[10] This is because the latlon goal is designed to refer to a specific image file (e.g., 1126.IMG). Correspondingly, the planning operators that had been defined to acquire information such as latlon presumed actual file names. Unfortunately, &middle-file refers to a VICAR variable which will be bound to an actual file name only at the time that the VICAR script is run (i.e. when the plan is executed). Thus, the bug lies in the mismatch between this precondition and the operators which can determine latlon information for a file. This bug was then fixed by defining operators which could utilize the VICAR variable information at runtime and perform the correct steps to compute the needed latlon information.

raised by a domain expert analyst which at first guess appeared to be primarily in the decomposition rules or operators. For 11 of these 22 problems (selected randomly) we used the debugging tools in refining the domain theory. For the other 11 problems we did not use the debugging tools. When tools were allowed, we estimated that the tools were applicable in 7 out of the 11 problems. These 7 problems were solved in an average of 10 minutes each. The other 4 took on average 41 minutes. The total 11 problems where the tools were used took on average 21 minutes each to correct. In the 11 problems solved without use of the tools, after fixing all 11 problems, we estimated that in 6 out of the 11 problems that the debugging tools would have helped. These 6 problems took on average 43 minutes each to solve. The remaining 5 problems took on average 40 minutes to solve. The second set of 11 problems took on average 42 minutes to solve.

Table 2. Empirical Impact of Completion Analysis Tools

Set	Tools Applicable	Average Time	Tools Not Applicable	Average Time	Overall Average
Tool	7/11	10 min.	4/11	41 min.	21 min.
No Tool	6/11	43 min.	5/11	40 min.	42 min.

5 Discussion

One area for future work is development of explanation facilities to allow the user to introspect into the planning process. Such a capability would allow the user to ask such questions as "Why was this operator added to the plan?" and "Why is this operator ordered after this operator?", which can be answered easily from the plan dependency structure. More difficult (but also very useful) questions are of the form "Why wasn't operator O2 used to achieve this goal?" or "Why wasn't this problem classified as problem class P?". We are currently investigating using completion analysis tools to answer this type of question. The completion analysis techniques are related to theory refinement techniques from machine learning [14, 9]. However, these techniques presume multiple examples over which to induce errors. Additionally, reasoning about planning operators requires reasoning about the specialized planning knowledge representations and constraints. This paper has described two classes of knowledge base development tools. Static analysis tools allow for efficient detection of certain classes of unachievable goals and can quickly focus user attention on the unachievable goals. Static analysis techniques can also be used to verify that domain coverage is achieved. Completion analysis tools allow the user to quickly focus on which goals (or subgoals) are preventing the planner from achieving a goal set believed achievable by the knowledge base developer. These tools are currently in use and we have presented empirical evidence documenting the usefulness of these tools in constructing, maintaining, and verifying the MVP planning knowledge base.

References

1. Chien, S.: Using AI Planning Techniques to Automatically Generate Image Processing Procedures: A Preliminary Report. Proc. AIPS94, Chicago, IL, June 1994, pp. 219-224.
2. Chien, S.: Automated Synthesis of Complex Image Processing Procedures for a Large-scale Image Database. Proc. First IEEE Int. Conf. on Image Processing, Austin, TX, Nov 1994, Vol 3, pp. 796-800.
3. Chien, S., Estlin, T., Wang, X., Govindjee, A., Hill, R.: Automated Generation of Antenna Operations Procedures: A Knowledge-based Approach. Submitted to Telecommunications and Data Acquisition.
4. Chien, S., Estlin, T., Wang, X.: Hierarchical Task Network and Operator-based Planning: Competing or Complementary. JPL Technical Document D-13390 Jet Propulsion Laboratory, California Institute of Technology, January 1996.
5. Davis, R.: Interactive Transfer of Expertise: Acquisition of New Inference Rules. Artificial Intelligence 12 (2) 1979, pp. 121-157.
6. DesJardins, M.: Knowledge Development Methods for Planning Systems. Working Notes of the AAAI Fall Symposium on Learning and Planning: On to Real Applications, New Orleans, LA, Nov 1994, pp. 34-40.
7. Etzioni, O.: Acquiring Search Control Knowledge via Static Analysis. Artificial Intelligence, 62 (2) 255-302, 1993.
8. Gil, Y., Tallis, M.: Transaction- based Knowledge Acquisition: Complex Modifications Made Easier. Proc. of the Ninth Knowledge Acquisition for Knowledge-based Systems Workshop, 1995.
9. Ginsberg, A., Weiss, S., Politakis, P.: Automatic Knowledge Based Refinement for Classification Systems. Artificial Intelligence, 35 pp. 197-226, 1988.
10. Iwasaki, Y., Friedland, P.: The Concept and Implementation of Skeletal Plans. Automated Reasoning 1, 1 (1985), pp. 161-208.
11. Lansky, A.: Localized Planning with Diverse Plan Construction Methods. TR FIA-93-17, NASA Ames Research Center, June 1993.
12. LaVoie, S., Alexander, D., Avis, C., Mortensen, H., Stanley, C., Wainio, L.: VICAR User's Guide, Version 2, JPL Internal Doc.D-4186, Jet Propulsion Laboratory, California Inst. of Tech., Pasadena, CA, 1989.
13. O'Keefe, R., O'Leary, D.: Expert System Verification and Validation: A Survey and Tutorial. AI Review, 7:3-42, 1993.
14. Mooney, R., Ourston, D.: A Multistrategy Approach to Theory Refinement. in Machine Learning: A Multistrategy Approach, Vol. IV, R.S. Michalski and G. Teccuci (eds.), pp.141–164, Morgan Kaufman, San Mateo,CA, 1994.
15. Pemberthy, J., Weld, D.: UCPOP: A Sound Complete, Partial Order Planner for ADL. Proc. of the Third Int. Conf. on Knowledge Representation and Reasoning, October 1992, pp. 103-114.
16. Ryu, K., Irani, K.: Learning from Goal Interactions in Planning: Goal Stack Analysis and Generalization. Proc 1992 National Conference on Artificial Intelligence (AAAI92), pp. 401-407.
17. Stefik, M.: Planning with Constraints (MOLGEN: Part 1). Artificial Intelligence 16, 2(1981), pp. 111-140.
18. Wang, X.: Learning by observation and practice: An incremental approach for planning operator acquisition. In Proc. 1995 Intl. Conf. on Machine Learning (ML95).

Configuring Service Recovery Planning with the CommonKADS Library

V. Arlanzón, A. Bernaras, I. Laresgoiti

LABEIN, Information Technologies Department
Parque Tecnológico, edificio 101, 48016 ZAMUDIO, Bizkaia (Spain)
Telephone: +34 4 489 2404; Fax: + 34 4 489 2540
E-mail: {amaia,lares}@labein.es

Abstract

It has become clear that KBS development, if intended to meet existing industrial quality standards, will have to follow a well structured engineering approach. This, in turn, might increase the reliability of the product and reduce the development costs, thus increasing productivity. CommonKADS is a methodology for KBS development supported by a library of reusable modeling components. This methodology and its library can provide the means for the methodological approach required in the development of knowledge intensive systems. Service recovery planning is a knowledge intensive process whose aim is to drive safely an electrical network from a disturbance situation to its normal operating condition. Many types of knowledge are required in a service recovery planning application, and thus, we consider that the effort spent using a structured methodology for its design will be paid for by the identification of components and structured knowledge that can be reused in related applications. It is for this reason that we have attempted to model this real-world problem using the reusable components provided by the CommonKADS library. In this paper we present this modeling process and its results. We also present some conclusions with respect to the use of the CommonKADS library.

1. Introduction

Access to electrical energy at consumption sites requires three complex processes: *generation*, *transportation*, and *distribution*. Generation is the process of transforming `raw´ energy (e.g., hydraulic, thermal, nuclear, and solar) into a more manageable and useful form such as electrical energy. Ideally, the consumption sites should be near the generation sites. However, economic, social, and political factors typically make this impossible. Hence, energy needs to be transported from generation to consumption sites, often over large distances (hundreds of kilometers). To minimize losses during transportation, the electrical voltage is made high (132 kV or above) before it is placed on the transport network. To make energy available to the customers at the consumption sites, this voltage is made low (66 kV and below), before it is placed on the distribution network.

To ensure the electricity transportation network remains within the desired safety and economical constraints, it is equipped with a sophisticated data acquisition system. This system collects large amounts of data about the state of the network, which are sent to a central dispatching control room (DCR) for analysis by control engineers (CEs) who are supported by a KBS, [Abel *et al.* 93]. As a result of this analysis a CE may detect a disturbance and deem it necessary to alter the configuration of the network. This is done either by sending commands from the console through the telemetry system to the network elements, or by giving orders over the phone to engineers in the field when telemetry is not available.

Whenever a non-planned and sudden disconnection of the network occurs, an emergency situation is signaled to the operators in the DCR. Alarm messages related to changes in network elements are displayed on various screens. Quick and accurate restorative actions must be performed to return the network to normal operating levels and conditions [Corera et al. 93].

Essentially, the goal of the restoration process is to safely transfer the system from an undesirable situation, the result of an unexpected event on the network, to its normal operating condition. A normal operating condition is the one that meets the economical exploitation objectives of a utility, subject to the safety constraints of the equipment.

A service recovery planning application is a knowledge based system which supports operators during this restoration process. To provide effective support, this KBS requires a range of types of knowledge.

Experience from previous efforts of building KBS applications, specifically in the power transport field, [Laresgoiti 88], [Jennings 92], shows a clear need for a methodological approach. We consider that the effort spent using a method for its design will be paid for by the identification of components and structured knowledge that can be reused in related applications. It is for this reason that we have attempted to model this real-world problem using the library of reusable components that the CommonKADS methodology provides. In this paper we present this modeling process and its results. We also present some conclusions with respect to the use of the CommonKADS library.

2. The CommonKADS Library

CommonKADS is a comprehensive methodology for the development of knowledge based systems. It has been under development for a decade, mainly within the two ESPRIT projects KADS-I (P1098) and KADS-II (P5248). KADS-I focused mainly on knowledge acquisition which, at the time, was considered a major bottleneck in knowledge based systems development. Later, it was gradually extended into a full knowledge engineering methodology. CommonKADS has become a common point of reference in Europe [Schreiber et al. 94].

According to CommonKADS, KBS development entails the construction of a set of engineering models of problem-solving behaviour in its concrete organization and application context. The set of models defined by CommonKADS can be viewed as a means to capture the different sources and types of requirements that play a role in real-world applications.

Effective modeling can be supported by libraries of reusable elements that are potentially available for all aspects modeled in a project. To give such a broad range of support, the CommonKADS expertise modeling library contains three categories of elements: modeling components (small modeling elements that can be used and reused to provided content to a model), generic models (skeletal plans, indicating the form of models and the constraints on how this form can be filled), and modeling operations (steps in modeling for elaborating a generic model based on modeling components). The primary access to the Library is by problem types [Breuker and Van de Velde 94]. A model is selected from the library on the basis of answers to a series of questions regarding features of a given task.

3. Model Definition

The CommonKADS expertise model describes knowledge (and its structure) related to knowledge intensive problems. It provides three basic knowledge categories: task knowledge (related to the task and its decomposition), inference knowledge (related to the basic reasoning steps required to achieve a task and the knowledge roles involved), and domain knowledge (related to facts of the domain relevant for the reasoning process).

The following sections describe the task and inference knowledge related to service recovery planning. Although the domain knowledge is not described in this paper, it can be found in [Bernaras *et al.* 95] and [Bernaras *et al.* 96] in the form of an ontology for the electrical network domain.

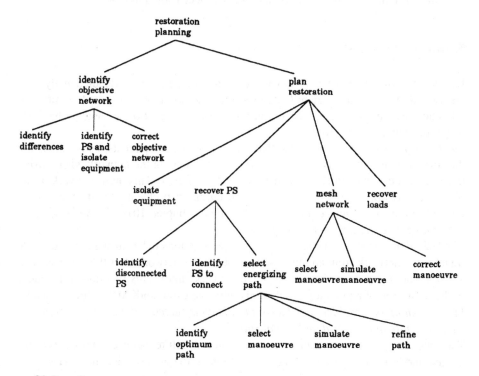

PS: Power Sources

Figure 1. The Configuration Function in CommonKADS

4. Task knowledge

This section presents the task knowledge for service recovery planning. Figure 1 shows a graphical representation of the task hierarchy, which is based on previous experience of building a KBS for service recovery planning [Corera *et al.* 93]. The interest of building this task hierarchy is that it provides a basis for guiding our inference selection, and for tailoring the result to fit this real-world problem. As can be seen in figure 1, the service recovery planning application has a main task called *restoration planning*, which has two sub tasks: *identify objective network* and *plan restoration*:

- Identify Objective Network: The goal of this task is to identify the network configuration that it is possible to have after the application of the restoration process (called objective network), considering that the objective network identified should be electrically possible.
- Plan Restoration: The goal of this task is to plan the sequential ordering of the set of operations that have to be performed in order to take the network from a reference state (state of the network after the occurrence of a disturbance) to the objective state, without exceeding the transport capabilities of the equipment forming the network. This task ensures that all the intermediate states between the reference and the objective network are electrically possible.

5. Inference knowledge

Here we describe the inference knowledge for this model. After a detailed analysis of the two main sub tasks identified in section 4, we have identified a different inference structure for each, because, although they are part of he same global task, they represent different problems.

Identify objective network is a task that, given a set of components, constraints, and the current state of the network, tries to find a new state of the network where, using the components available, the constraints are satisfied. This new network is an objective network. This is considered a configuration problem according to one of the definitions in the CommonKADS Library (chapter 10): *"... the process of assembling a configuration from objects."*

The task *plan restoration* generates a sequence of actions to be carried out in order to transform a network from an initial state (state of the network after the occurrence of a disturbance) to a desired state (objective network state). This function corresponds to the definition of a planning problem given in the CommonKADS Library (chapter 11): *"Planning is a problem in which a plan is constructed ... based on the inputs of an initial state of the world and a goal state."*

The following sections show how each inference structure has been chosen from the library, and how these structures have been adapted to our case when necessary.

5.1 Inference Structure Selection for identify objective network

Figure 2 shows the basic inference structure of the configuring function in CommonKADS. The elements of figure 2 are related to our configuration problem in the following way: the components of the network, their compositional structures, and technical constraints are the *configuration environment model*, our requirements specification are the *user requirements*, the objective network is the *solution space*, and the task identify objective network is the *configuring* function.

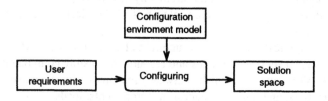

Figure 2. The Configuring Function in CommonKADS.

A configuration model is selected from the library on the basis of answers to a series of questions regarding features of the configuration task. In order to choose between different expansions for the configuring function, we answered the questions as follows:

Q1:   Is it enough when only the existence of suitable configurations is stated (or is an optimal configuration to be chosen from the suitable ones)?

Ans: Yes. In fact, there is a set of optimality criteria, but it has been previously applied to determine the suitable configurations. So each of them are supposed to be an optimal one.

Q2:   Are the user requirements phrased in terms such that they directly can be used in the search for suitable configurations (or do they have to be transformed first)?

Ans: The requirements have been phrased by experts, with expert knowledge about the electrical domain, so no transformation is needed.

These answers lead us to choose the structure shown in figure 3:

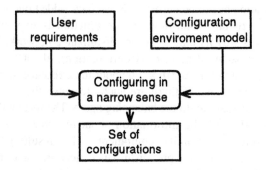

Figure 3. Basic expansion of the configuring function.

The configuration space is usually quite big or even unlimited. There are different possible expansions for *configuration in a narrow sense*. That is, configuration problem solving can be considered as an intelligent way to restrict search of a suitable configuration, in a initially unlimited solution space, in an efficient way in order to find a locally optimal solution [Breuker and Van de Velde 94]. How this search can be performed depends on the features of the application domain, and gives the possible expansion for *configuration in a narrow sense* function. Our selection has been based on the answers to the following questions:

Q1:   Is the application domain hierarchically structured?

Ans: No in our case. The different elements of the electrical domain are at the same level.

Q3:   Is the application domain structure flat and allows a partitioning of the component set into resources and resource requesting components?

Ans: Yes. We can distinguish between resources: lines, transformers, and generators; and resource requesting components: loads.

Q4:   If so (Q3 = yes), can you prioritize the resource requesting components according to a cost/profit ratio?

Ans: Yes. All these ratios are known as part of the domain knowledge.

Q5:   If so (Q3 = yes), can you linearize the resources according to restrictions they impose on the usage of resources requesting components?

Ans: No in our case.

These answers lead us through the decision tree to select expansion MR2 from the library, figure 4.a, a resource-oriented approach, where components can be viewed as resources or as resource requesting components. Suitable configurations can be determined by balancing the requested and provided resources. In this configuration user requirements are expressed as Configuration specification.

As it is shown in figure 4.b, we have refined the MR2 inference structure for our specific domain. Some modifications were required in the refinement process, as might be expected. The part of the inference structure involving specifying and prioritizing the resources and resource-requesting components remains very similar. The *configuration specification*, is the initially desired configuration, i.e., the pre disturbance network. Since this configuration was valid before the disturbance occurred, it could be considered as our user requirements. These user requirements are used to get a configuration which is valid in the new circumstances. The validity of the new configuration has to be verified. So we have added one more inference to the MR2 inference structure, *load-flow*, whose function is to verify the resulting configurations. This is why its inputs are pre disturbance network, locally balanced network and globally balanced network (Configuration), all of them configuration states. The verification gives us information about the existence, or not, of elements with an undesirable behaviour. If there are such elements, the configuration is not valid and it will be necessary to do the balancing again. The local balancing balances an area of the network, with the information about resources, resource requesting components, and the out-of-limits equipment. The resulting local balanced configurations, together with the pre disturbance network, and the out-of-limits equipment, are used in the global balancing to find the final configuration. We will call the resulting inference structure a verified-resource-oriented expansion.

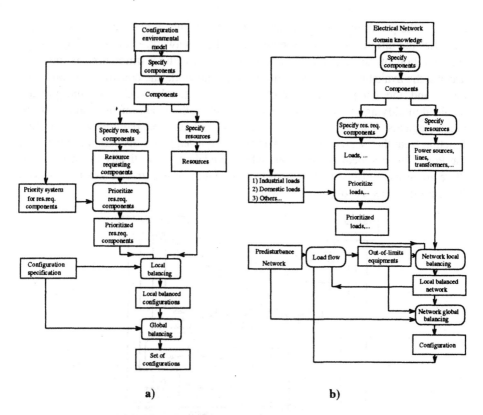

Figure 4. Expansions MR2 for Resource-oriented approach.
a) Domain independent expansion, b) Domain specific refined expansion

In the task model for service recovery planning (figure 1), the *identify objective network* task has three sub tasks, *identify differences, identify PS and isolate equipment* and *correct objective network*. These sub tasks take into account the current state of the network to identify differences with the objective network, the damaged equipment to isolate it, and the elements of the network to correct it. The configuration identified through the modified MR2 inference structure does not cover these tasks. So the structure needs to be modified to cover them. The point that allows more changes in the domain specific MR2 (figure 4.b) is the *configuration specification* input in figure 4.a.

To generate an structure that covers completely our reasoning process a new *configuration specification* is defined, starting from the current state of the network, and with the aim of defining a desired state as close as possible to the pre disturbance network. The pre disturbance network could, itself, be valid as the new state, since it was the working state before the fault occurred. However, it is not possible to restore the pre disturbance network due to some damaged equipment as a result of the fault. Thus, the desired state should be as close as possible to the pre disturbance state, but without the damaged equipment.

To arrive at this desired state, the current state of the network, which is also referred to as *Reference Network*, needs to be modified until the differences between this state and the pre disturbance state are minimal. For this, a distance function, which identifies the differences between both states of the network, is defined. The current configuration of the network is modified to reduce these differences taking into account the available components that form the network, the constraints imposed by them, and the compositional structure of the network. The new configuration obtained modifying the previous one, must meet all the requirements imposed by all these elements. The verification of the new configuration requires a verification function from the *Electrical Network Domain Knowledge*. In this case the function is the Power-Flow system of equations which models mathematically the network. If there are any unfulfilled requirement the configuration is corrected again, otherwise it is considered as the objective network.

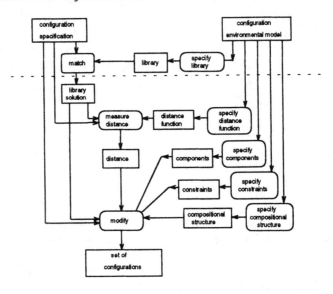

Figure 5. Expansion MC1 for Case-based approach in the CommomKADS Library

The CommonKADS Library contains an inference structure for transformation, MC1, which uses a similar reasoning process within a case-based approach, see figure 5. A case-based approach is defined considering that "...*the configuration environment model must contain a library of previously collected pairs of configuration specifications and optimal configurations...*" [Breuker and Van de Velde 94].

Strictly speaking, our problem is not a case-based problem (there is no library anywhere), but the kind of transformation performed by both reasoning processes is the same. We will call our problem a single-case-based problem.

We start with the pre disturbance state of the network (figure 6.b), that can be considered as a *configuration specification* (because we want to find a configuration as close to it as possible). In our case, there is no library, thus there is no library solution to modify, but we modify the current state of the network, or *Reference Network*. Obviously this is not a solution for our problem, indeed it is our starting point, but we can consider that it plays a similar role in our case, as the library solution in a case-based approach. The rest of both processes are similar (see figures 5 under the dotted line and 6.a). We select a *distance function* from the *Electrical Network Domain Knowledge* (*configuration environmental model* in MC1). We identify differences between both states: *Pre disturbance network* and *Reference Network* (*configuration specification* and *library solution*) and modify one of them: *Reference Network* (*library solution*) to reduce those differences. Up to this point we can adapt the inference structure MC1 to our case.

This inference structure, MC1, finishes at this point, modifying the *library solution* and obtaining in this way a set of configurations. In our case, however, the configuration obtained has to be verified. The inferences related to the verification can be added to the rest of inferences. We define the inference *specify verification function* from the *Electrical Network Domain Knowledge* (figure 6.b).

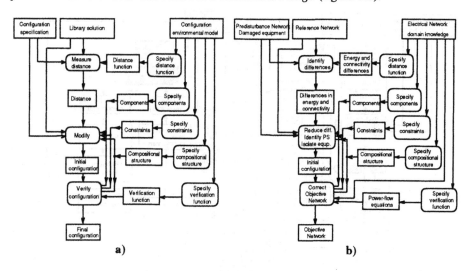

Figure 6. Modified expansions MC1
a) Domain independent expansion, b) Domain specific expansion

This function, in our case the *power-flow equations*, acts on the *initial configuration*, obtained from MC1, to verify it and obtain in this way the objective network. As figure 6.b shows, these inferences and domain knowledge are modeled in our modified version of MC1, and we will call it the verified-single-case-based expansion.

So far, we have seen that the resolution of our problem requires is a verified-resource-oriented expansion, and also a verified-single-case-based expansion. However, these two expansions can be combined to form a single inference structure for our configuration problem.

The combination of the modified MC1 and MR2 structures is made in the following way: the *configuration environmental model* is the same in both cases, as well as *specify components* and *components*. Each modified structure has an inference where Power-flow equations are applied to the state of the network to verify it. In the modified MC1, this state is the *initial configuration* and, in the modified MR2, it is the specification of the network we want to arrive at. This configuration was supposed to be the *pre disturbance network* but now it is the output of the modified MC1 structure. Indeed this is the reason to introduce MC1. So in order to couple both inference structures, we consider that the *initial configuration* obtained from the modified MC1 is the configuration specification for the modified MR2 (do not confuse it with the configuration specification for MC1), and we call it the *desired configuration*. We apply the power-flow equations (*verification function*) to the *desired configuration* in the *verify configuration* inference. The rest of the structure is the same as the modified MR2. So we can consider that the inference *correct objective network* in figure 6.b involves verifying and balancing inferences. The domain-specific version of the model is shown in figure 7.

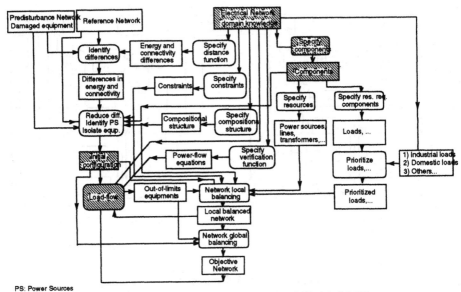

PS: Power Sources

Figure 7. Combination of the modified MR2 and MC1

5.2   Inference Structure Selection for plan restoration

Having configured an inference structure for the sub task *identify objective network,* next, we present the configuration of an inference structure for the sub task *plan restoration,* thus covering the two main sub tasks in figure 1. Planning is a task where a plan is constructed to go from an initial state of the world to a goal state. Planning also uses a single static role, the plan model, which defines what a plan is and what it is made of. The plan model includes a description of the world (world description), and a description of a plan itself (plan description) [Breuker and Van de Velde 94]. This definition is shown in figure 8.

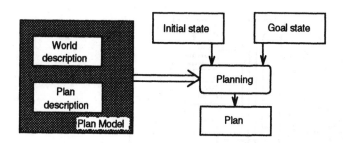

Figure 8. The Planning Function in CommonKADS

The double arrow corresponds to static knowledge of the plan model. We can consider our sub task *plan restoration* as a planning problem, where our initial state is the current state of the network and the goal state is the objective network identified in the configuration task. The plan is the set of steps we have to carry out to transform the network from its actual state to the objective network state.

We have consulted the corresponding chapter of the CommonKADS Library in order to select an inference structure for this particular planning problem [Breuker and Van de Velde 94, Chapter 11]. But in this case, there are no questions whose answers can lead us to select an inference structure in the library. The library only contains information about certain families of planning methods.

We consider our problem as linear planning. Linear planners are those that use a domain model that assumes a linear plan (completely ordered). Our plan will be a set of actions to be carried out strictly in order. This corresponds exactly with the previous definition. This point leads us to select the inference structure shown in figure 9. The inference structure selected from the library, fits quite well our problem, so there is no need to modify it any further.

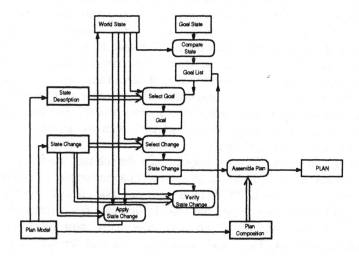

Figure 9. Function structure for linear planners

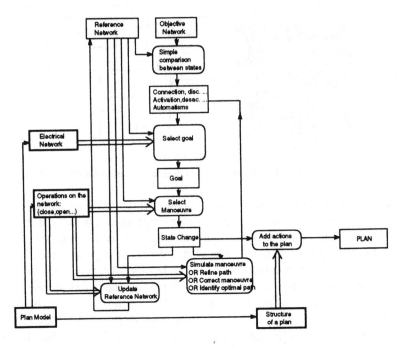

Figure 10. Domain specific structure for linear planners

Figure 10 shows how this structure is adapted to our particular case. The inputs to the process are the *reference network* (current state of the network), and the *objective network* identified in the configuration process. With a simple comparison between them, the *goal list* is identified, containing all the connections, disconnections, activations, and changes in automatisms that could be done to arrive at the *goal state*. With the information about the *reference network* and about the *electrical network* (state description), one of these subgoals is selected according to the tasks being executed (*isolate equipment, recover power sources, mesh network, recover loads*). A maneuver is selected in *select a maneuver* according to the information about the operations on the network and the *reference network*. These two elements are used to verify the selected change (*simulate maneuver, refine path, correct maneuver, identify optimal path*). If the change is correct the list of connections, disconnections etc. is modified. The *reference network* and *operations on the network* are also used to *update the reference network*. The selected change is added to the list of actions previously selected, with the information about the structure of a plan, forming the plan.

The inferences in figure 10 can be mapped onto the sub task hierarchy for the task *plan restoration*, figure 1. This task presents a situation completely different to that of the configuration problem. While in the previous task, *identify objective network*, the inferences belong only to one sub task, in this case this distribution is not so clear. As we execute some of the sub tasks sequentially, most inferences belong to more than one sub task. The criteria used to select a goal depends on the sub task being executed: *isolate equipment, recover power sources, mesh network* or *recover loads*. There are two important points to be made about this mapping:

The first point is that the plan resulting from the planning task hierarchy in figure 1 is also a hierarchical plan, where actions have subactions. Since this plan is linear our planning problem fits well in the family of linear planners provided by the library.

However, the selected inference structure for linear planners also seems to assume a non-hierarchical plan, i.e., there are no inferences related to decomposition and aggregation of actions. In this respect, the library solution does not provide a full solution to our problem.

The second point is that according to the inference structure from the library it seems that all inferences have more or less the same complexity. This is not the case in service recovery planning. In fact, the inference *verify state* is very complex and requires a large amount of knowledge, being the most important in the planning task. This is why several tasks in our task structure use this inference, using different knowledge for each task. The verification process in this case has consequences such as invalidating steps of the plan, inputting new conditions on other goals, or even generating new goals to achieve.

6. Conclusions

Real-world problems often require complex solutions and, when using a library, they require complex component selection and configuration. It is clear that trying to fit a particular problem to the problem types in the library supports abstraction. Abstracting from a particular domain with the library helps in getting a better understanding of the type of problem at hand. This, together with the solutions given in the library help in understanding what can be reused from previous knowledge and experiences.

It is frustrating, though, to find such little support in the library for important and reusable problem types such as planning. Further work is suggested in this area to develop a more complete version of the library.

We found that, in those problems for which a range of components is provided (such as configuration), the questions are, at times, somewhat ambiguous, and thus difficult to answer. Still, they seem to be good enough to drive the questioning to a set of components that, in our case, fits the task, at least partially. We have shown in section 5.1 how the resource-oriented approach to configuration covered only some of the sub tasks of *identify objective network*. To provide a complete solution, it has been necessary, first, to improve the inference structure to obtain a verified-resource-oriented expansion to cover the verification of the results (not considered in any of the library components). It has also been necessary to combine the resulting structure with a verified-single-case-based expansion to cover all the sub tasks of *identify objective network*.

From this experience some areas for improvement have been identified:

Generic types of inferences should be included: the solutions in the library do not include verification inferences. As we have seen, these are critical in real-world problems, and thus they should be included in further developments of the library solutions.

<u>Transformation and modification operators need to be better described</u>: reusing inference structures might involve creating new inferences, or modifying existing ones, to cover reasoning steps required for a specific problem (such as adding the load-flow inference to the MR2 structure). These are important operations in the library which need further research.

<u>Composition operators should cover the combination of `generic models´</u>: Real-world problems might involve configuring not only by expanding functions (as it is currently) but also by combining inference structures related to different ways of solving problems (e.g., a resource-oriented approach, with a case-based approach). As far as the current structure of the library is concerned, this possibility does not seem to have been considered (a problem is either resource-oriented or case-based, but the questioning does not provide the means to put them together), and thus, the composition operators only define the relation between a generic model and its modeling components. In our case, it might be argued that we should not have put together MR2 and MC1 in the first place, since the use of the case-based approach inference structure is not complete, and thus, it is not really a case-based problem. On the other hand, if one of the main modeling principles of the library is the provision of basic elements that can be configured to provide a solution to a problem, the main question still remains, what is the appropriate level of granularity for those elements? In our case, the lever of granularity required is lower than the one provided in MC1. This lower level allows us to have a complete inference structure for our problem, and, without it, the reusability of the library elements would not have been complete.

<u>An operator for the combination of types of problems is necessary</u>: A problem might relate to more than one problem type in the library (e.g., service recovery planning involves configuration and planning). The library, however, does not offer enough support in this preliminary design phase. For example, it would be useful to have support for the decomposition of a problem into smaller problems (following the divide and conquer strategy) and for the integration of the solutions.

<u>It is important that the library supports (and even requires) explicit identification of new assumptions</u>: The assumptions, or features, of the library problem types and their solutions might not always be applicable, and the selected and configured solution might need to be modified to account for the different or new assumptions. For example, the configuration problem presented in this paper is different from the ones addressed by the library, in the following aspects:

<u>Energy configuration</u>: The configuration of an electrical network during restoration does not involve configuring a network from components that may exist in a stock and arranging them appropriately. It involves configuring components that are already placed in the network and the only possible actions are to open or close their connections (but they cannot be moved, for example). This kind of configuration really involves configuring the energy flow through the network. This has to be done in a very small time frame and with the components already arranged in the network. It is not possible, thus, to add new components or modify the existing network.

<u>Initial Configuration</u>: The state of the initial configuration in the library is taken as known and fix, this means that the initial configuration is taken as a starting

point to proceed from. Although this is the case in many problems, it is not in ours because the achieved final configuration may require modifications to the starting point. The only situation in which the library solution could be appropriate would be in the case a complete blackout, with all the components disconnected. This is an extremely unlikely situation.

Configuration specification: The solutions in the library also consider a fixed specification for the configuration problem. In our case, however, the objective would be to achieve the same energy flow configuration as the one the network had before the disturbance occurred but without using the damaged equipment. This objective might be impossible to reach, which means that, instead of deducing that a solution does not exists, the specification has to be relaxed in order to achieve a configuration, as close as possible, to the desired one.

Tailoring solutions is not straightforward, but we should not expect it to be. A library such as the CommonKADS library is useful and it helps in putting the problem being modeled in perspective with respect to the task, and the basic reasoning inferences required to solve it. The basic principle that library components are configured to form a full model depending on specific features of a problem is one of the main assets of this library, and our proposal is that further research concentrate on developing this principle to a fuller extent to support effective modeling of complex real-world problems such as the one presented in this paper.

7. Acknowledgments

The work reported here was carried out in the course of the KACTUS project. This project is partially funded by the ESPRIT Program of the CEC as project number 8145. The partners in the project are Cap Gemini Innovation (F), Cap Programator (S), DELOS (I), FINCANTIERI (I), IBERDROLA (ESP), LABEIN (ESP), Lloyd's Register (UK), University of Karlsruhe (D), SINTEF (N), STATOIL (N), University of Amsterdam (NL). This paper represents the author's point of view and does not necessarily reflect that of the KACTUS consortium. The authors also acknowledge the support provided by the CICYT (ref. TIC95-1261-CE).

The authors would like to thank Wouter Jansweijer for reviewing the KACTUS deliverable that this paper is extracted from, and Tim Smithers for his valuable comments on a previous draft of this document.

References

[Abel et al. 93] E. Abel, I. Laresgoiti, J. Perez, J. M. Corera, J. Echavarri (1993). Multiagent approach to analyze disturbances in electrical networks. In Proceedings of Expert System Application to Power Systems IV---ESAP'93, Melbourne, Australia. CRL Publishing Ltd.

[Bernaras et al. 95] Amaia Bernaras, Iñaki Laresgoiti, Nerea Bartolomé (1995). Interoperability and Reuse of Ontologies in Electrical Networks. In Proceedings of The Impact of Ontologies on Reuse, Interoperability and Distributed Processing, London, UK

[Bernaras *et al.* 96] Amaia Bernaras, Iñaki Laresgoiti, Nerea Bartolomé, José Corera (1996). An Ontology for Fault Diagnosis in Electrical Networks. Proceedings of the International Conference on Intelligent Systems Applications to Power Systems, pp. 199-203, ISAP´96, Florida, USA. Editors O.A.Mohammed & K.Tomsovic

[Breuker and Van de Velde 94] Joost Breuker and Walter Van de Velde (1994). Expertise model Document Part II: The CommonKADS Library. Technical Report KADS-II/TM.2/VUB/TR/054/3.0, VUB.

[Corera *et al.* 93] J. M. Corera, J. Echavarri, I. Laresgoiti, J.M. Lazaro, J. Perez (1993). On-line Expert System for Service Restoration. In Proceedings of Expert System Application to Power Systems IV---ESAP´93, Melbourne, Australia. CRL Publishing Ltd.

[Jennings *et al.* 92] N.R. Jennings, E. H. Mamdani, I. Laresgoiti, J. Perez, J. Corera (1992). GRATE: a general framework for co-operative problem solving. Intelligent Systems Engineering, Vol 1, 2, winter 1992.

[Laresgoiti *et al.* 88] I. Laresgoiti, J. Perez, J. Amantegui, J. Echavarri (1988). LAIDA: Development of an Expert System for Disturbance Analysis in Electrical networks. In Proceedings of the Symposium on Expert System Applications to Power Systems, Stockholm-Helsinki, August 1988.

[Wielinga *et al.* 94] Bob J. Wielinga, Hans Akkermans, Heshem Hassan, Olle Olsson, Klas Orsvärn, Guus Schreiber, Peter Terpstra, Walter Van de Velde, Steve Wells (1994). Expertise Model Definition Document Research Report KADS-II/M2/UvA/026/5.0, University of Amsterdam.

[Schreiber *et al.* 94] Guus Schreiber, Bob Wielinga, Hans Akkermans, Walter Van de Velde, Robert de Hoog (1994). CommonKADS: A comprehensive methodology for KBS development. IEEE Expert, 9 (6) 1994.

Domain and System Influences in Problem Solving Models for Planning[†]

Hugh Cottam and Nigel Shadbolt.

University of Nottingham, AI Group, Dept of Psychology,
University Park, Nottingham NG7 2RD.

Abstract . The field of knowledge level modelling has achieved great success when applied to various domains, yet has thus far largely neglected the generic areas of planning, scheduling and resource allocation. In this paper we outline the development and use of a knowledge level modelling approach within the domain of planning for Search and Rescue. Existing problem solving models for planning are almost exclusively derived from the analysis of systems. We argue that this makes their suitability for directly assisting knowledge acquisition debatable. Our approach makes a clear distinction between domain derived knowledge level models and those derived from systems. We describe how the combination of these two types of model can achieve definite benefits within the course of KBS development.

1. Introduction

This paper discusses insights derived from a project commissioned by the Defence Research Agency Flight Systems Division. The project was entitled "Acquiring and Using Planning Knowledge for Search and Rescue" and was motivated by the requirement for the Flight Systems Division of DRA Farnborough to find ways in which their knowledge engineering work within planning system development could be made more efficient and reusable. This was coupled with the mutual interest of the AI Group at Nottingham and AIAI at Edinburgh, in the development of methodologies to assist in knowledge acquisition for planning systems.

A central goal of the project was the development of a generic approach to assist in the reliable capture of knowledge related to planning, scheduling and resource allocation. This would involve the construction of a knowledge level model to describe the structure of problem solving in the SAR domain. The aim was that this model would be suitable for re-use in similar domains. This paper will describe in detail the accomplishment of this goal and its relation to other work on problem solving models for planning. For a more general overview of the SAR project see [Cottam *et al.*, 1995.].

The increased use of intelligent decision support systems has created a demand for efficient acquisition, implementation and maintenance of the knowledge required by such systems. This has led to the construction of methodologies for KBS development that facilitate a generic approach to knowledge acquisition. e.g. KADS

[†] The work described has been done under contract to the Defence Research Agency Flight Systems Division, Farnborough. The project was a joint effort between the AI Group at Nottingham and AIAI at Edinburgh.

[Breuker *et al.*, 1987.] or VITAL [O'Hara *et al.*, 1992]. These methodologies rely heavily upon the concept of a generic problem-solving model (PSM in this context refers to the model used to drive KA not the problem solving method). Generic PSMs resulted from the discovery that when a certain number of PSMs were purged of their domain-specific content, the resulting structures seemed invariant over various domains. Users of knowledge level methodologies have thus built up extensive libraries of generic PSMs, aimed at facilitating the reuse of both knowledge engineering effort and system software itself.

Such generic approaches have achieved great success when applied to various domains, yet have thus far largely neglected the areas of planning, scheduling and resource allocation. This point should be clarified as it might well be argued that there are in fact a number of existing generic PSMs for planning. e.g. *CommonKADS Library for Expertise Modelling* [Breuker & van de Velde, 1994]. The important observation to be made about these existing PSMs for planning is that they are almost exclusively system derived. This raises an important discussion point concerning the origin of the generic PSMs associated with a methodology. The originators of a methodology may deduce the ontological elements for use in such models, yet the structure of generic models must be inferred or validated inductively. There are several established generic PSMs that have originated as a result of system analysis, as opposed to human expert analysis. e.g. the heuristic classification model of Mycin [Clancey, 1985]. However the strength of a model such as heuristic classification is not simply the initial system analysis, but its proven efficacy for knowledge acquisition. This observation has important implications for the construction of generic PSMs within the generic area of planning. Existing planning PSMs have resulted as an attempt to extend the use of knowledge level methodologies, yet are derived from the knowledge level analysis of well known operational planning architectures. Because such planning PSMs model how computers plan rather than how humans plan, their efficacy for human expert knowledge acquisition is debatable, and they may enforce an unsuitable system architecture upon the domain.

Most methodologies for model based knowledge acquisition expect that generic PSMs will require modification once selected for use in a particular domain (or constructing from several smaller generic PSMs). The model selection/construction/modification process is also the least well supported of the knowledge acquisition stages. This process is aided to a degree by the organisation and classification of the PSM libraries [Valente & Löckenhoff, 1993] [O'Hara, 1993]. Specifically with regard to the CommonKADS planning model library, it is suggested that the availability of knowledge to play certain static roles within a model will give guidance to PSM selection [Valente, 1994]. This does not however provide any validation of the actual structure of the PSM. There is a clear danger when applying system derived PSMs to knowledge acquisition. The knowledge engineer may tend to force the characterisation of the domain to fit the "off the shelf" model. These system derived PSMs await validation through their use and refinement in the context of knowledge acquisition.

Our observations on the nature of existing PSMs for planning, led us to the goal of constructing an explicit PSM for the SAR domain from a combination of domain analysis and wider ontological considerations. Thus the structure of the PSM was domain driven, which we considered to be of great importance in order to avoid imposing a pre-conceived PSM upon the domain. Once shorn of its domain specific content this model can be compared to generic PSMs such as those mentioned earlier from the CommonKADS library (see section 5). The applicability of the resulting generic PSM could then be considered for other domains.

It is the intention of this paper to demonstrate that had we attempted to utilise one of the existing CommonKADS models directly, then this would have hindered rather than assisted the knowledge acquisition and would have lead to a system that did not preserve the structure of planning for SAR. We also aim to show that system derived models can be utilised to great effect in knowledge acquisition by using them as a means of critiquing domain derived models.

2. Ontologies for Planning

Initially the ontological issues regarding the entities that would constitute a PSM for planning were addressed, and possible structures of PSMs for planning in the SAR domain were then considered. There is widespread interest in ontologies to support knowledge sharing across a range of domains and, at this time, a rapidly growing interest in the development of ontologies for planning [Tate, 1994]. These ontologies establish a set of consistent terms to describe the entities that constitute a plan and the relationships between such entities. The ontologies thus represent "what" is reasoned about in planning, but do not explicitly represent "how" planning is performed. It was our objective to merge generic planning ontologies with a knowledge level modelling approach in order to formulate a planning PSM for the SAR domain.

An example of a generic planning ontology is that proposed by [Tate, 1994] which has been adopted as a base for the US ARPA working group on Plan Ontology, and as a component of Enterprise modelling ontologies [Fraser & Tate, 1995]. These efforts are being undertaken for a variety of purposes, one of which is to assist the knowledge acquisition process. Other developments that have much in common with the Plan Ontology work are the Workflow Management Coalition glossary [1994] and the Process Interchange Format standards [Lee, 1994].

The generic planning entities that were defined as a result of the Plan Ontology work [Tate, 1995] include the following:

Activity	This is a behaviour performed by one or more agents.
Agent	This is an entity that can perform or participate in behaviour, or hold some purpose.
Issue	An implied or pending constraint upon a plan. These are requirements remaining to be addressed in the plan.
Activity Decomposition	A set of sub-activities or sub-activity constraints. There are normally multiple ways of decomposing the activity.

Constraints There are three main types of constraint:
  Implied Constraints These represent future constraints that will be added to the plan as a result of handling unsatisfied requirements.
Plan Level Constraints Actions in the plan associated with begin and end time points.
Detailed Constraints These are of two main sub types:
  Ordering Constraints These define temporal relationships between actions.
  Variable Constraints These are co-designation and non-co-designation constraints on plan objects.

Additional detailed constraints may include authority constraints, that define agent to agent relationships such as the authority of one agent over another, or delegation. These generic planning entities represent abstractions of the possible items that may exist within a particular planning domain. The range of generic entities defined in the Plan Ontology will in general be a superset of the entities required for a specific domain. They therefore also define a superset of the knowledge roles or information types that will be contained within our planning PSM.

3. Planning for Search and Rescue

Planning for search and rescue is based at the Rescue Co-ordination Centre (RCC) near Edinburgh. The RCC have responsibility for the support of military flying and to provide cover for Royal Flights, yet their most common role is in support and co-ordination of civilian emergencies. The RCC's geographical area of responsibility covers the Northern UK and extends out into the Atlantic and North Sea. The RCC have direct responsibility for the allocation, application and co-ordination of military assets for SAR (including SAR helicopters, RAF Nimrods and RAF mountain rescue teams). They may however have to co-ordinate with a number of civilian emergency authorities such as fire, police, ambulance, coastguard and civilian mountain rescue teams. They might also take responsibility for overall co-ordination of a rescue incident that includes the allocation and application of these civilian rescue assets. An incident can vary in scale from retrieving a walker with a sprained ankle to handling a large aircrash.

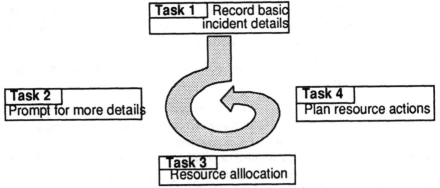

Figure 1: High Level Task Decomposition

Figure 1 shows the high level tasks identified in the RCC's workflow. This task decomposition was necessary to gain a wider picture of the RCC's work flow, including the interaction and nature of the high level tasks outlined. Tasks 2, 3 & 4 in Figure 1 were considered to be knowledge intensive. Task 4 is the RCC making decisions about the actions that resources should take when applied to an incident. This is where detailed planning takes place and it is here that we concentrated our KA for the actual PSM construction.

In addition to our KA goals, the task decomposition and workflow analysis also act as a means of defining user requirements and of assigning a focus for the deployment of KBS support. It became apparent during this analysis that there were key knowledge structures in the RCC's reasoning that had no explicit representation. A good example of this is the RCC's plans, which have no explicit representation outside the minds of the operators. The reason for this is that the plans are simply changing too rapidly to be practically recorded in a paper based environment. A system incorporating multiple views upon a consistent maintainable knowledge-base was a clear requirement for any significant KBS support at the RCC. This would then form a framework around which plans could be represented and visualised. It also became clear to us at this stage that an appropriate solution would be a mixed initiative rather than a "black box" planner. The system should follow the RCC's natural idiom as far as possible, and should act as an assistant rather than taking control away from the operator.

4. Knowledge Level Problem Solving Models

Within our discussion of planning for SAR (task 4), we shall refer to outline plan templates, executable plans, goals and actions. An outline plan template consists of a set of partially ordered high level goals that define the requirements of an incident. The template is generic to a generic class of incident e.g. maritime rescue requiring search and involving lifeboats, helicopters and nimrod aircraft. There would be a certain set of goals associated with the handling of this type of incident. However another generic incident class would be associated with a different set of goals e.g. a mountain rescue not requiring search and involving a mountain rescue team and a helicopter. Planning within the RCC can be viewed as the process of moving from an outline plan template to an executable plan. An executable plan is a set of ordered physical actions to be taken at the RCC. The reasoning process of the RCC enables this transition between outline plan template and executable plan. We identified a library of outline plan templates which were then indexed according to a hierarchical organisation of generic incident classes. The first stage of RCC problem solving is situation assessment in order to define the incident class and to enable the selection of an outline plan template.

Planning for SAR is a progressive task that spans the temporal duration of a particular resource's application to an incident. This process involves the use of heuristic expert knowledge in order to make planning decisions in a domain where future data and constraints on planning are unpredictable. Due to this unpredictability, the decomposition of outline goals, and instantiation into planned physical actions, is usually not performed until the situation demands it. The RCC often resort to this least commitment strategy when planning. In this manner, the maximum amount of factual knowledge about the current situation is gathered before decision making. Oftentimes the RCC must hold back from taking physical actions, because if they wait for a small amount of time their factual knowledge of the situation will have increased so as to make a more effective decision possible.

4.1 Critiquing the Domain PSM Using a System Derived PSM

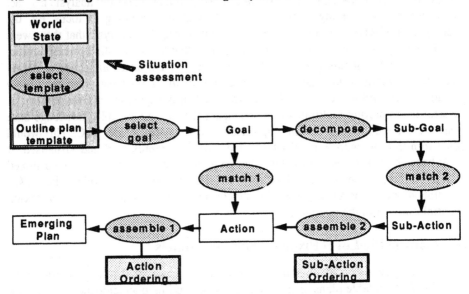

Figure 2: Domain Problem Solving Model for asset utilisation in SAR

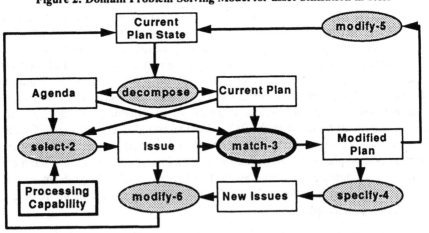

Figure 3: System Problem Solving Model

Figure 2 shows a knowledge level model representing the inference layer for problem solving within task 4, from the perspective of a single search and rescue incident. The model represents the inference types and domain roles that exist within task 4 reasoning. The shaded boxes represent support knowledge for a particular inference. This is a KADS like model that is expressed in domain terminology. It was constructed through a lengthy process of second stage KA involving taped structured interviews, video tape analysis, protocol analysis, incident documentation and structured analysis of specific incident cases. The model represents the process of reasoning from an outline plan to an executable plan; converting outline goals into an ordered set of physical actions to be carried out by the RCC. A detailed description of Figure 2 is given in section 4.2.

The domain PSM (Figure 2) was validated via a process of lengthy discussion with multiple domain experts. This discussion was based upon relating the model back to specific incidents in SAR, in order to confirm that all cases could be characterised accurately within the model. A knowledge level methodology advises that the next stage in the development lifecycle should be the population and refinement of the PSM with domain knowledge. At this point we departed from the suggested course of development. Rather than launching directly into the domain knowledge acquisition, we wanted first to consider operationalisation issues.

The reason for this is a common problem occurring in KBS development that relies upon a domain inferred PSM. Either during the design process or the actual implementation, it often becomes apparent that there are vital knowledge elements missing from the original PSM. This potential incompleteness of the PSM is a recognised problem in domain driven knowledge acquisition [Ford & Bradshaw, 1993]. Our proposed method of overcoming this was to select a generic system based planning PSM, and attempt to establish a mapping into this from the domain based PSM. The rationale behind this was that the system PSM would be complete and sufficient, because it represented an operationalised architecture. If a clear mapping existed between the elements of the PSMs, then the system PSM may aid us in anticipating any omissions in the domain PSM, that would compromise its ability to produce decisions.

The system PSM that we selected for this purpose was derived from the Open Planning Architecture (O-Plan) [Currie & Tate, 1991]. The O-Plan system is a generic computational planning architecture. The generic nature of the system and the fact that initial CommonKADS models of O-Plan had already been proposed [Kingston, 1995], made this an attractive option for our purpose. We established the existence of a mapping from the ontological elements in the domain PSM to corresponding elements in the O-Plan PSM (Figure 3). This approach successfully aided us in the identification of knowledge omissions in our domain PSM, prior to the completion of KA. This two model approach presents a number of advantages:

- comparison between domain and system based PSMs facilitates the early identification of omissions in the domain PSM, without enforcing a system structure upon it.

- the explicit mapping between the two types of PSM provides a mapping between domain-specific terminology and generic planning terminology.

Both the system PSM (Figure 3) and the domain inferred PSM (Figure 2) possess inference steps which allow the transition from one form of knowledge to another. In this section we describe the inference steps and knowledge roles in the domain based PSM, and how these items map to the O-Plan based PSM. Although the two models initially bear little resemblance to each other, there is in actual fact a clear mapping between both the ontological elements and inference steps that are depicted in the domain PSM to corresponding items within the O-Plan PSM. Both structures represent the matching of goals to possible actions. Both PSMs also facilitate the decomposition of goals and identify the selection of the next goal as an important inference step in the planning process. The comparison showed that the O-Plan PSM had a richer representation for the selection of goals, highlighting the necessity for knowledge that supports this inference step in the architecture of any intended system. The comparison had therefore successfully identified weaknesses in the domain based PSM.

4.2 The Mapping Between the Models

The following is an explanation of the knowledge roles and inference steps in the domain PSM (Figure2), accompanied by their mappings into the O-Plan PSM (Figure 3):

4.2.1 Goal Selection

Select template -- The input to this is the world state, and the output is an outline plan template consisting of outline goals that correspond to a generic type of incident. They have a partial temporal ordering, yet it is only when the RCC plan the application of resources to an incident that these goals are more fully defined and ordered. In complex situations it may be the case that no outline plan template exists and one will have to be constructed. This then requires a knowledge of temporal constraints on the goals that make up an outline plan template. This template maps to the initial agenda in the O-Plan PSM. The outline plan template is a set of outline goals to be resolved, and the agenda consists of a set of issues to be resolved. In this case, the goals in the domain map to outstanding issues in the O-Plan PSM. The outline plan template in the domain PSM is selected at the commencement of planning for an incident.

Select Goal -- This represents the selection of an outline goal from the outline plan template. The selection step is often simple, corresponding to the default ordering of goals defined in the outline plan template. However, in a complex or rapidly changing situation, the selection of goals becomes more knowledge intensive. It is here that our model comparison was informative, as it suggested the existence of certain types of control knowledge affecting goal selection. It is clear that in the O-Plan PSM there is a much richer representation of the knowledge affecting which goal/issue to resolve next. These are described in the O-Plan PSM as three possible expansions of the *match-3* inference step, which is marked in bold in Figure 3 to indicate its importance. The three expansions represent three different ways in which O-Plan can attempt the resolving of issues. The expansions are depicted in the O-Plan PSM as three separate inference structures. Two of these structures have clear mappings to the domain PSM (the decompose expansion is described in the next section, Figure 4). The third does not and represents knowledge about goal selection that is not accounted for in the domain PSM. In O-Plan this knowledge drives a backward chaining search process that decides which issues to resolve when the present issue's conditions are not satisfied (see Figure 5). Issues are selected in order to achieve actions that will satisfy the original unsatisfied conditions. This backward chaining process caused by interaction between issues had not been considered in the domain PSM. All that had been considered was a knowledge of basic dependencies between goals, of the form Goal A must be satisfied before Goal B can be considered. The comparison between PSMs suggested a deeper form of knowledge about interdependencies between conditions necessary to resolve goals and the actions that satisfy them. This knowledge will provide important support to the user when incidents become complex and the default ordering of goals described by the outline plan template may not be applicable. The SAR domain has examples of the need for this "backward chaining" e.g. if the RCC are in charge of an incident involving mountain rescue in poor visibility the default ordering of the outline goals may not apply. The outline plan template for this incident places "scramble resources" before "ascertain weather". The outline goal "scramble resources" decomposes to "scramble helicopter", "scramble mountain rescue team" or both, depending upon the world state. A condition of this decomposition will be that visibility at the incident scene is sufficient for a helicopter to operate. If the visibility condition is unknown then the outline goal "ascertain weather" will be initiated in order to effect an action that will satisfy or negate this condition.

4.2.2 Goal Decomposition
Decompose -- This inference step decomposes a goal into a sub-goal. Similarly in O-plan issues may be decomposed into sub-issues. There is a clear correspondence with one expansion of the *match-3* inference step in the O-Plan PSM (Figure 4). The degree to which goals are decomposed by RCC varies. Some high level goals match to high level actions that consist of an invariant ordered set of physical actions. The existence of such invariant high level actions and their suitability to satisfy high level goals are factors affecting the degree to which goals must be decomposed. In some cases goals will have to be decomposed to the granularity of physical actions. It would seem that decomposition increases when an incident and its associated goals are out of the ordinary. Intuitively the level of reasoning increases in the exceptional cases.

4.2.3 Matching Goals to Actions
These inference steps involve finding actions that can fulfil (or help to fulfil) goals. There will generally be multiple actions that can fulfil a particular goal. The match therefore depends upon the present world state. There is a mapping between these two inference types and the third method of expanding *match-3* in the O-Plan PSM.

Match 1 -- The input to this is a high level goal. The output is a high level action. This step will require a knowledge of high level actions that satisfy high level goals, and the conditions that make the match valid.

Match 2 -- The input to this is a low level goal, corresponding to a physical action. The output is a lower level action. This is similar to the Match 1 inference type, though it is actually matching to a physical action.

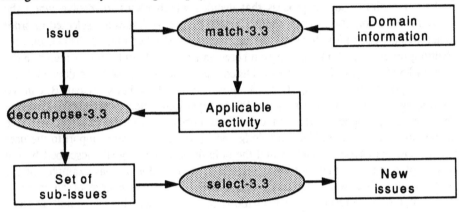

Figure 4: Expansion of match-3 for issue decomposition

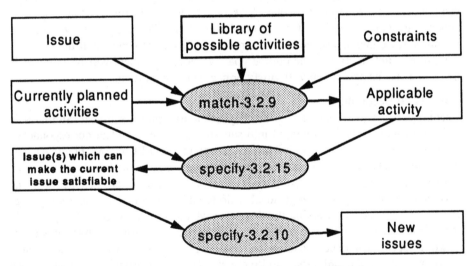

Figure 5: Expansion of match-3 for backward chaining

4.2.4 Assembling the Executable Plan

Assemble 1 -- The input to this is a high level action, corresponding to an outline goal. This high level action consists of a set of ordered physical actions or of sub-actions. The output is the current executable plan. As discussed earlier the executable plan is gradually formulated throughout the course of the resources application to the incident. This is supported by a knowledge of action ordering, though a lot of this ordering will have been decided at the goal ordering stage.

Assemble 2 -- The input to this is a set of lower level actions; the lowest level being physical actions. The output is a higher level action; the highest being those that actually make up the executable plan (i.e. those that correspond to the high level goals).

There is no replication of these assembly inference steps in the O-Plan PSM, although typically any set of actions in O-Plan have ordering constraints instantiated during planning and are therefore assembled implicitly within the plan. The explicit assembly of actions is however important to the RCC, as it serves to summarise what has been done (or what is intended to be done), in order to achieve goals. This reflects the nature of the RCC's planning, which proceeds in small chunks corresponding to the outline goals in the template. There may be activity in several chunks at once, though this tends to be the exception rather than the norm.

There are clearly three inference steps in Figure 3 (besides the "backward chaining" expansion of *match-3*) that are not represented in the domain PSM. The *modify-6* step describes how the actions carried out in the plan modify the world state (world state is part of current plan state as it includes constraints). This could be included in the domain PSM as a step from emerging plan back to world state. The *modify-5* and *specify-4* steps describe how intended actions in the plan cause new issues to arise, and this therefore modifies the current plan state. These are not represented in the domain PSM, and this form of knowledge has not been observed in the domain. This is probably due to the previously mentioned least commitment strategy of the RCC decreasing the amount of intended actions that exist within their plans. This type of knowledge may be important in forms of SAR incident that we have not yet witnessed, and we regard this as an important area for future KA.

5. Comparison with Existing PSMs for Planning

In this section we compare our domain PSM developed for knowledge acquisition in SAR (Figure 2) with two of the planning models available in the CommonKADS library [Valente, 1994]. These are high level models of the inference structures of a non-linear planner (Figure 6) and a skeletal planner (Figure 7). We also compare the CommonKADS planning models to the O-Plan PSM, in order to consider how effective these models would have been if used in the critiquing role described above.

Initially the SAR domain seemed to match a form of non-linear planning such as described in Figure 6. However with hindsight the concept of outline plan templates became very important within the knowledge acquisition. In actual fact planning for SAR lies in-between non-linear planning and the skeletal planning described in Figure 7. At the RCC non-linear planning takes place around a framework of default skeletal plans (outline plan templates). This is caused by particular types of rescue incident possessing a common structure. The goals and their ordering are thus implicitly defined by the type of incident, yet more detailed explicit knowledge may override this when necessary. Had we used either of the models below as the basis of a PSM for knowledge acquisition, we would have neglected one of the major defining characteristics of the expert problem solving that we were attempting to model.

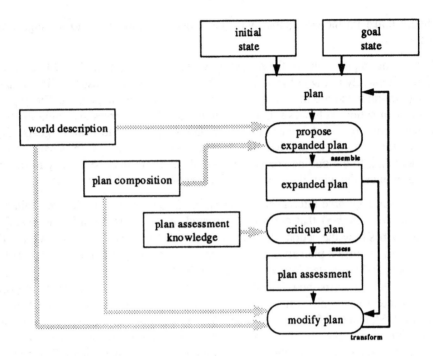

Figure 6: CommonKADS function structure for non-linear planner

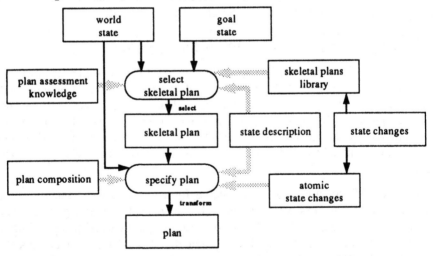

Figure 7: CommonKADS function structure for skeletal planner

Because planning for SAR is a continuous process the initial state and goal state are constantly changing. Planning takes place by selecting a high level goal which then becomes decomposed into sub-goals. They continue being decomposed until appropriate actions can be assigned to the sub-goals. This takes place in the context of the actions that have already been executed and the high level goals that are still to be addressed. Goals and the actions that will achieve the goals thus become very prevalent within the RCC's problem solving. Each high level goal is a planning cycle in itself. Both the non-linear planner model and the skeletal planner model are not broken down as far as the level of actions and goals, though it would be reasonable to refine either of these models to include these entities. However we believe that if this approach had been used, too much emphasis would have been placed on knowledge roles such as plan assessment knowledge, initial states and goal states. In the context of the RCC these knowledge roles are much less prevalent than would be suggested PSMs such as Figures 6 and 7. By less prevalent we mean that although these roles are present within the domain they are seldom actually utilised in problem solving. Therefore it would not be fruitful for us to attempt to base our PSM around such secondary knowledge roles.

The key characteristic of the domain PSM is that it represents planning in situations of high unpredictability. Because this effectively limits the amount of planning that can be usefully carried out the knowledge roles that are most prevalent in problem solving are different from those in domains of greater predictability. It is possible that the system PSMs shown in Figures 5 and 6 would be more applicable in such domains.

Off the shelf system models are useful in informing us about the knowledge roles and inference steps that are necessary for the operationalisation of the knowledge in a system. The O-Plan PSM is the most suitable in this instance as it is already decomposed to the level of goals and actions (called issues and activities in the O-Plan terminology), enabling us to establish a mapping between the domain PSM and the system PSM.

6. Summary of Methodology

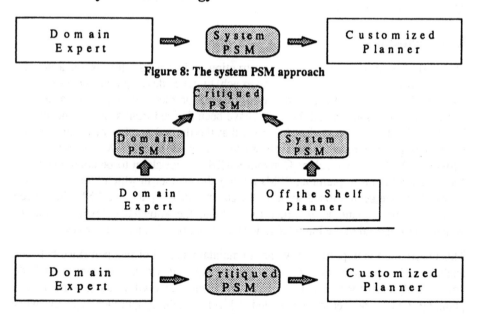

Figure 8: The system PSM approach

Figure 9: The critiqued domain PSM approach

If we consider the generic PSM as a framework that the knowledge engineer must map their domain level knowledge into, then it is vital that the structure of this framework is as close to that of the domain as possible. The greater the difference between the structure of the generic PSM and the structure of problem solving in the domain then the greater the difficulty that will be encountered by the knowledge engineer in mapping the domain entities into the PSM. Figures 7 and 8 illustrate the difference between the recommended approach and our own. The crux of our approach is to arrive at a PSM that is not just sufficient to characterise the problem solving, but whose problem solving structure reflects accurately that in the domain. Thus our goal in knowledge engineering is emulation of the domain. We accept that this may not always be considered a priority in the knowledge engineering process. If the purpose of using a knowledge modelling technique is just to support modular KBS design then utilising a system derived PSM may prove more useful. System derived PSMs are also very important in situations where a pre-defined operational system is to be deployed in a particular domain [Major *et al*, 1994], though a two model approach might present advantages in this situation.

Because our PSM had to be inferred directly from the domain this changes the emphasis of KA, and also the emphasis of the methodology developed as a result of the project. The methodology developed concentrates on supporting the earlier stages of KA. Support is provided in the form of techniques and advice on the construction and critiquing of domain inferred PSMs in planning type domains. The methodology also provides a new generic PSM for planning, that is hoped will have applicability in a number of other areas. Many domains that involve some form of resource allocation appear to have a similar structure in their problem solving to the PSM we have uncovered.

7. Conclusions

The work described represents the construction and demonstrated use of a domain driven knowledge level modelling approach to KBS development in a planning domain. We make a definite distinction between problem solving models that are inferred from the domain and those that have been derived from systems. Indeed one insight derived from the project has been that the limited number of existing PSMs for planning are almost exclusively system derived models. We recognise that current model libraries (such as CommonKADS) do not claim to be comprehensive, and this system bias in planning PSMs reflects the manner in which knowledge level approaches have been utilised so far in the generic area of planning. PSMs have been harnessed within planning in order to facilitate the knowledge level analysis of systems, as opposed to the knowledge level acquisition of human expertise.

This observation is important if we are to maintain a level of independence between analysis and implementation within KBS development. Domain derived models do not presently exist for the support of system development within the generic area of planning. Our work merges a knowledge level modelling approach with the work that has been done on ontologies for planning, in order to formulate a generic approach to the acquisition and utilisation of knowledge for planning systems. The approach was tested and refined through the development of a knowledge-based system for the support of planning for search and rescue.

The distinction that we have made between domain and system based models, led us to investigate possible benefits that could be gained by exploring the mappings between these models. In the context of the SAR demonstrator development, we discovered that the comparison of these models enabled us to identify omissions in the domain model. It also enabled us to identify specific areas for future KA. We believe this twin model approach may have more general applicability for KBS development.

During a KBS development lifecycle there must be iteration between the developmental stages. Later stages of development iteratively inform and revise the earlier stages. It is expected that this iterative cycle will improve the final product. The price paid is that a large amount of iteration in the development lifecycle increases the effort expended. Approaches that enable the detection of shortcomings in the earlier stages represent a potentially large saving in development effort. The two model approach described demonstrates such a saving in the case of domain driven knowledge level modelling for planning.

This approach offers a high degree of support and advice for the early stages of KA in planning domains. It principally supports the construction of a high level PSM that reflects the structure of problem solving in a planning domain (this construction may be replaced by generic PSM selection as a comprehensive library of generic domain derived PSMs is evolved). It also offers a high degree of support for converting the completed PSM into the high level system design (including the appropriate system knowledge structures).

The project has produced a new generic model for planning and has discovered a set of generic plans for SAR in the form of outline plan templates. It has made important observations on the derivation of PSMs, and clearly outlined the distinction between those that are system derived and those that are derived from the analysis of expert problem solving. This distinction was explored in depth within the context of the SAR demonstrator development. The project has discovered both the implications of the distinction and methods by which we can effectively exploit these to our advantage.

The early stages of KA support contained in the methodology as it currently stands require further validation and refinement through the practical application of the methodology in other planning domains. We need to derive more domain PSMs in other planning domains. A process of comparison can then take place both between these domain PSMs and with system PSMs. Such a comparison might be informative in suggesting modifications to present planners in order to more effectively deploy them in selected domains.

8. References.

Breuker, J. and van de Velde, W.(Eds.). (1994) *CommonKADS Library for Expertise Modelling*. IOS Press, Amsterdam, September 1994.

Breuker, J., Wielinga, B., Van Someren, M., De Hoog, R., Schreiber, G., De Greef,P.,Bredeweg, B., Wielemaker, L., Billault, J-P., Davoodi, M. and Hayward, S. (1987)
Model driven knowledge acquisition: interpretation models.
KADS-I Project Deliverable, University of Amsterdam, Holland 1987.

Clancey, W.J. (1985) *Heuristic classification.*
Artificial Intelligence, 27: 289-350, 1985.

Cottam, H., Shadbolt, N., Kingston, J., Beck, H. and Tate, A. (1995)
Knowledge Level Planning in the Search and Rescue Domain.
In Bramer, M.A., Nealon, J.L. and Milne, R., (eds.) Research and Development in Expert Systems XII: Proceedings of BCS SGES Expert Systems' 95, pages 309-326. SGES Publications. 1995.

Currie, K.W. and Tate, A. (1991) *O-Plan: The Open Planning Architecture.*
Artificial Intelligence, 52 (1): 49-86, 1991. Also available as AIAI-TR-67.

Ford, K.M. and Bradshaw, J.M.(Eds.). (1993)
Knowledge acquisition as modelling. New York: Wiley. 1993.

Kingston, J.K. (1995) *CommonKADS Models for Planning tasks.*
forthcoming AIAI technical report, 1995.

Major, N., Cupit, J. & Shadbolt, N. (1994)
Applying the REKAP methodology to situation assessment.
in the Proceedings of the European Knowledge Acquisition Workshop, EKAW 94. Brussels. Also published in Voss, H. and Studer, R. (Eds.) Proceedings of the 4th International KADS Meeting, Bonn, Germany. Arbeitspapiere der GMD, 832, March 1994.

Motta, E., O'Hara, K., Shadbolt, N., Stutt, A. & Zdrahal, Z. (1994).
A VITAL Solution to the Sisyphus II Elevator Design Problem.
Proceedings of the Eighth Banff Knowledge Acquisition for Knowledge Based Systems Workshop, Banff, Alberta, Canada. 1994.

O'Hara, K., Shadbolt, N. R., Laublet, P., Zacklad, M. & Le Roux, B. (1992).
Knowledge acquisition methodology.
VITAL deliverable DD212. Nottingham University, UK. 1992.

O'Hara, K. (1993). *A Representation of KADS-I Interpretation Models Using a Decompositional Approach.* In C. Lockenhoff, D. Fensel & R. Studer (eds.) 3rd KADS Meeting (Siemens AG, Munich) 147-69. 1993.

Tate, A. (1994) *"Plan Ontology", a paper to the Workshop on Ontology Development and Use.* San Diego, California, USA, November 1994. (Also available as AIAI Technical Report AIAI-TR-161, and through URL: ftp://ftp.aiai.ed.ac.uk/pub/document/1994/94-krsl-plans.html)

Valente, A. (1994) *Planning models for the CommonKADS library.*
ESPRIT Project P5248 KADS-II
KADS-II/M2.3/UVA/56/1.0, University of Amsterdam, 1994.

Valente, A. and Löckenhoff, C. (1993)
Organization as guidance: A library of assessment models.
In Proceedings of the Seventh European Knowledge Acquisition Workshop (EKAW 93) pages 243-262, 1993.

Author Index

Springer-Verlag
and the Environment

We at Springer-Verlag firmly believe that an international science publisher has a special obligation to the environment, and our corporate policies consistently reflect this conviction.

We also expect our business partners – paper mills, printers, packaging manufacturers, etc. – to commit themselves to using environmentally friendly materials and production processes.

The paper in this book is made from low- or no-chlorine pulp and is acid free, in conformance with international standards for paper permanency.

Lecture Notes in Artificial Intelligence (LNAI)

Lecture Notes in Computer Science